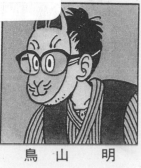

鳥　山　明

Recently, the neighborhood where I live has started to get more developed, with new roads and shops being built. It's pretty convenient, but on the other hand, it's getting rarer and rarer to see weasels, pheasant or quail. The noise level has increased too. Being a country boy, I prefer a nice quiet lifestyle so I can really take it easy and reeee-lax. I know it might be inconvenient in some ways, but I'd like to live way, way out in the country. This is the sort of thing that I end up thinking about.

–Akira Toriyama, 1987

Artist/writer Akira Toriyama burst onto the manga scene in 1980 with the wildly popular **Dr. Slump**, a science fiction comedy about the adventures of a mad scientist and his android "daughter." In 1984 he created his hit series **Dragon Ball**, which ran until 1995 in Shueisha's best-selling magazine **Weekly Shonen Jump**, and was translated into foreign languages around the world. Since **Dragon Ball**, he has worked on a variety of short series, including **Cowa!**, **Kajika**, **SandLand**, and **Neko Majin**, as well as a children's book, **Toccio the Angel**. He is also known for his design work on video games, particularly the **Dragon Warrior** RPG series. He lives with his family in Japan.

DRAGON BALL VOL. 6
SHONEN JUMP Manga Edition

STORY AND ART BY
AKIRA TORIYAMA

Translation/Mari Morimoto
English Adaptation/Gerard Jones
Touch-Up Art & Lettering/Wayne Truman
Cover Design/Izumi Evers & Dan Ziegler
Graphics & Design/Sean Lee
Senior Editor/Jason Thompson

DRAGON BALL © 1984 by BIRD STUDIO. All rights reserved.
First published in Japan in 1984 by SHUEISHA Inc., Tokyo.
English translation rights arranged by SHUEISHA Inc.

Some art has been modified from the original Japanese edition.

The stories, characters, and incidents
mentioned in this publication are entirely fictional.

In the original Japanese edition, DRAGON BALL and DRAGON
BALL Z are known collectively as the 42-volume series DRAGON
BALL. The English DRAGON BALL Z was originally volumes 17–42
of the Japanese DRAGON BALL.

Printed in Canada

Published by VIZ Media, LLC
P.O. Box 77010
San Francisco, CA 94107

10 9 8
First printing, March 2003
Eighth printing, May 2017

SHONEN JUMP MANGA

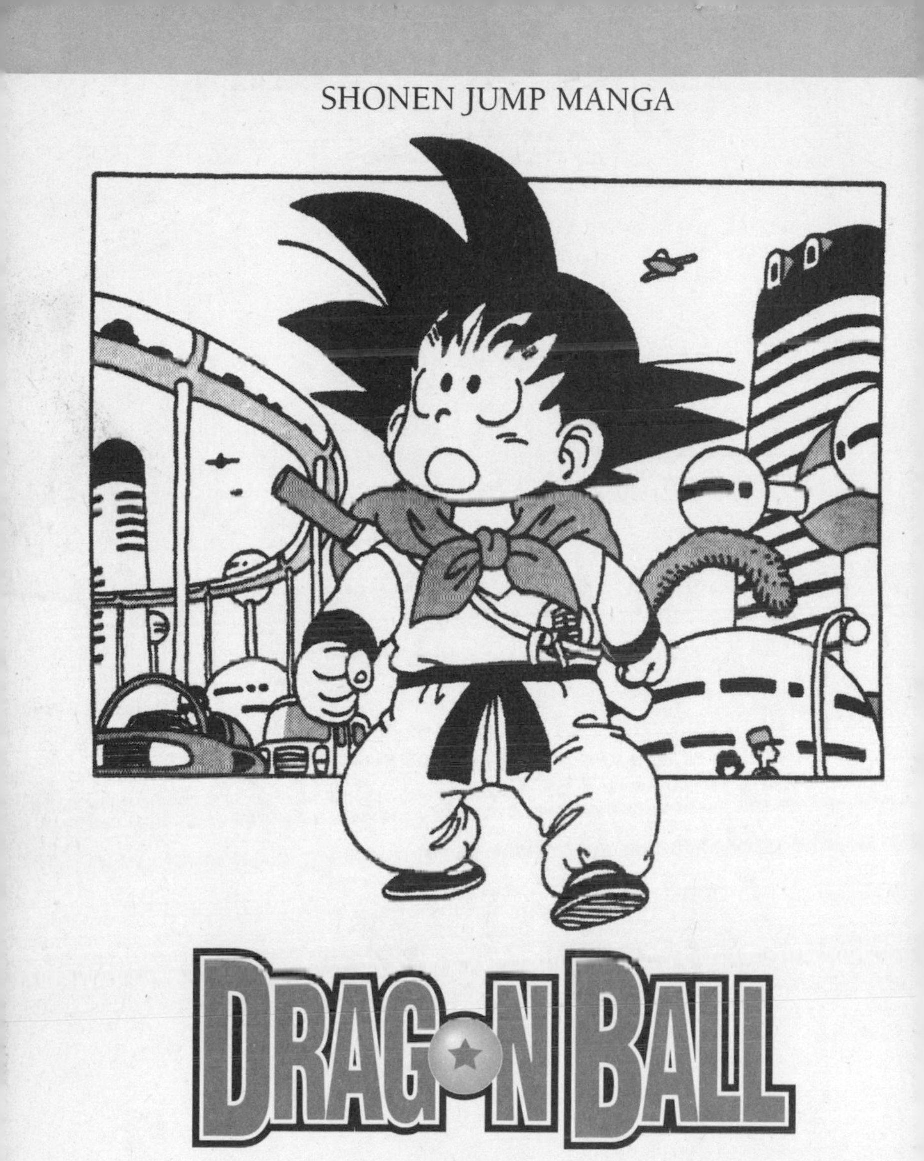

DRAGON BALL

Vol. 6

DB: 6 of 42

STORY AND ART BY
AKIRA TORIYAMA

THE MAIN CHARACTERS

Son Goku

Monkey-tailed young Goku has always been stronger than normal. His grandfather Gohan gave him the *nyoibô*, a magic staff, and Kame-Sen'nin gave him the *kinto'un*, a magic flying cloud. However, the *kinto'un* was recently destroyed by Colonel Silver, forcing Goku to find alternate means of transportation!

Oolong

Immature, shapeshifting Oolong was the only member of the group who got his wish with the Dragon Balls.

Bulma

A genius inventor, Bulma met Goku on her quest for the seven magical Dragon Balls.

Pu'ar

Yamcha's shapeshifting friend.

Yamcha

Yamcha used to be a desert bandit, but he went to the city to be Bulma's boyfriend. He uses "Fist of the Wolf-Fang" kung-fu.

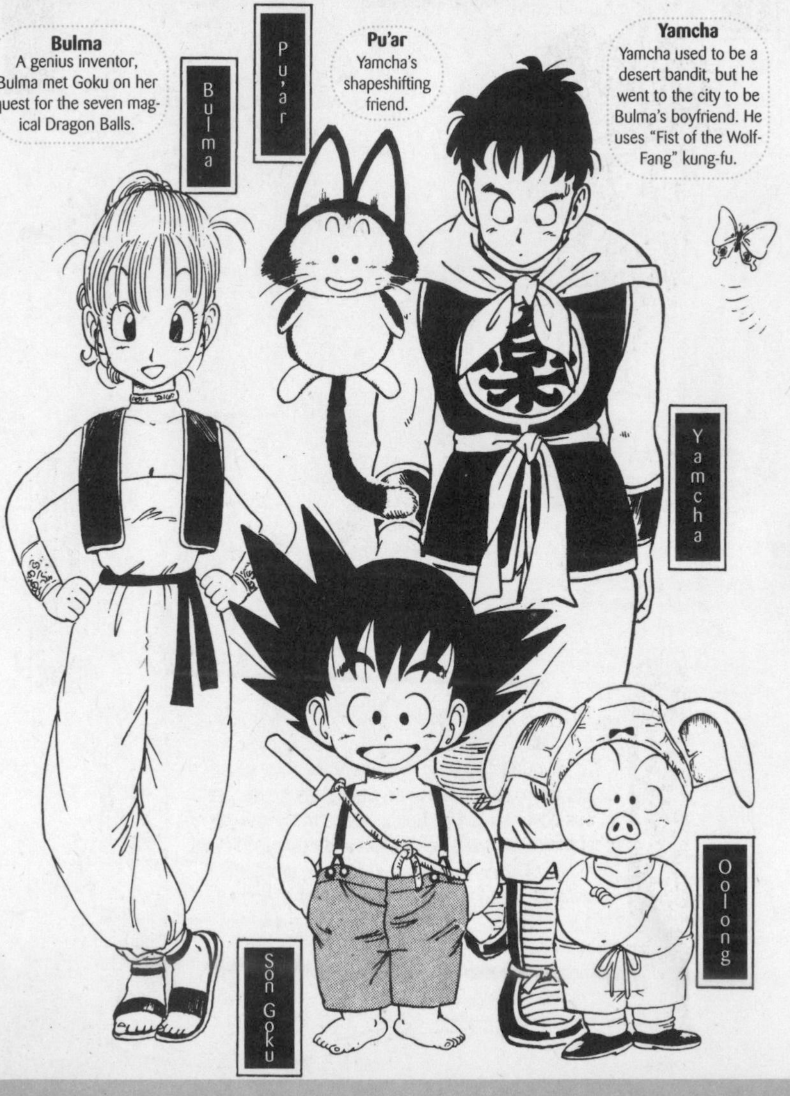
Pu'ar
Bulma
Yamcha
Oolong
Son Goku

Sergeant Major Purple

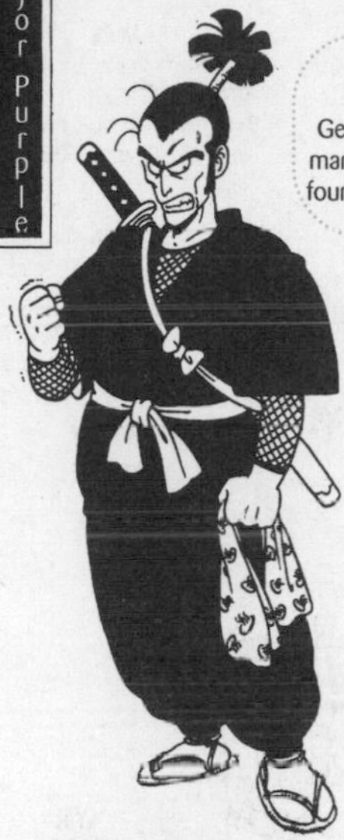

Sergeant Major Purple
General White's right-hand man, a ninja who guards the fourth level of Muscle Tower.

General White

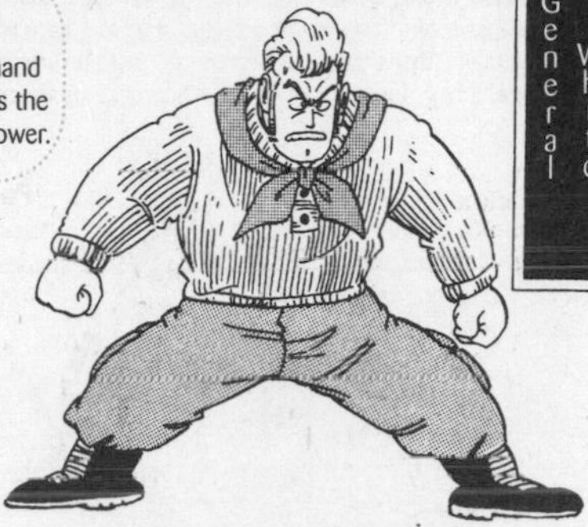

General White
The diabolical boss of Muscle Tower. He kidnapped the mayor of Jingle Village to force the peaceful villagers to help him find a Dragon Ball. Now he waits on the sixth level of his tower, mocking Goku's efforts to climb to the top...

Kame-Sen'nin (The "Turtle Hermit")
A lecherous but powerful martial artist (also known as the *muten-rôshi*, or "Invincible Old Master") who trained Goku's grandfather, Son Gohan, as well as Goku himself. He taught Goku the *kamehameha* attack.

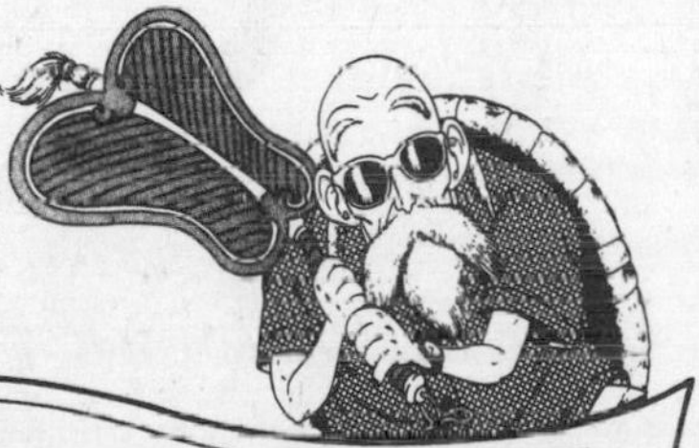

Kame-Sen'nin

Legend says that whoever gathers the seven magical "Dragon Balls" will be granted any one wish. Son Goku, a young boy from the mountains, first heard the legend from a city girl named Bulma. After many dangerous adventures with Bulma, Goku trained under the great martial artist Kame-Sen'nin and competed in the "Strongest Under the Heavens" fighting tournament. Afterwards, Goku resumed his quest for the Dragon Balls, only to find that a powerful enemy, the Red Ribbon Army, was also searching for them. Now, Goku faces a perilous challenge in Muscle Tower, the Red Ribbon Army's arctic base!

DRAGON BALL 6

IT'S THE
CONTENTS.
SHEESH.

ドラゴンボール

DRAGON BALL

Tale 61 • The 4 1/2 Tatami Mat Flip

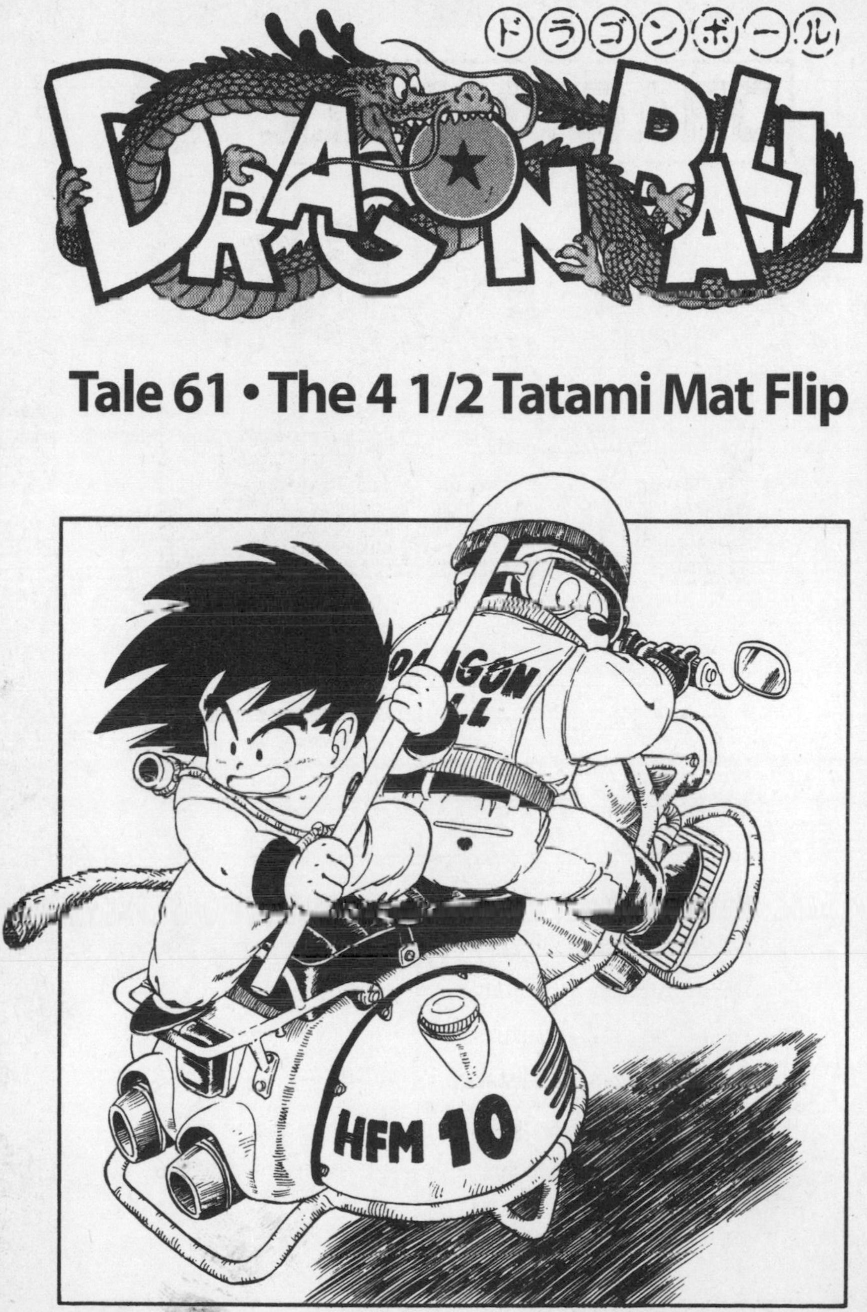
HFM 10

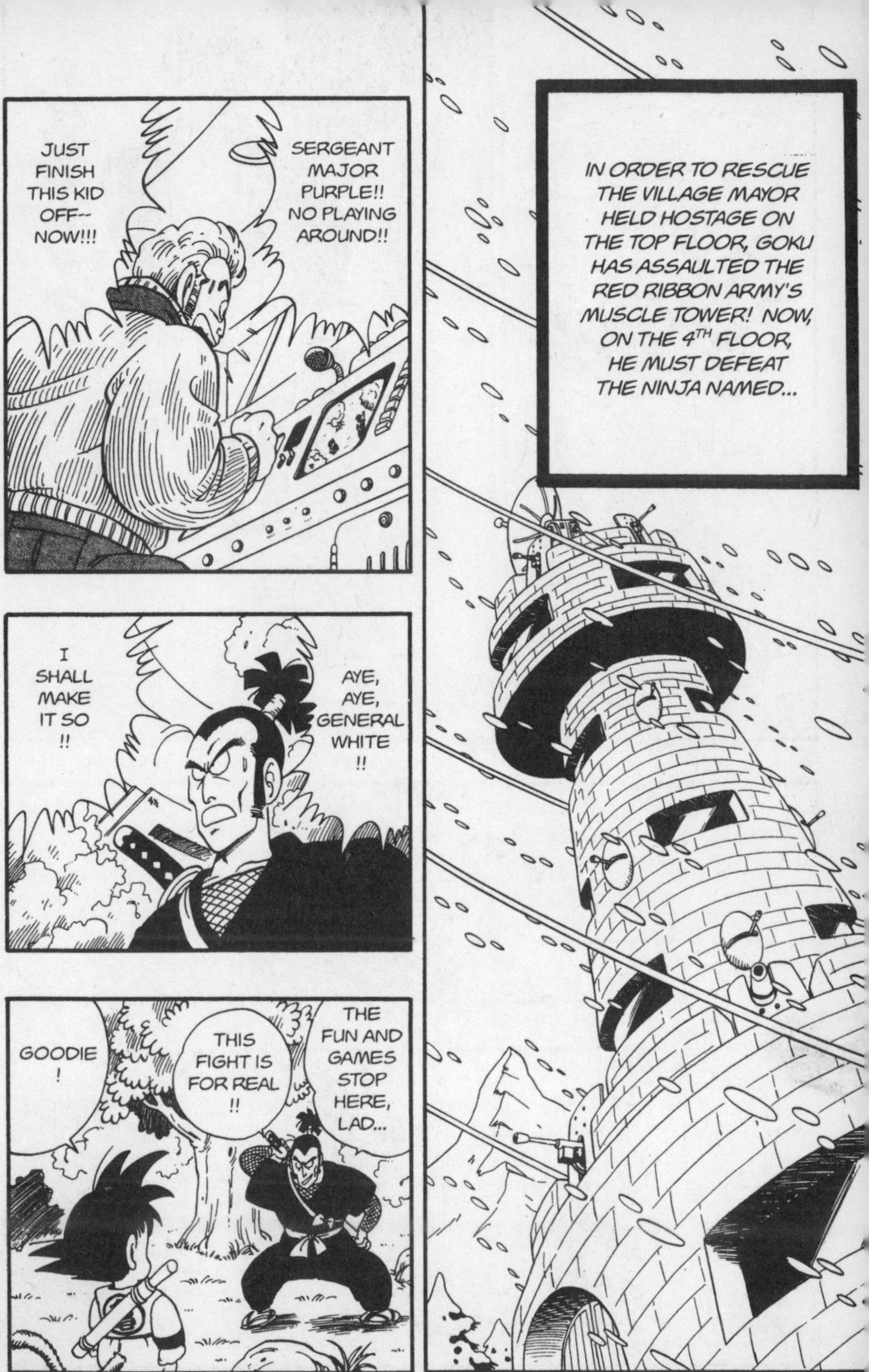
IN ORDER TO RESCUE THE VILLAGE MAYOR HELD HOSTAGE ON THE TOP FLOOR, GOKU HAS ASSAULTED THE RED RIBBON ARMY'S MUSCLE TOWER! NOW, ON THE 4TH FLOOR, HE MUST DEFEAT THE NINJA NAMED...
SERGEANT MAJOR PURPLE!! NO PLAYING AROUND!!
JUST FINISH THIS KID OFF-- NOW!!!
AYE, AYE, GENERAL WHITE !!
I SHALL MAKE IT SO !!
THE FUN AND GAMES STOP HERE, LAD...
THIS FIGHT IS FOR REAL !!
GOODIE !

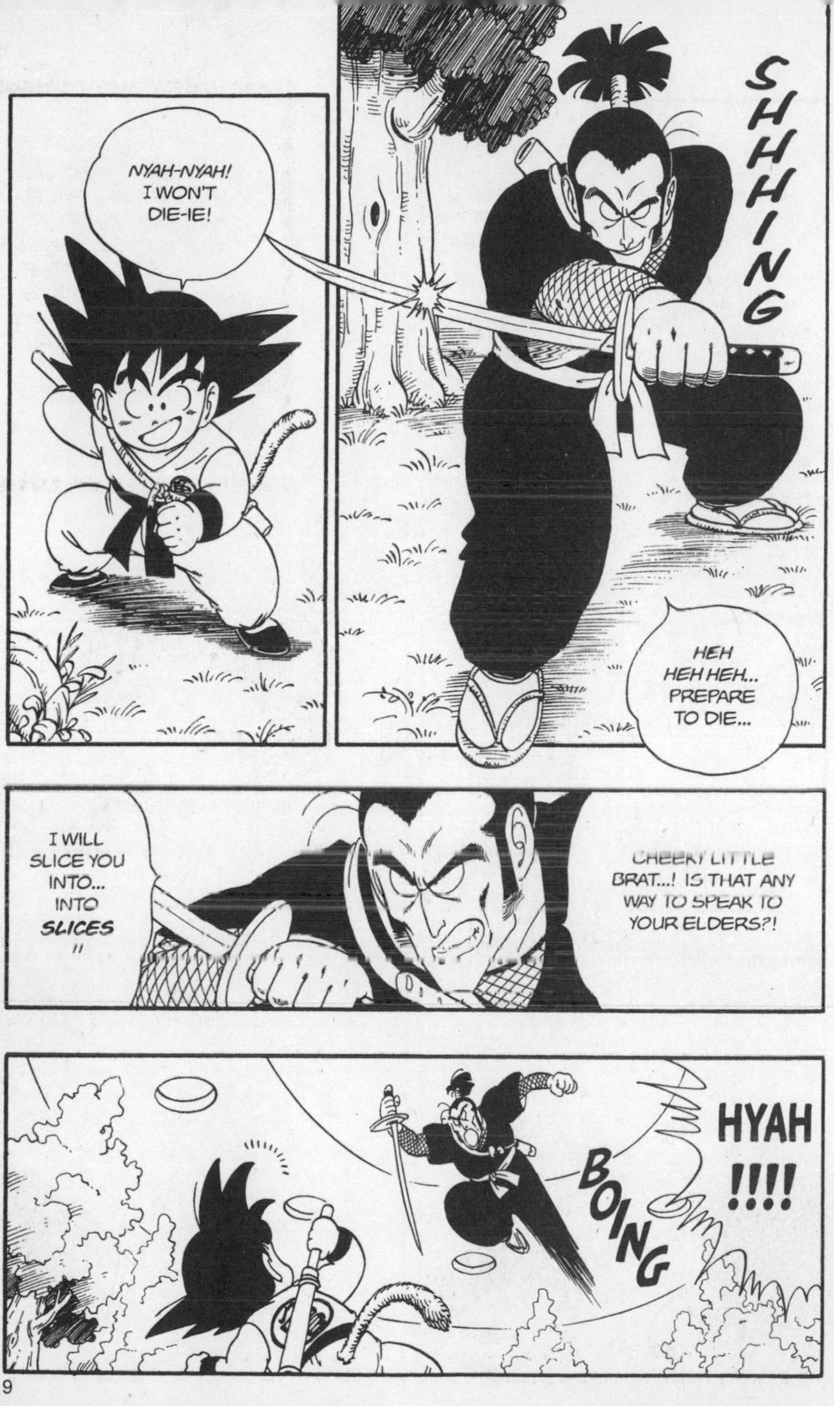
SHHHING
HEH HEH HEH... PREPARE TO DIE...
NYAH-NYAH! I WON'T DIE-IE!
CHEEKY LITTLE BRAT...! IS THAT ANY WAY TO SPEAK TO YOUR ELDERS?!
I WILL SLICE YOU INTO... INTO SLICES
HYAH !!!!
BOING

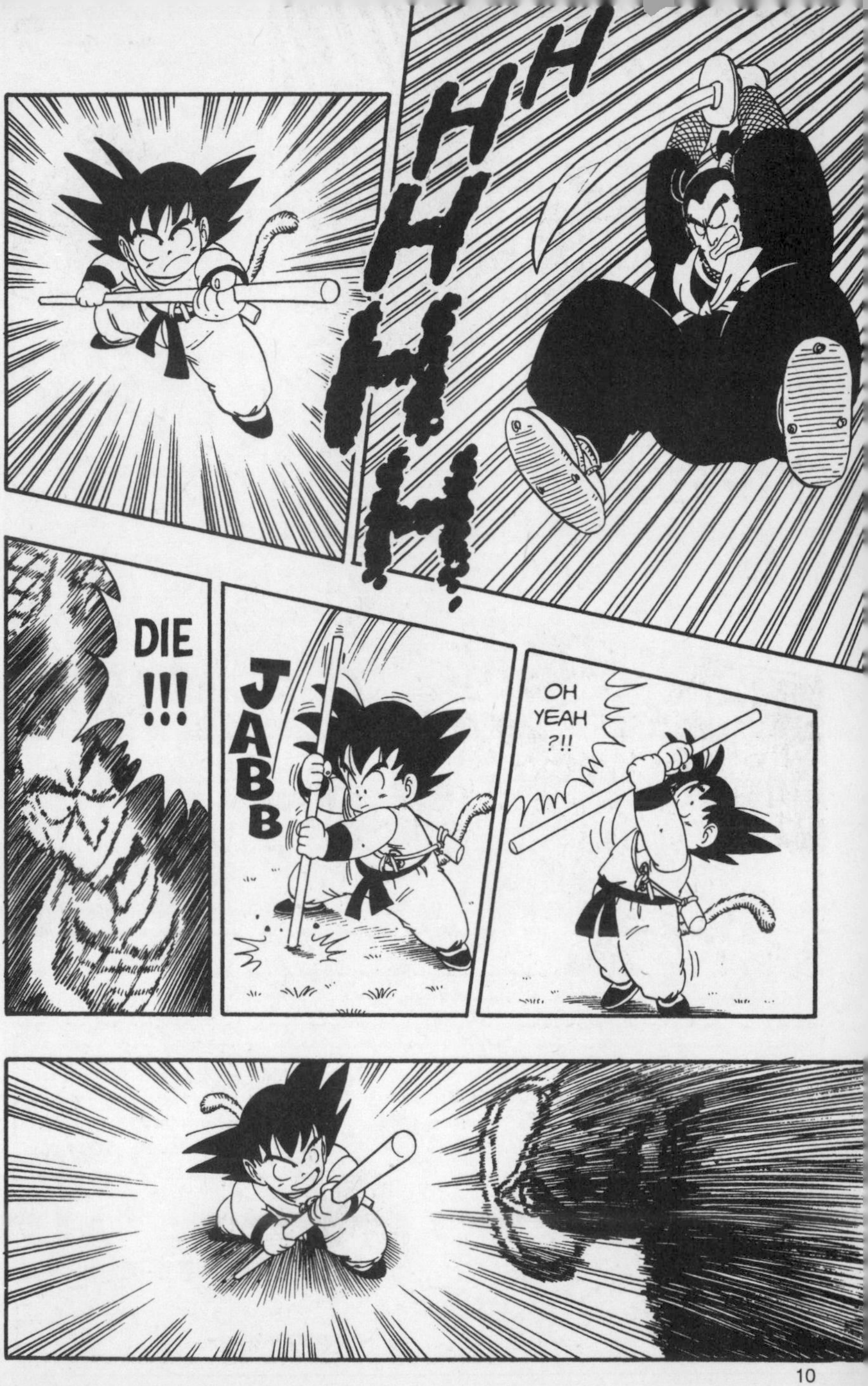
HHHHHH!
OH YEAH ?!!
JABB
DIE !!!

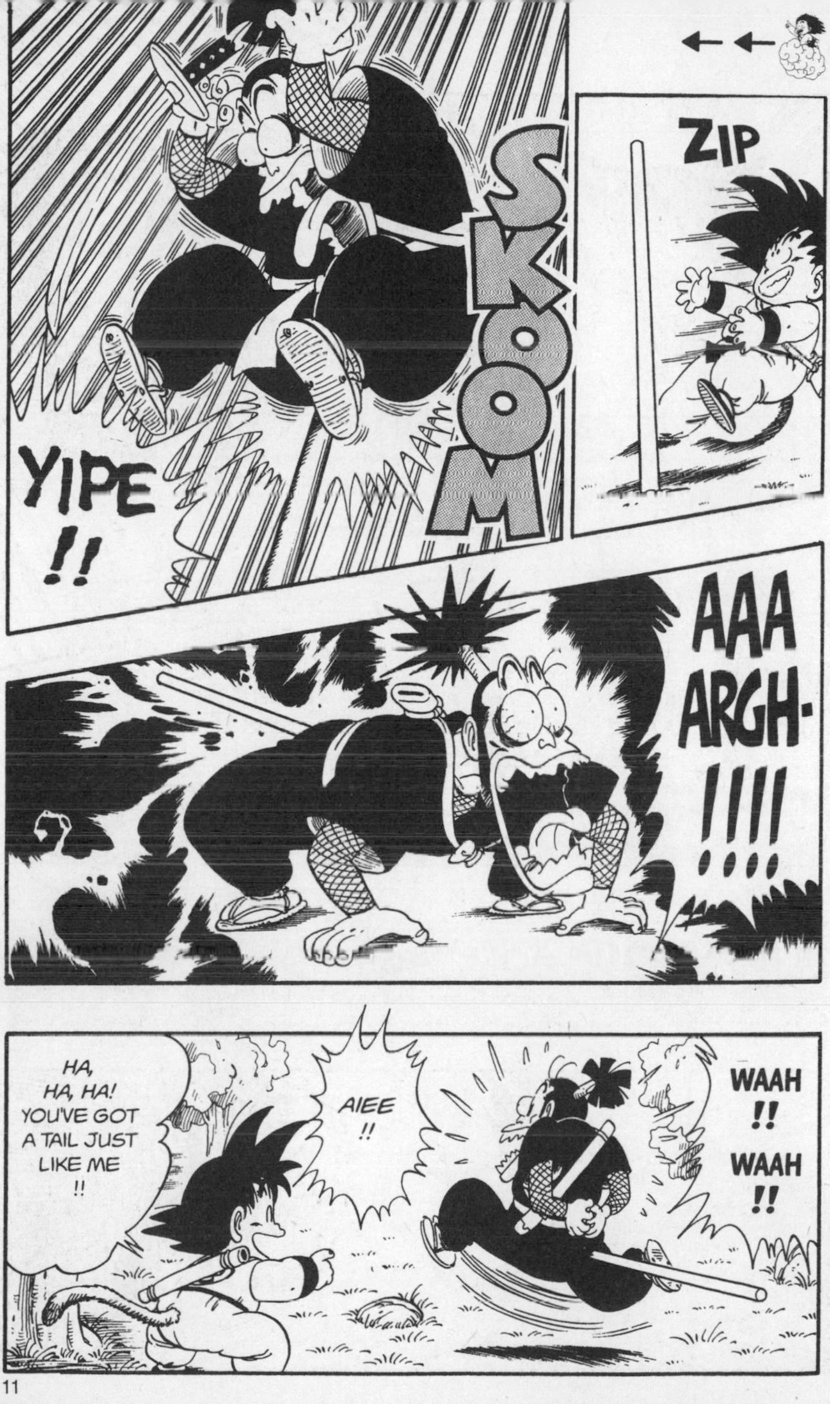
ZIP
SKOOM
YIPE !!
AAA ARGH- !!!!
WAAH !! WAAH !!
AIEE !!
HA, HA, HA! YOU'VE GOT A TAIL JUST LIKE ME !!

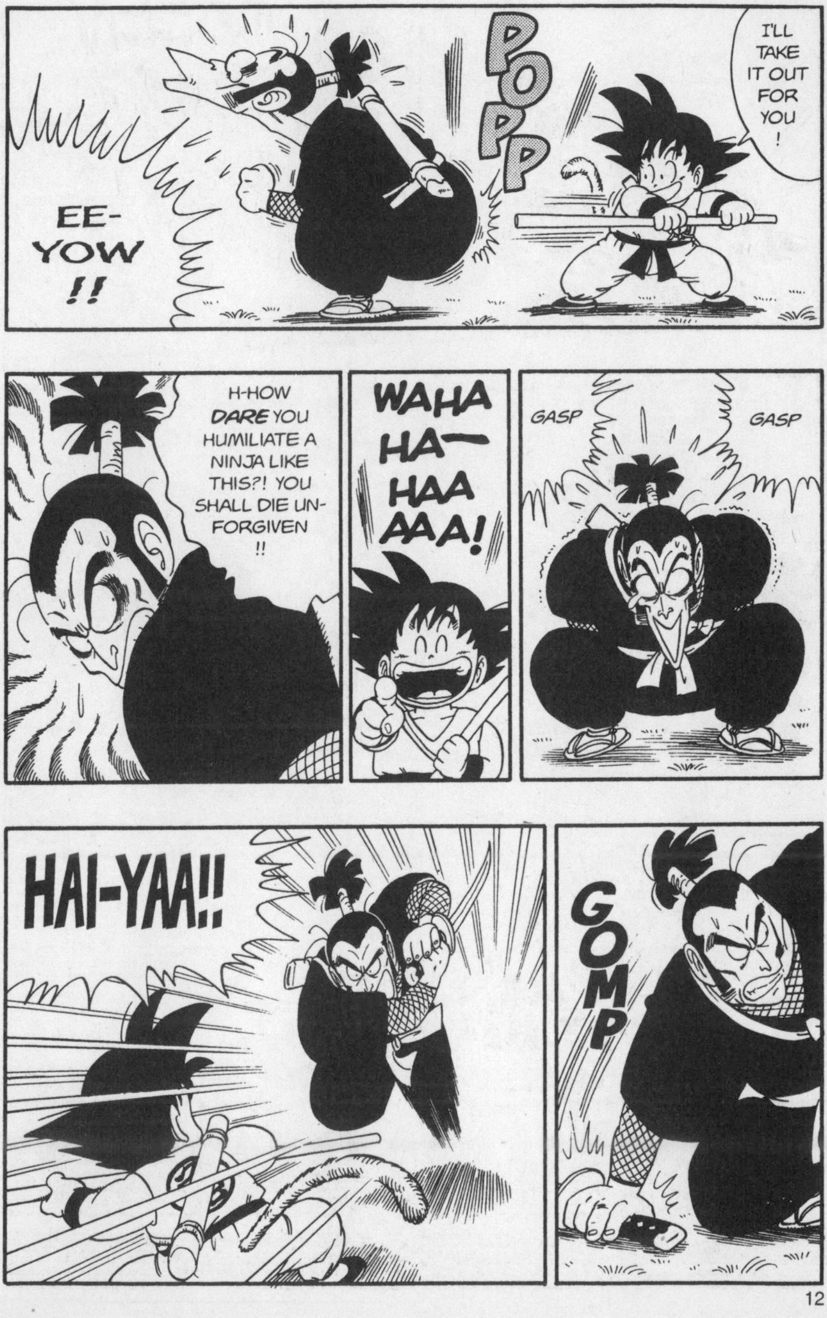
I'LL TAKE IT OUT FOR YOU!
POPP
EE-YOW!!
GASP
GASP
WAHAHA-HAAAAA!
H-HOW DARE YOU HUMILIATE A NINJA LIKE THIS?! YOU SHALL DIE UN-FORGIVEN!!
GOMP
HAI-YAA!!

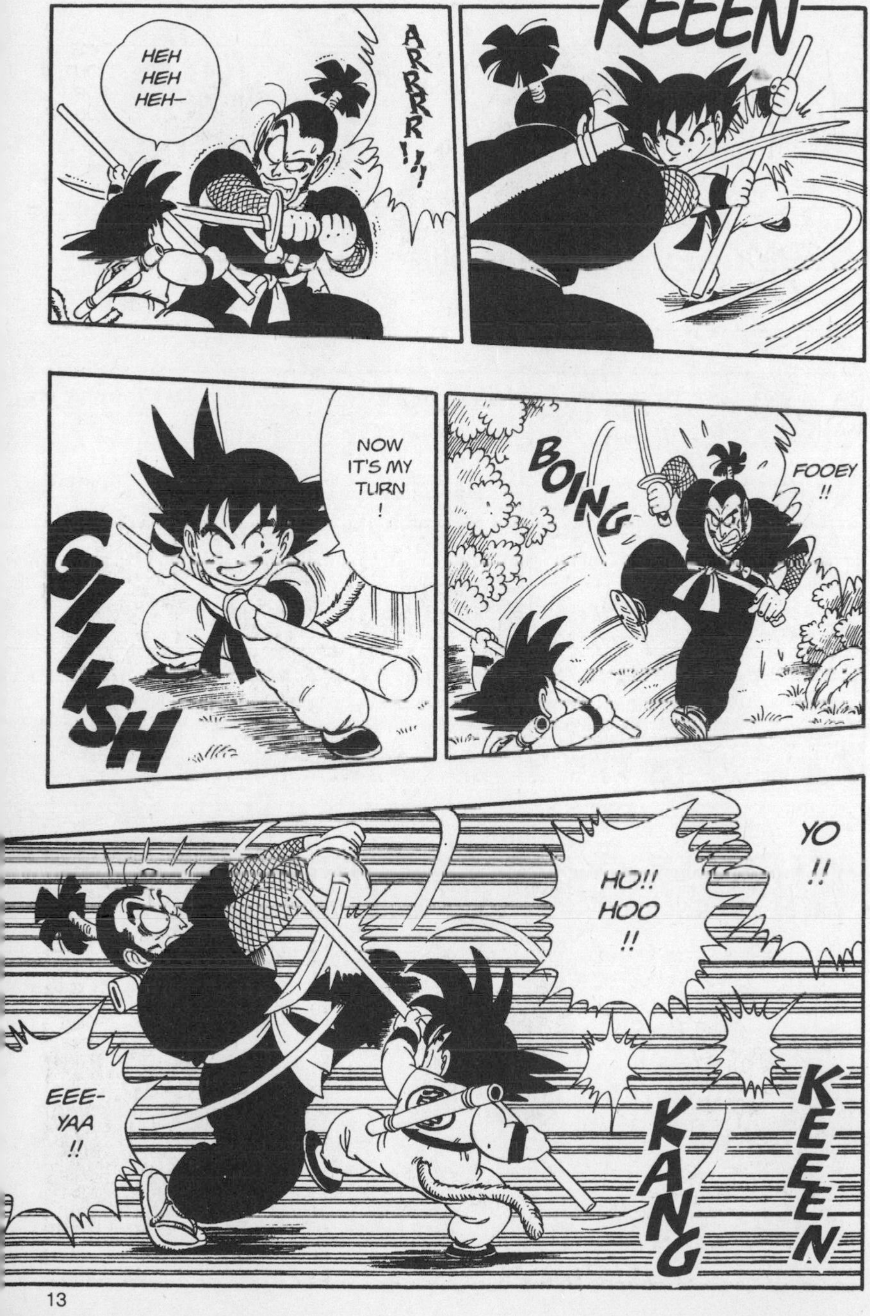
KEEEN
ARRRR!!!
HEH HEH HEH—
FOOEY !!
BOING
NOW IT'S MY TURN !
GIIISH
YO !!
HO!! HOO !!
KEEEN
KANG
EEE-YAA !!

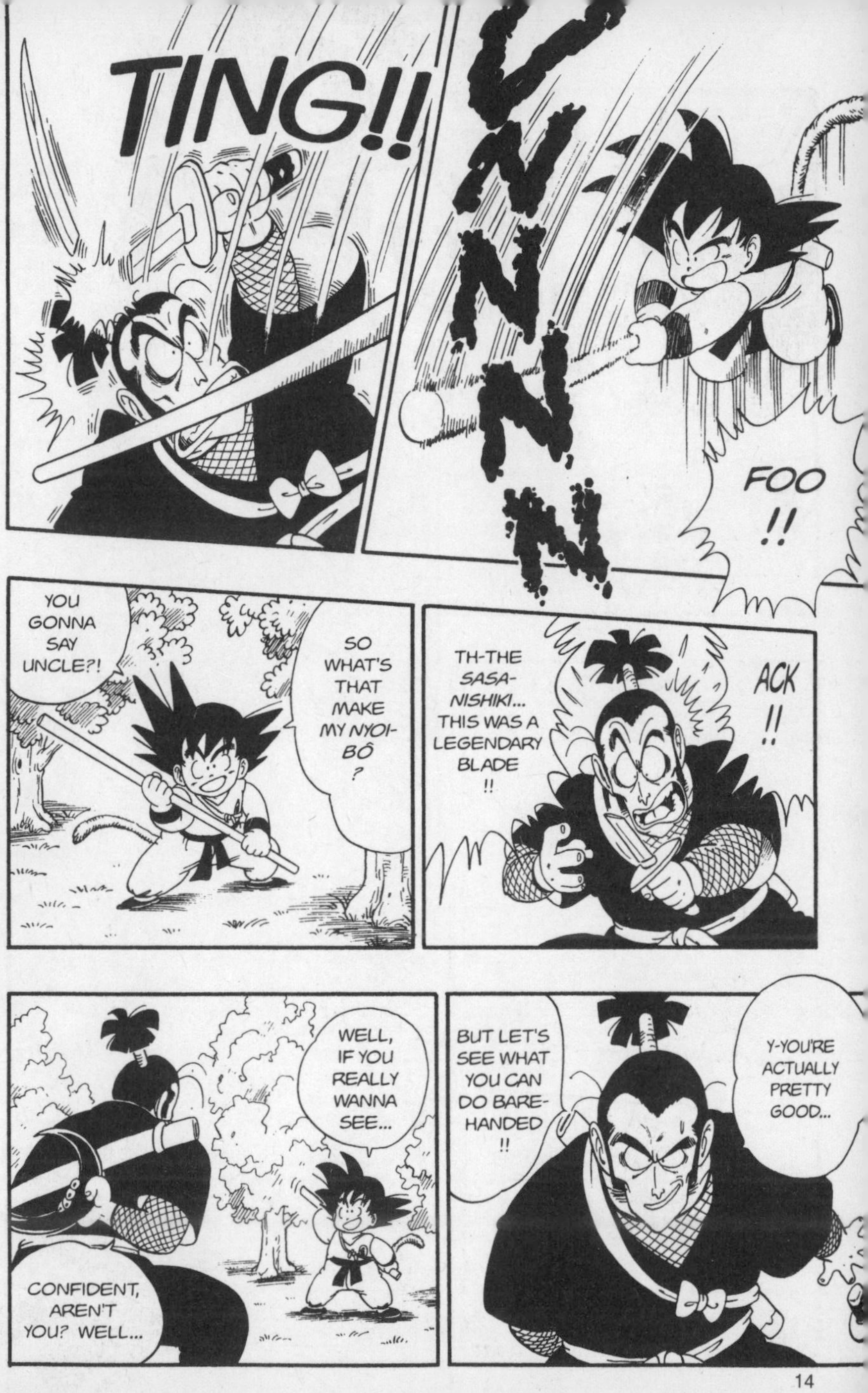
FOO!!
TING!!
ACK!!
TH-THE SASA-NISHIKI... THIS WAS A LEGENDARY BLADE!!
SO WHAT'S THAT MAKE MY NYOI-BÔ?
YOU GONNA SAY UNCLE?!
Y-YOU'RE ACTUALLY PRETTY GOOD...
BUT LET'S SEE WHAT YOU CAN DO BARE-HANDED!!
WELL, IF YOU REALLY WANNA SEE...
CONFIDENT, AREN'T YOU? WELL...

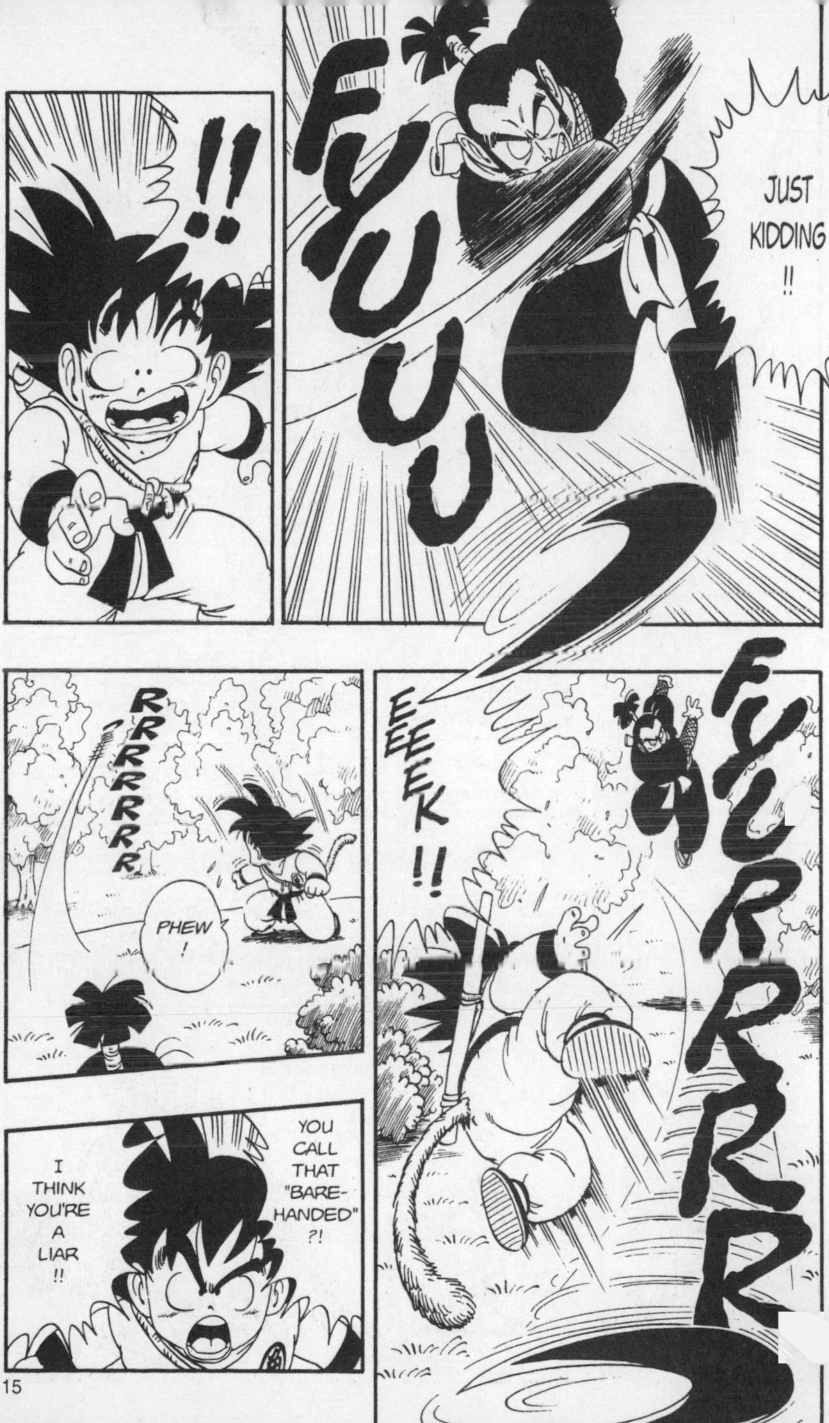
FYUUU
JUST KIDDING !!
!!
FURRRR
EEEEK !!
RRRRRRRR
PHEW !
YOU CALL THAT "BARE-HANDED" ?!
I THINK YOU'RE A LIAR !!

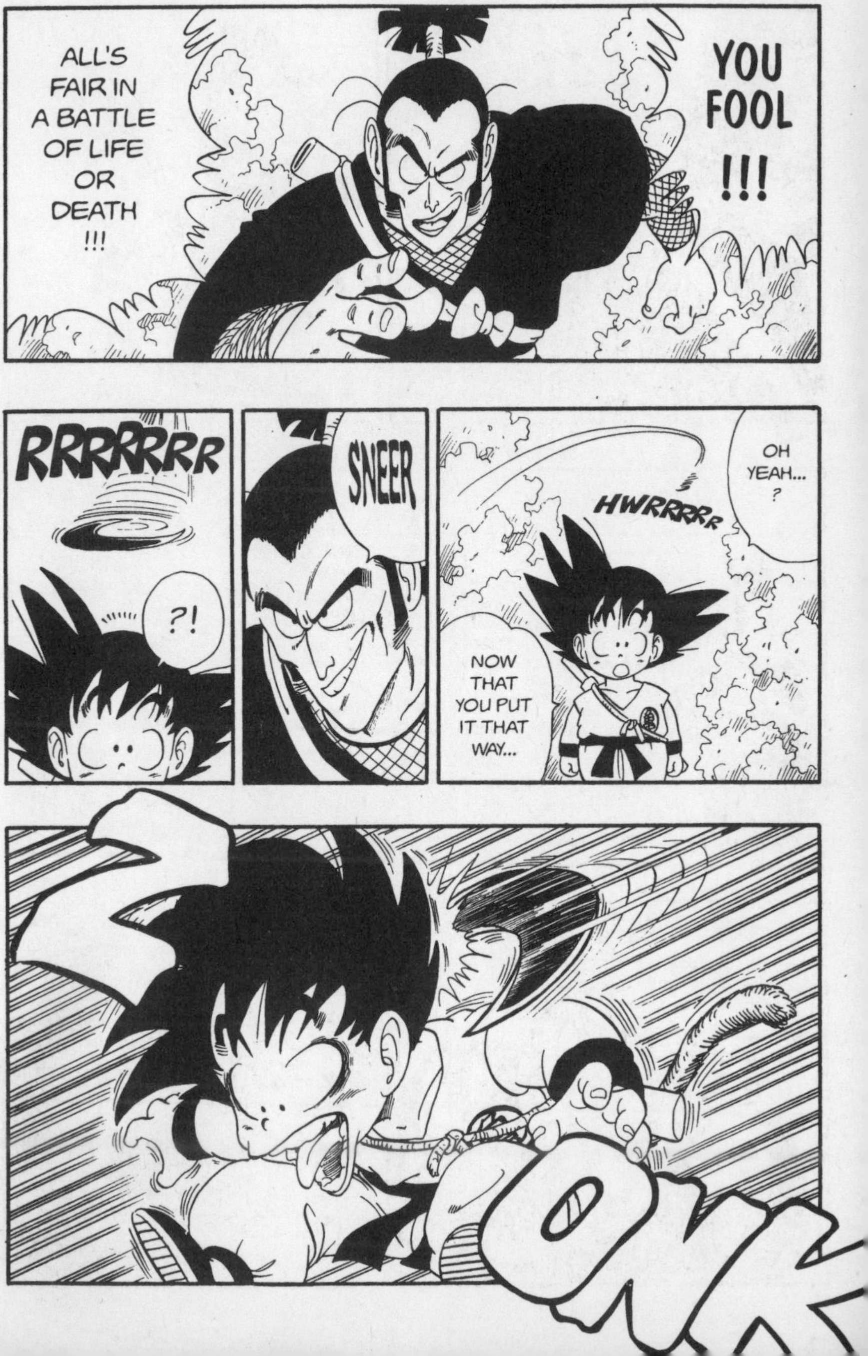
YOU FOOL !!!
ALL'S FAIR IN A BATTLE OF LIFE OR DEATH !!!
OH YEAH... ?
HWRRRRRR
NOW THAT YOU PUT IT THAT WAY...
SNEER
RRRRRRR
?!
ONK

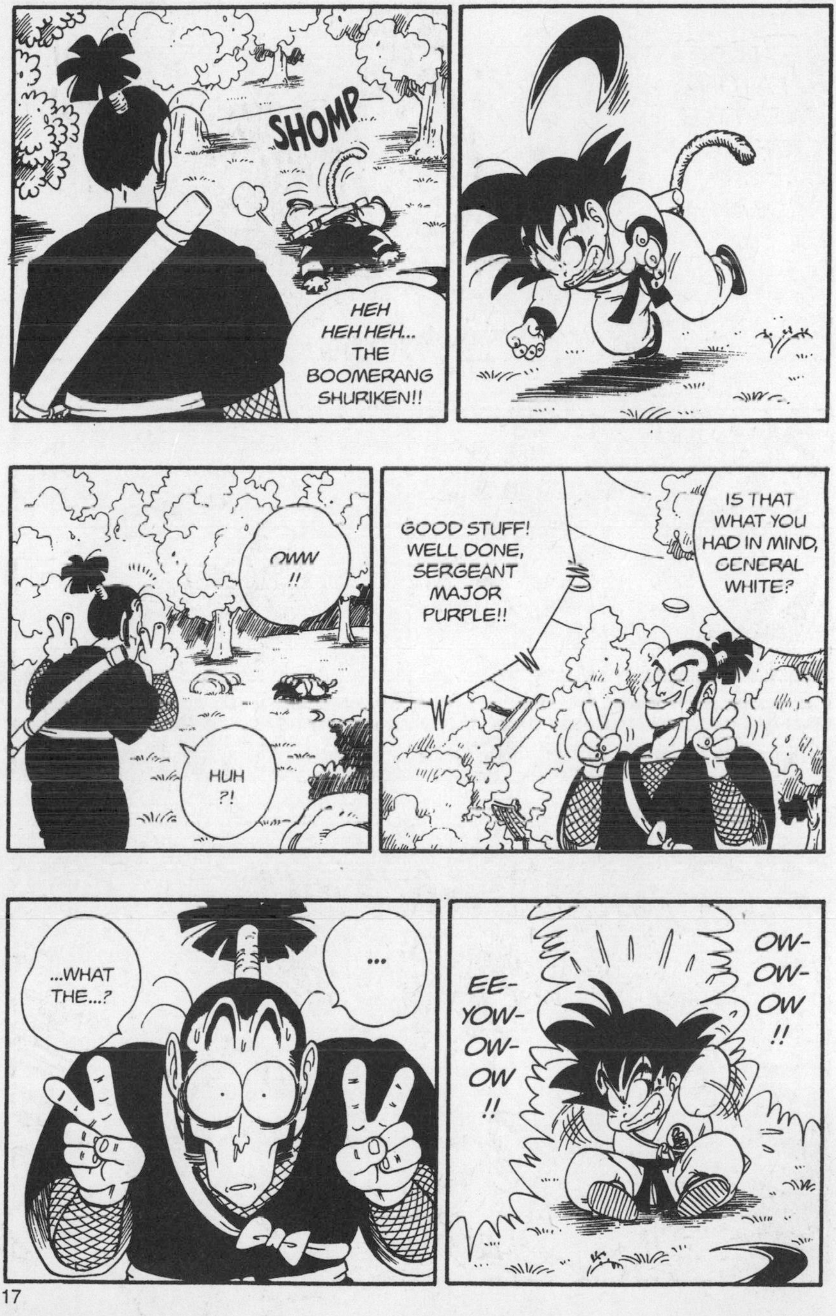
SHOMP
HEH HEH HEH... THE BOOMERANG SHURIKEN!!
IS THAT WHAT YOU HAD IN MIND, GENERAL WHITE?
GOOD STUFF! WELL DONE, SERGEANT MAJOR PURPLE!!
OWW !!
HUH ?!
OW-OW-OW !!
EE-YOW-OW-OW !!
...
...WHAT THE...?

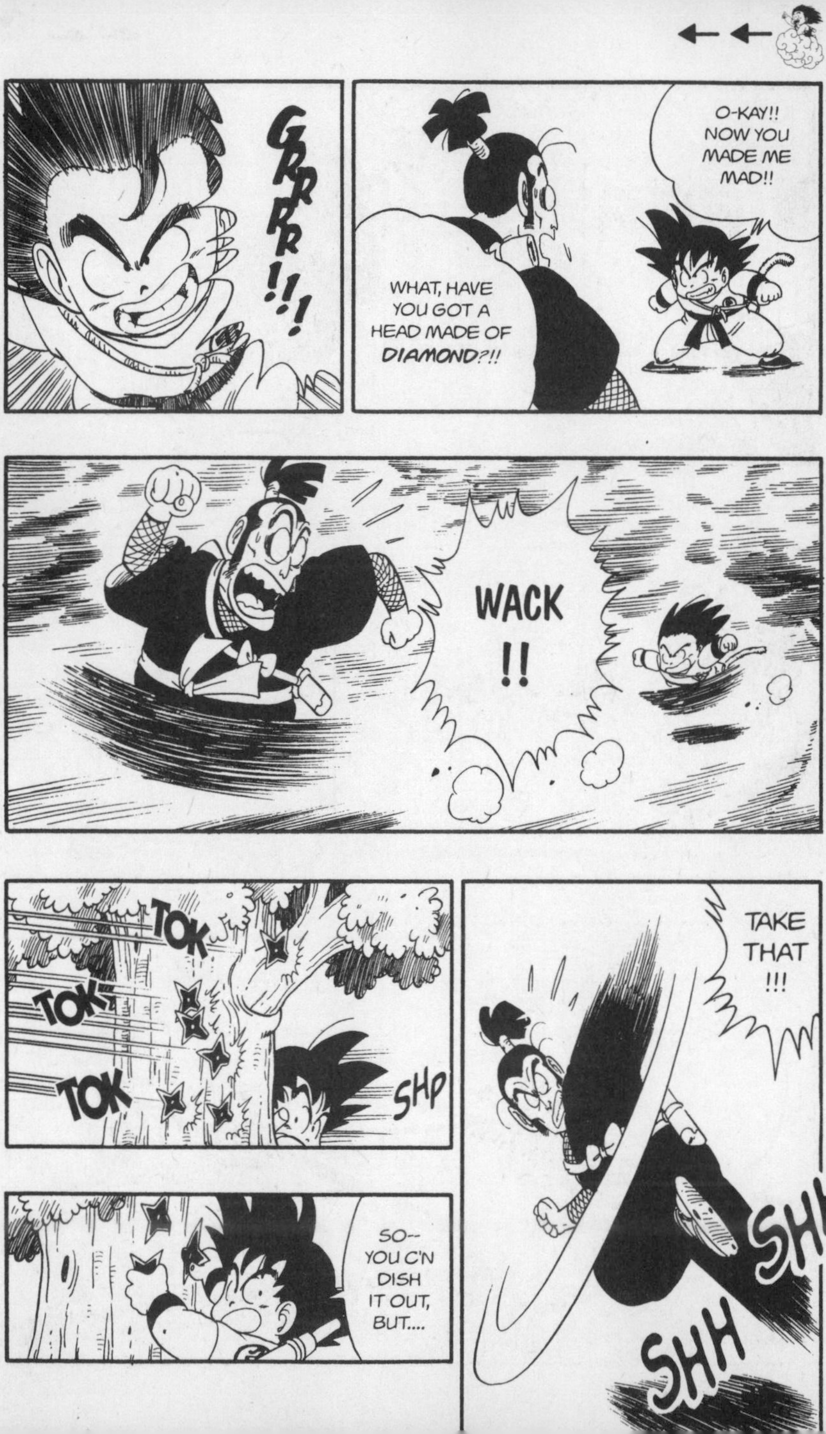
O-KAY!! NOW YOU MADE ME MAD!!
WHAT, HAVE YOU GOT A HEAD MADE OF DIAMOND?!!
GRRRR!!!
WACK !!
TAKE THAT !!!
SHH
SHH
SHH
TOK
TOK
TOK
SHP
SO-- YOU C'N DISH IT OUT, BUT....

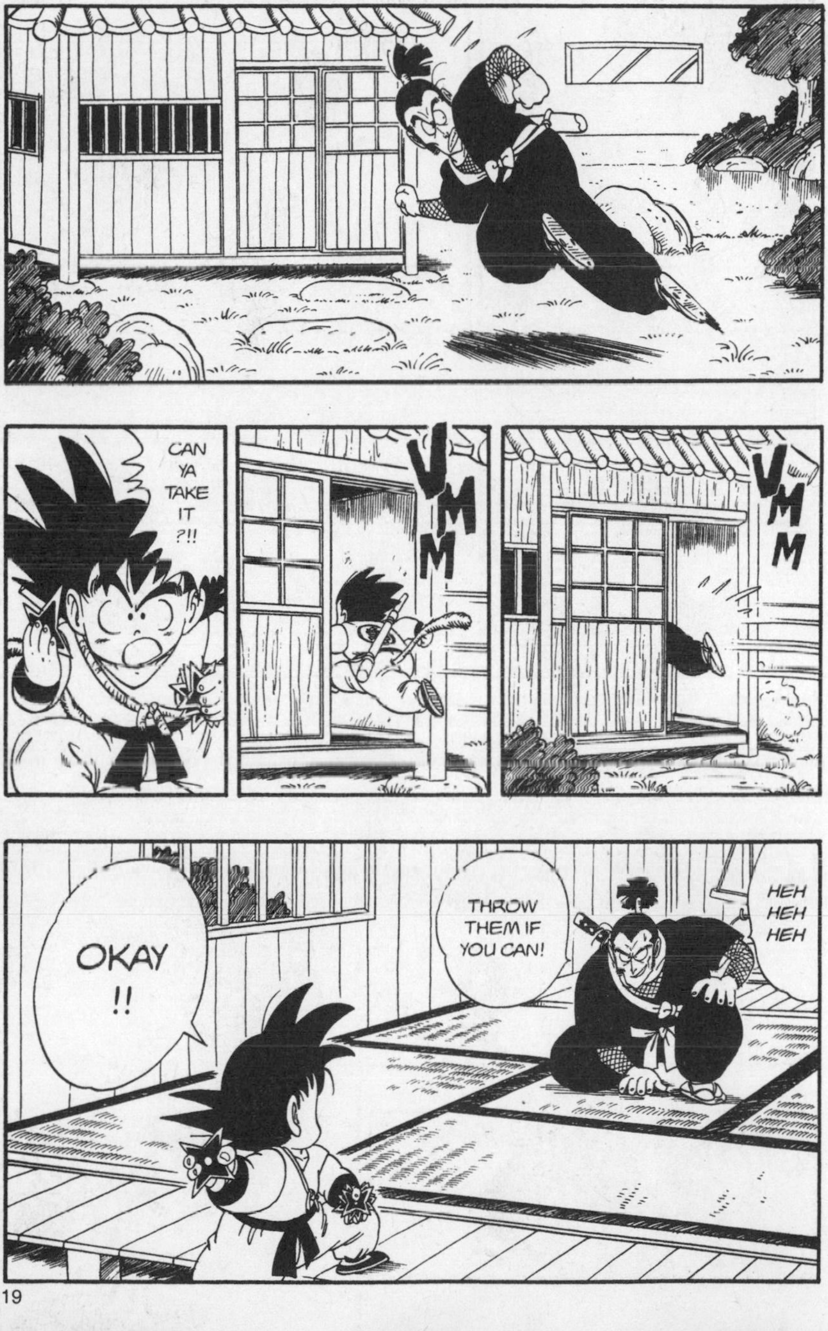
VMM
VMM
CAN YA TAKE IT ?!!
HEH HEH HEH
THROW THEM IF YOU CAN!
OKAY !!

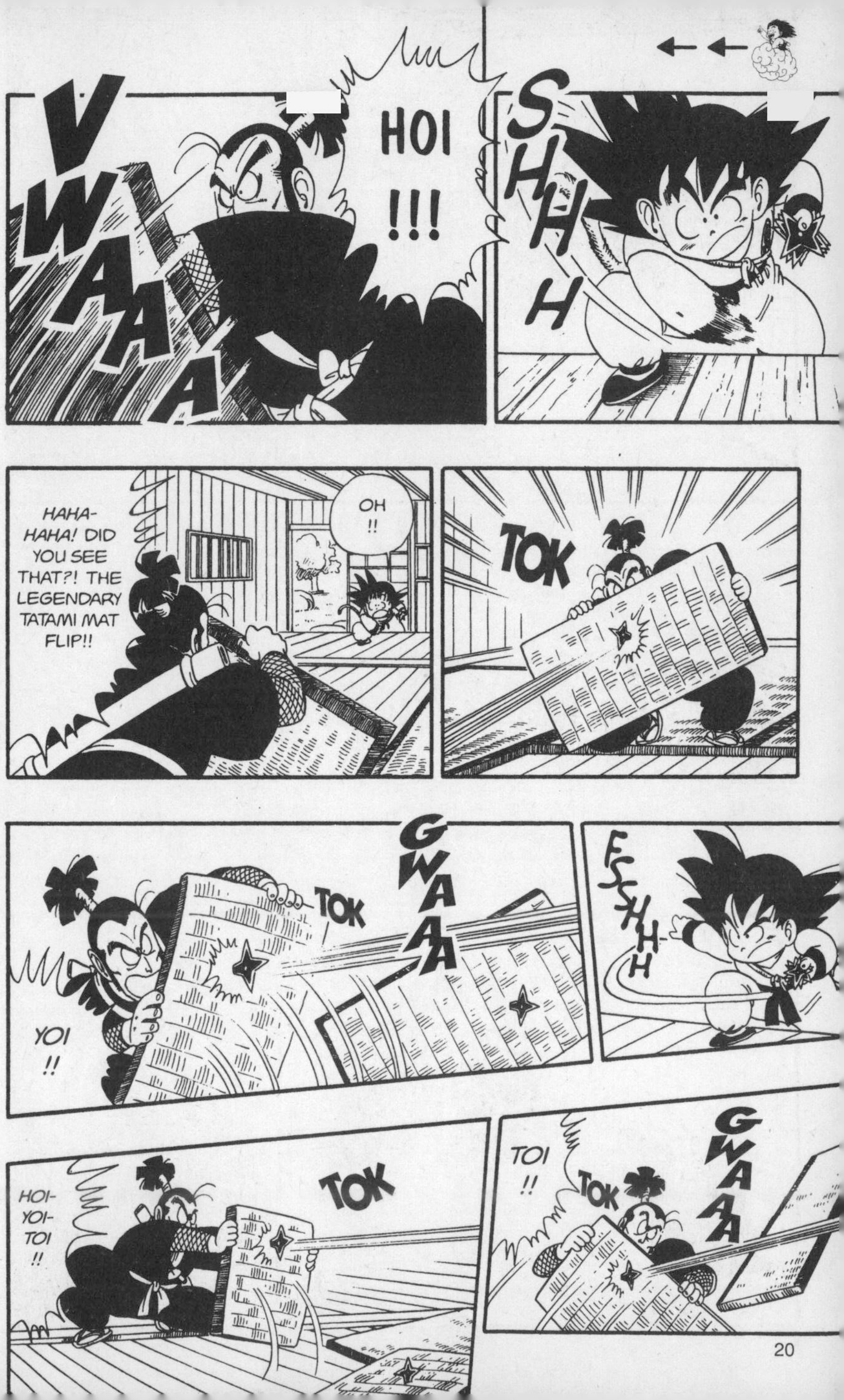
SHHHH
HOI!!!
VWAAAA
TOK
OH!!
HAHA-HAHA! DID YOU SEE THAT?! THE LEGENDARY TATAMI MAT FLIP!!
FSHHH
GWAAAA
TOK
YOI!!
GWAAAA
TOI!!
TOK
TOK
HOI-YOI-TOI!!

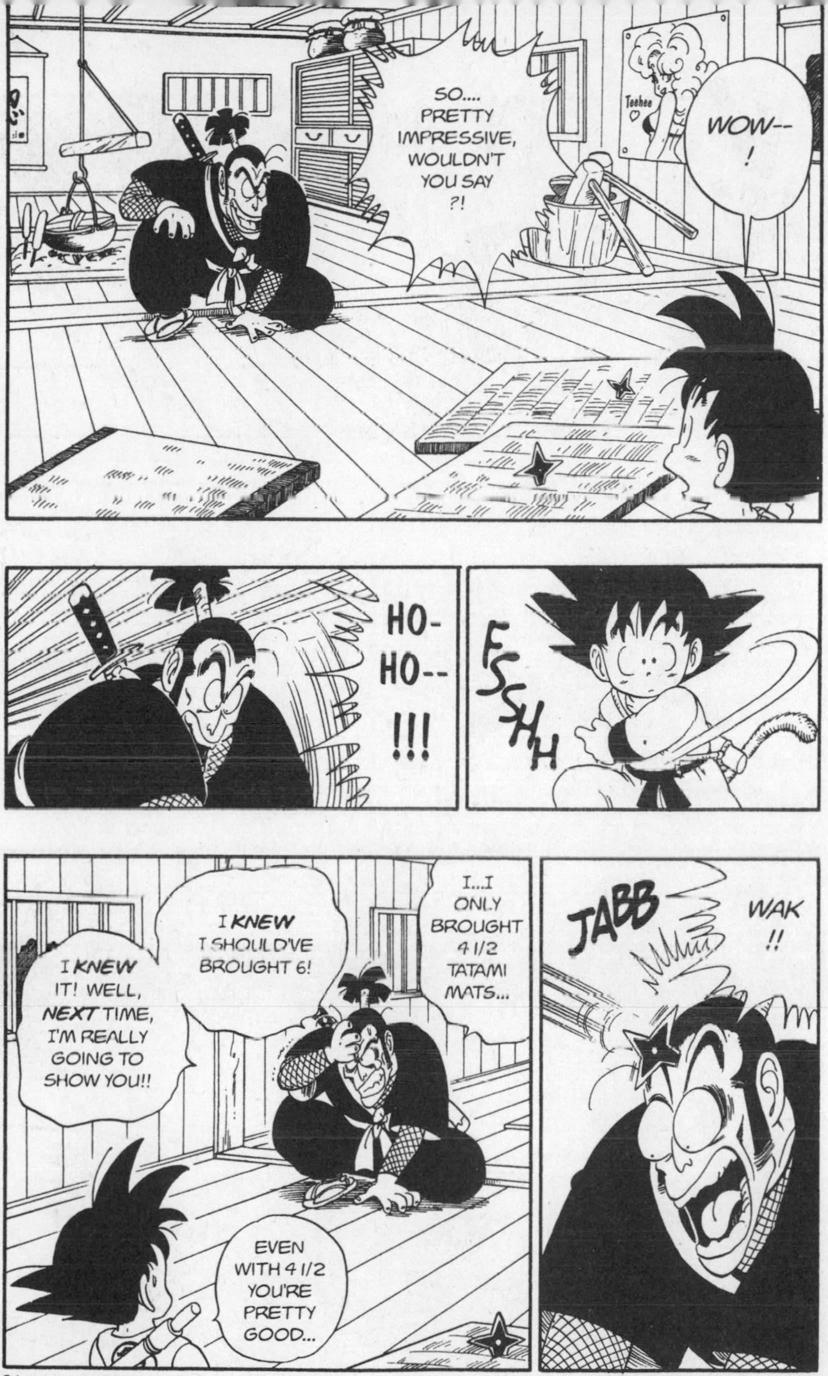
WOW--!
Teehee
SO.... PRETTY IMPRESSIVE, WOULDN'T YOU SAY ?!
FSSHH
HO-HO--!!!
WAK !!
JABB
I...I ONLY BROUGHT 4 1/2 TATAMI MATS...
I KNEW I SHOULD'VE BROUGHT 6!
I KNEW IT! WELL, NEXT TIME, I'M REALLY GOING TO SHOW YOU!!
EVEN WITH 4 1/2 YOU'RE PRETTY GOOD...

ドラゴンボール

DRAGON BALL

Tale 62 • The Ninja Split!

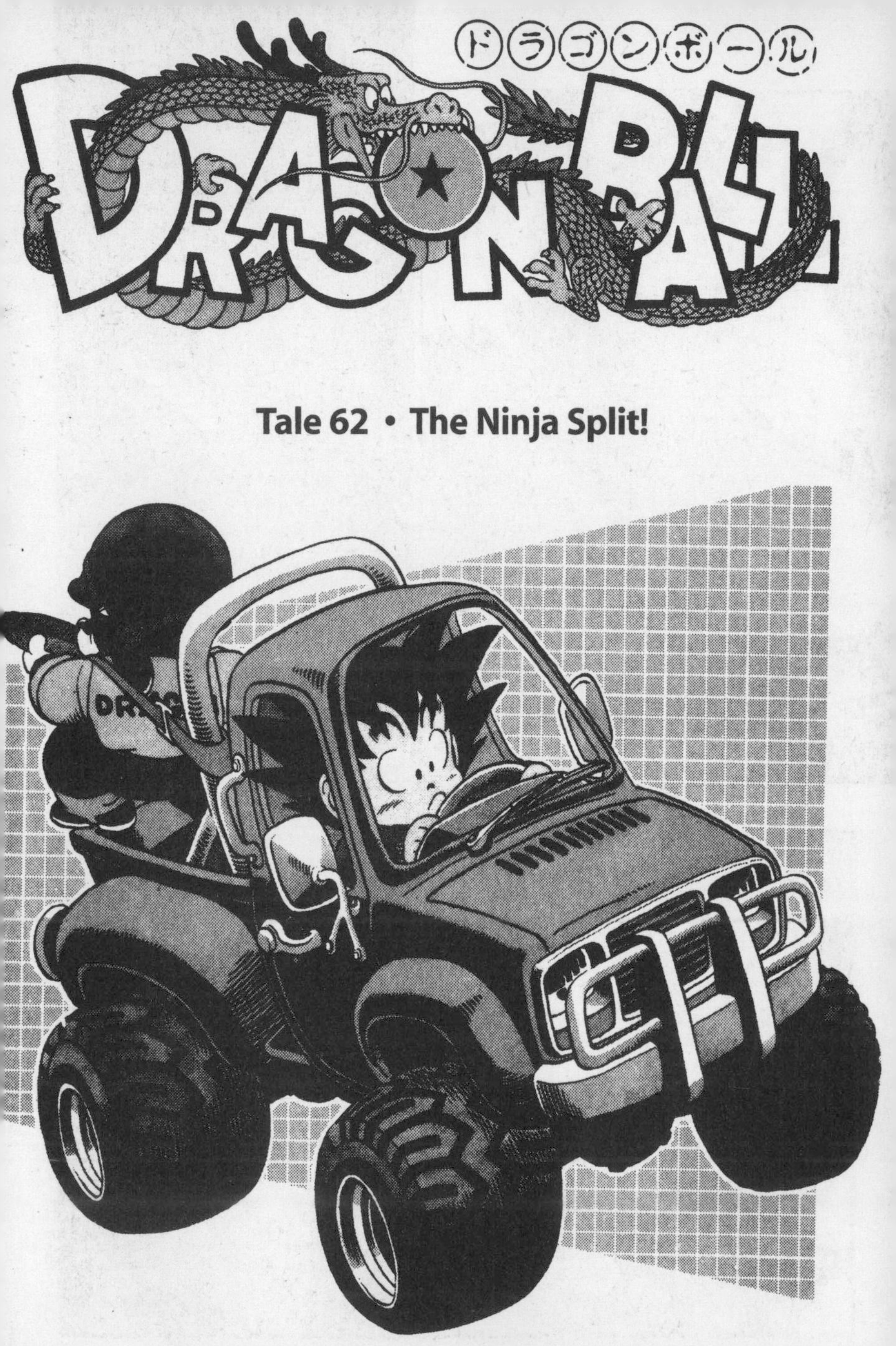

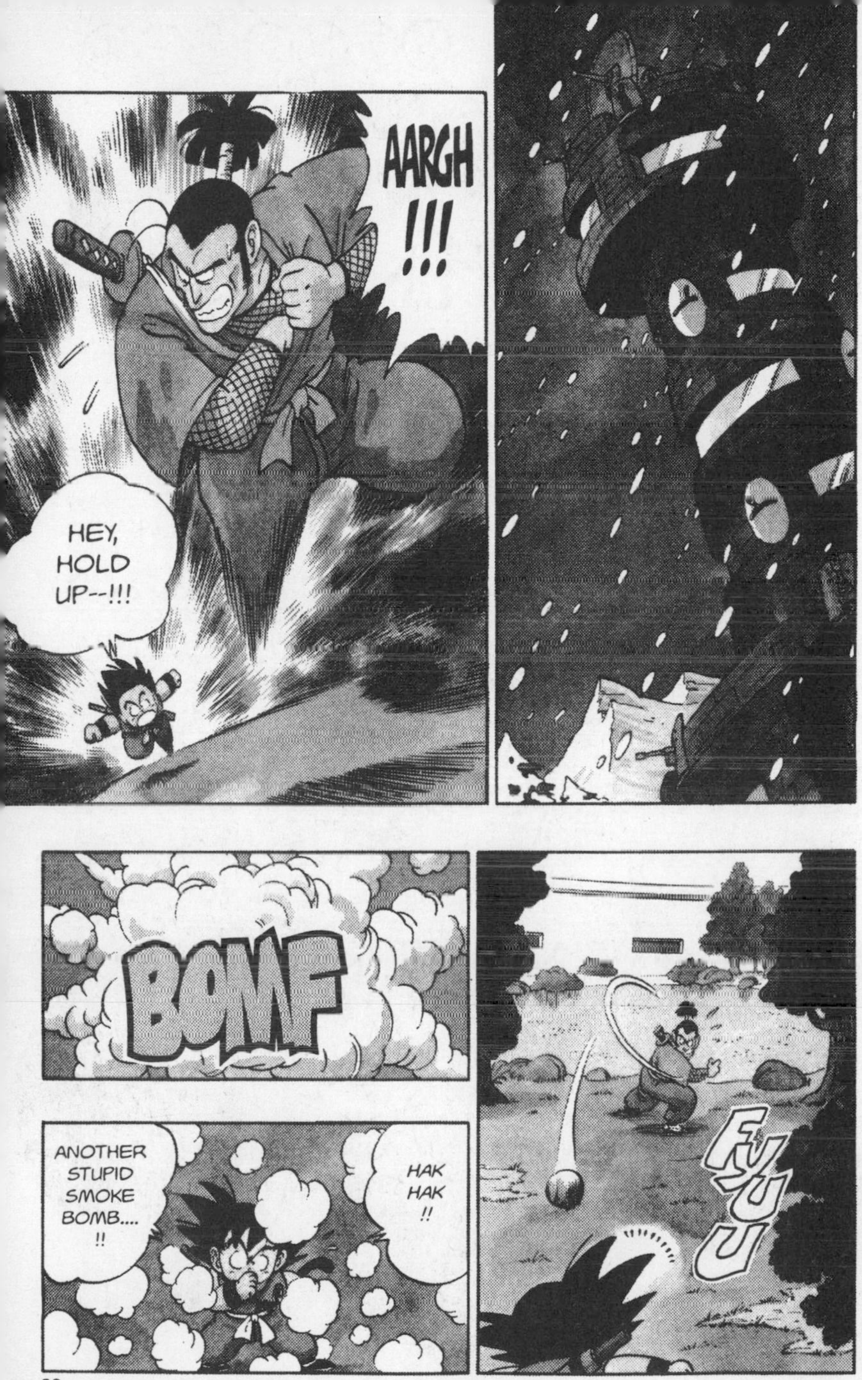
AARGH !!!
HEY, HOLD UP--!!!
FYUUU
BOMF
HAK HAK !!
ANOTHER STUPID SMOKE BOMB.... !!

SON GOKU

HERO OF THE ANCIENT CHINESE FABLE **SAIYÛKI** ("JOURNEY TO THE WEST")

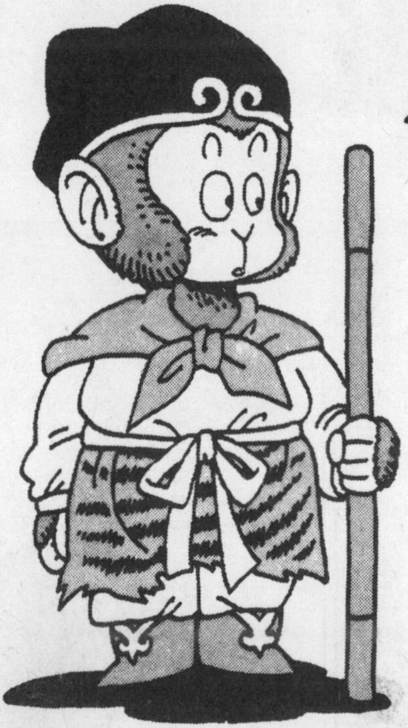

SON GOKU

HERO OF ***DRAGON BALL***

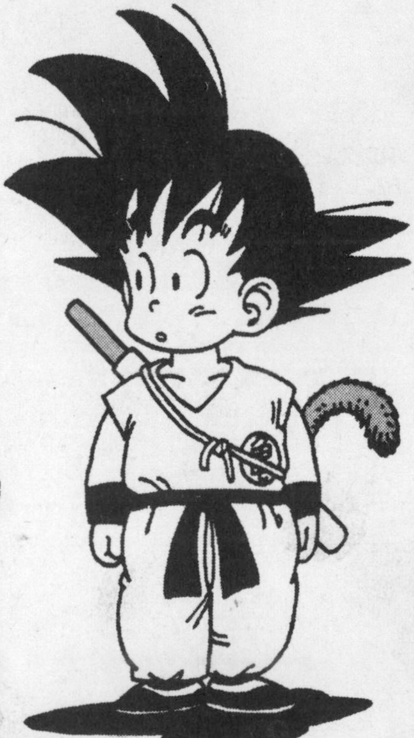

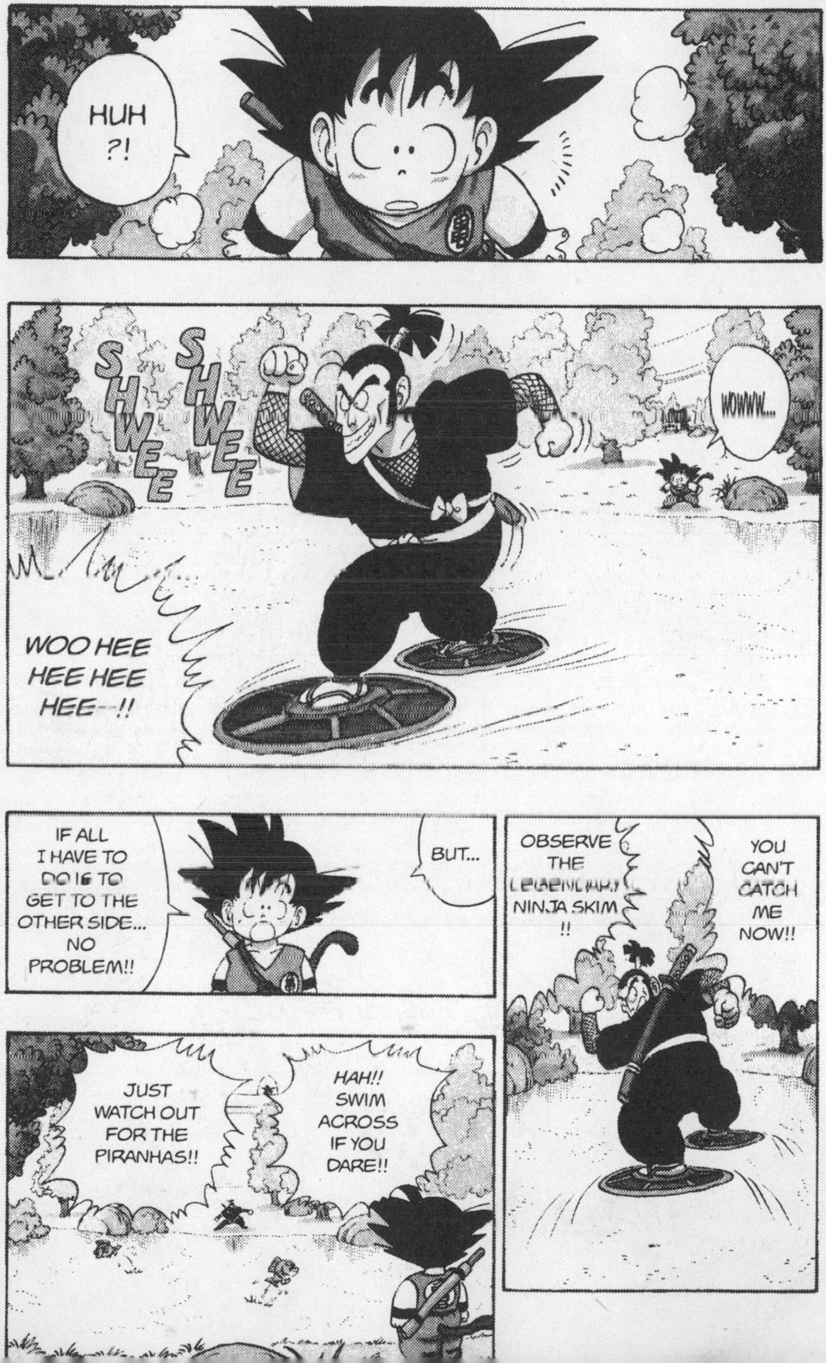
HUH ?!
WOWWW...
SHWEE
SHWEE
WOO HEE HEE HEE HEE--!!
YOU CAN'T CATCH ME NOW!!
OBSERVE THE LEGENDARY NINJA SKIM !!
BUT...
IF ALL I HAVE TO DO IS TO GET TO THE OTHER SIDE... NO PROBLEM!!
HAH!! SWIM ACROSS IF YOU DARE!!
JUST WATCH OUT FOR THE PIRANHAS!!

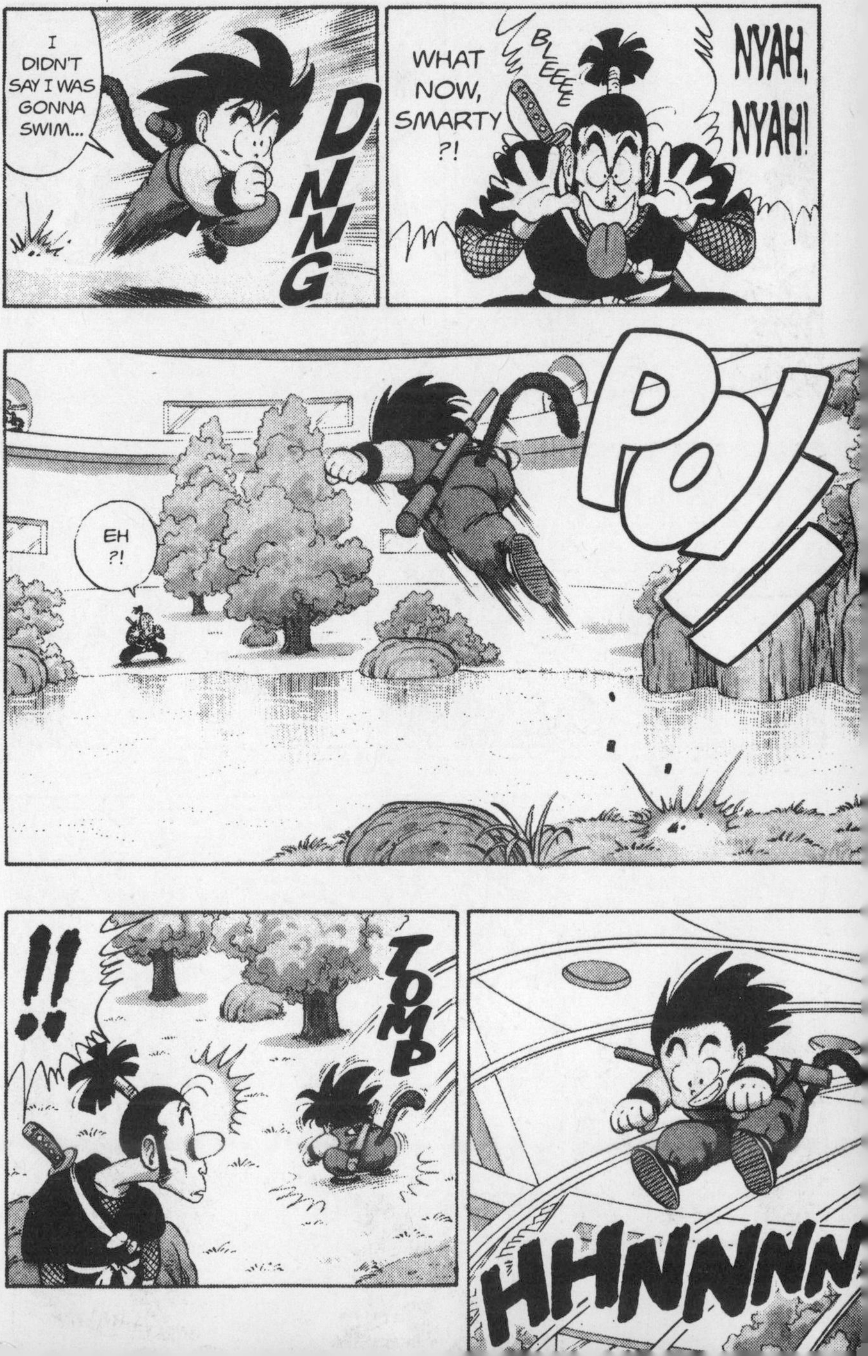
NYAH, NYAH!
BLEEEE
WHAT NOW, SMARTY?!
I DIDN'T SAY I WAS GONNA SWIM...
DNNG
POY
EH?!
HHNNNNN
TOMP
!!

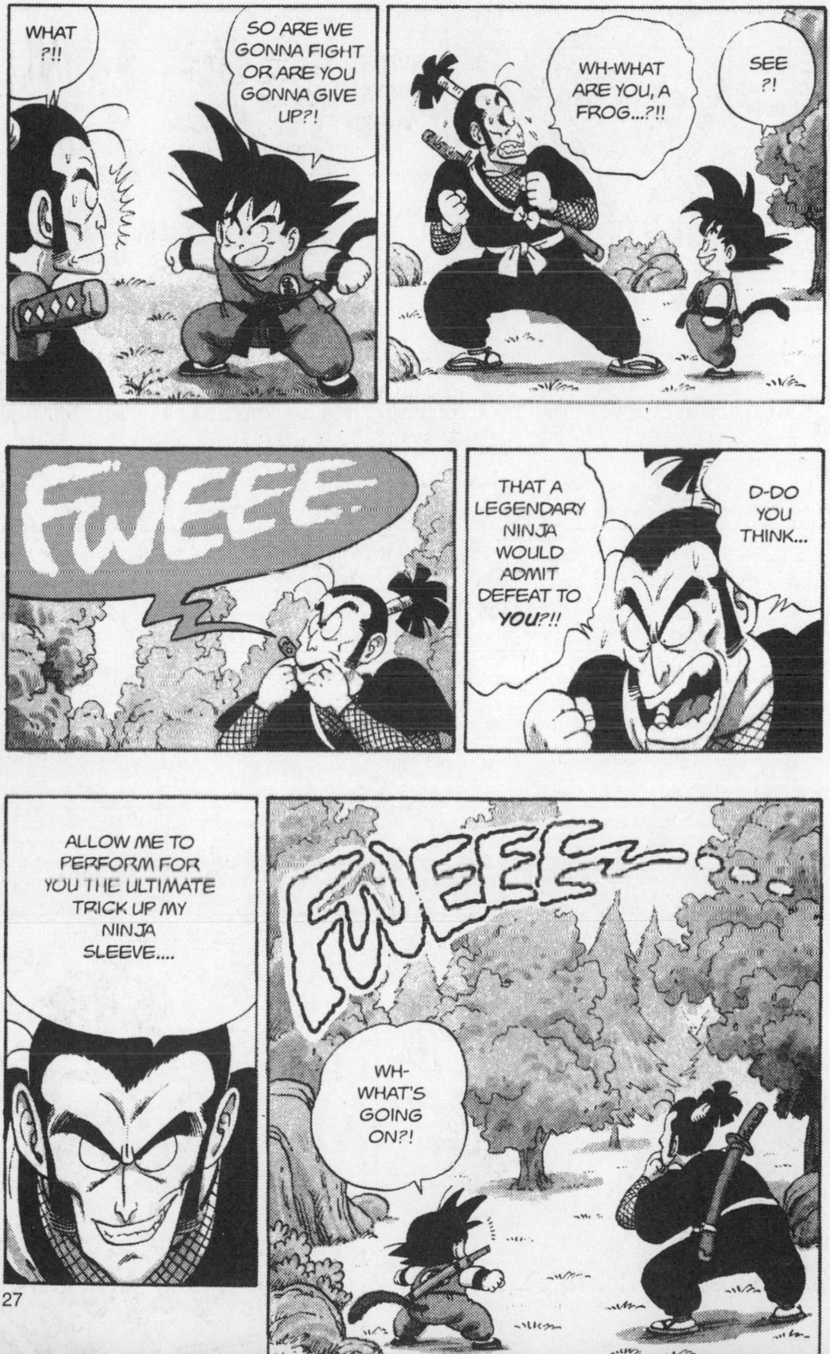
SEE ?!
WH-WHAT ARE YOU, A FROG...?!!
SO ARE WE GONNA FIGHT OR ARE YOU GONNA GIVE UP?!
WHAT ?!!
D-DO YOU THINK...
THAT A LEGENDARY NINJA WOULD ADMIT DEFEAT TO *YOU*?!!
FWEEE
FWEEE
WH- WHAT'S GOING ON?!
ALLOW ME TO PERFORM FOR YOU THE ULTIMATE TRICK UP MY NINJA SLEEVE....

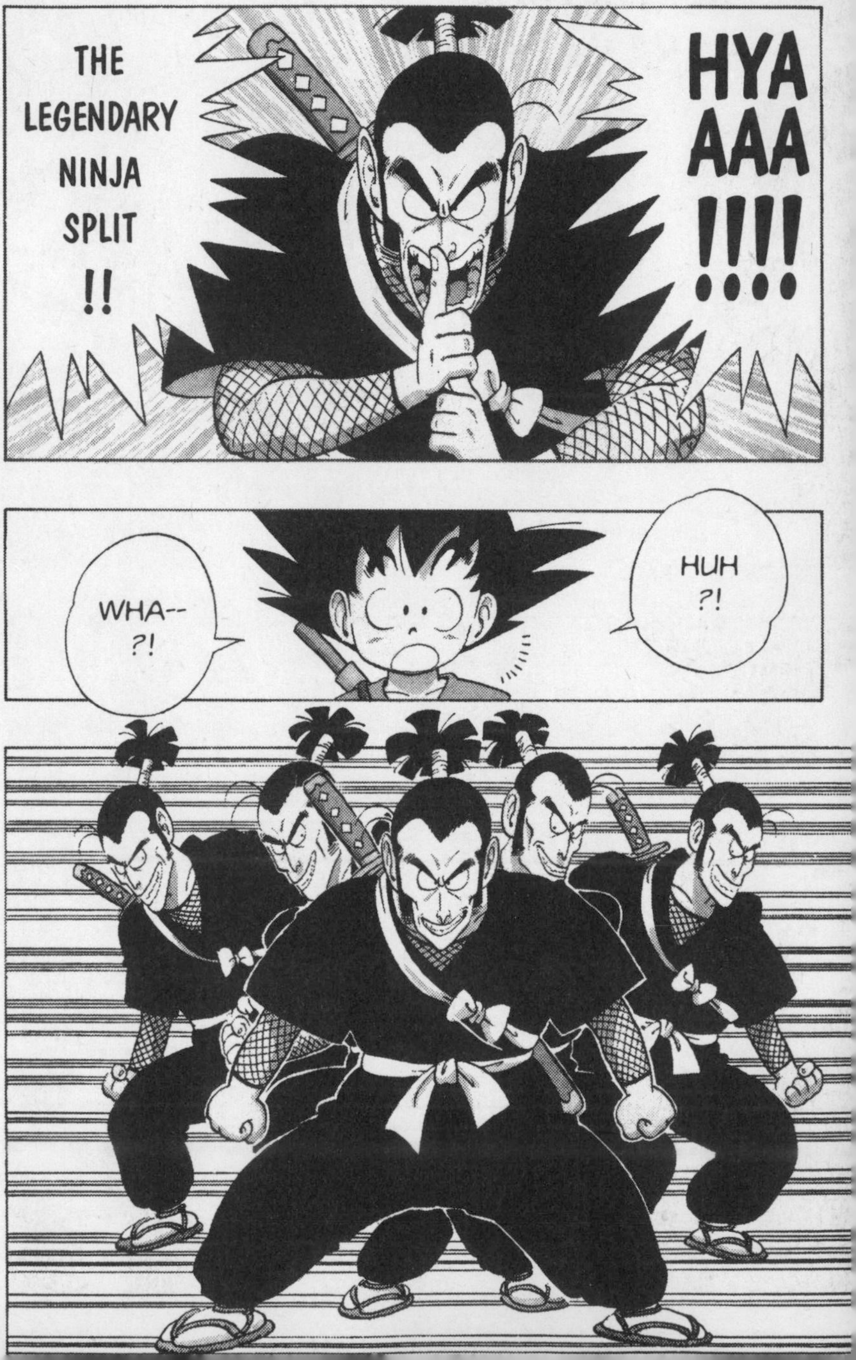
HYA AAA !!!!
THE LEGENDARY NINJA SPLIT !!
HUH ?!
WHA-- ?!

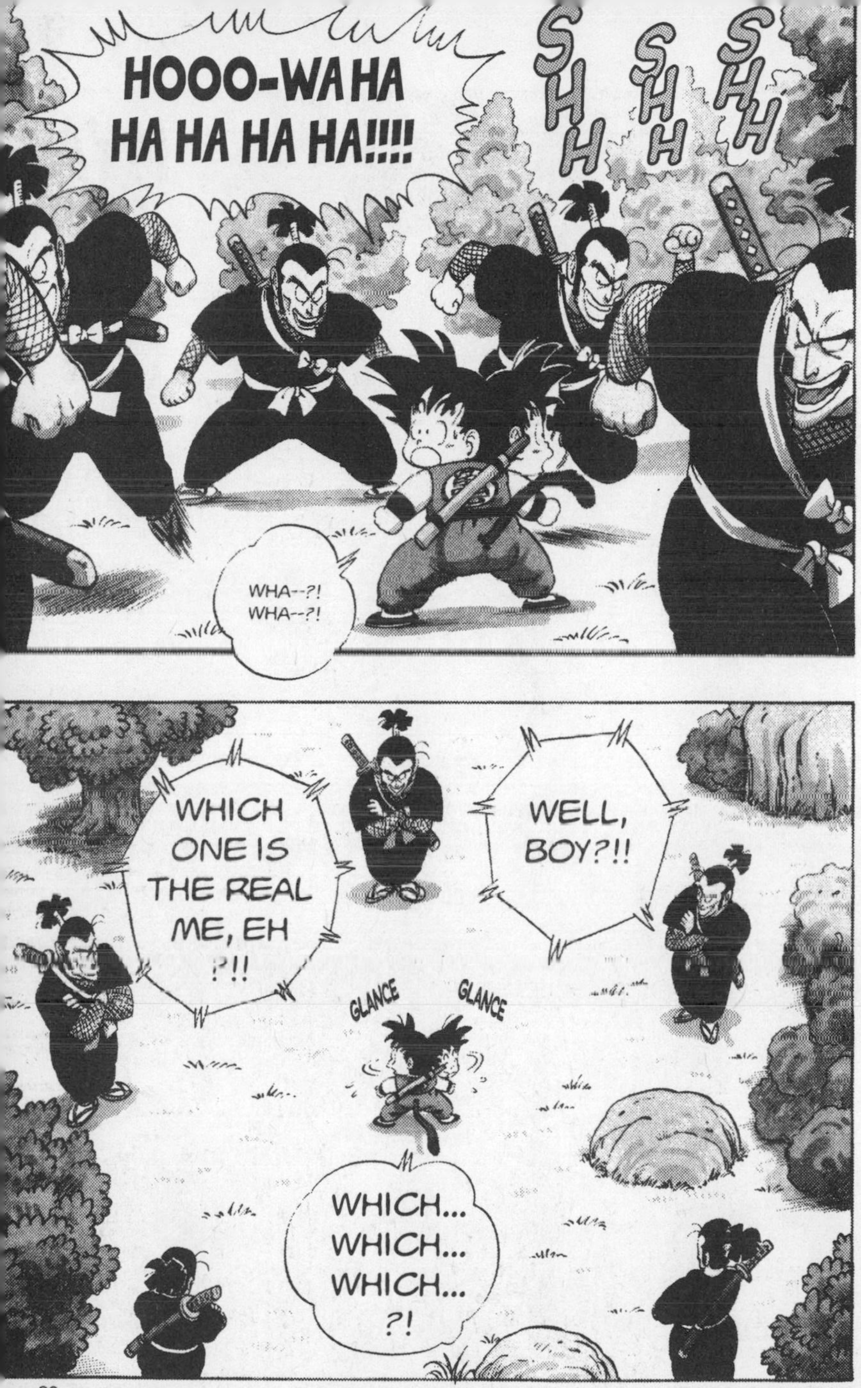
SHHH
SHHH
SHHH
HOOO-WAHA HA HA HA HA!!!!
WHA--?! WHA--?!
WELL, BOY?!!
WHICH ONE IS THE REAL ME, EH ?!!
GLANCE
GLANCE
WHICH... WHICH... WHICH... ?!

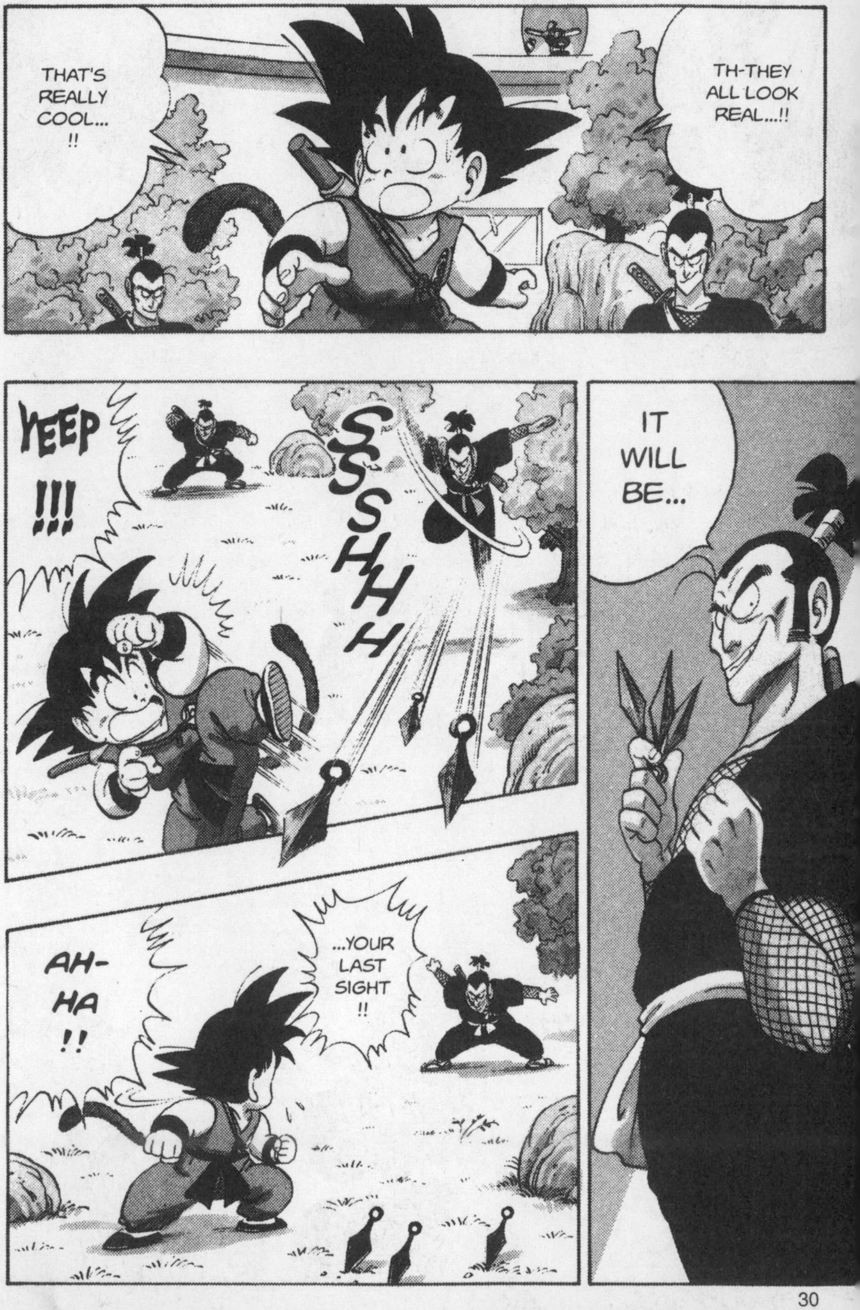
TH-THEY ALL LOOK REAL...!!
THAT'S REALLY COOL... !!
IT WILL BE...
SSSHHHH
YEEP !!!
...YOUR LAST SIGHT !!
AH-HA !!

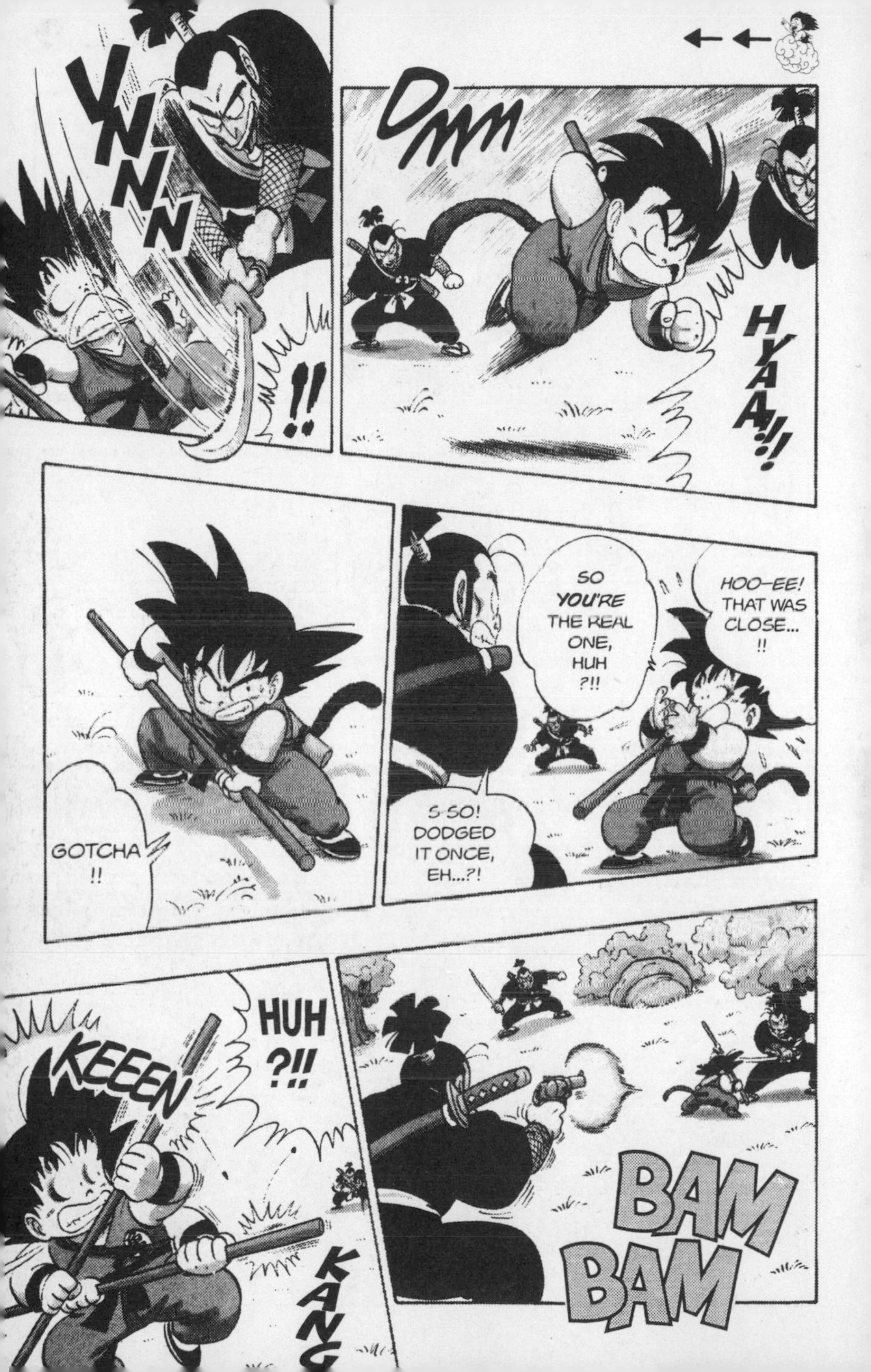
OMM
HYAA!!
VNNNN
!!
HOO-EE! THAT WAS CLOSE... !!
SO YOU'RE THE REAL ONE, HUH ?!!
S-SO! DODGED IT ONCE, EH...?!
GOTCHA !!
BAM BAM
HUH ?!!
KEEEN
KANG

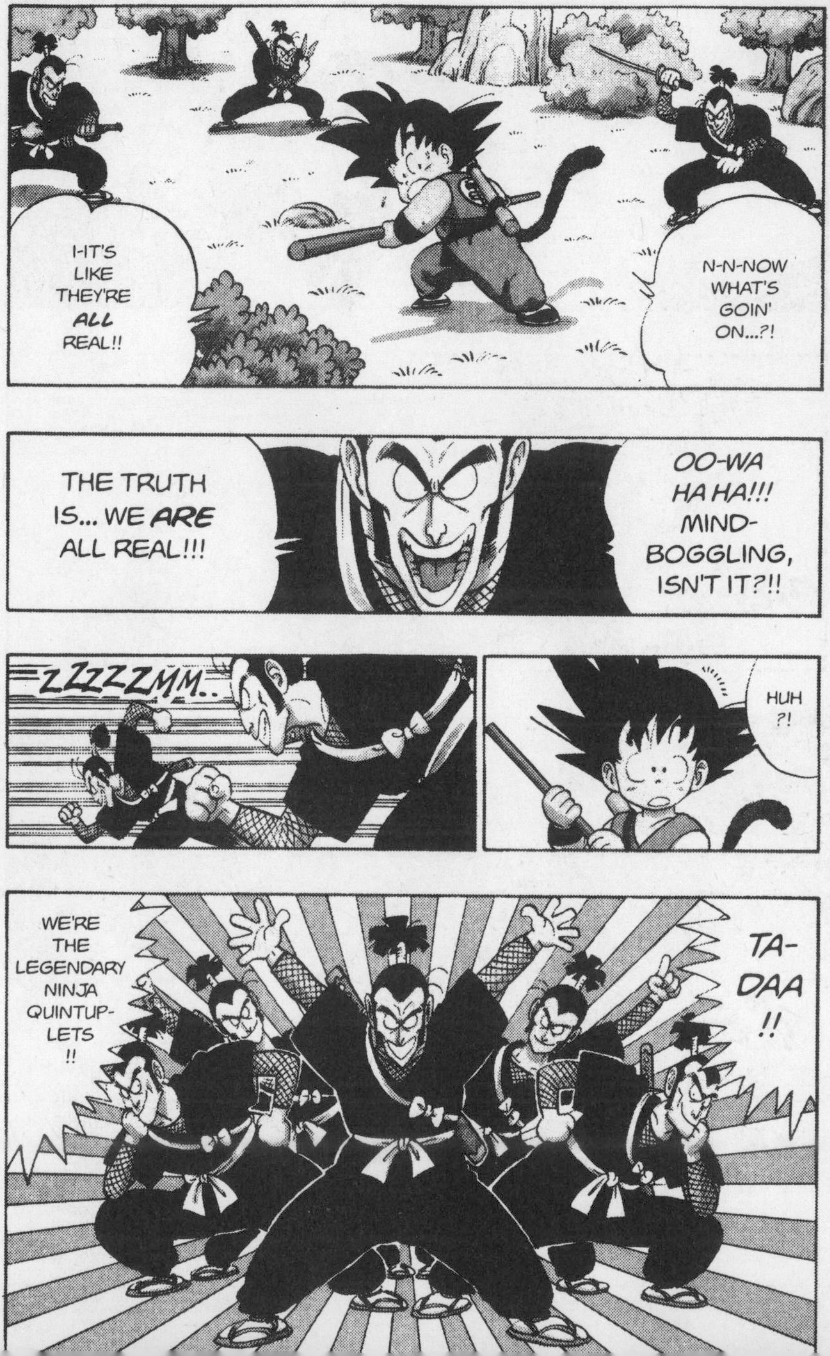
N-N-NOW WHAT'S GOIN' ON...?!
I-IT'S LIKE THEY'RE ALL REAL!!
OO-WA HA HA!!! MIND-BOGGLING, ISN'T IT?!!
THE TRUTH IS... WE ARE ALL REAL!!!
HUH ?!
ZZZZZMM..
TA-DAA !!
WE'RE THE LEGENDARY NINJA QUINTUP-LETS !!

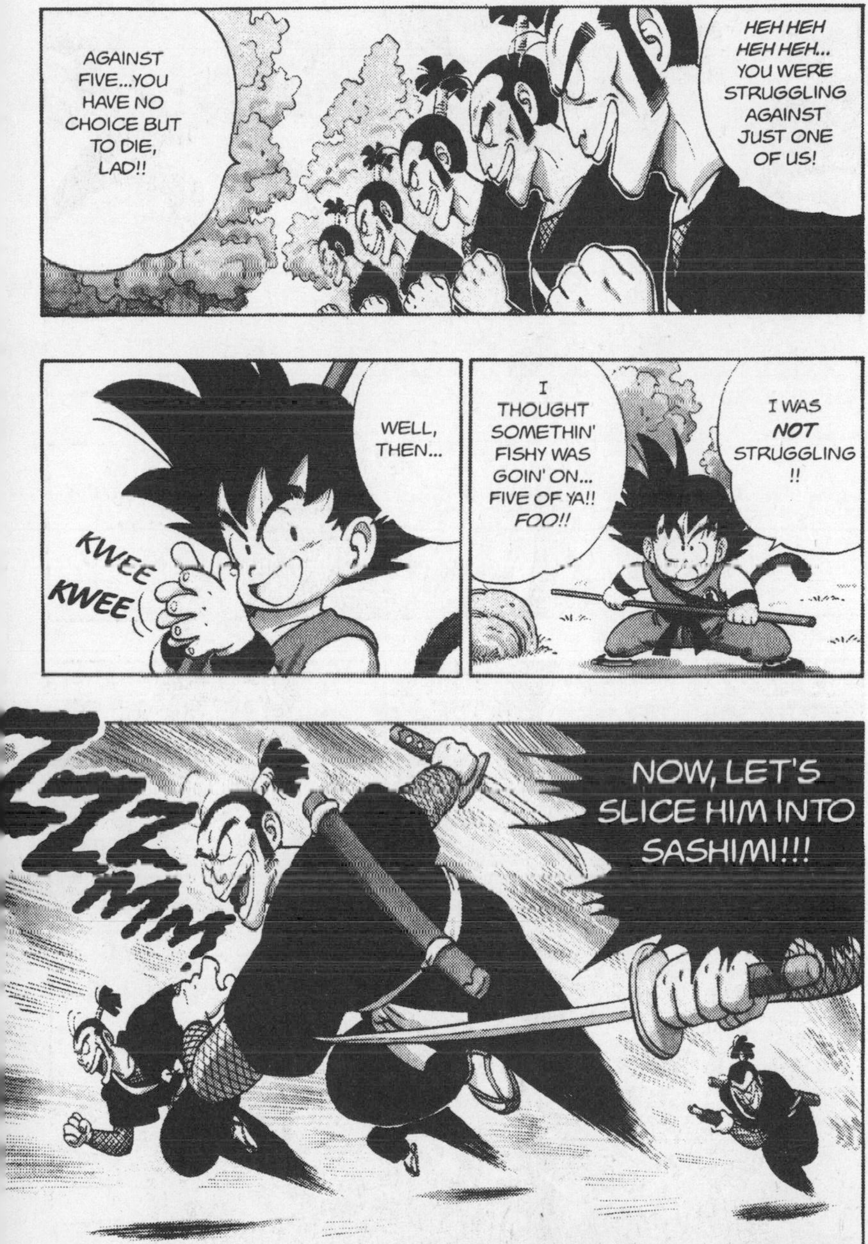
HEH HEH HEH HEH... YOU WERE STRUGGLING AGAINST JUST ONE OF US!
AGAINST FIVE...YOU HAVE NO CHOICE BUT TO DIE, LAD!!
I WAS NOT STRUGGLING !!
I THOUGHT SOMETHIN' FISHY WAS GOIN' ON... FIVE OF YA!! FOO!!
WELL, THEN...
KWEE KWEE
NOW, LET'S SLICE HIM INTO SASHIMI!!!
ZZZMM

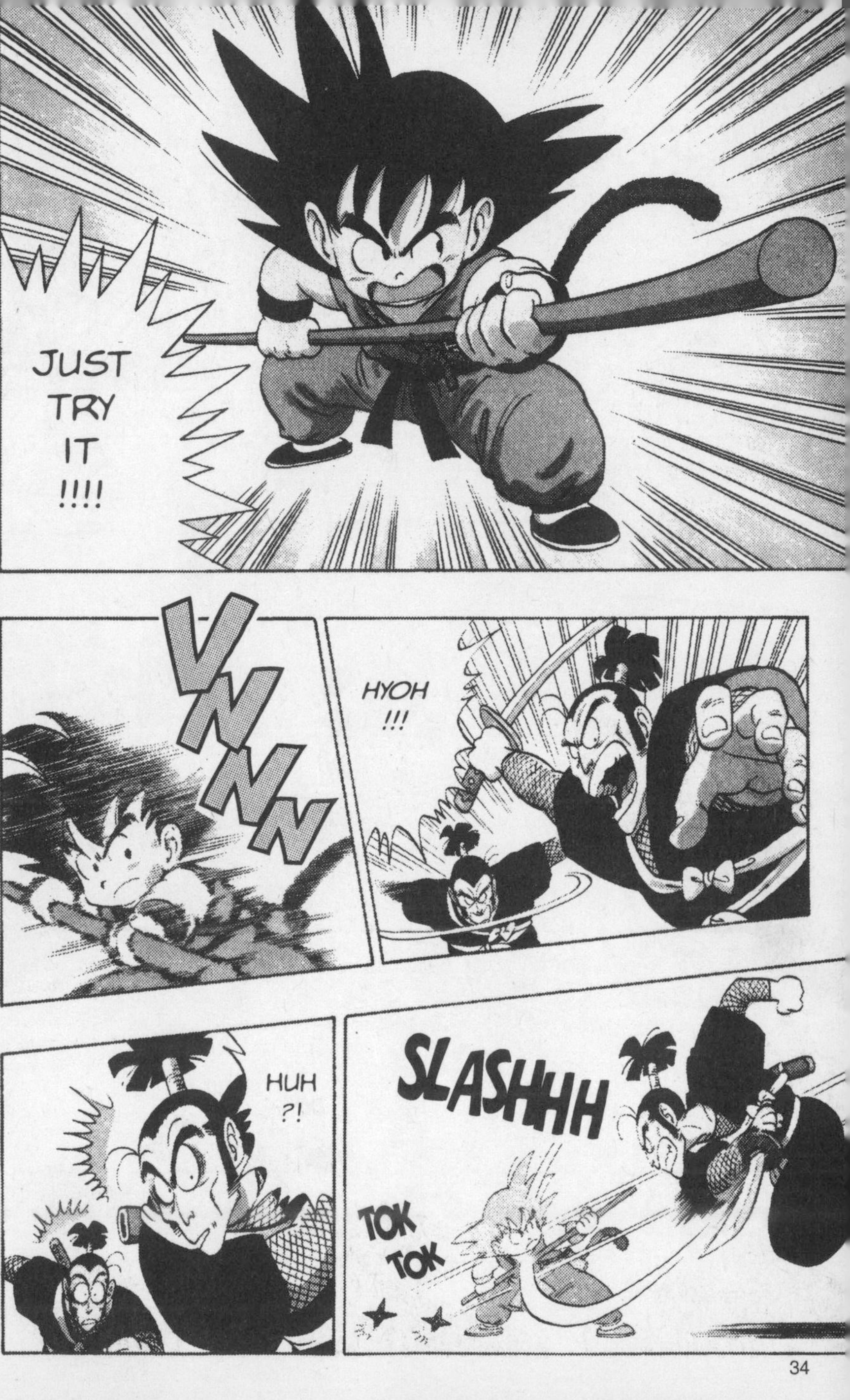
JUST TRY IT !!!!
HYOH !!!
VNNNN
SLASHHH
TOK TOK
HUH ?!

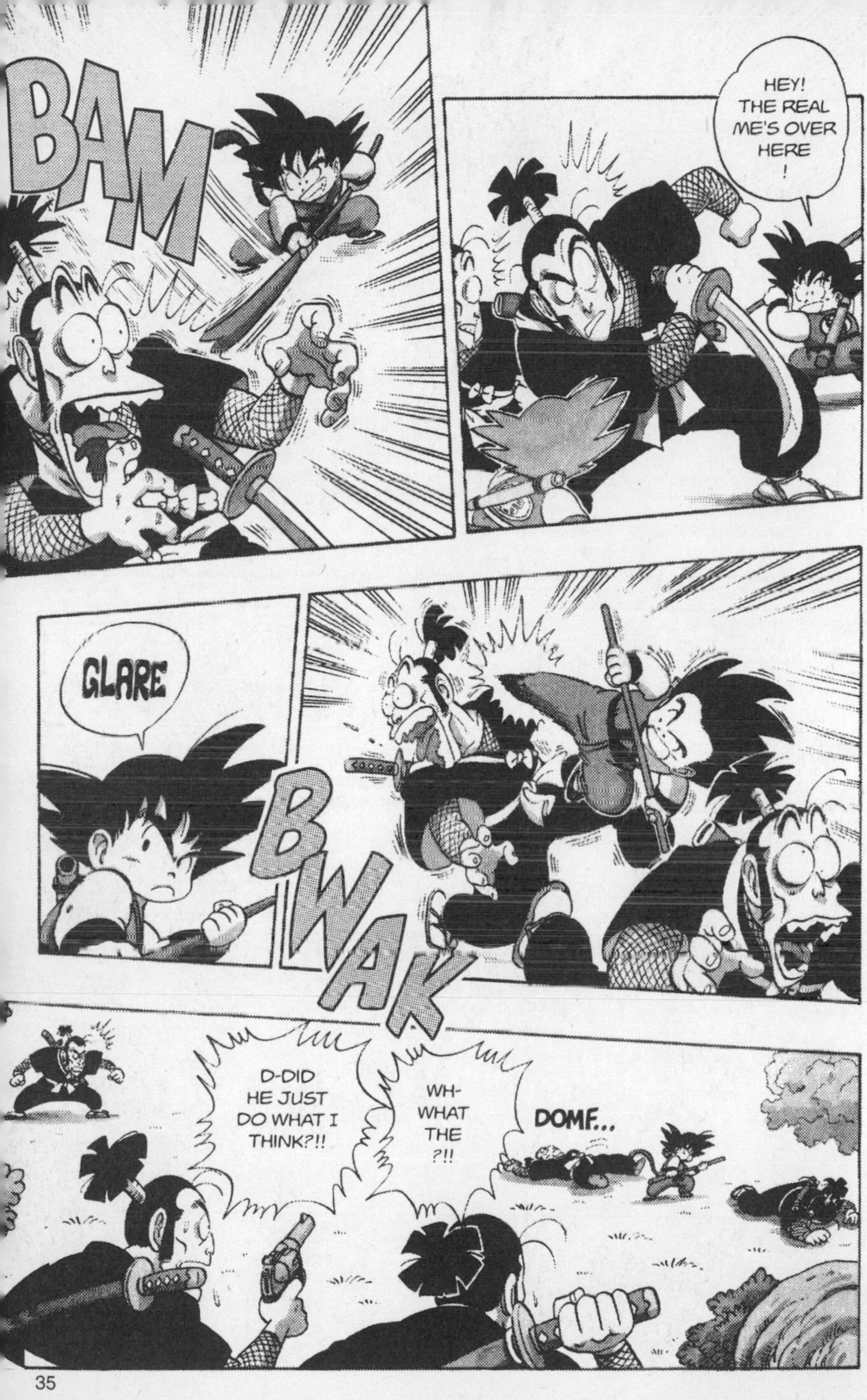
HEY! THE REAL ME'S OVER HERE !
BAM
BWAK
GLARE
DOMF...
WH- WHAT THE ?!!
D-DID HE JUST DO WHAT I THINK?!!

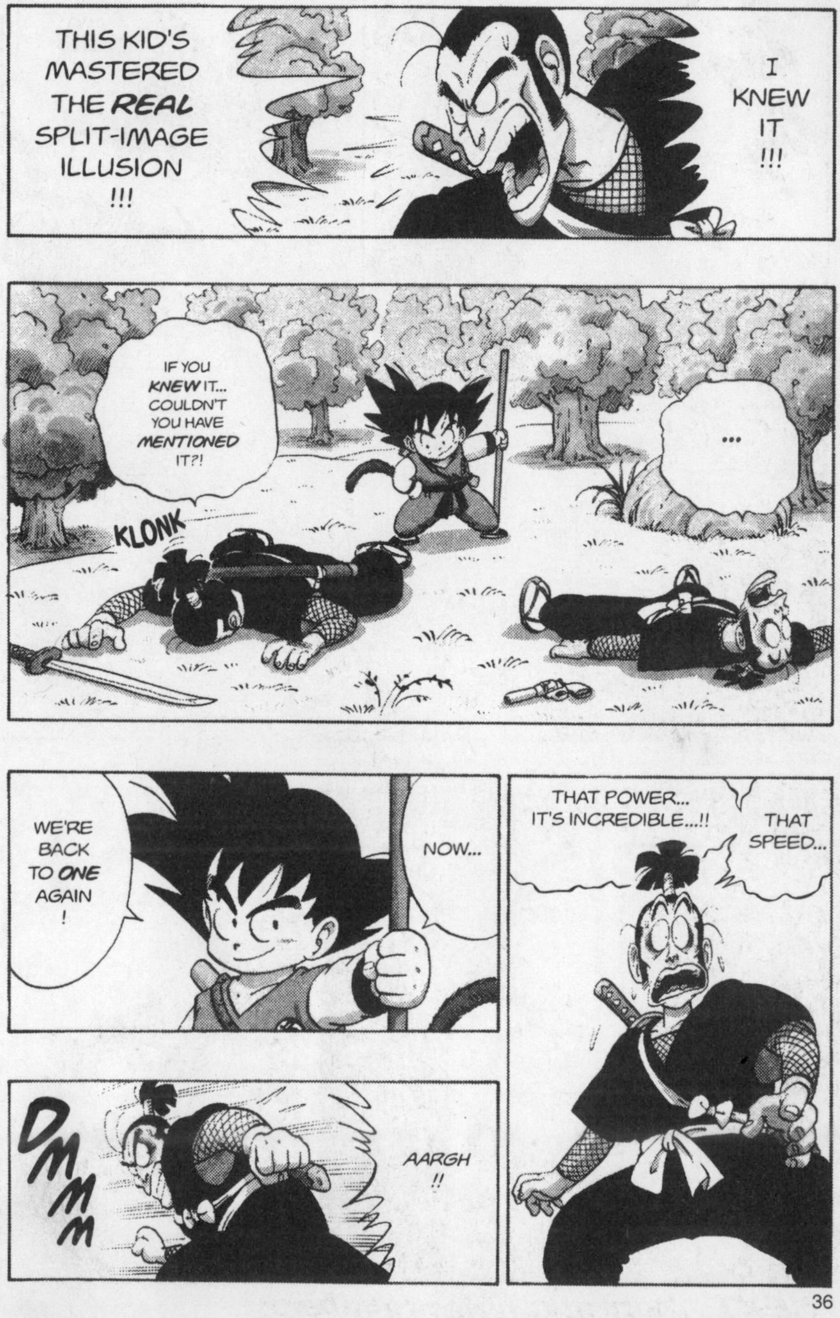
I KNEW IT !!!
THIS KID'S MASTERED THE REAL SPLIT-IMAGE ILLUSION !!!
...
IF YOU KNEW IT... COULDN'T YOU HAVE MENTIONED IT?!
KLONK
THAT SPEED...
THAT POWER... IT'S INCREDIBLE...!!
NOW...
WE'RE BACK TO ONE AGAIN !
AARGH !!
DMMM

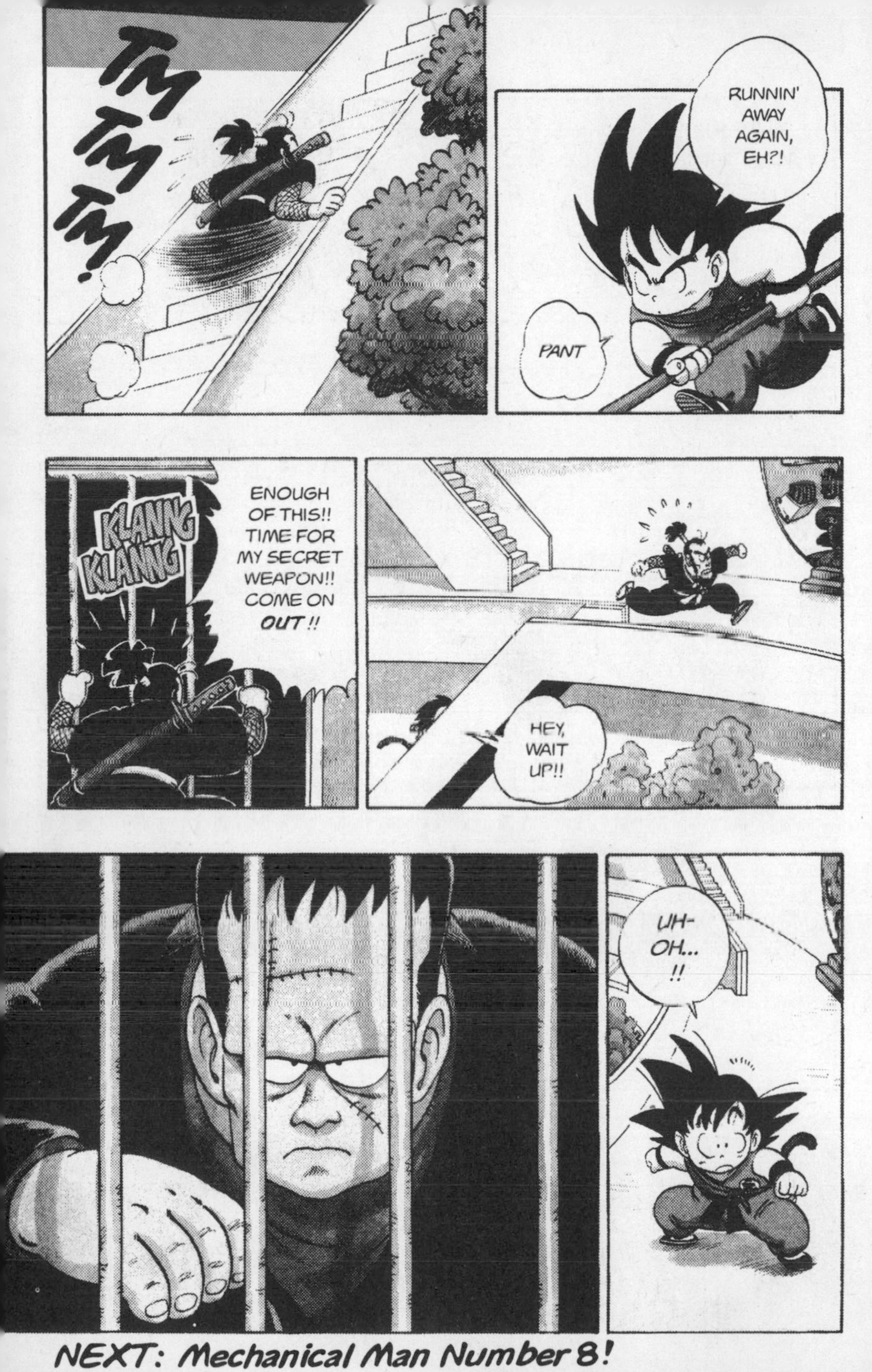
RUNNIN' AWAY AGAIN, EH?!
PANT
TM TM TM!
HEY, WAIT UP!!
ENOUGH OF THIS!! TIME FOR MY SECRET WEAPON!! COME ON OUT!!
KLANNG KLANNG
UH-OH... !!

NEXT: Mechanical Man Number 8!

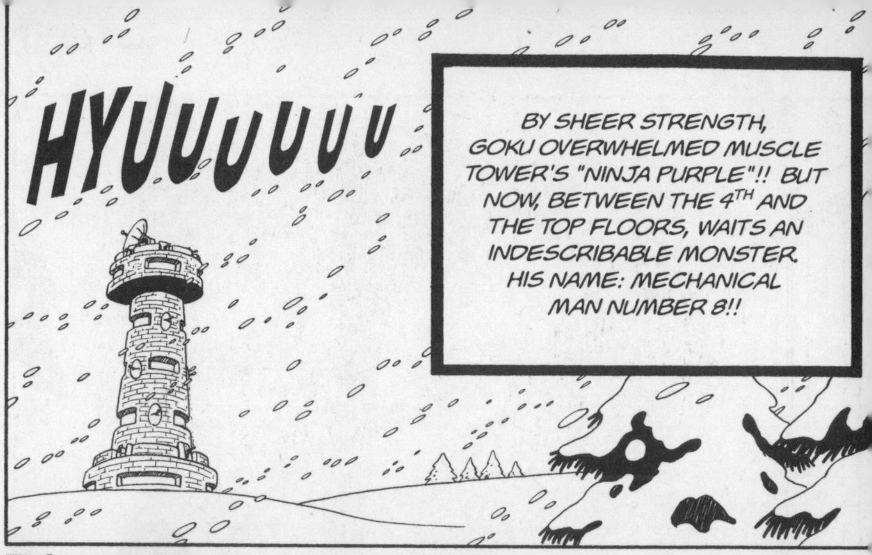
BY SHEER STRENGTH, GOKU OVERWHELMED MUSCLE TOWER'S "NINJA PURPLE"!! BUT NOW, BETWEEN THE 4TH AND THE TOP FLOORS, WAITS AN INDESCRIBABLE MONSTER. HIS NAME: MECHANICAL MAN NUMBER 8!!
HYUUUUUUU

Tale 63 • Mechanical Man No. 8

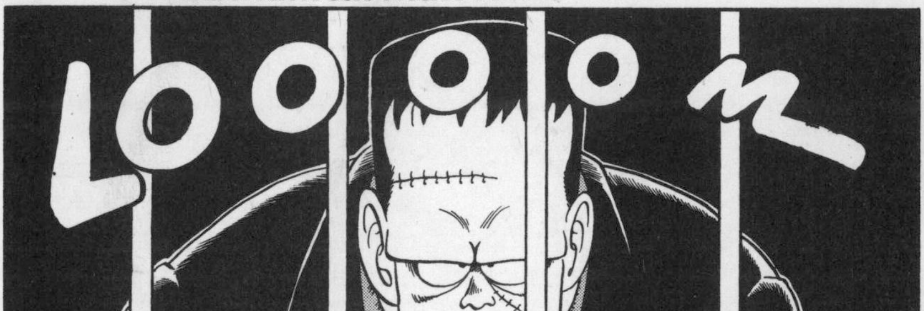
LOOOOM

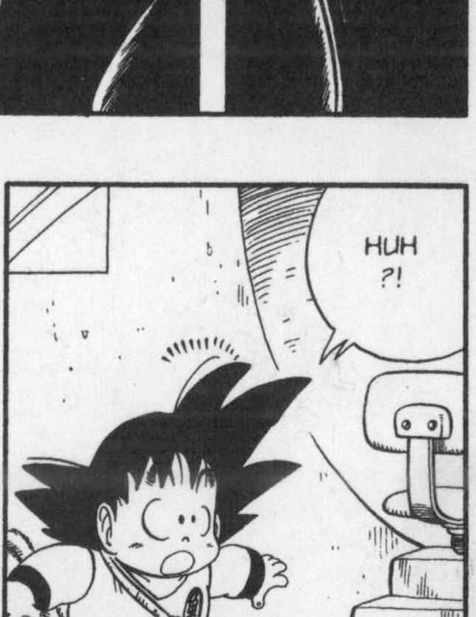
HUH ?!

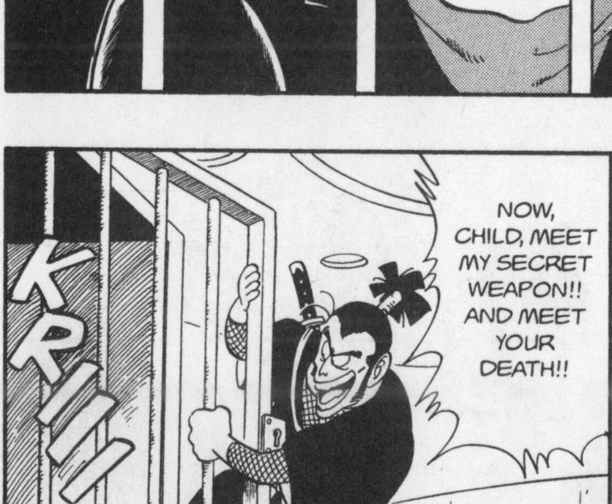
NOW, CHILD, MEET MY SECRET WEAPON!! AND MEET YOUR DEATH!!
KRIIII

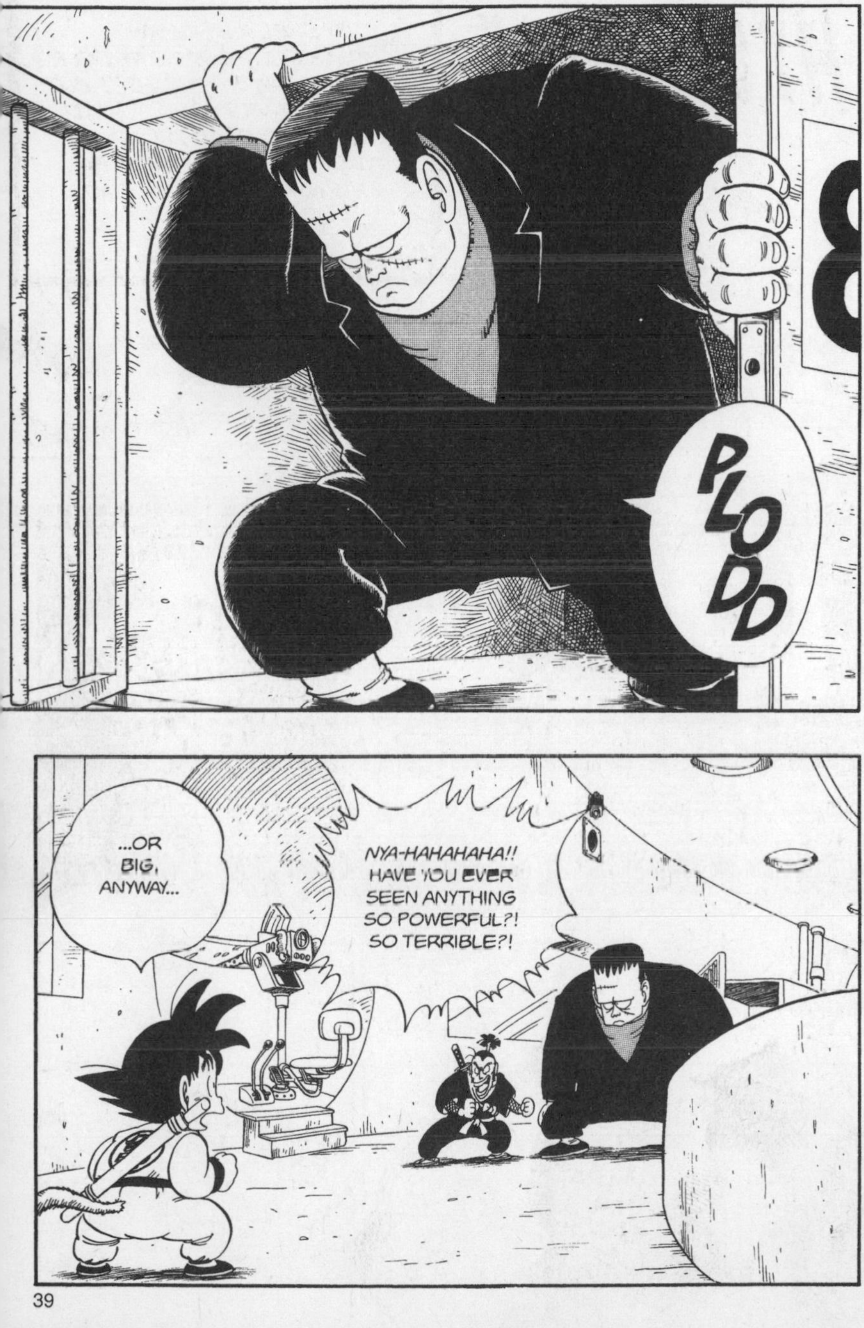
PLODD
NYA-HAHAHAHA!! HAVE YOU EVER SEEN ANYTHING SO POWERFUL?! SO TERRIBLE?!
...OR BIG, ANYWAY...

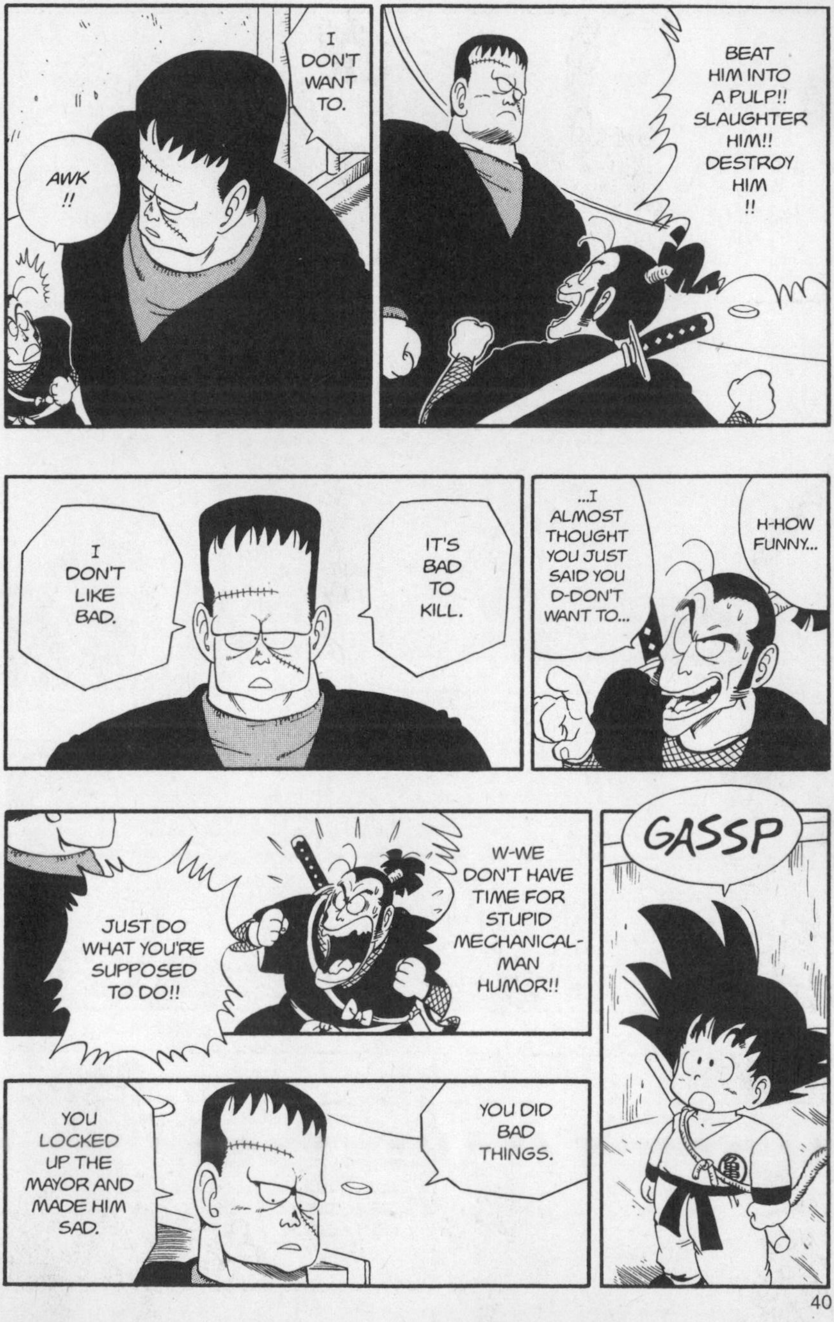
BEAT HIM INTO A PULP!! SLAUGHTER HIM!! DESTROY HIM !!
I DON'T WANT TO.
AWK !!
H-HOW FUNNY...
...I ALMOST THOUGHT YOU JUST SAID YOU D-DON'T WANT TO...
IT'S BAD TO KILL.
I DON'T LIKE BAD.
GASSP
W-WE DON'T HAVE TIME FOR STUPID MECHANICAL-MAN HUMOR!!
JUST DO WHAT YOU'RE SUPPOSED TO DO!!
YOU DID BAD THINGS.
YOU LOCKED UP THE MAYOR AND MADE HIM SAD.

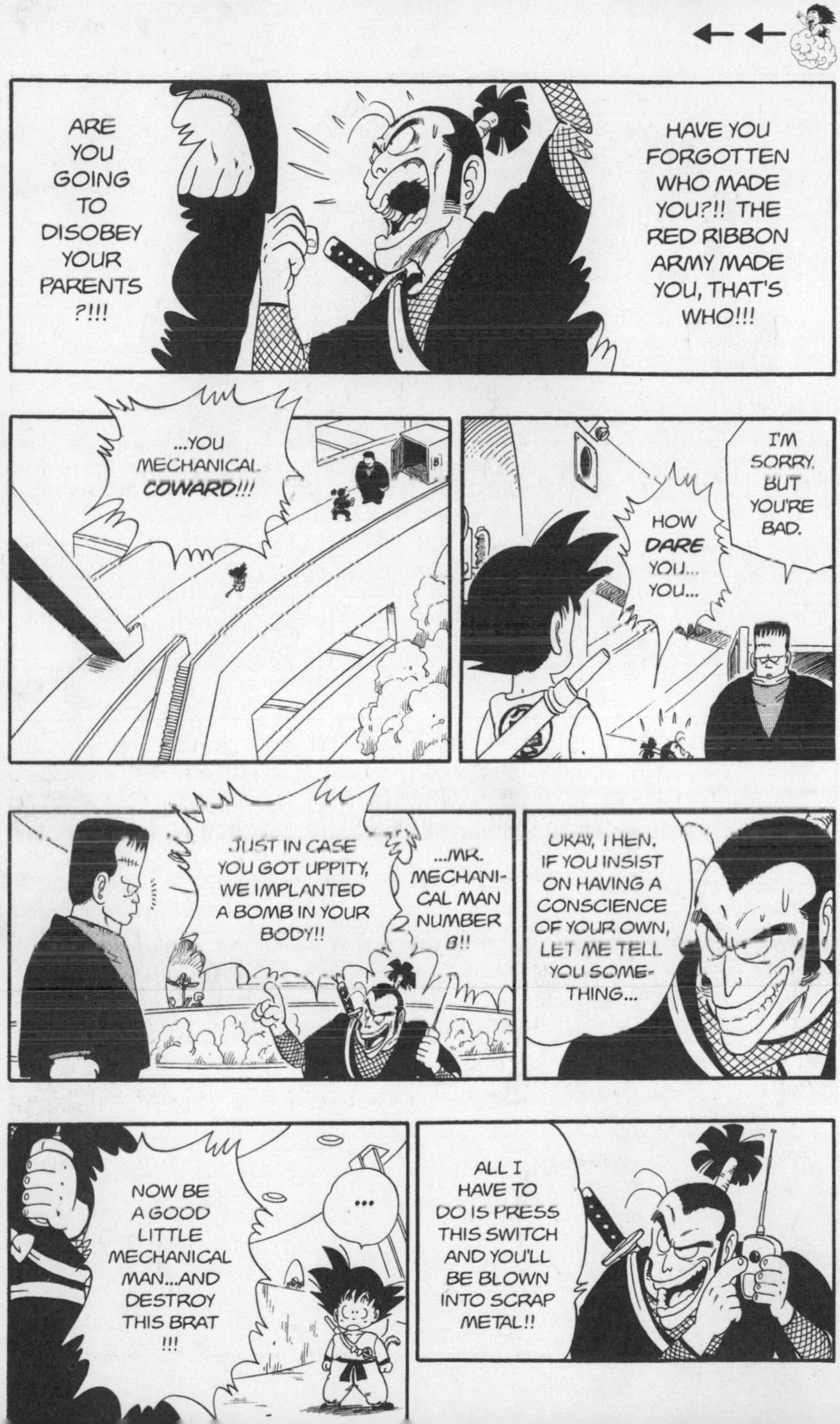
HAVE YOU FORGOTTEN WHO MADE YOU?!! THE RED RIBBON ARMY MADE YOU, THAT'S WHO!!!
ARE YOU GOING TO DISOBEY YOUR PARENTS ?!!!
I'M SORRY. BUT YOU'RE BAD.
HOW **DARE** YOU... YOU...
...YOU MECHANICAL **COWARD**!!!
OKAY, THEN. IF YOU INSIST ON HAVING A CONSCIENCE OF YOUR OWN, LET ME TELL YOU SOME-THING...
...MR. MECHANI-CAL MAN NUMBER 8!!
JUST IN CASE YOU GOT UPPITY, WE IMPLANTED A BOMB IN YOUR BODY!!
ALL I HAVE TO DO IS PRESS THIS SWITCH AND YOU'LL BE BLOWN INTO SCRAP METAL!!
...
NOW BE A GOOD LITTLE MECHANICAL MAN...AND DESTROY THIS BRAT !!!

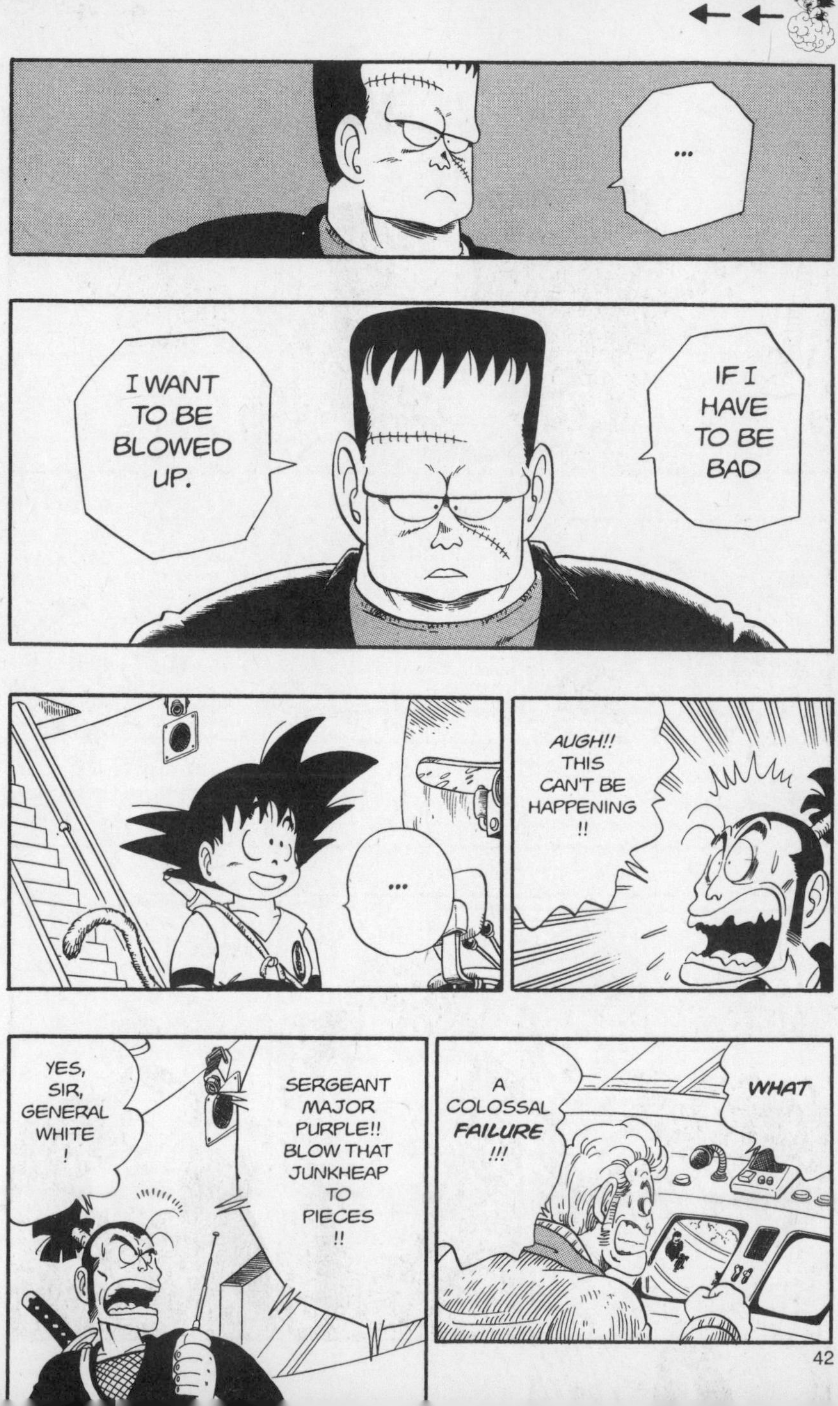
...
IF I HAVE TO BE BAD
I WANT TO BE BLOWED UP.
AUGH!! THIS CAN'T BE HAPPENING !!
...
WHAT
A COLOSSAL FAILURE !!!
SERGEANT MAJOR PURPLE!! BLOW THAT JUNKHEAP TO PIECES !!
YES, SIR, GENERAL WHITE !

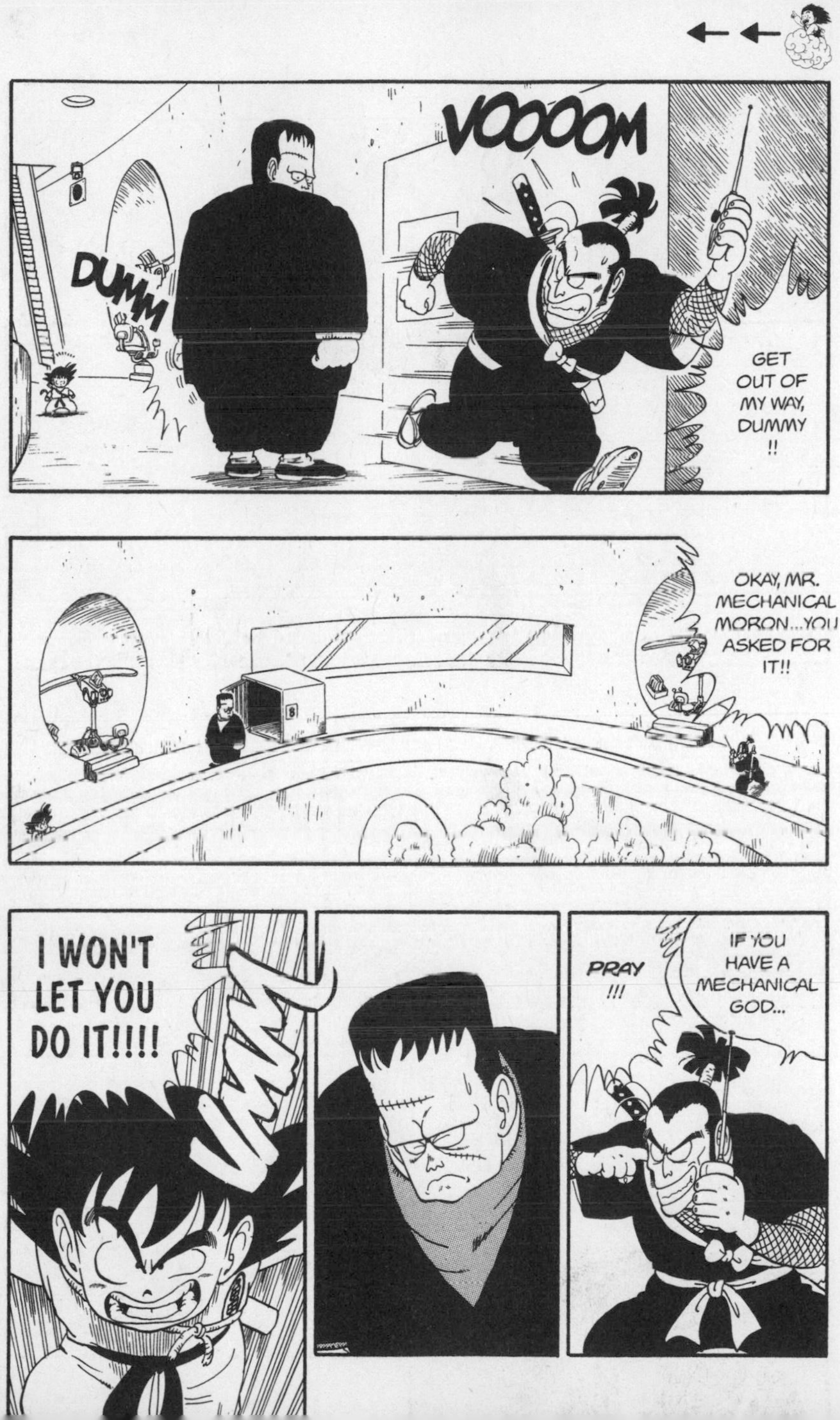
VOOOOM
GET OUT OF MY WAY, DUMMY !!
DUMM
OKAY, MR. MECHANICAL MORON...YOU ASKED FOR IT!!
IF YOU HAVE A MECHANICAL GOD...
PRAY !!!
I WON'T LET YOU DO IT!!!!!

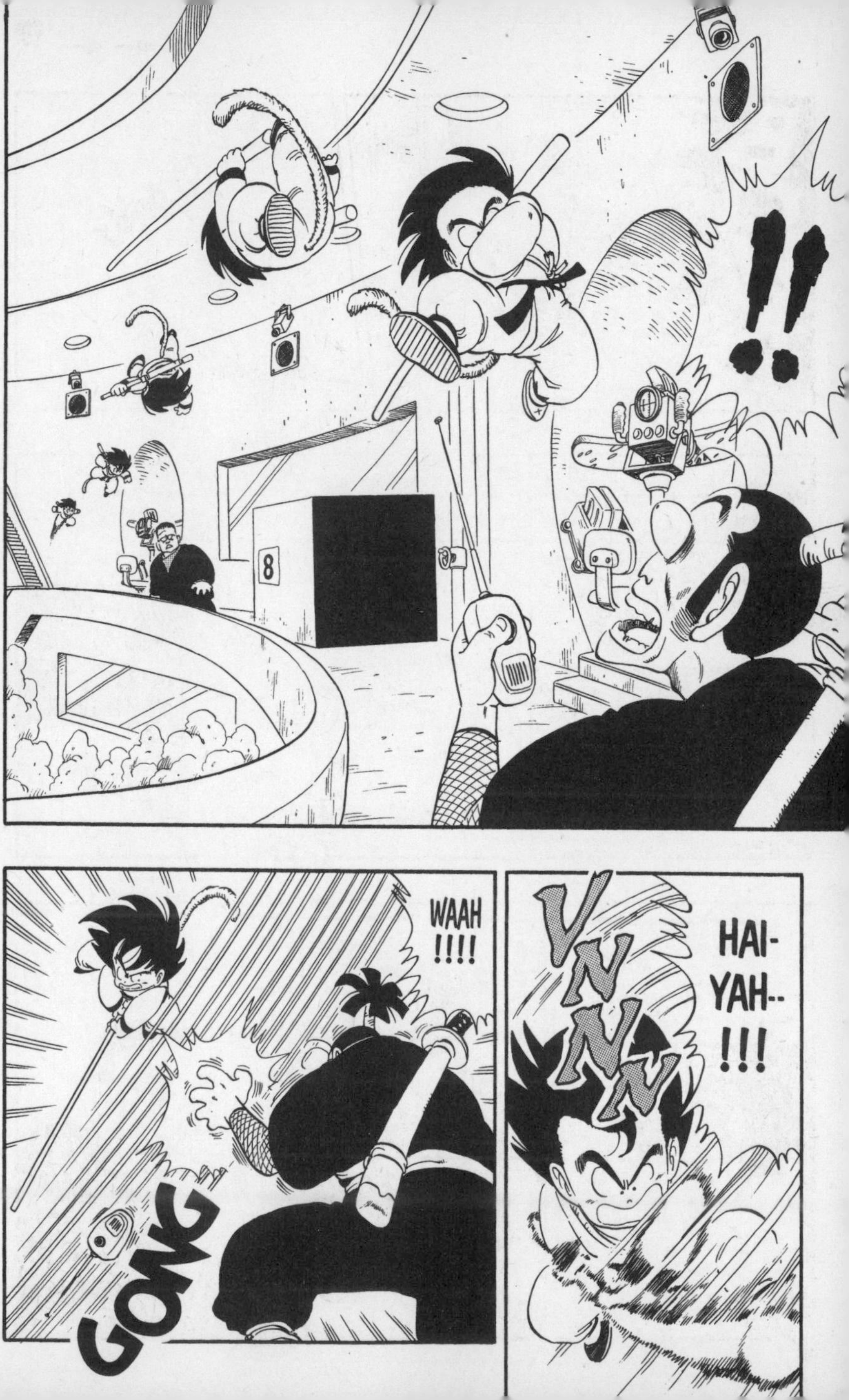
!!
VNNN
HAI-YAH--!!!
WAAH !!!!
GONG

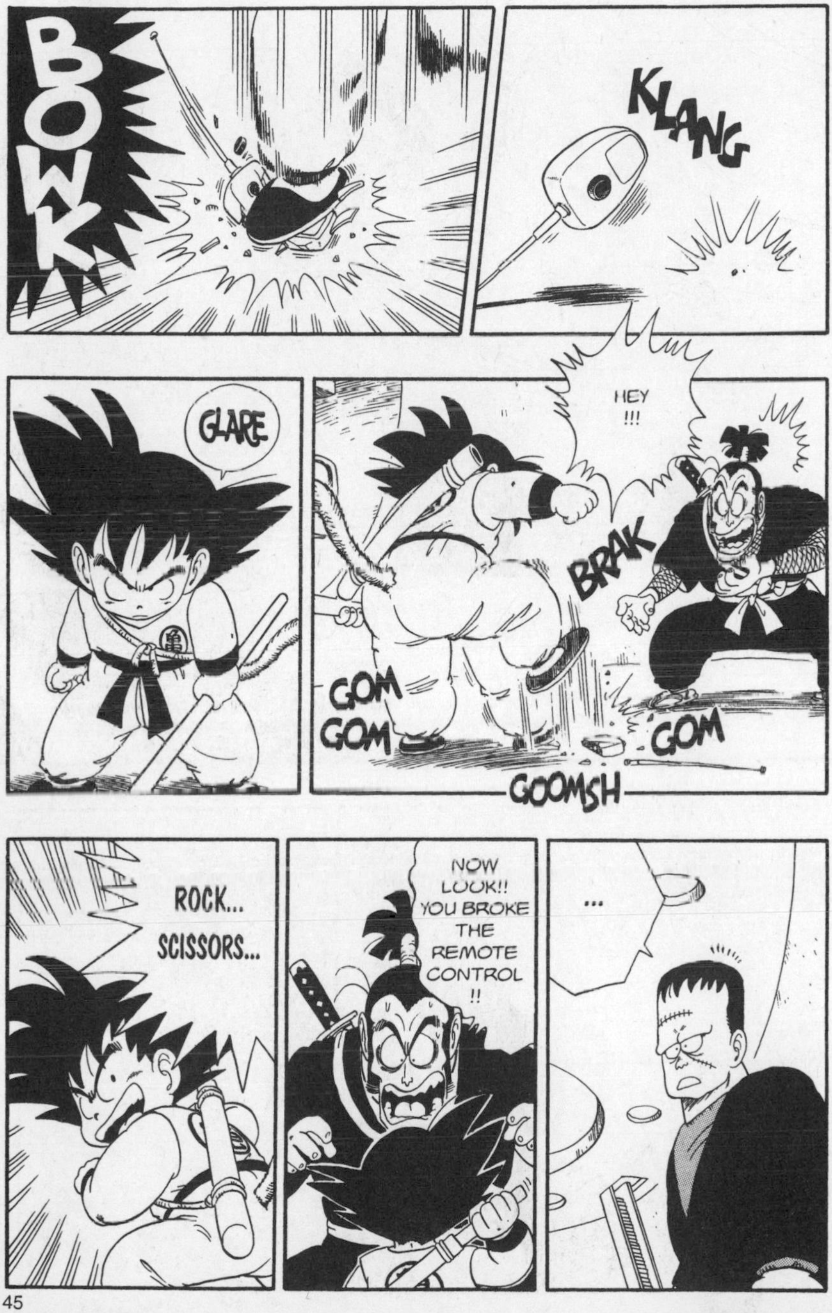
KLANG
BOWK
HEY !!!
BRAK
GOM
GOM GOM
GOOMSH
GLARE
...
NOW LOOK!! YOU BROKE THE REMOTE CONTROL !!
ROCK... SCISSORS...

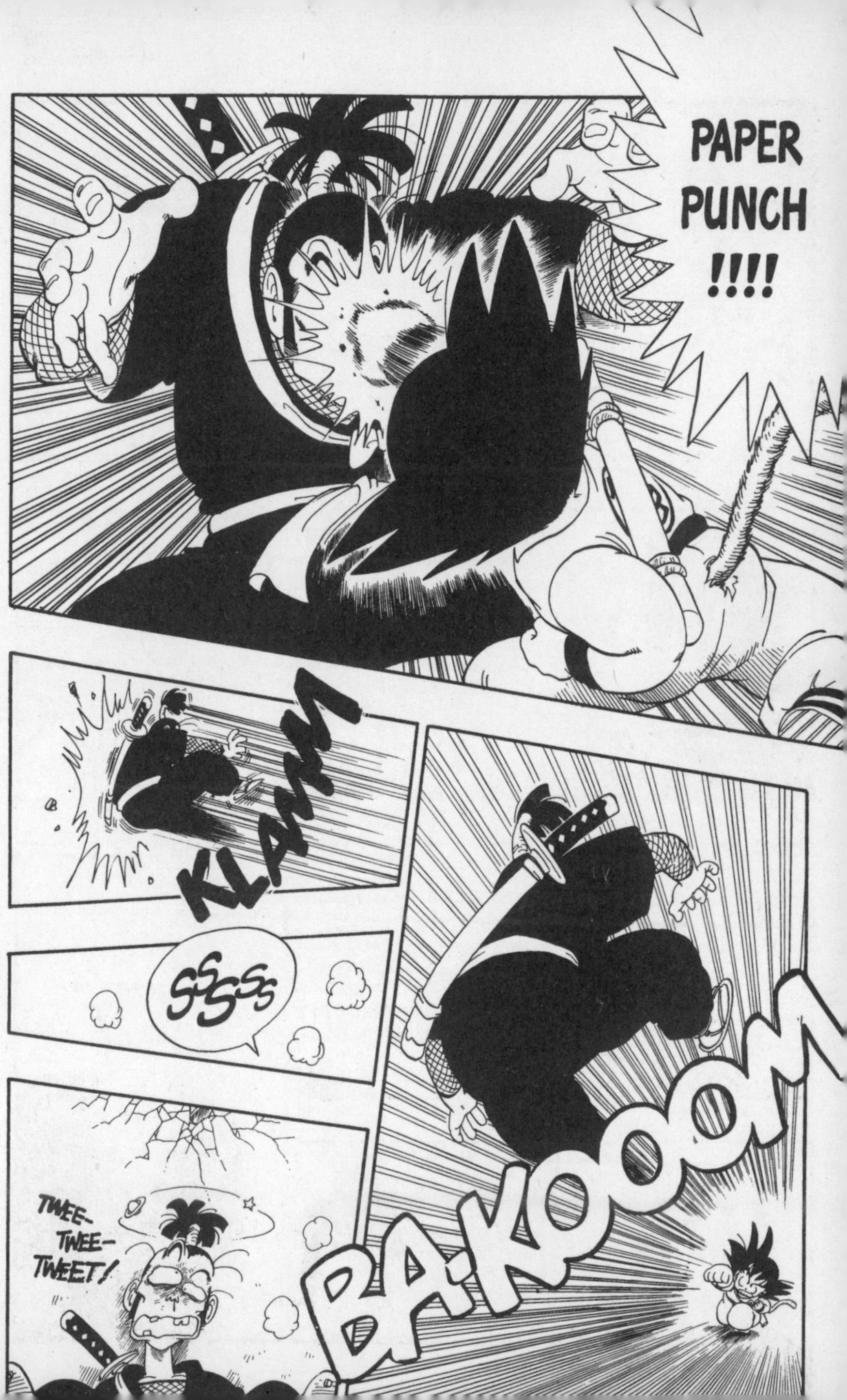
PAPER PUNCH!!!!
BA-KOOOOM
KLAMM
SSSSS
TWEE-TWEE-TWEET!

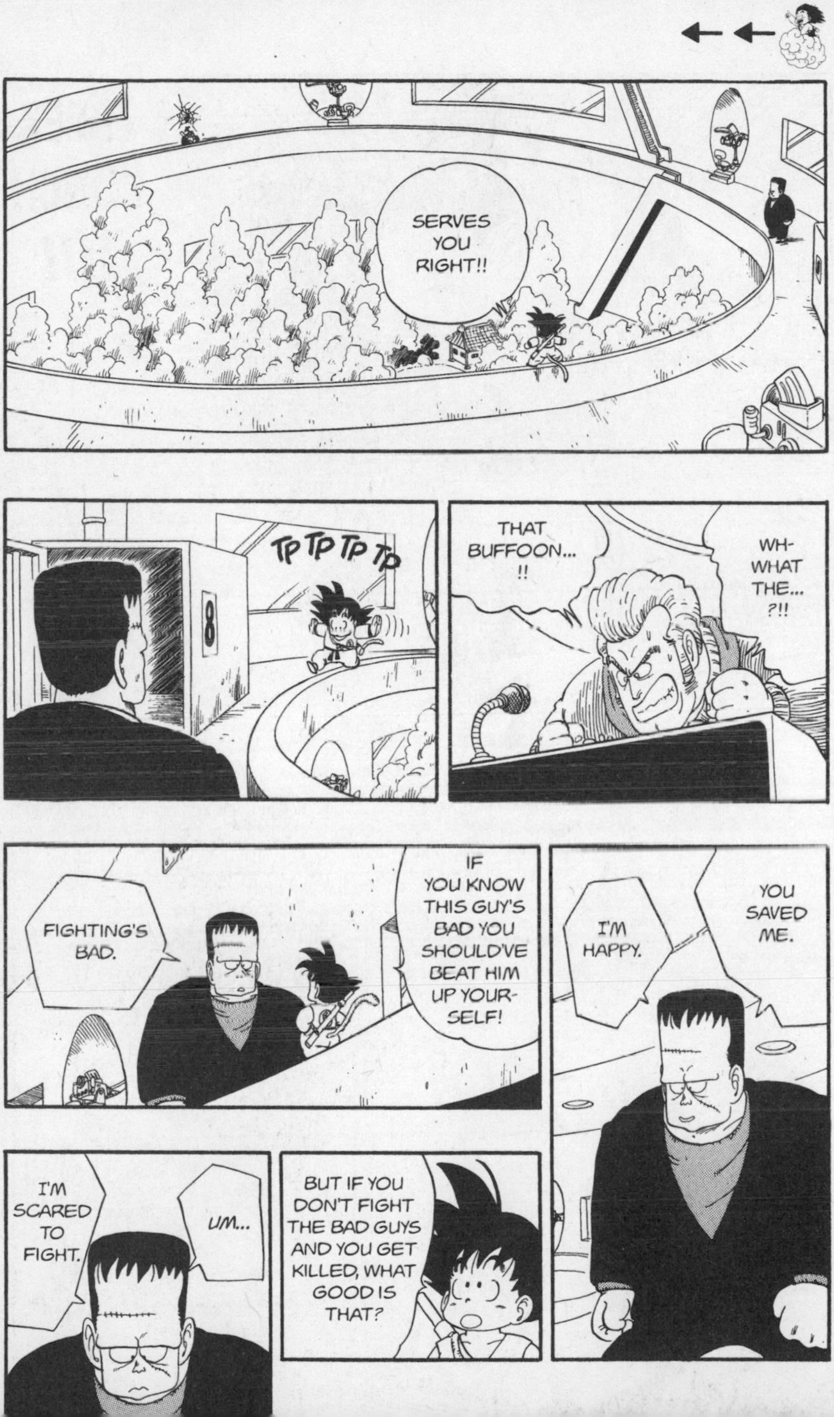
SERVES YOU RIGHT!!
WH- WHAT THE... ?!!
THAT BUFFOON... !!
TP TP TP TP
YOU SAVED ME.
I'M HAPPY.
IF YOU KNOW THIS GUY'S BAD YOU SHOULD'VE BEAT HIM UP YOUR-SELF!
FIGHTING'S BAD.
BUT IF YOU DON'T FIGHT THE BAD GUYS AND YOU GET KILLED, WHAT GOOD IS THAT?
UM...
I'M SCARED TO FIGHT.

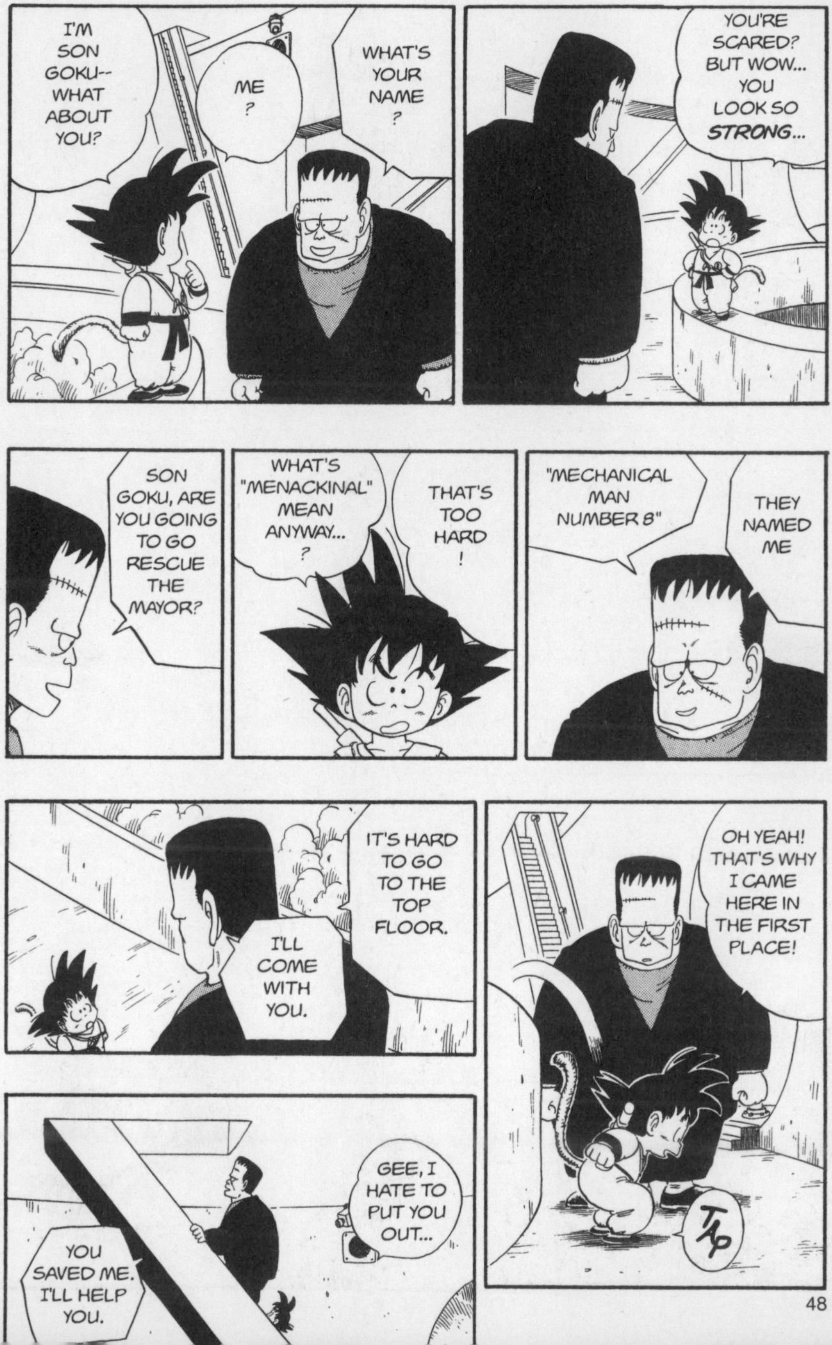
YOU'RE SCARED? BUT WOW... YOU LOOK SO **STRONG**...
WHAT'S YOUR NAME ?
ME ?
I'M SON GOKU-- WHAT ABOUT YOU?
THEY NAMED ME
"MECHANICAL MAN NUMBER 8"
THAT'S TOO HARD !
WHAT'S "MENACKINAL" MEAN ANYWAY... ?
SON GOKU, ARE YOU GOING TO GO RESCUE THE MAYOR?
OH YEAH! THAT'S WHY I CAME HERE IN THE FIRST PLACE!
TAP
IT'S HARD TO GO TO THE TOP FLOOR.
I'LL COME WITH YOU.
GEE, I HATE TO PUT YOU OUT...
YOU SAVED ME. I'LL HELP YOU.

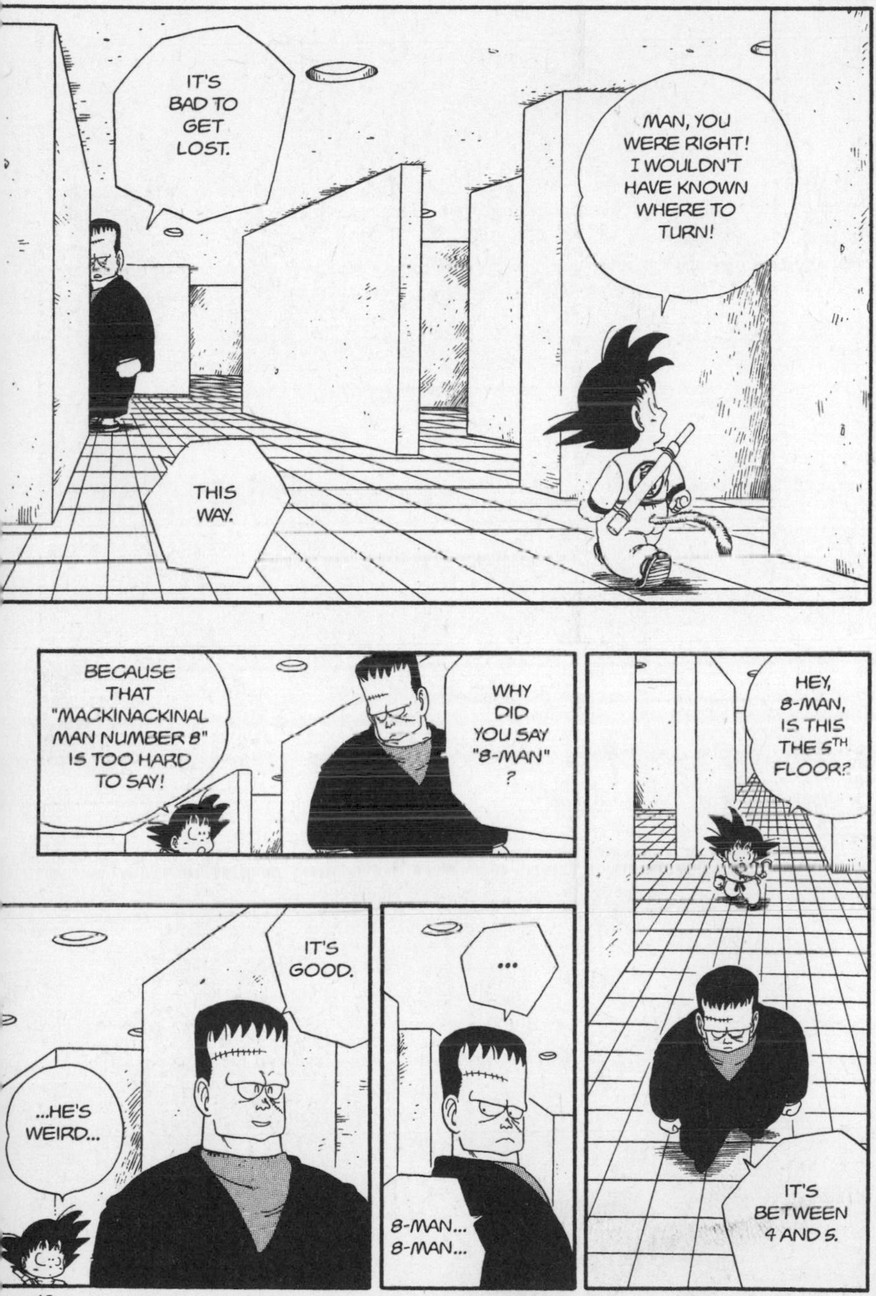
MAN, YOU WERE RIGHT! I WOULDN'T HAVE KNOWN WHERE TO TURN!
IT'S BAD TO GET LOST.
THIS WAY.
HEY, 8-MAN, IS THIS THE 5TH FLOOR?
IT'S BETWEEN 4 AND 5.
WHY DID YOU SAY "8-MAN" ?
BECAUSE THAT "MACKINACKINAL MAN NUMBER 8" IS TOO HARD TO SAY!
...
8-MAN... 8-MAN...
IT'S GOOD.
...HE'S WEIRD...

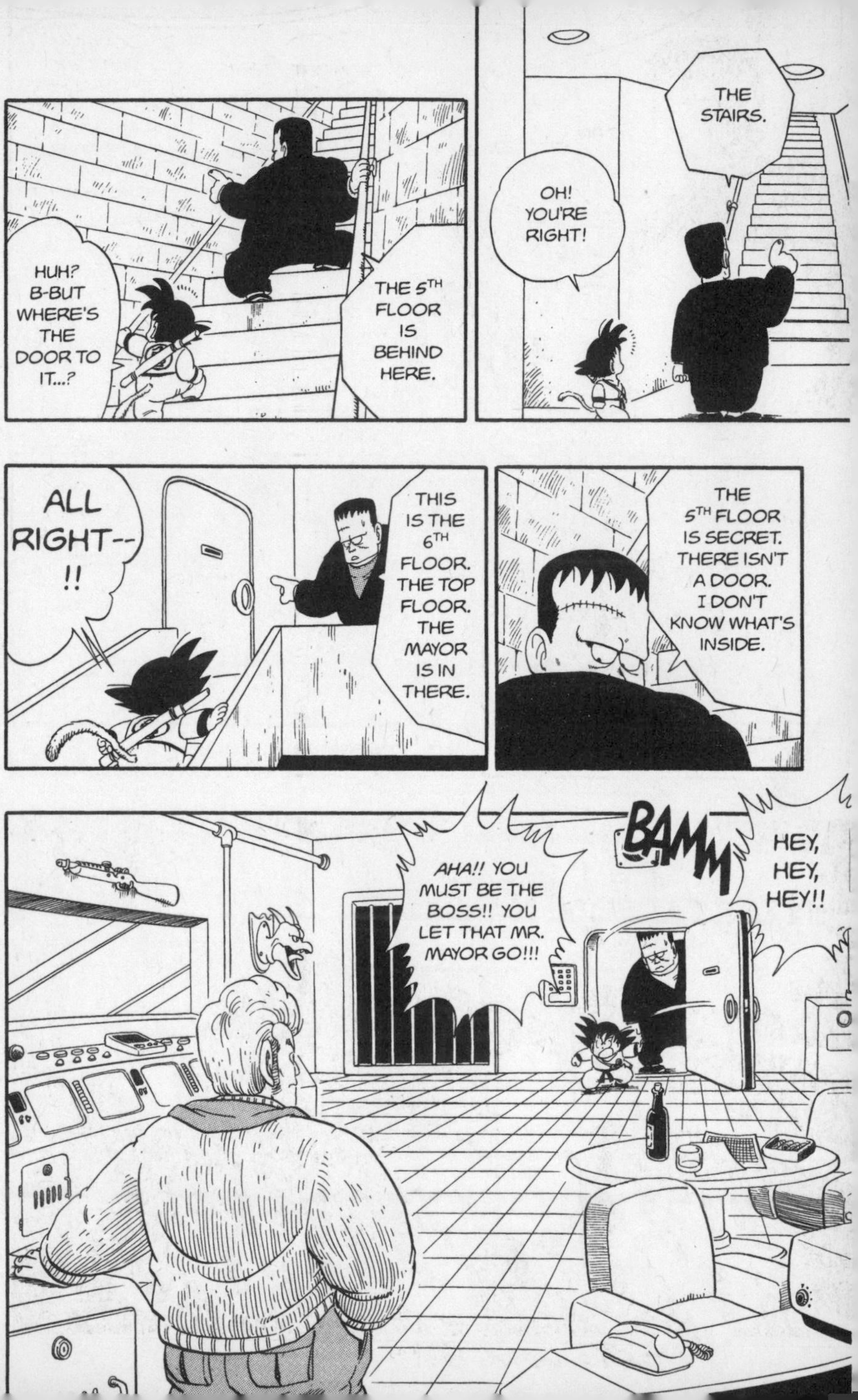
THE STAIRS.
OH! YOU'RE RIGHT!
THE 5TH FLOOR IS BEHIND HERE.
HUH? B-BUT WHERE'S THE DOOR TO IT...?
THE 5TH FLOOR IS SECRET. THERE ISN'T A DOOR. I DON'T KNOW WHAT'S INSIDE.
THIS IS THE 6TH FLOOR. THE TOP FLOOR. THE MAYOR IS IN THERE.
ALL RIGHT--!!
BAMM
HEY, HEY, HEY!!
AHA!! YOU MUST BE THE BOSS!! YOU LET THAT MR. MAYOR GO!!!

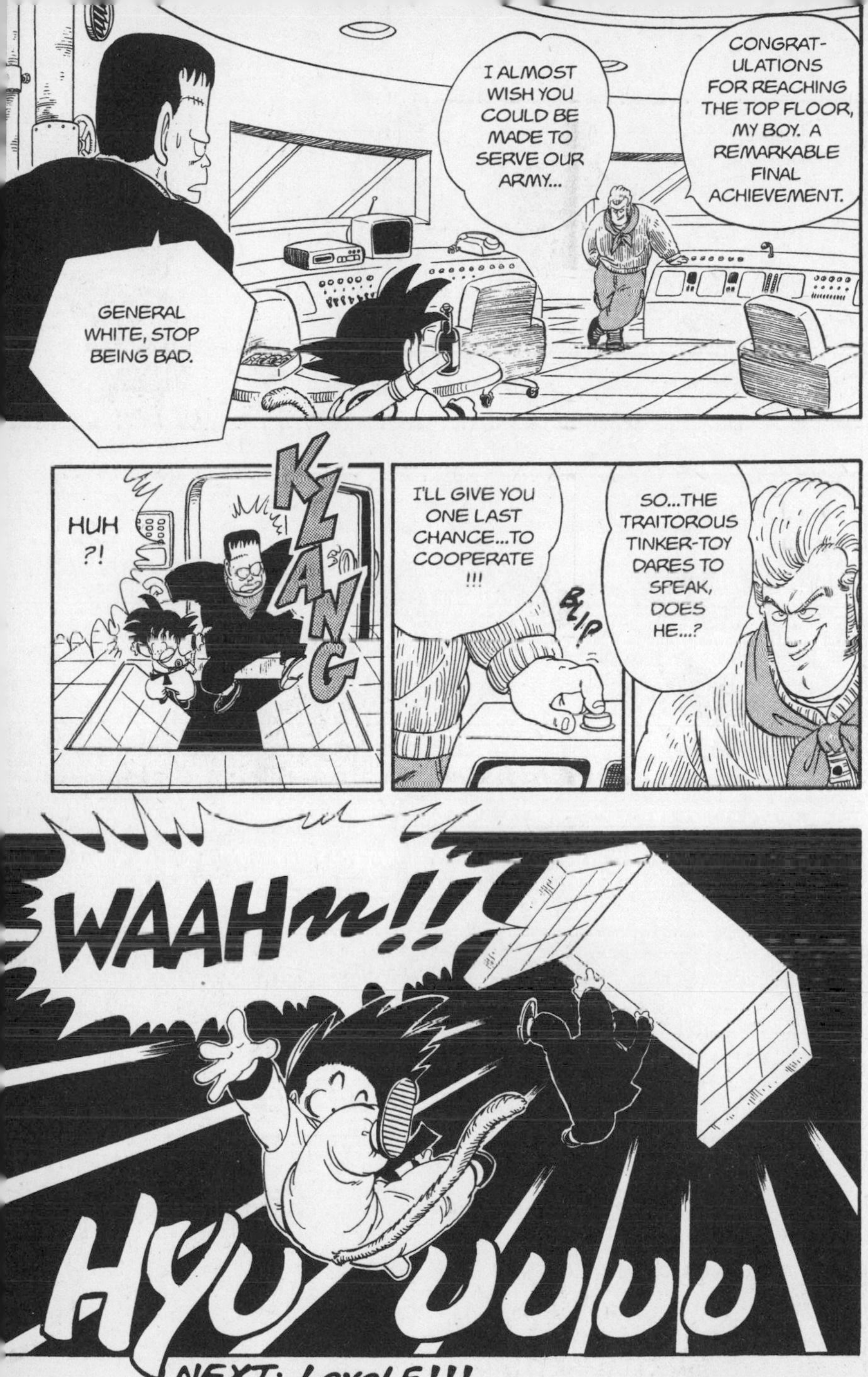
CONGRAT-ULATIONS FOR REACHING THE TOP FLOOR, MY BOY. A REMARKABLE FINAL ACHIEVEMENT.
I ALMOST WISH YOU COULD BE MADE TO SERVE OUR ARMY...
GENERAL WHITE, STOP BEING BAD.
SO...THE TRAITOROUS TINKER-TOY DARES TO SPEAK, DOES HE...?
I'LL GIVE YOU ONE LAST CHANCE...TO COOPERATE !!!
BLIP
KLANG
HUH ?!
WAAHn!!
HYUUUUU

NEXT: Level 5!!!

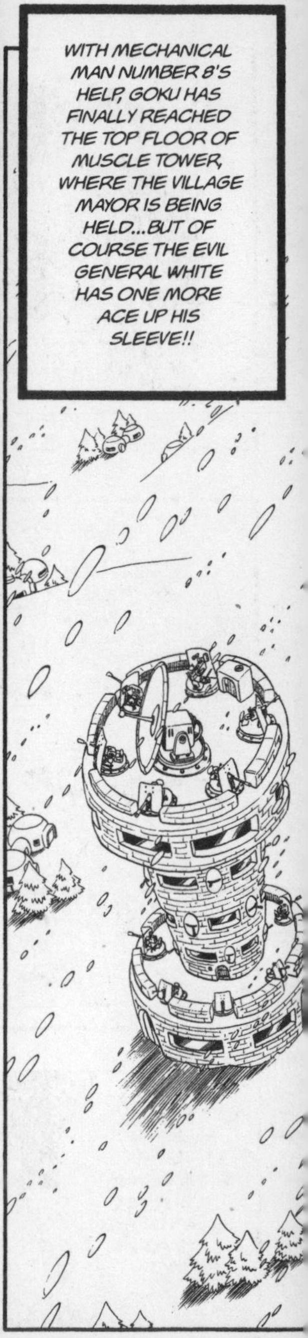
WITH MECHANICAL MAN NUMBER 8'S HELP, GOKU HAS FINALLY REACHED THE TOP FLOOR OF MUSCLE TOWER, WHERE THE VILLAGE MAYOR IS BEING HELD...BUT OF COURSE THE EVIL GENERAL WHITE HAS ONE MORE ACE UP HIS SLEEVE!!

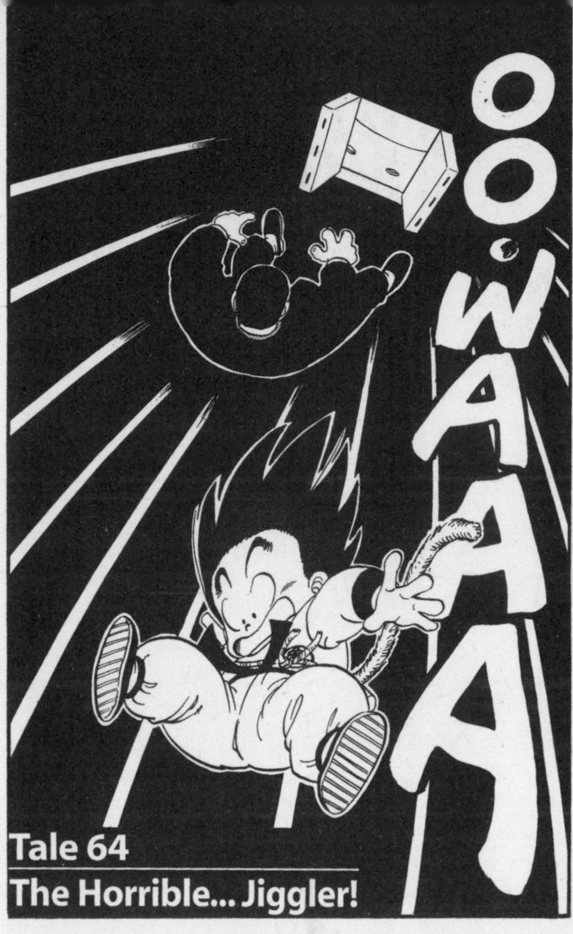
OOWAAAA

Tale 64
The Horrible... Jiggler!

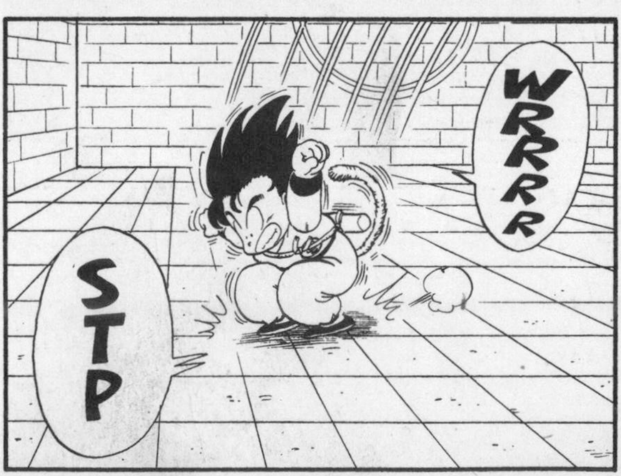
WRRRR
STP

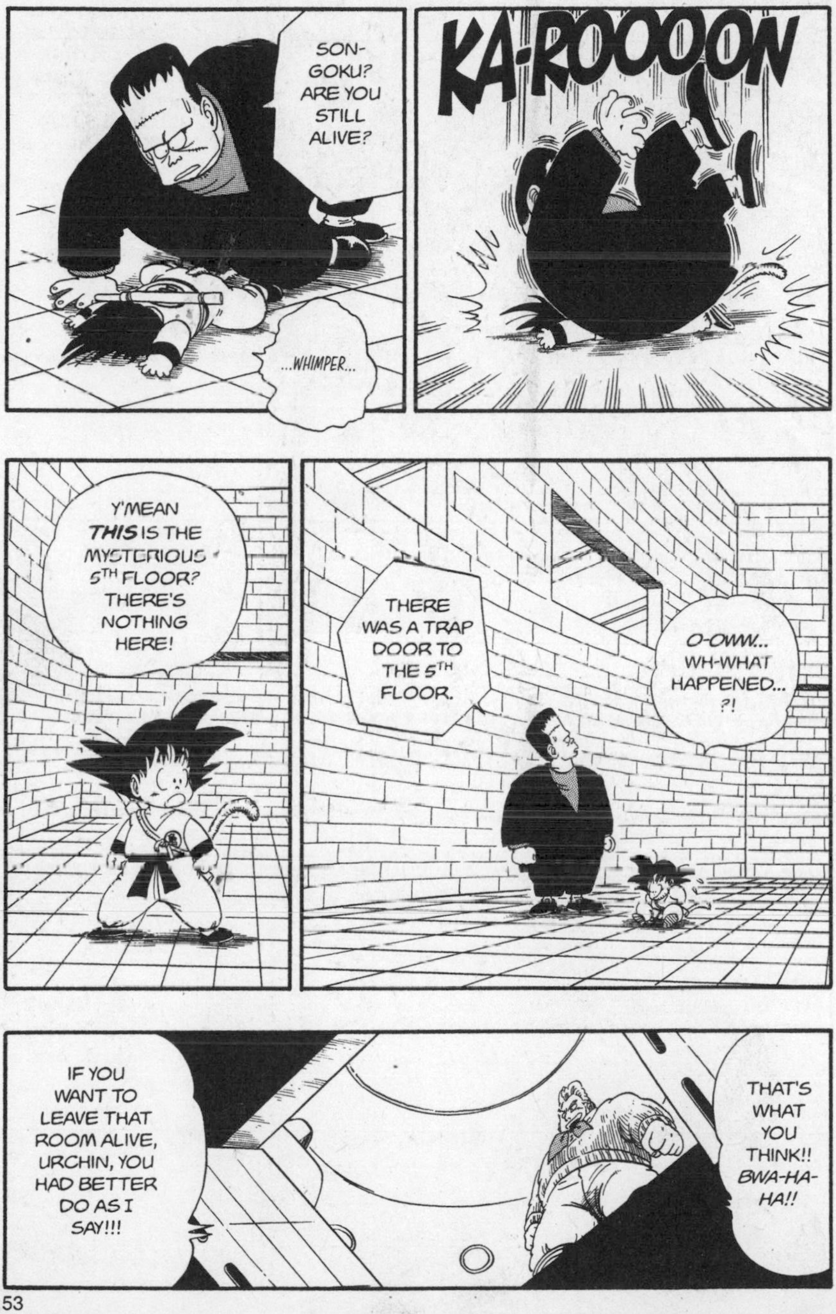
KA-ROOOOON
SON-GOKU? ARE YOU STILL ALIVE?
...WHIMPER...
O-OWW... WH-WHAT HAPPENED...?!
THERE WAS A TRAP DOOR TO THE 5TH FLOOR.
Y'MEAN *THIS* IS THE MYSTERIOUS 5TH FLOOR? THERE'S NOTHING HERE!
THAT'S WHAT YOU THINK!! *BWA-HA-HA!!*
IF YOU WANT TO LEAVE THAT ROOM ALIVE, URCHIN, YOU HAD BETTER DO AS I SAY!!!

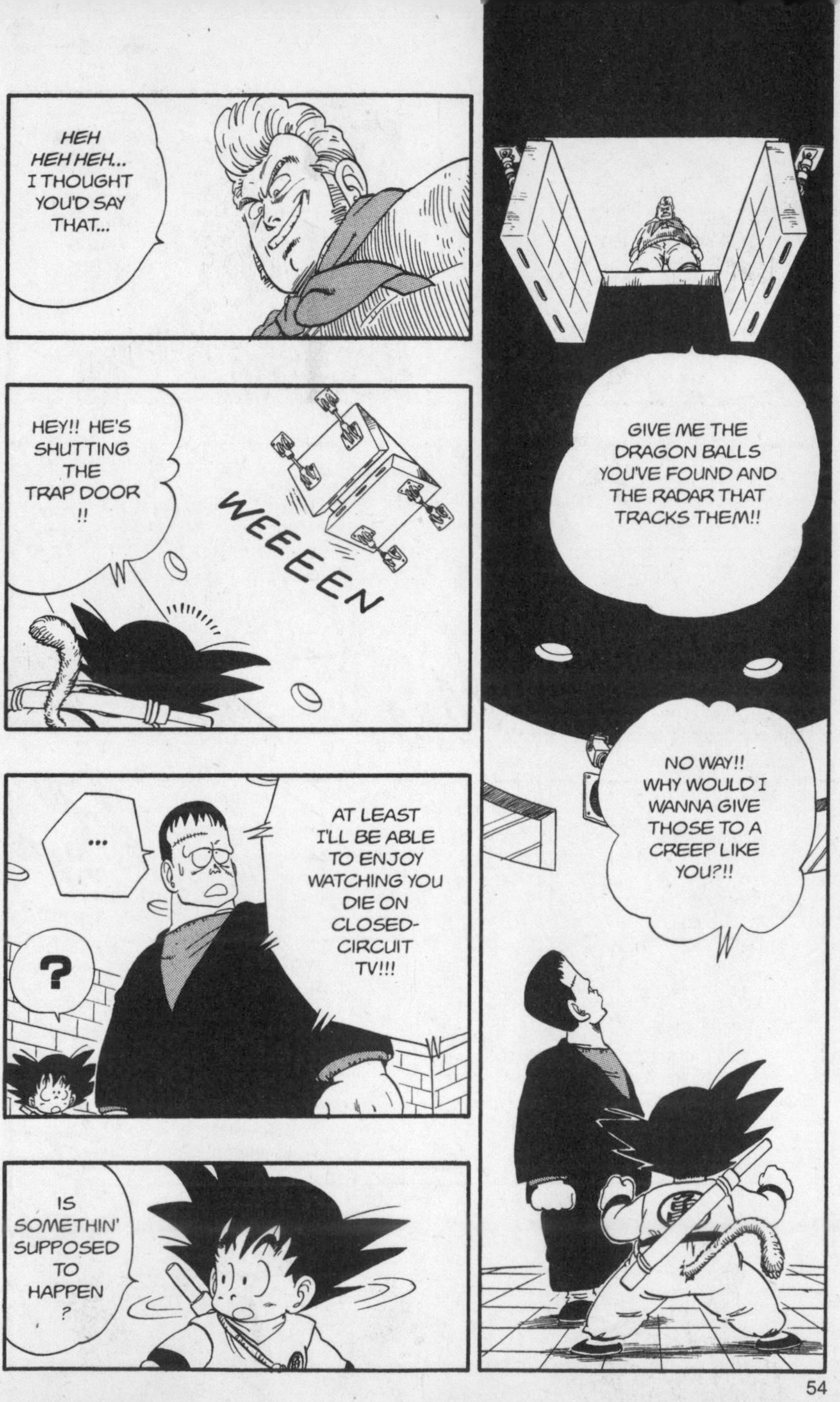
GIVE ME THE DRAGON BALLS YOU'VE FOUND AND THE RADAR THAT TRACKS THEM!!
NO WAY!! WHY WOULD I WANNA GIVE THOSE TO A CREEP LIKE YOU?!!
HEH HEH HEH... I THOUGHT YOU'D SAY THAT...
HEY!! HE'S SHUTTING THE TRAP DOOR !!
WEEEEN
AT LEAST I'LL BE ABLE TO ENJOY WATCHING YOU DIE ON CLOSED-CIRCUIT TV!!!
...
?
IS SOMETHIN' SUPPOSED TO HAPPEN ?

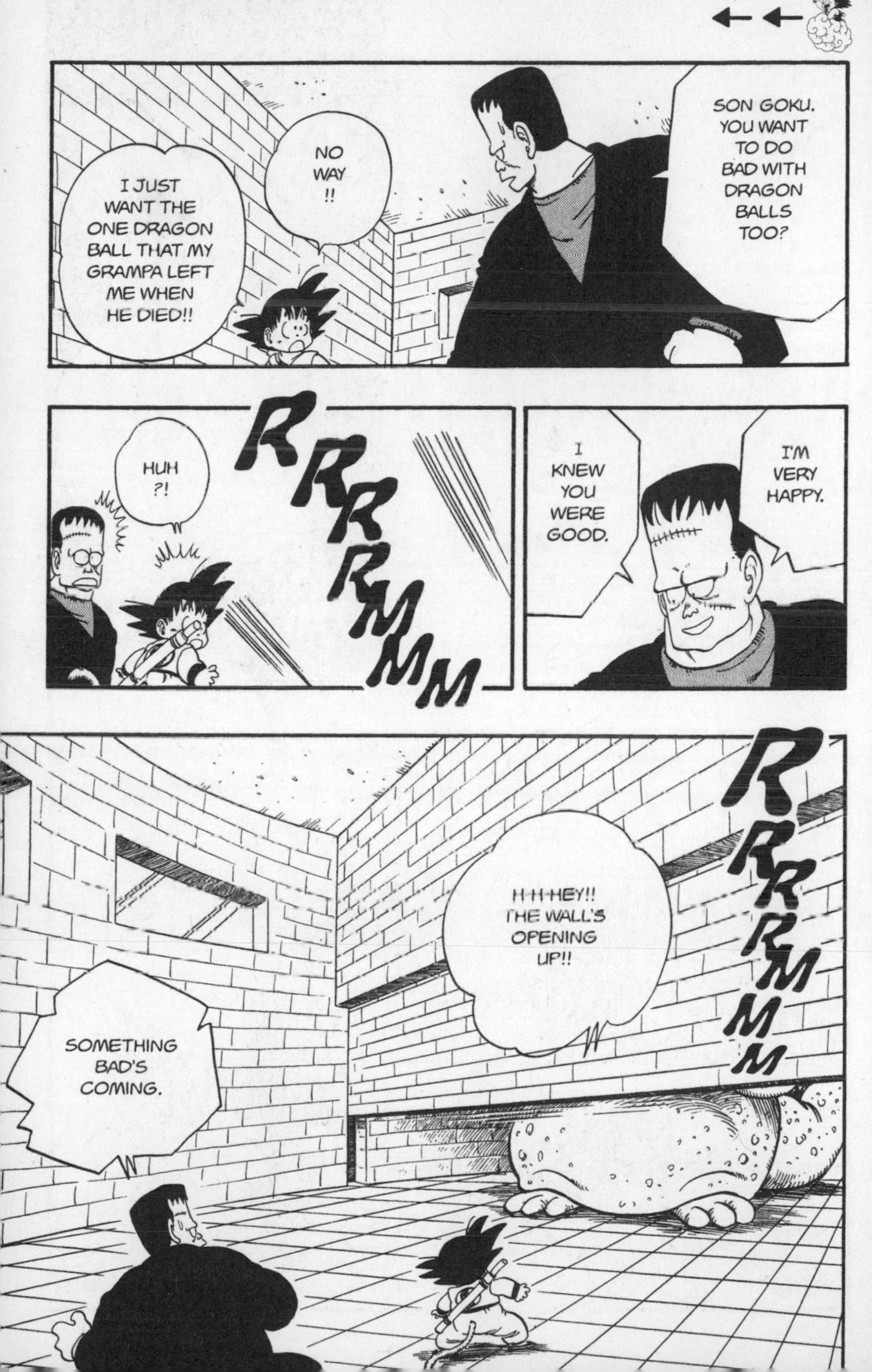
SON GOKU. YOU WANT TO DO BAD WITH DRAGON BALLS TOO?
NO WAY !!
I JUST WANT THE ONE DRAGON BALL THAT MY GRAMPA LEFT ME WHEN HE DIED!!
I'M VERY HAPPY.
I KNEW YOU WERE GOOD.
RRRRMMM
HUH ?!
RRRRMMM
H-H-HEY!! THE WALL'S OPENING UP!!
SOMETHING BAD'S COMING.

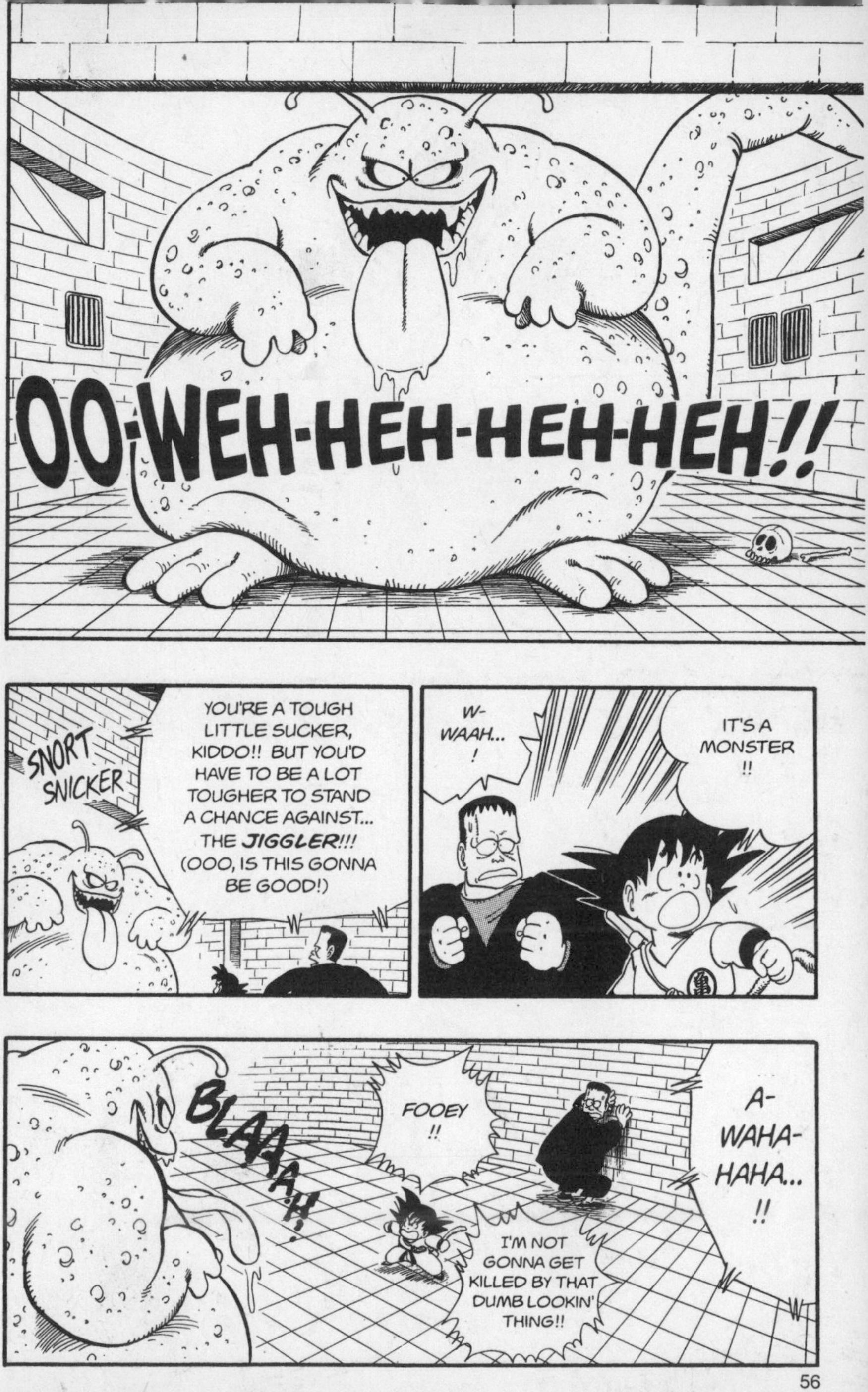
OO-WEH-HEH-HEH-HEH!!
SNORT SNICKER
YOU'RE A TOUGH LITTLE SUCKER, KIDDO!! BUT YOU'D HAVE TO BE A LOT TOUGHER TO STAND A CHANCE AGAINST... THE JIGGLER!!! (OOO, IS THIS GONNA BE GOOD!)
W-WAAH...!
IT'S A MONSTER!!
BLAAAAH!
FOOEY!!
I'M NOT GONNA GET KILLED BY THAT DUMB LOOKIN' THING!!
A-WAHA-HAHA...!!

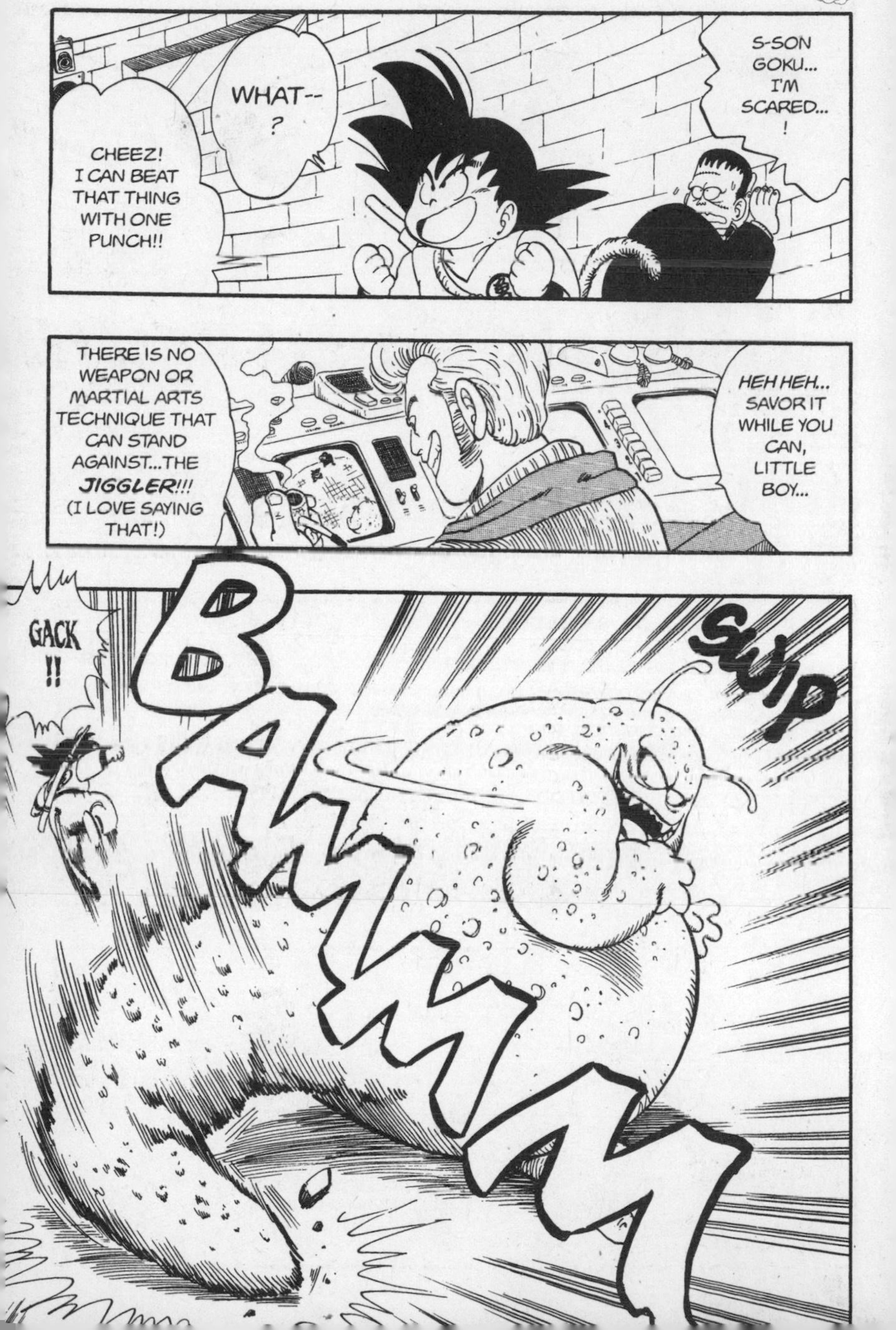
S-SON GOKU... I'M SCARED... !
WHAT-- ?
CHEEZ! I CAN BEAT THAT THING WITH ONE PUNCH!!
HEH HEH... SAVOR IT WHILE YOU CAN, LITTLE BOY...
THERE IS NO WEAPON OR MARTIAL ARTS TECHNIQUE THAT CAN STAND AGAINST...THE ***JIGGLER***!!! (I LOVE SAYING THAT!)
SLURP
BAMMMM
GACK !!

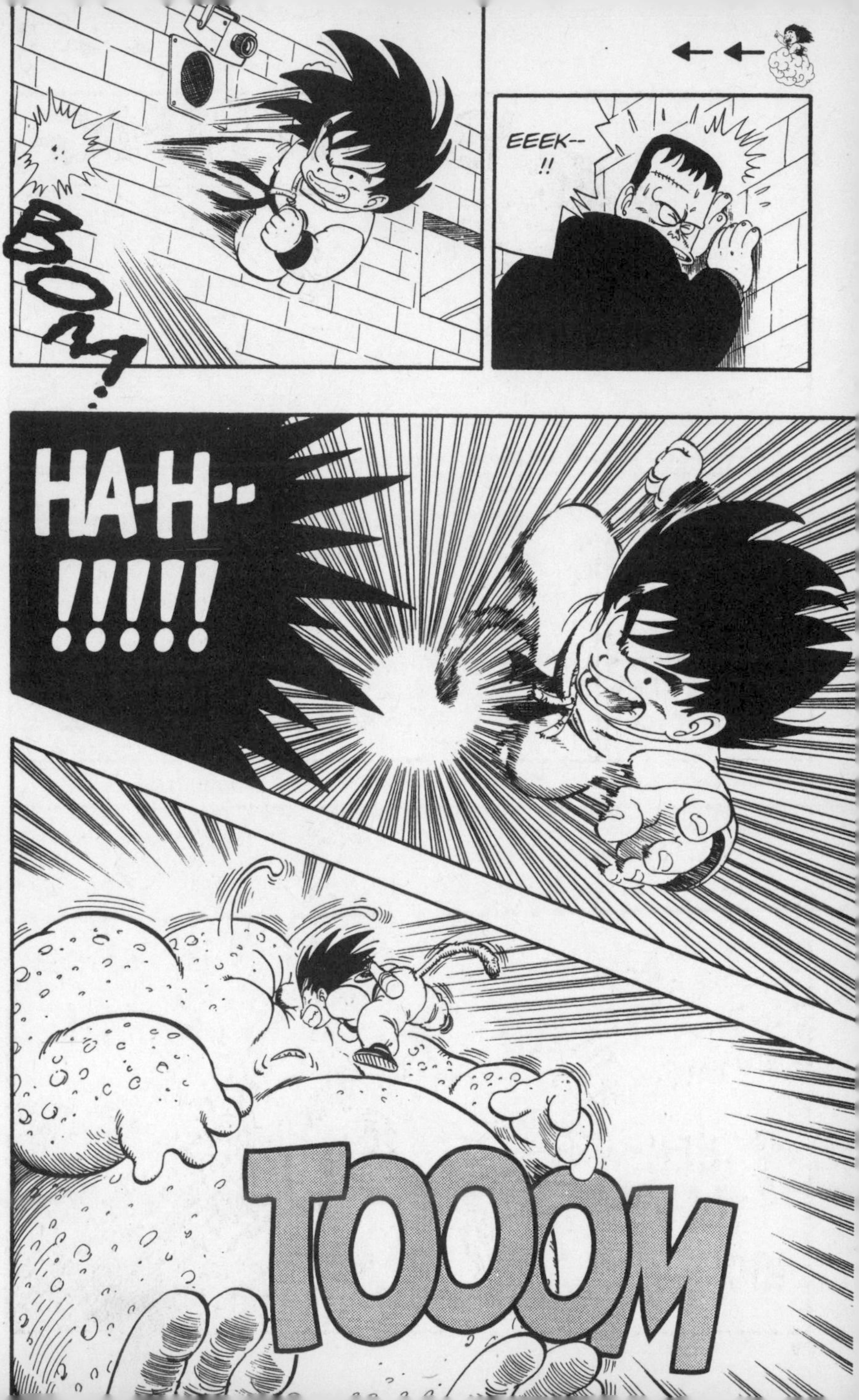
EEEK-- !!
BOM
HA-H-- !!!!!!
TOOOM

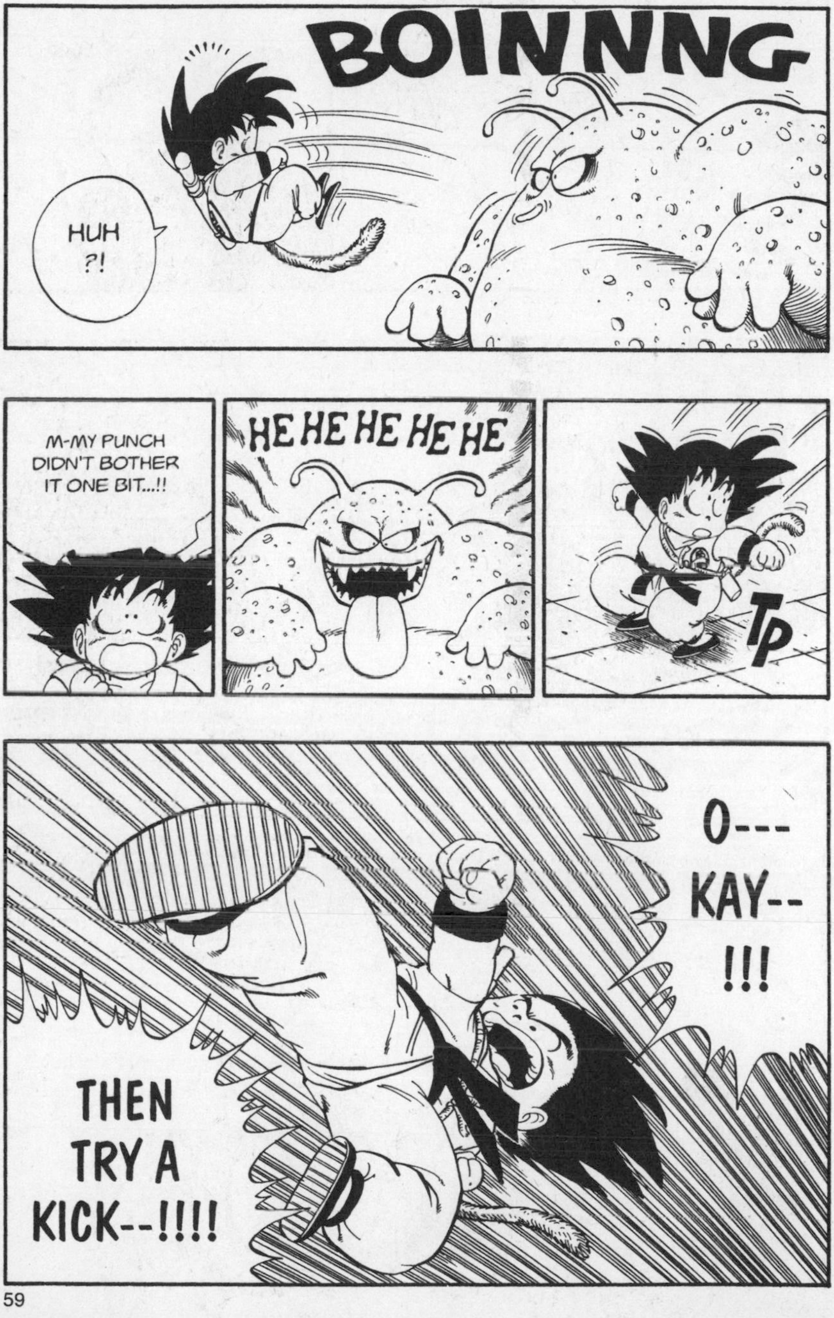
BOINNNG
HUH ?!
TP
HE HE HE HE HE
M-MY PUNCH DIDN'T BOTHER IT ONE BIT...!!
O--- KAY-- !!!
THEN TRY A KICK--!!!!

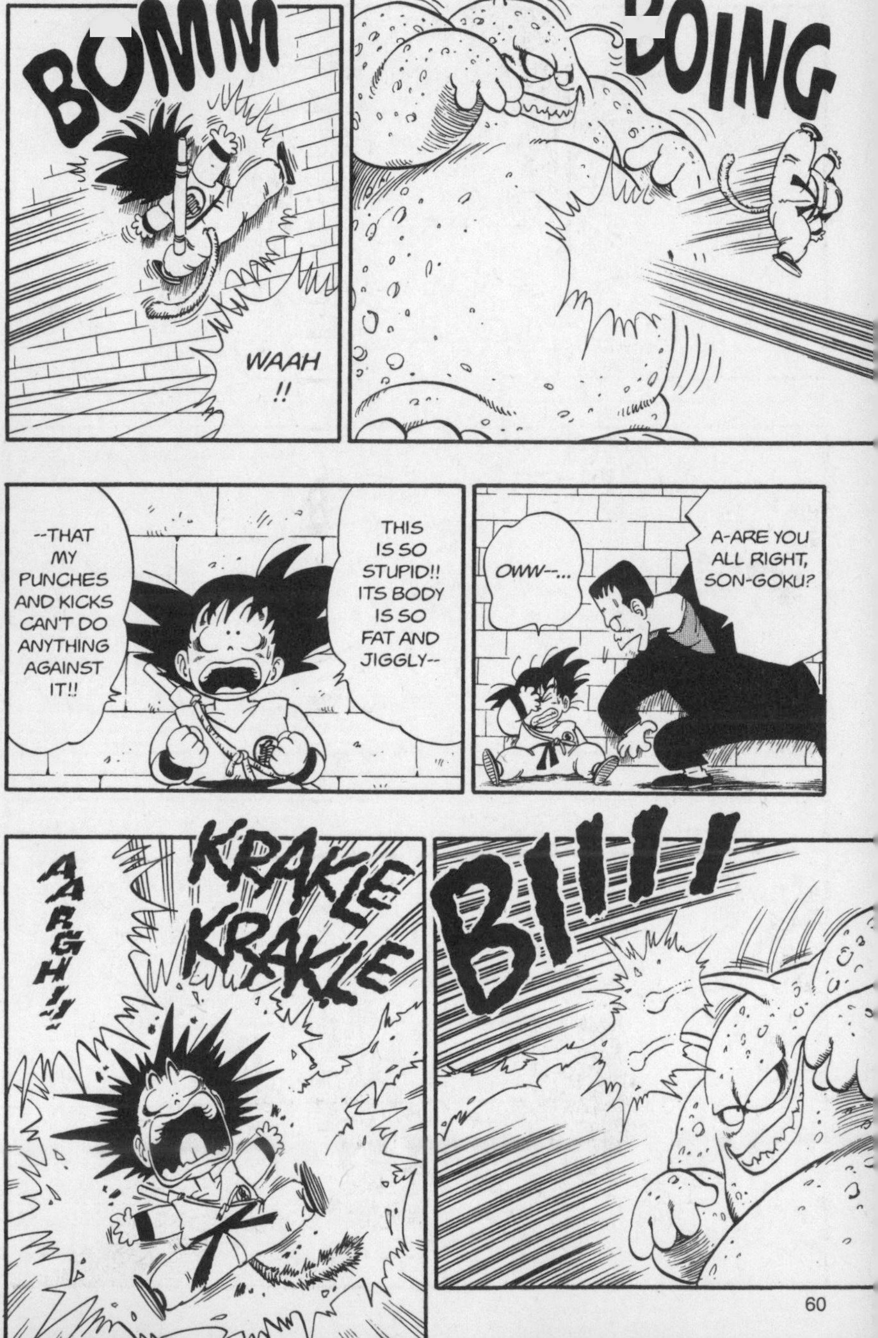
BOING
BOMM
WAAH !!
A-ARE YOU ALL RIGHT, SON-GOKU?
OWW--...
THIS IS SO STUPID!! ITS BODY IS SO FAT AND JIGGLY--
--THAT MY PUNCHES AND KICKS CAN'T DO ANYTHING AGAINST IT!!
BIIIII
KRAKLE KRAKLE
AARGH!!!

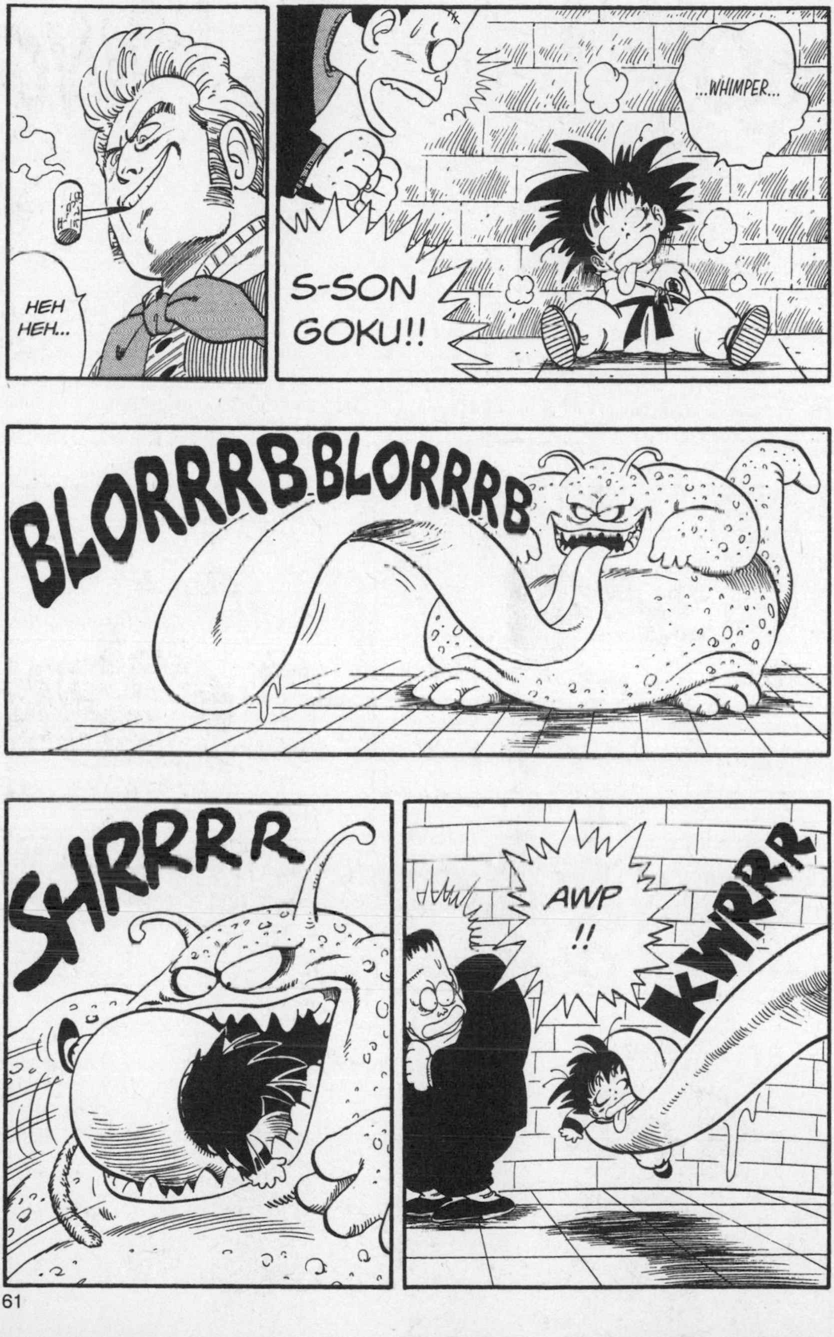
...WHIMPER...
S-SON GOKU!!
HEH HEH...
BLORRRB BLORRRB
KWRRR
AWP !!
SHRRRR

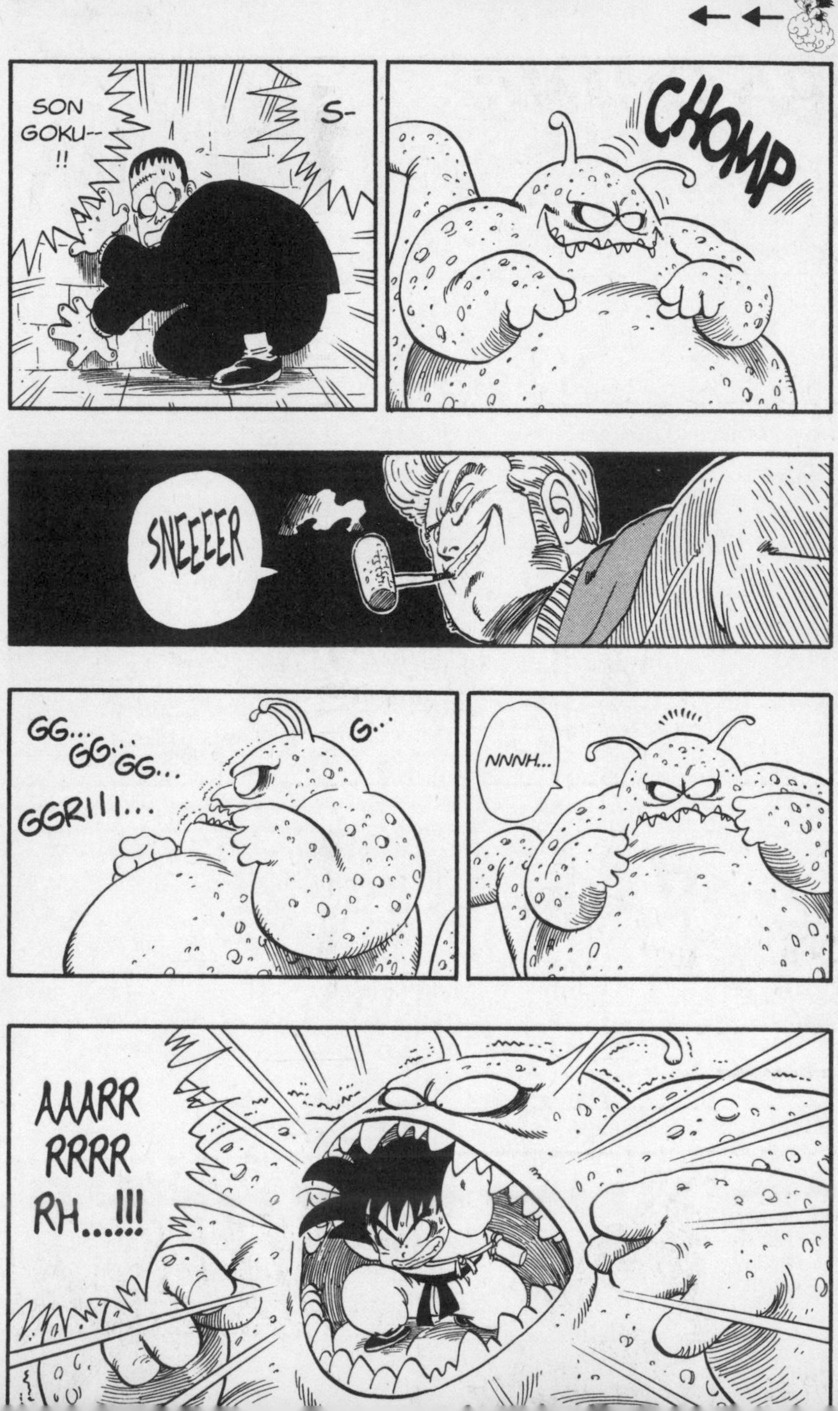
CHOMP
S-
SON GOKU--!!
SNEEEER
NNNH...
G...
GG... GG... GG...
GGRIIII...
AAARRRRRRRH.....!!!

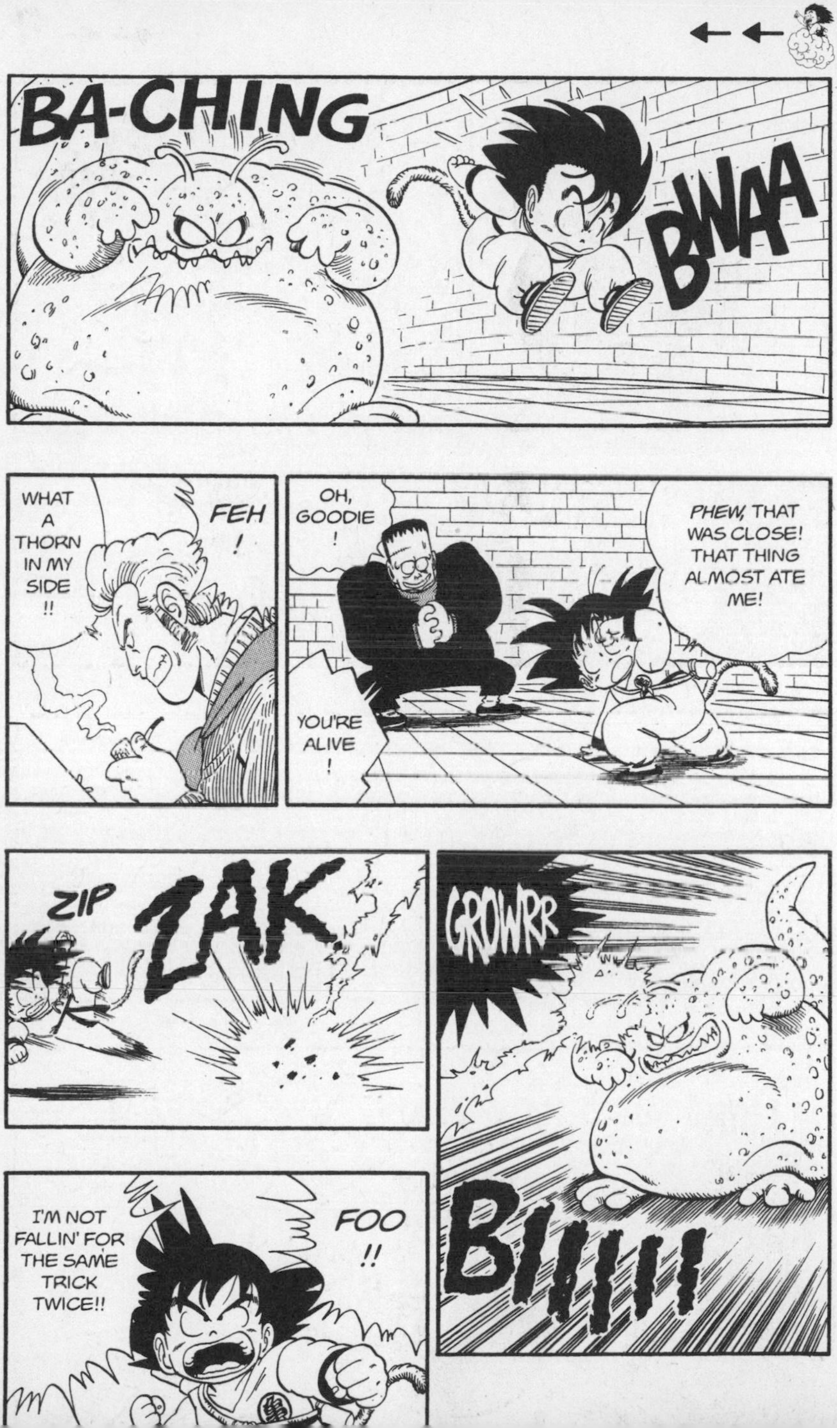
BWAA
BA-CHING
PHEW, THAT WAS CLOSE! THAT THING ALMOST ATE ME!
OH, GOODIE!
YOU'RE ALIVE!
FEH!
WHAT A THORN IN MY SIDE!!
GROWRR
BIIIII
ZAK
ZIP
FOO!!
I'M NOT FALLIN' FOR THE SAME TRICK TWICE!!

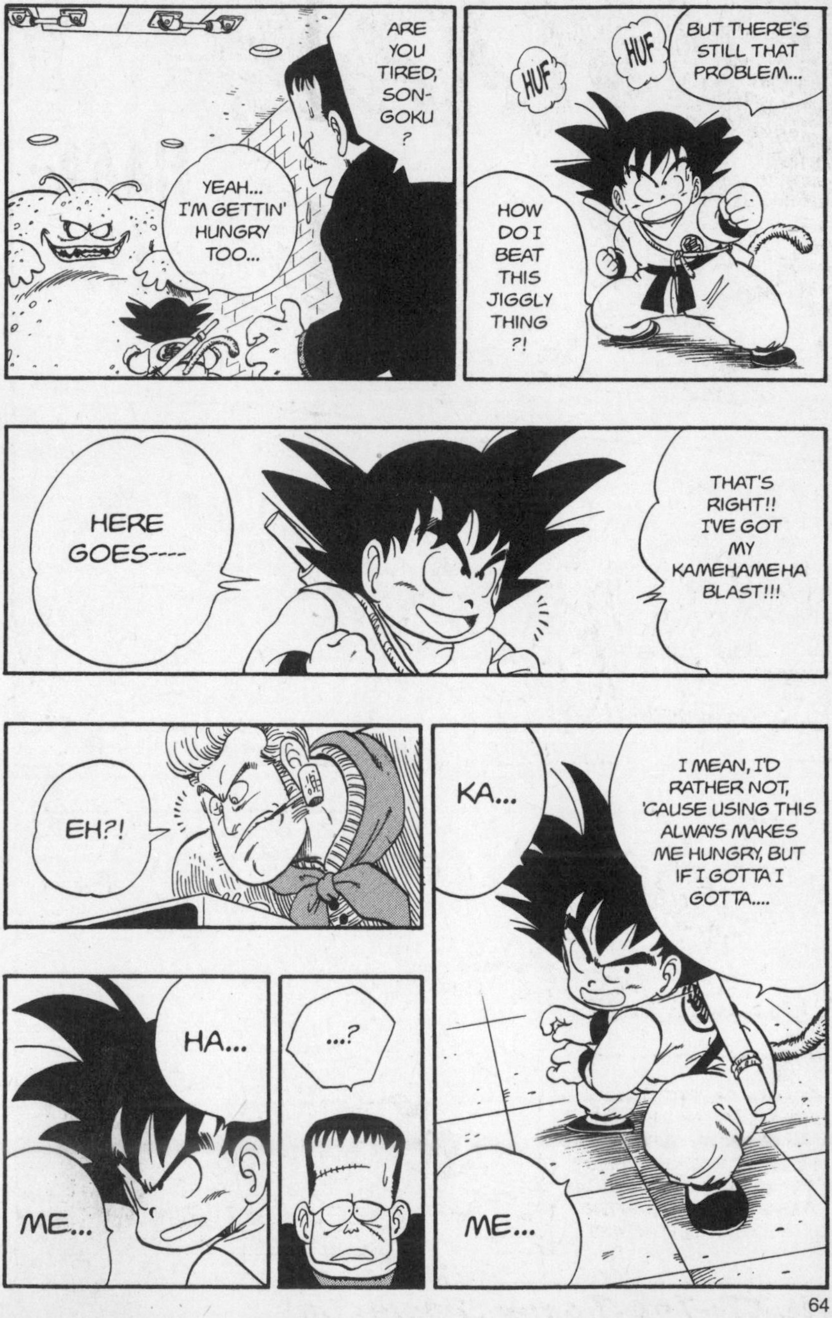
HUF
HUF
BUT THERE'S STILL THAT PROBLEM...
HOW DO I BEAT THIS JIGGLY THING ?!
ARE YOU TIRED, SON-GOKU ?
YEAH... I'M GETTIN' HUNGRY TOO...
THAT'S RIGHT!! I'VE GOT MY KAMEHAMEHA BLAST!!!
HERE GOES----
I MEAN, I'D RATHER NOT, 'CAUSE USING THIS ALWAYS MAKES ME HUNGRY, BUT IF I GOTTA I GOTTA....
KA...
ME...
EH?!
...?
HA...
ME...

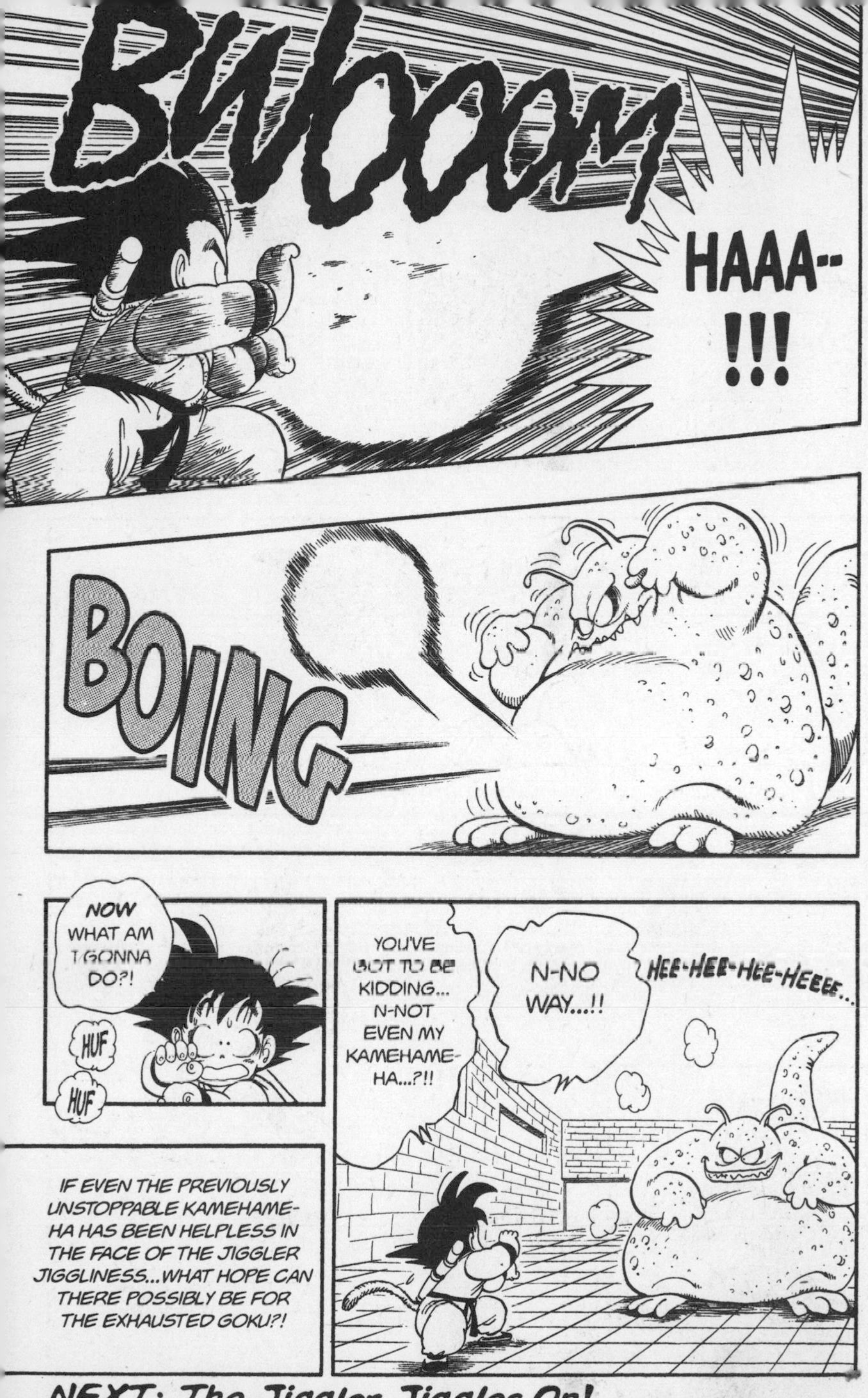
BWOOOM
HAAA--!!!
BOING
HEE-HEE-HEE-HEEEE...
N-NO WAY...!!
YOU'VE GOT TO BE KIDDING... N-NOT EVEN MY KAMEHAME-HA...?!!
NOW WHAT AM I GONNA DO?!
HUF
HUF
IF EVEN THE PREVIOUSLY UNSTOPPABLE KAMEHAME-HA HAS BEEN HELPLESS IN THE FACE OF THE JIGGLER JIGGLINESS...WHAT HOPE CAN THERE POSSIBLY BE FOR THE EXHAUSTED GOKU?!

NEXT: The Jiggler Jiggles On!

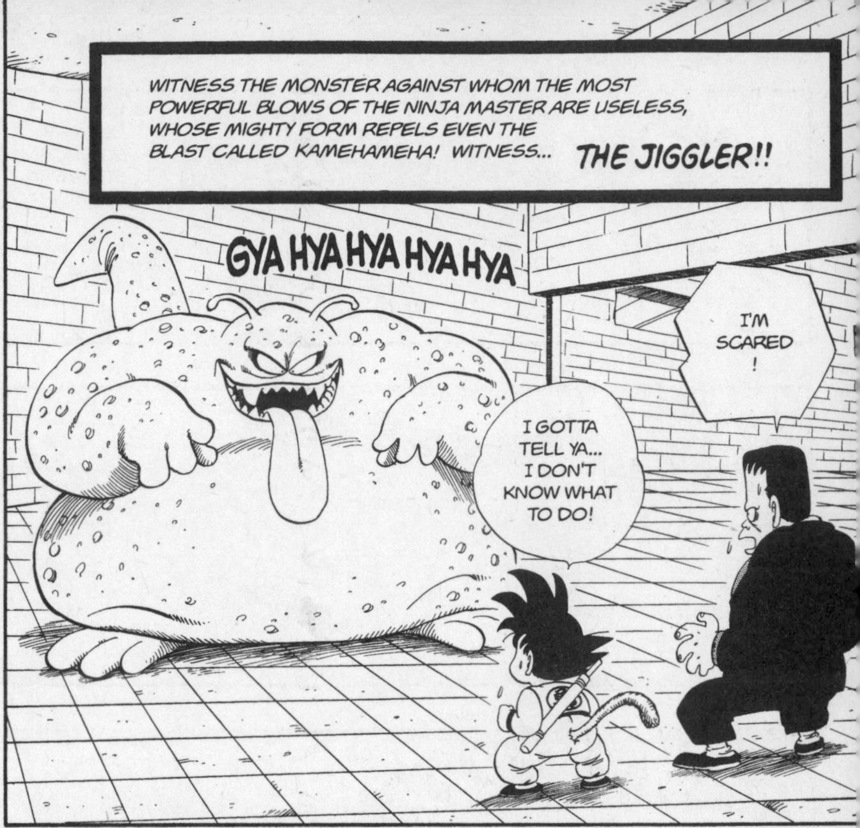
WITNESS THE MONSTER AGAINST WHOM THE MOST POWERFUL BLOWS OF THE NINJA MASTER ARE USELESS, WHOSE MIGHTY FORM REPELS EVEN THE BLAST CALLED KAMEHAMEHA! WITNESS... THE JIGGLER!!
GYA HYA HYA HYA HYA
I'M SCARED !
I GOTTA TELL YA... I DON'T KNOW WHAT TO DO!

Tale 65 • How to Unjiggle a Jiggler

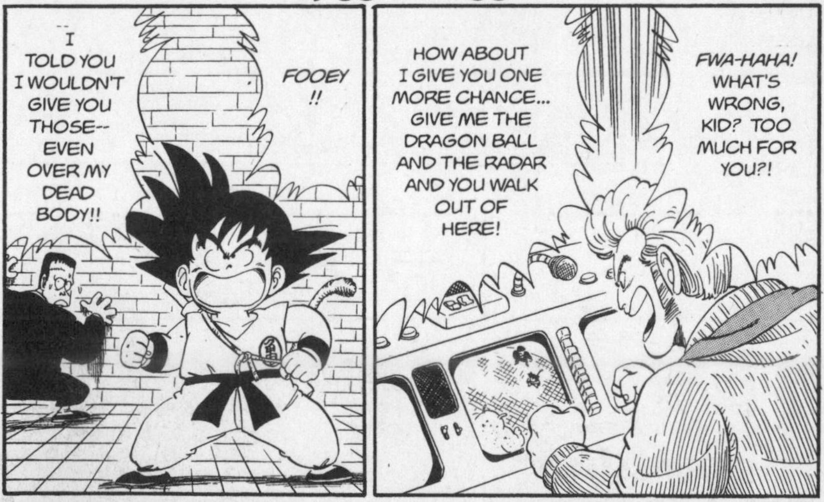
FWA-HAHA! WHAT'S WRONG, KID? TOO MUCH FOR YOU?!
HOW ABOUT I GIVE YOU ONE MORE CHANCE... GIVE ME THE DRAGON BALL AND THE RADAR AND YOU WALK OUT OF HERE!
FOOEY !!
I TOLD YOU I WOULDN'T GIVE YOU THOSE-- EVEN OVER MY DEAD BODY!!

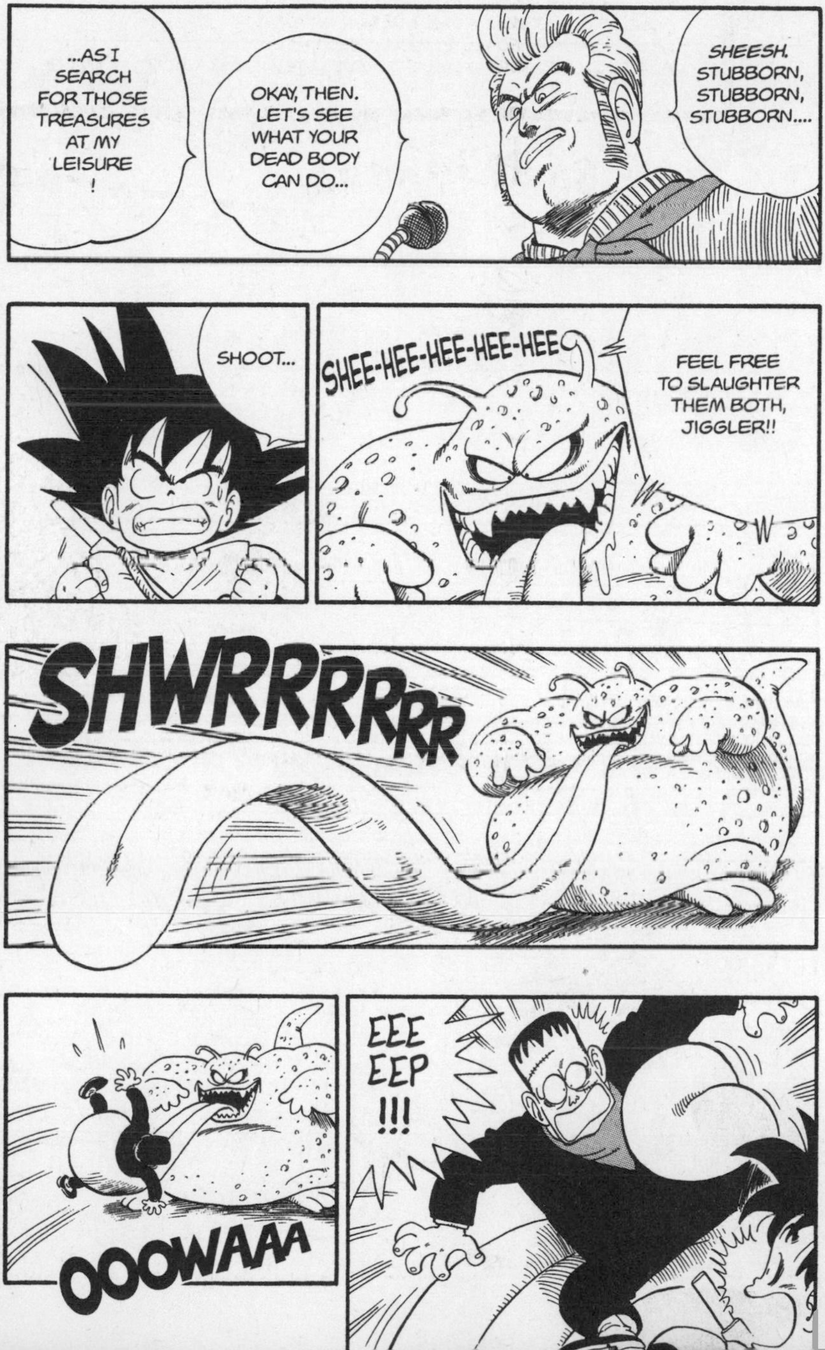
SHEESH. STUBBORN, STUBBORN, STUBBORN....
OKAY, THEN. LET'S SEE WHAT YOUR DEAD BODY CAN DO...
...AS I SEARCH FOR THOSE TREASURES AT MY LEISURE !
FEEL FREE TO SLAUGHTER THEM BOTH, JIGGLER!!
SHEE-HEE-HEE-HEE-HEE
SHOOT...
SHWRRRRRR
EEE EEP !!!
OOOWAAA

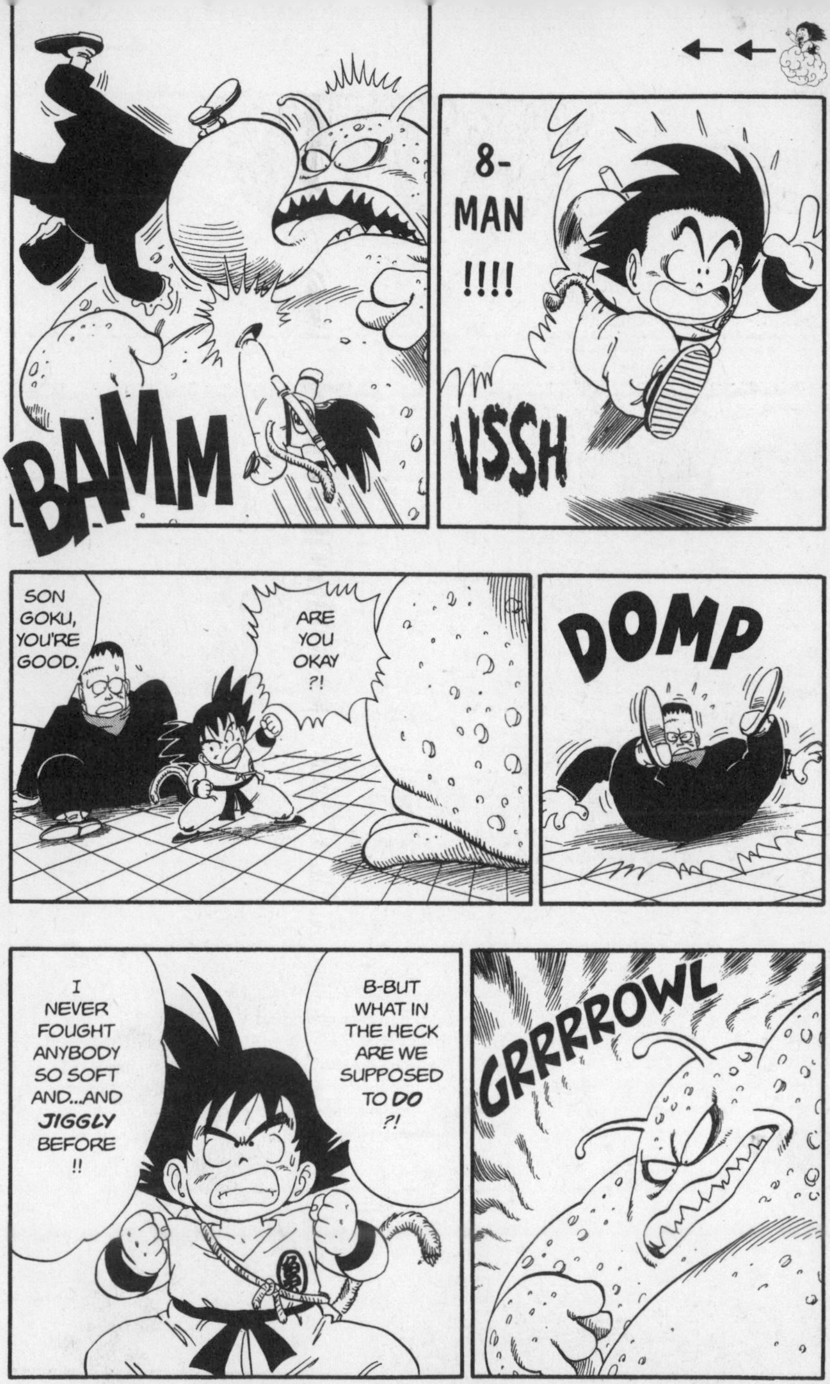
8-MAN!!!!
VSSH
BAMM
DOMP
ARE YOU OKAY ?!
SON GOKU, YOU'RE GOOD.
GRRRROWL
B-BUT WHAT IN THE HECK ARE WE SUPPOSED TO ***DO*** ?!
I NEVER FOUGHT ANYBODY SO SOFT AND...AND ***JIGGLY*** BEFORE !!

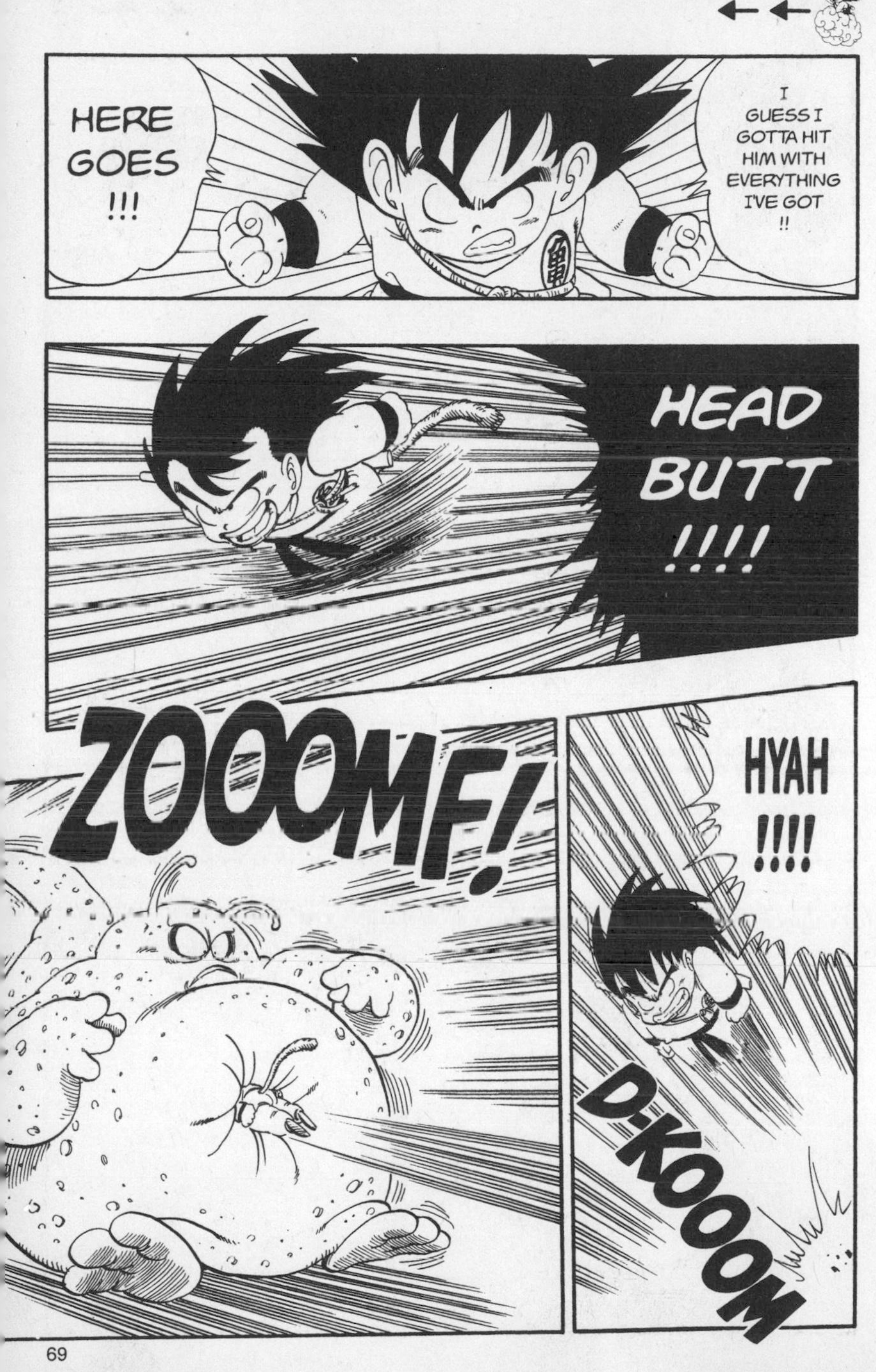
I GUESS I GOTTA HIT HIM WITH EVERYTHING I'VE GOT !!
HERE GOES !!!
HEAD BUTT !!!!
HYAH !!!!
D-KOOOM
ZOOOMF!

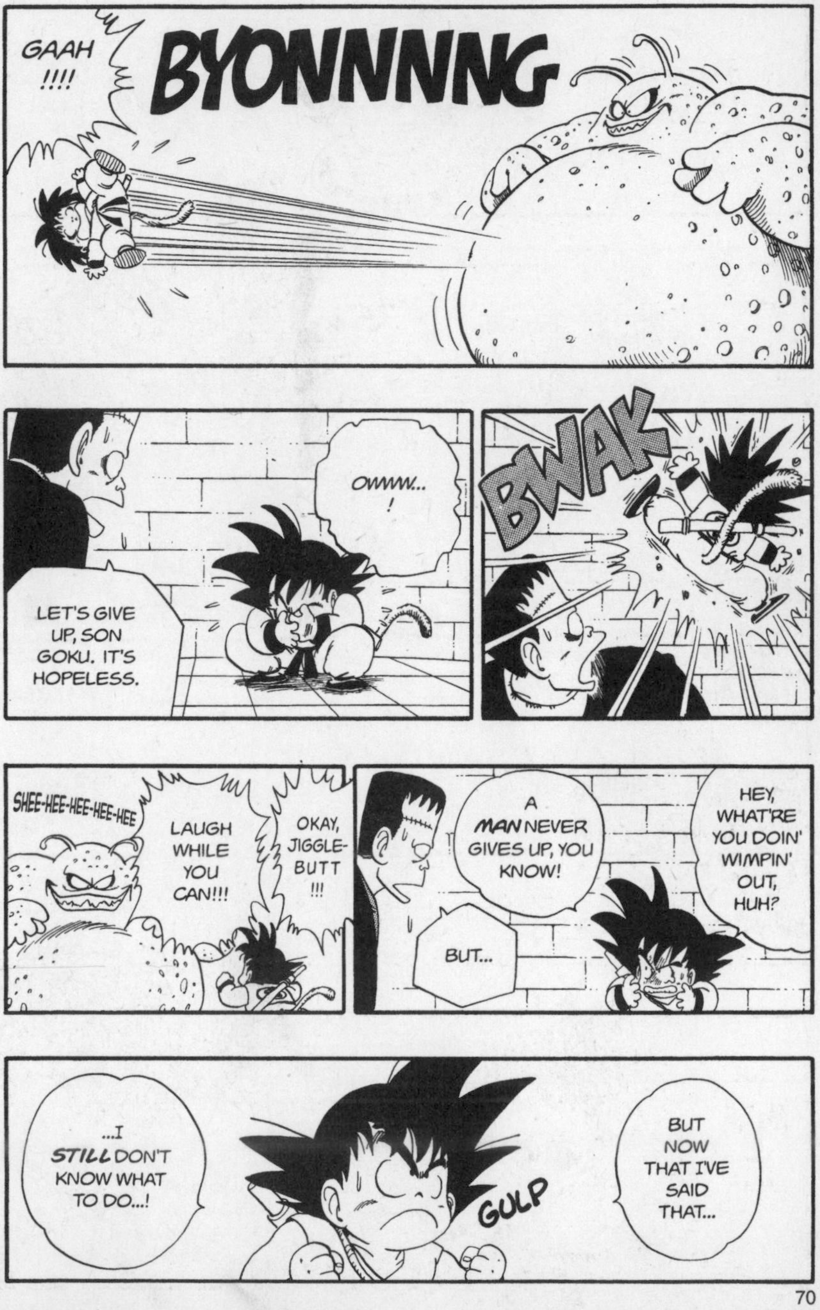
BYONNNNG
GAAH !!!!
BWAK
OWWW... !
LET'S GIVE UP, SON GOKU. IT'S HOPELESS.
HEY, WHAT'RE YOU DOIN' WIMPIN' OUT, HUH?
A MAN NEVER GIVES UP, YOU KNOW!
BUT...
OKAY, JIGGLE-BUTT !!!
LAUGH WHILE YOU CAN!!!
SHEE-HEE-HEE-HEE-HEE
BUT NOW THAT I'VE SAID THAT...
GULP
...I STILL DON'T KNOW WHAT TO DO...!

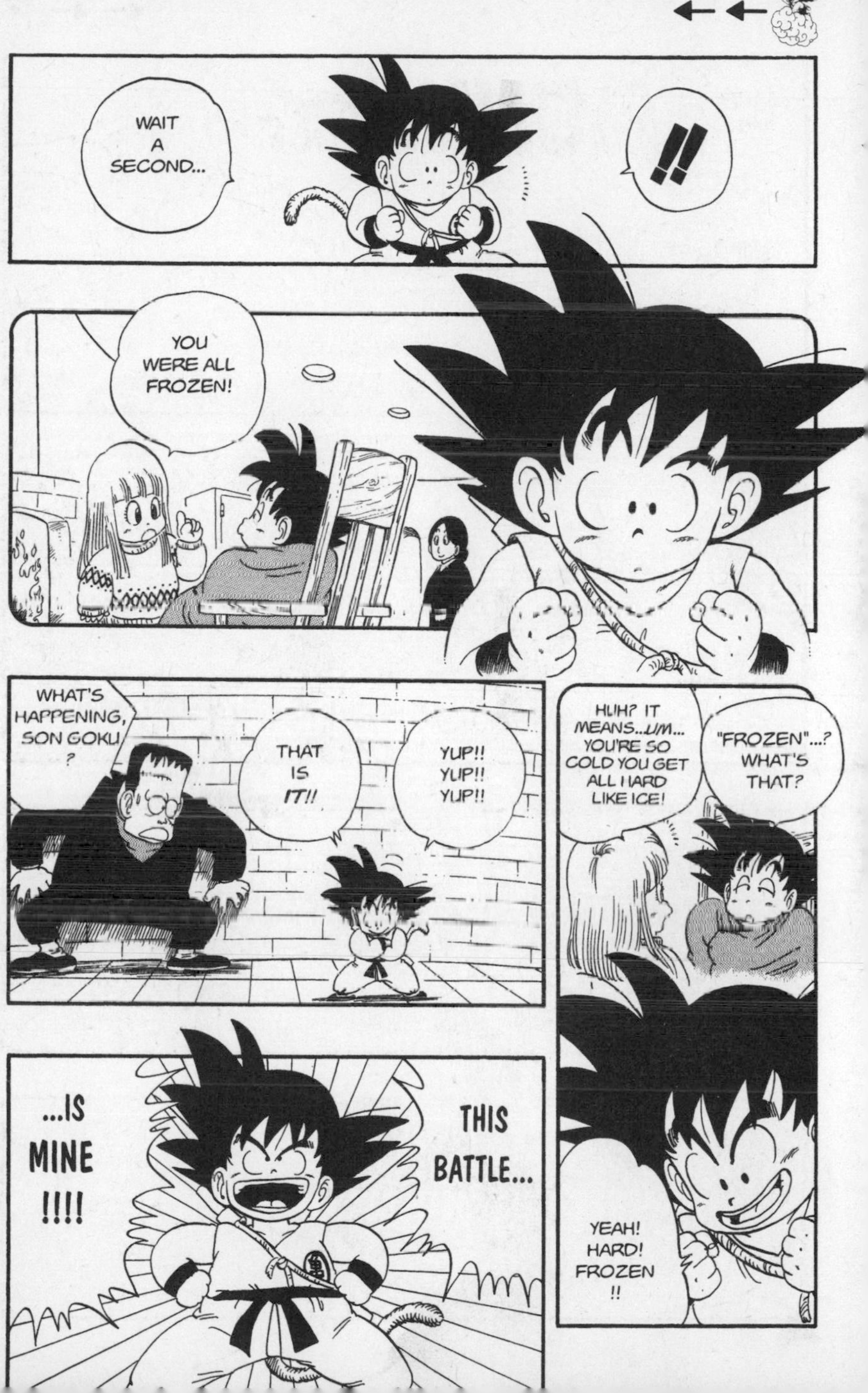
!!
WAIT A SECOND...
YOU WERE ALL FROZEN!
"FROZEN"...? WHAT'S THAT?
HUH? IT MEANS...UM... YOU'RE SO COLD YOU GET ALL HARD LIKE ICE!
YEAH! HARD! FROZEN !!
YUP!! YUP!! YUP!!
THAT IS IT!!
WHAT'S HAPPENING, SON GOKU ?
THIS BATTLE...
...IS MINE !!!!

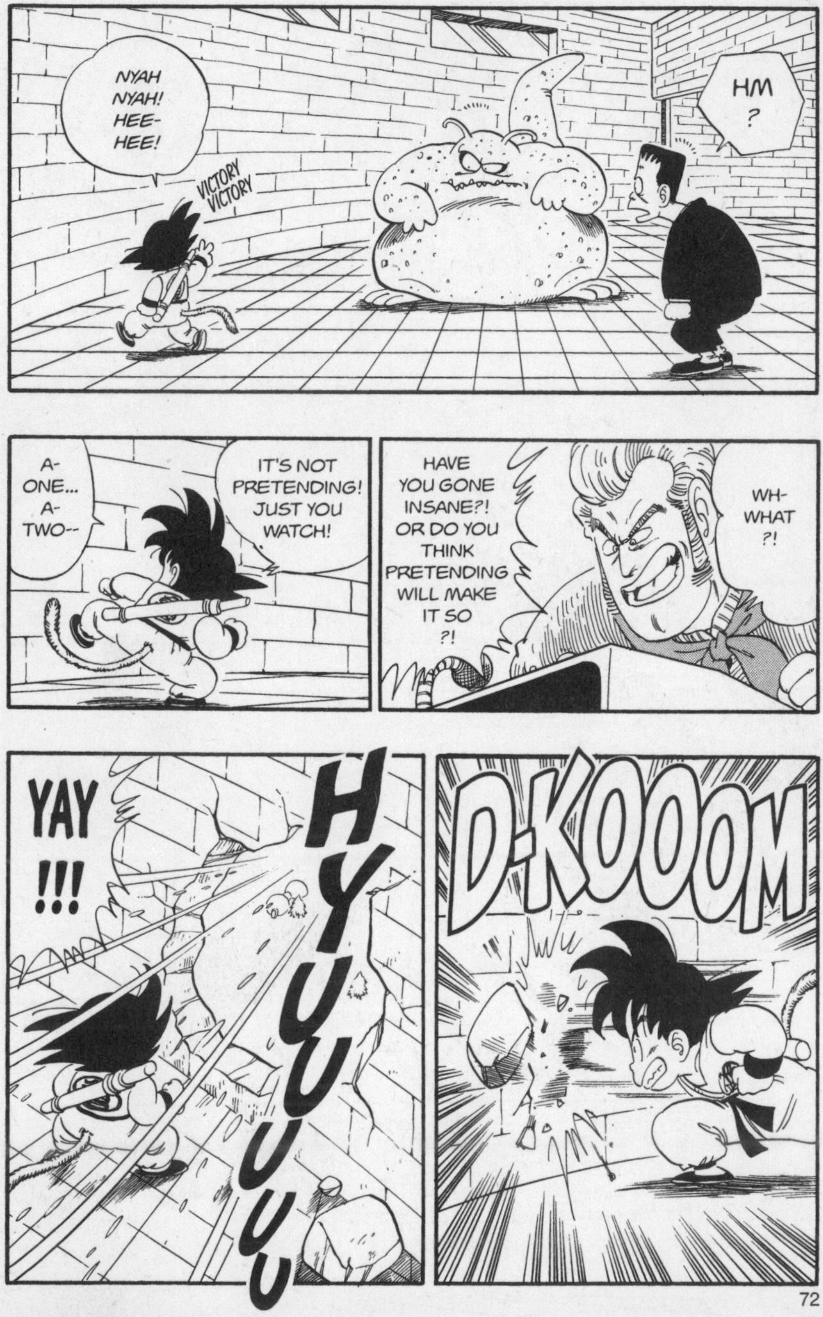
HM ?
NYAH NYAH! HEE-HEE!
VICTORY VICTORY
WH- WHAT ?!
HAVE YOU GONE INSANE?! OR DO YOU THINK PRETENDING WILL MAKE IT SO ?!
IT'S NOT PRETENDING! JUST YOU WATCH!
A- ONE... A- TWO--
D-KOOOM
HYUUUUUU
YAY !!!

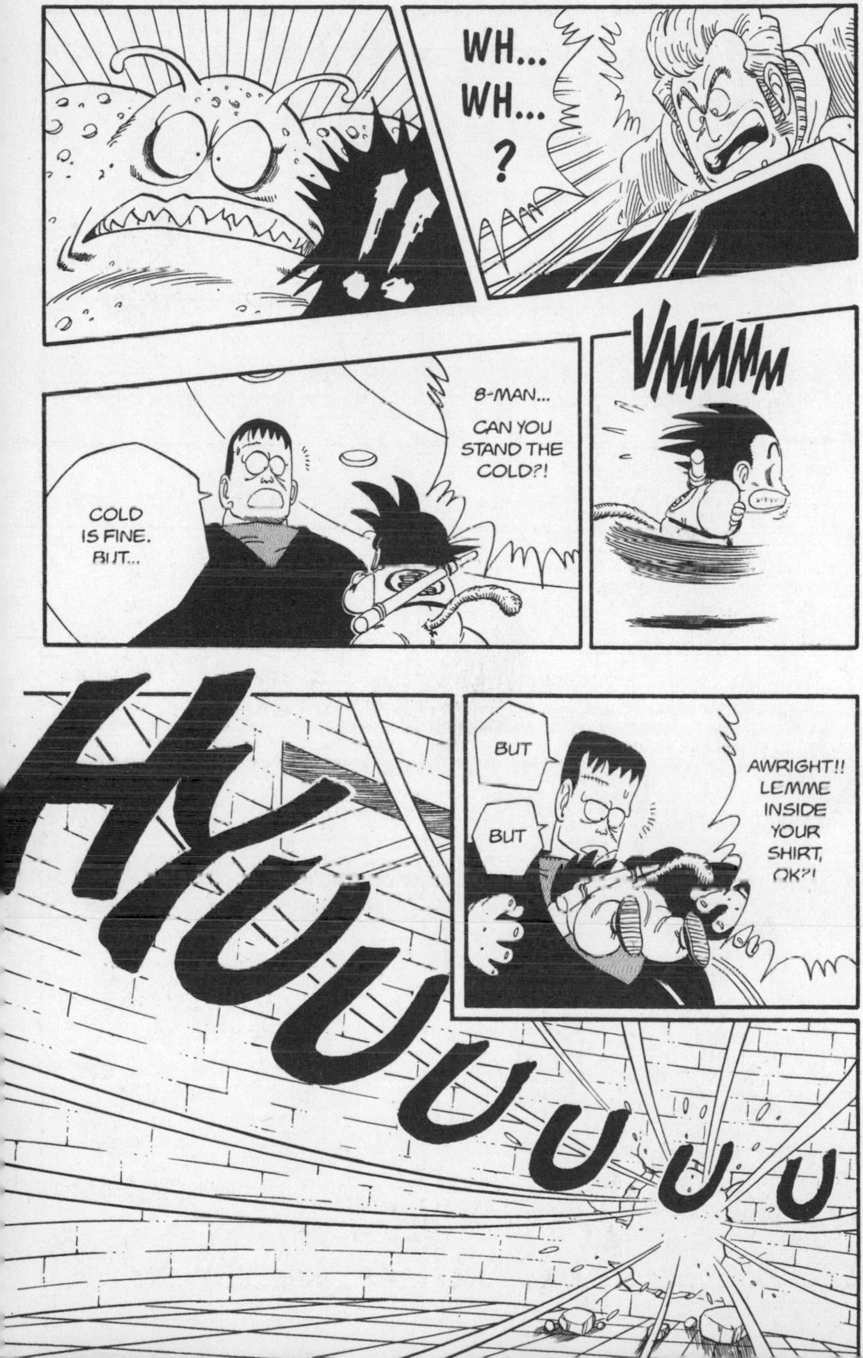
WH...
WH...
?
VMMMM
8-MAN...
CAN YOU STAND THE COLD?!
COLD IS FINE. BUT...
AWRIGHT!! LEMME INSIDE YOUR SHIRT, OK?!
BUT
BUT
HYUUUUUUU

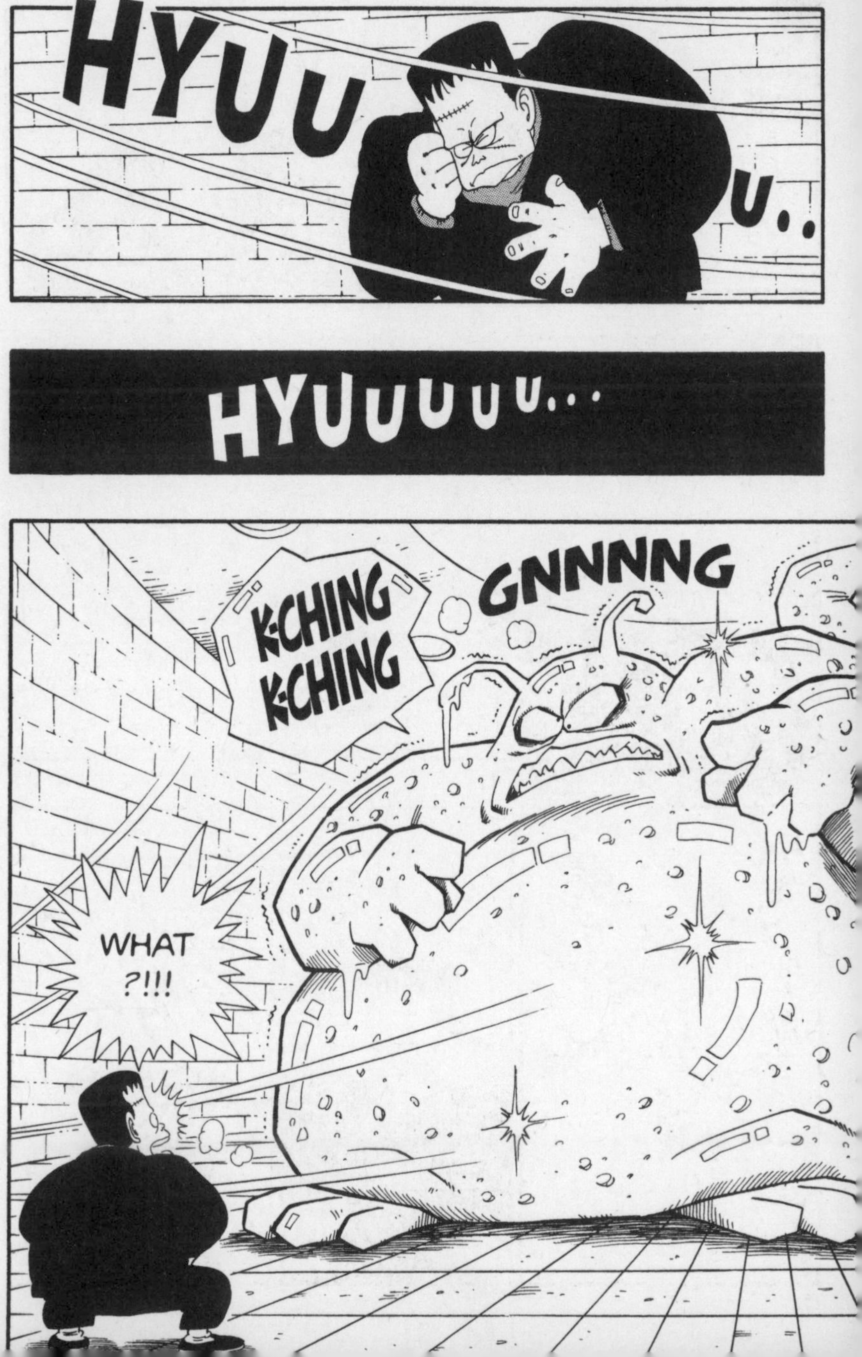
HYUUU..
HYUUUUU...
GNNNNG
K-CHING K-CHING
WHAT ?!!!

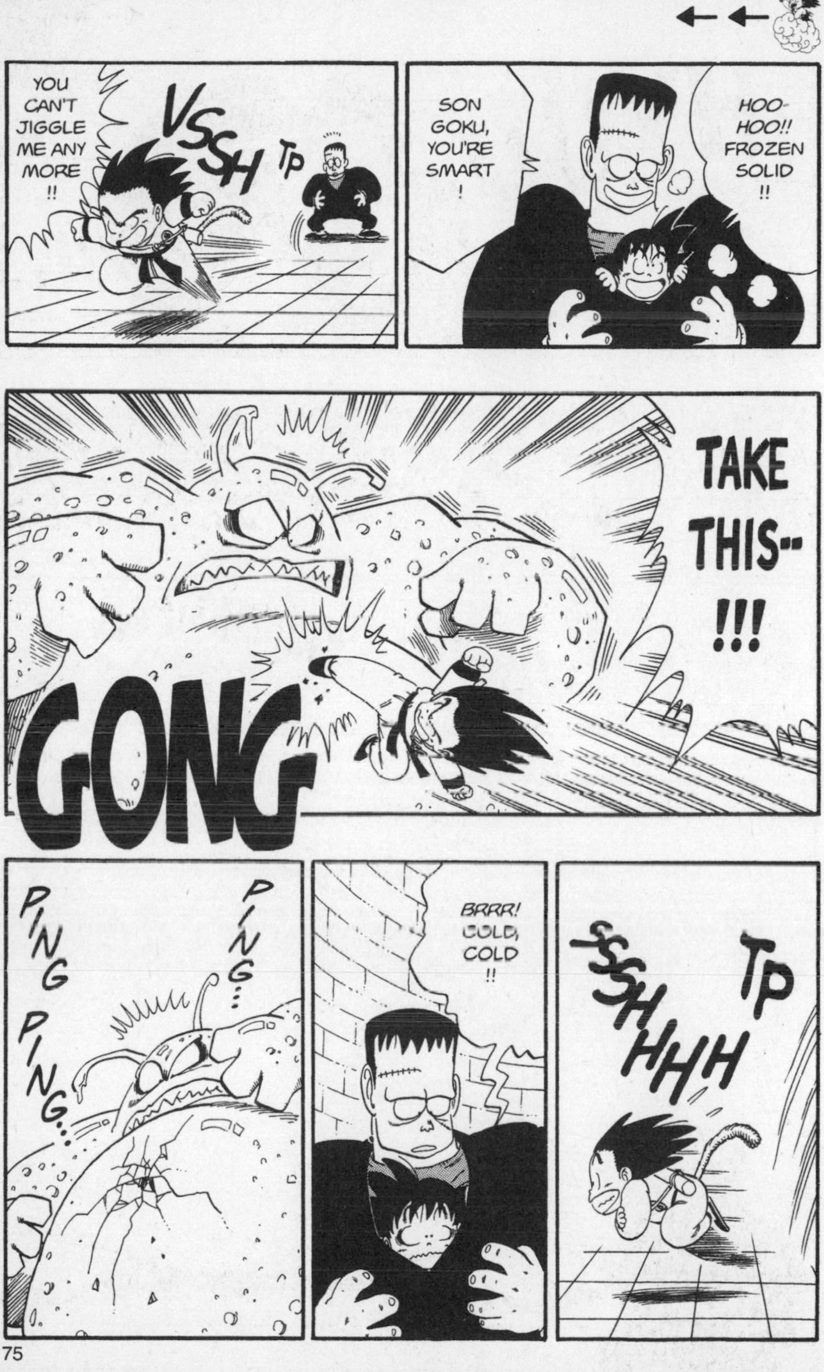
HOO-HOO!! FROZEN SOLID!!
SON GOKU, YOU'RE SMART!
YOU CAN'T JIGGLE ME ANY MORE!!
VSSH
TP
TAKE THIS--!!!
GONG
SSSHHHH
TP
BRRR! COLD, COLD!!
PING...
PING PING...

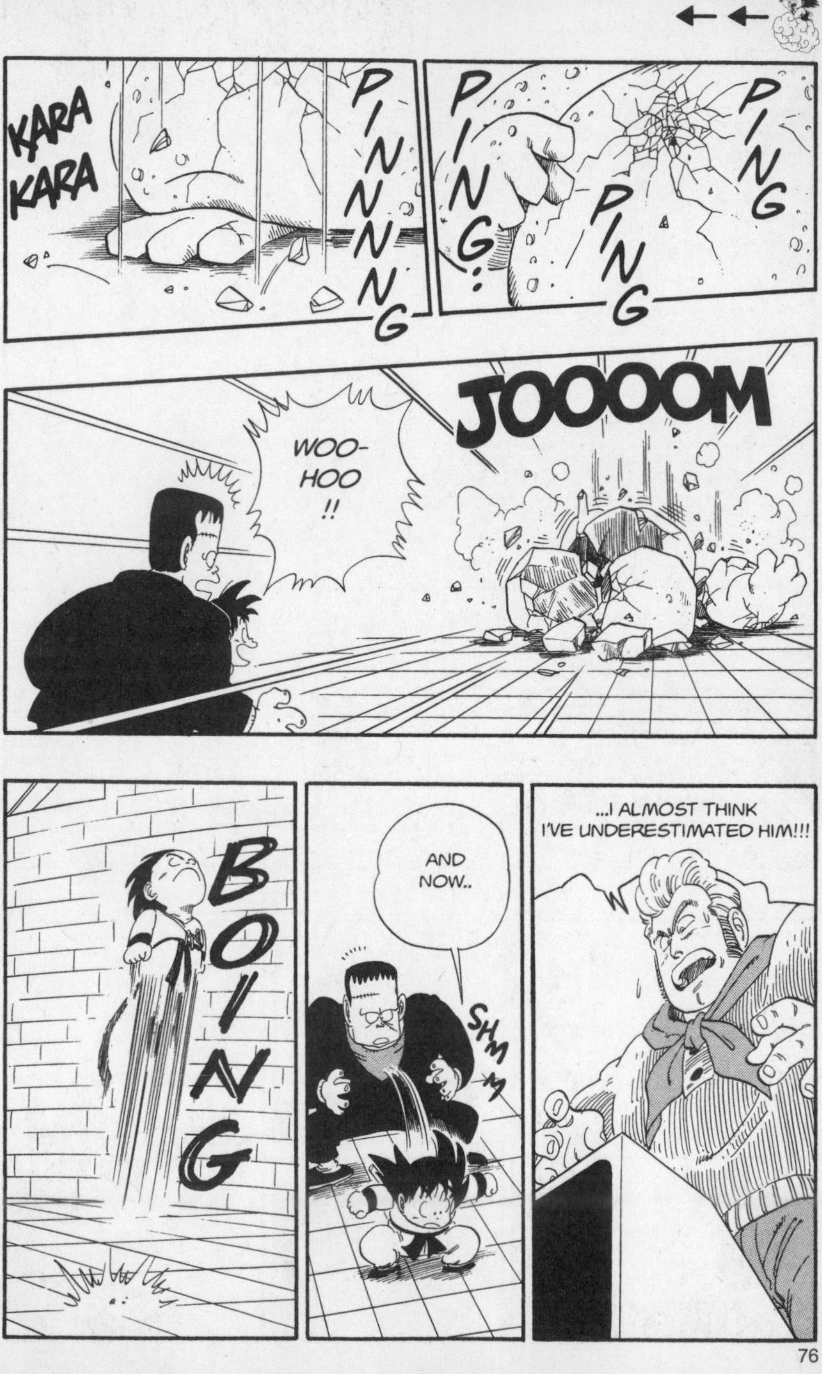
PING
PING
PING
PINNNNG
KARA KARA
JOOOOM
WOO-HOO!!
...I ALMOST THINK I'VE UNDERESTIMATED HIM!!!
AND NOW..
SHMM
BOING

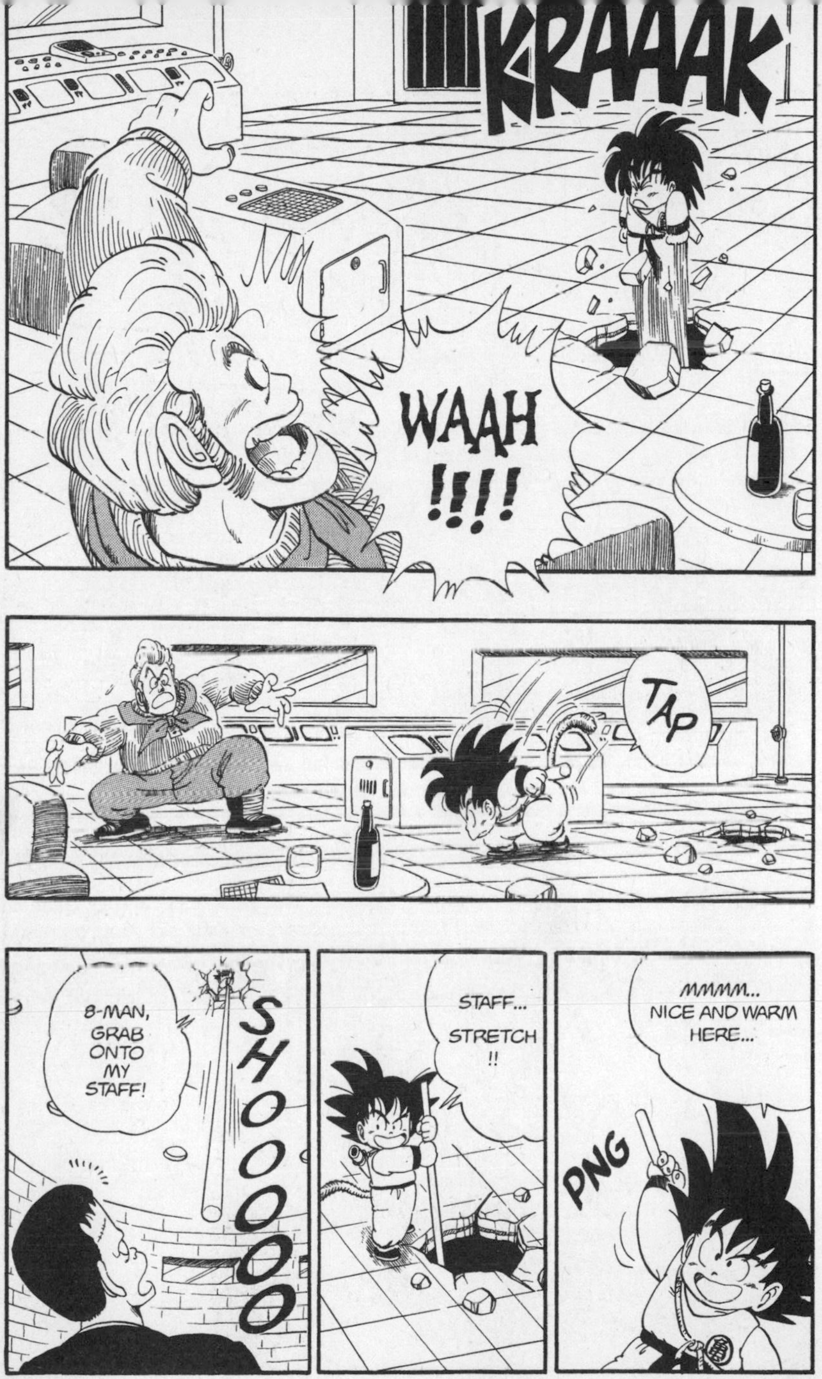
KRAAAK
WAAH !!!!
TAP
MMMM... NICE AND WARM HERE...
PNG
STAFF... STRETCH !!
8-MAN, GRAB ONTO MY STAFF!
SHOOOOO

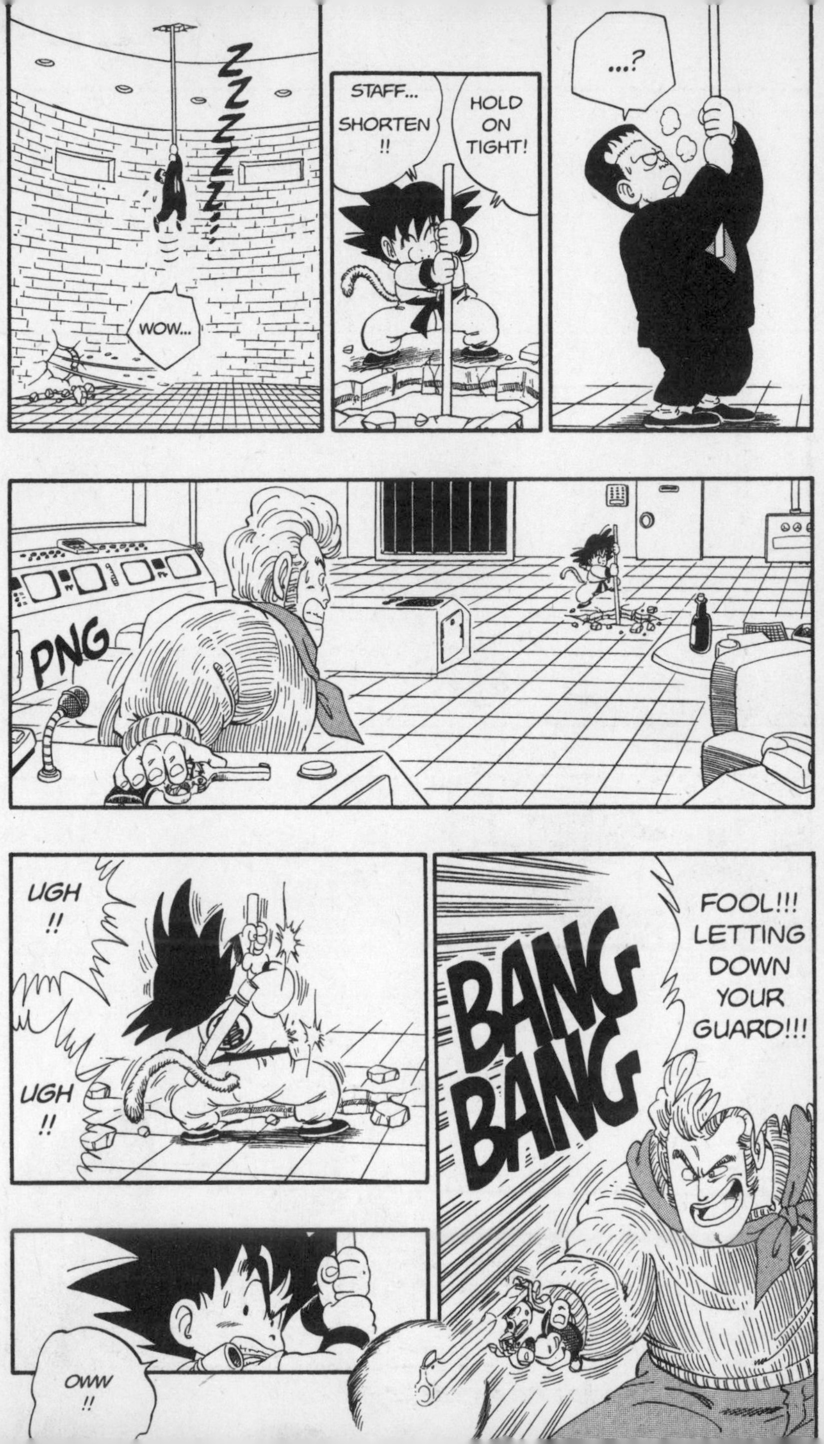
...?
HOLD ON TIGHT!
STAFF... SHORTEN !!
ZZZZZZ
WOW...
PNG
FOOL!!! LETTING DOWN YOUR GUARD!!!
BANG BANG
UGH !!
UGH !!
OWW !!

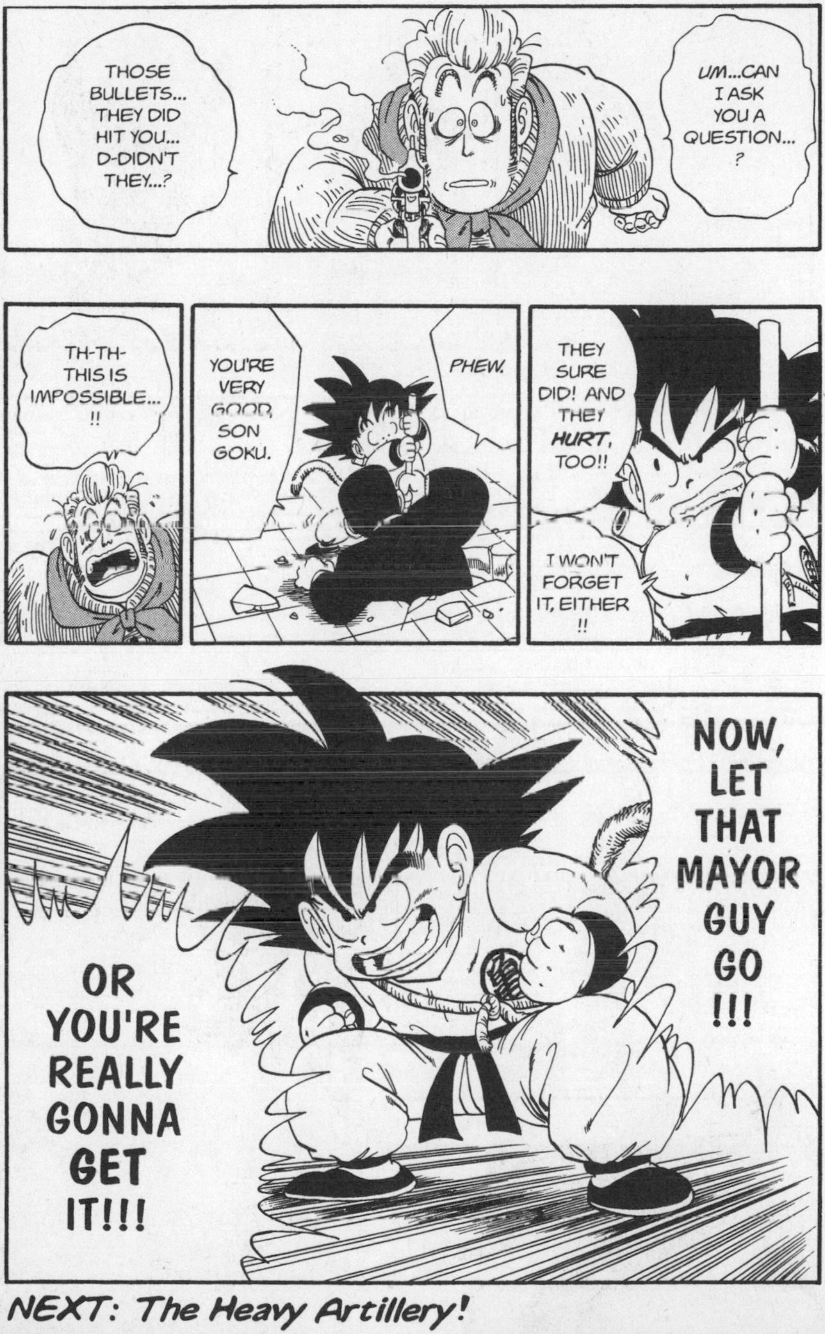
UM...CAN I ASK YOU A QUESTION... ?
THOSE BULLETS... THEY DID HIT YOU... D-DIDN'T THEY...?
THEY SURE DID! AND THEY HURT, TOO!!
I WON'T FORGET IT, EITHER !!
PHEW.
YOU'RE VERY GOOD, SON GOKU.
TH-TH-THIS IS IMPOSSIBLE... !!
NOW, LET THAT MAYOR GUY GO !!!
OR YOU'RE REALLY GONNA GET IT!!!

NEXT: The Heavy Artillery!

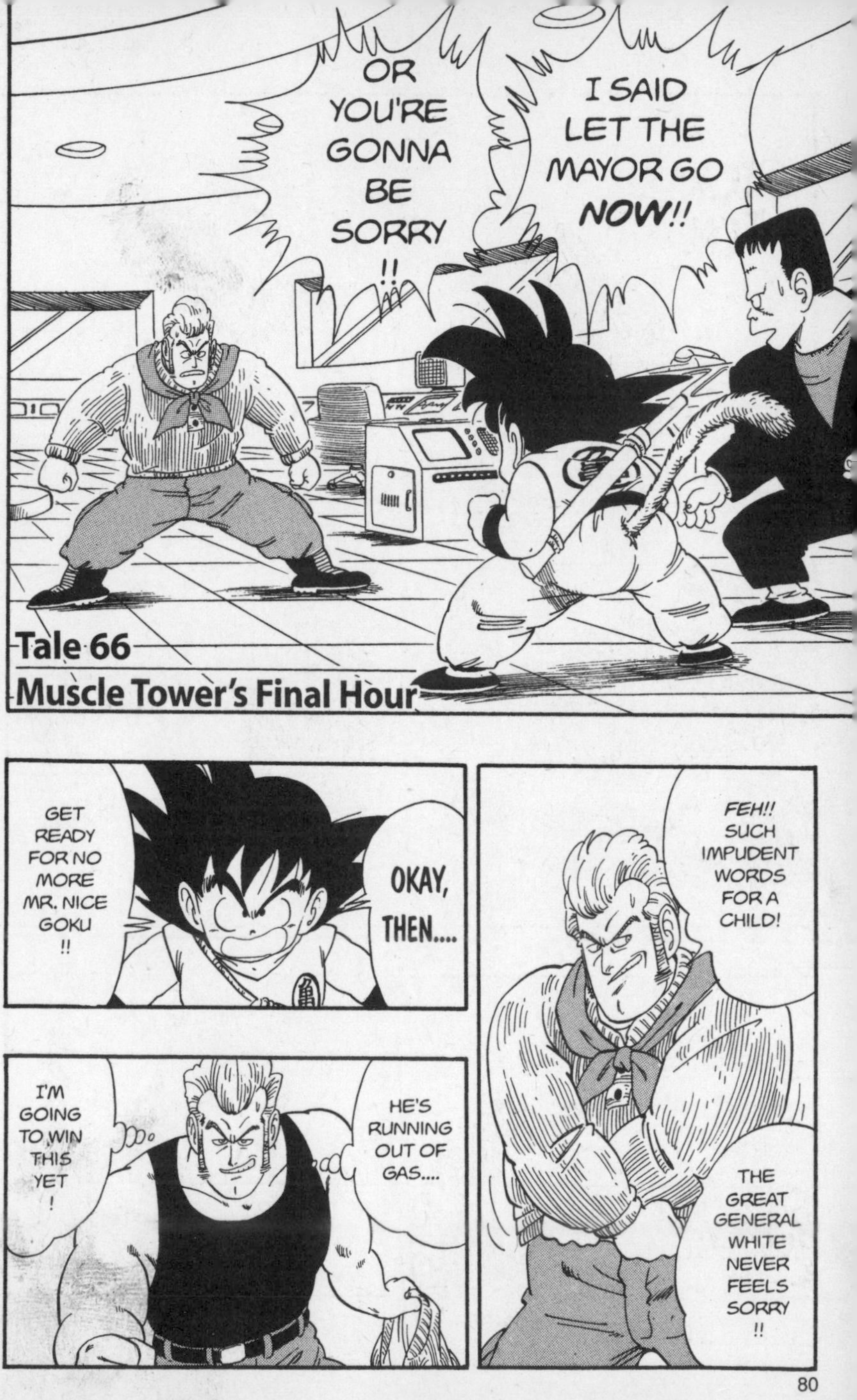
I SAID LET THE MAYOR GO NOW!!
OR YOU'RE GONNA BE SORRY!!
Tale 66
Muscle Tower's Final Hour
FEH!! SUCH IMPUDENT WORDS FOR A CHILD!
THE GREAT GENERAL WHITE NEVER FEELS SORRY!!
OKAY, THEN....
GET READY FOR NO MORE MR. NICE GOKU!!
HE'S RUNNING OUT OF GAS....
I'M GOING TO WIN THIS YET!

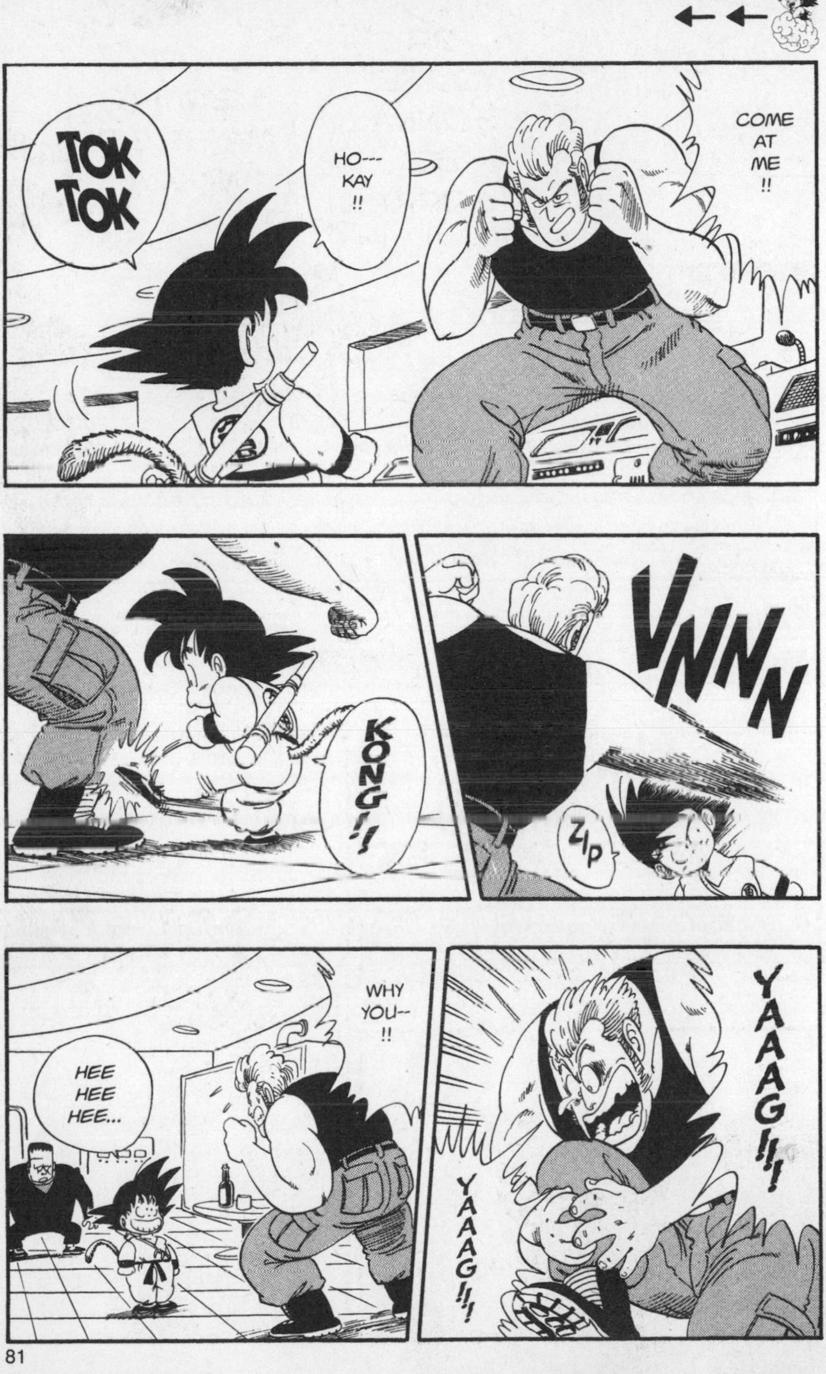
COME AT ME !!
HO--- KAY !!
TOK TOK
VNNN
ZIP
KONG!!
YAAAG!!!
YAAAG!!!
WHY YOU-- !!
HEE HEE HEE...

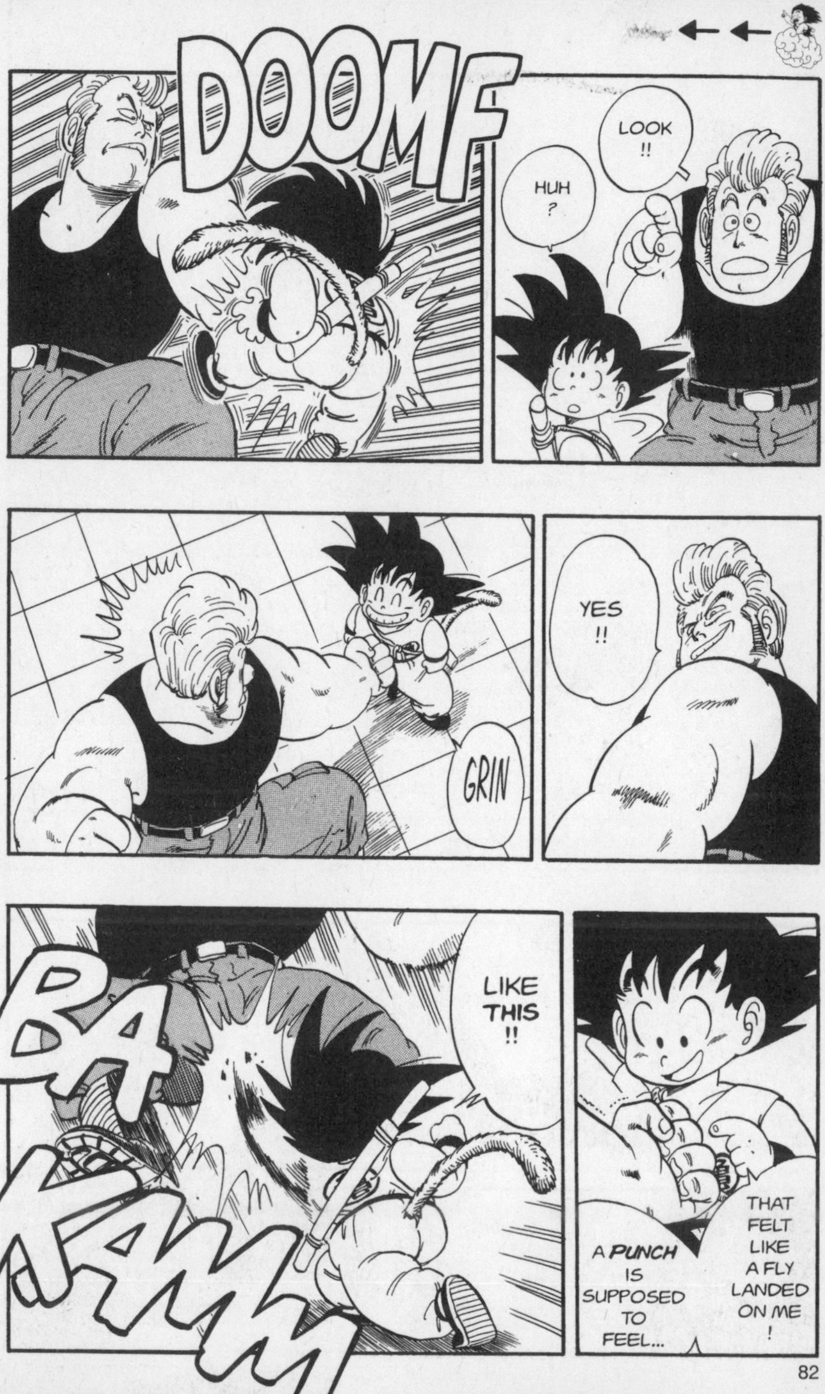
LOOK !!
HUH ?
DOOMF
YES !!
GRIN
THAT FELT LIKE A FLY LANDED ON ME !
A **PUNCH** IS SUPPOSED TO FEEL...
LIKE THIS !!
BA
KAMM

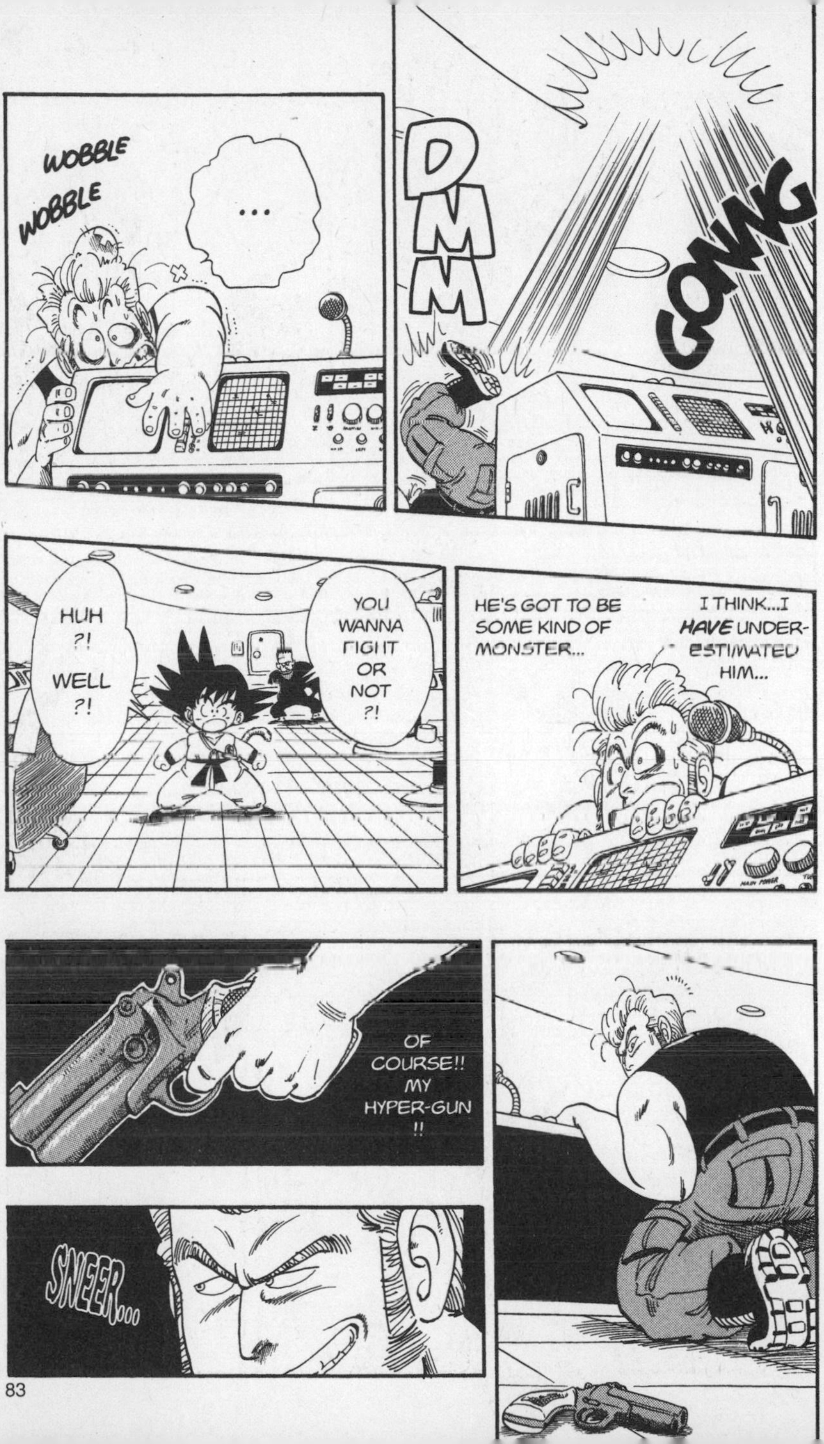
DMMM
GONNG
WOBBLE WOBBLE
...
I THINK...I HAVE UNDER-ESTIMATED HIM...
HE'S GOT TO BE SOME KIND OF MONSTER...
YOU WANNA FIGHT OR NOT ?!
HUH ?! WELL ?!
OF COURSE!! MY HYPER-GUN !!
SNEER...

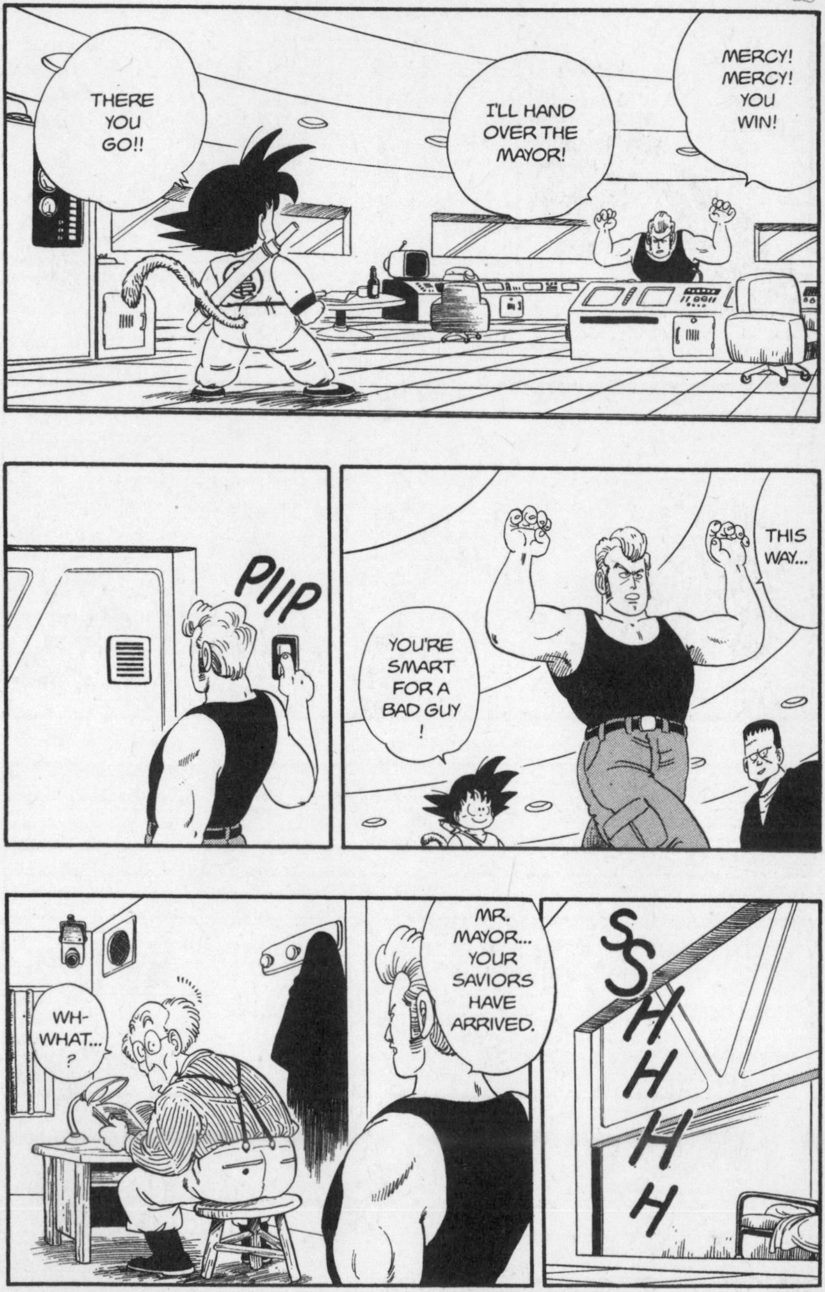
MERCY! MERCY! YOU WIN!
I'LL HAND OVER THE MAYOR!
THERE YOU GO!!
THIS WAY...
YOU'RE SMART FOR A BAD GUY!
PIIP
SSHHHH
MR. MAYOR... YOUR SAVIORS HAVE ARRIVED.
WH-WHAT...?

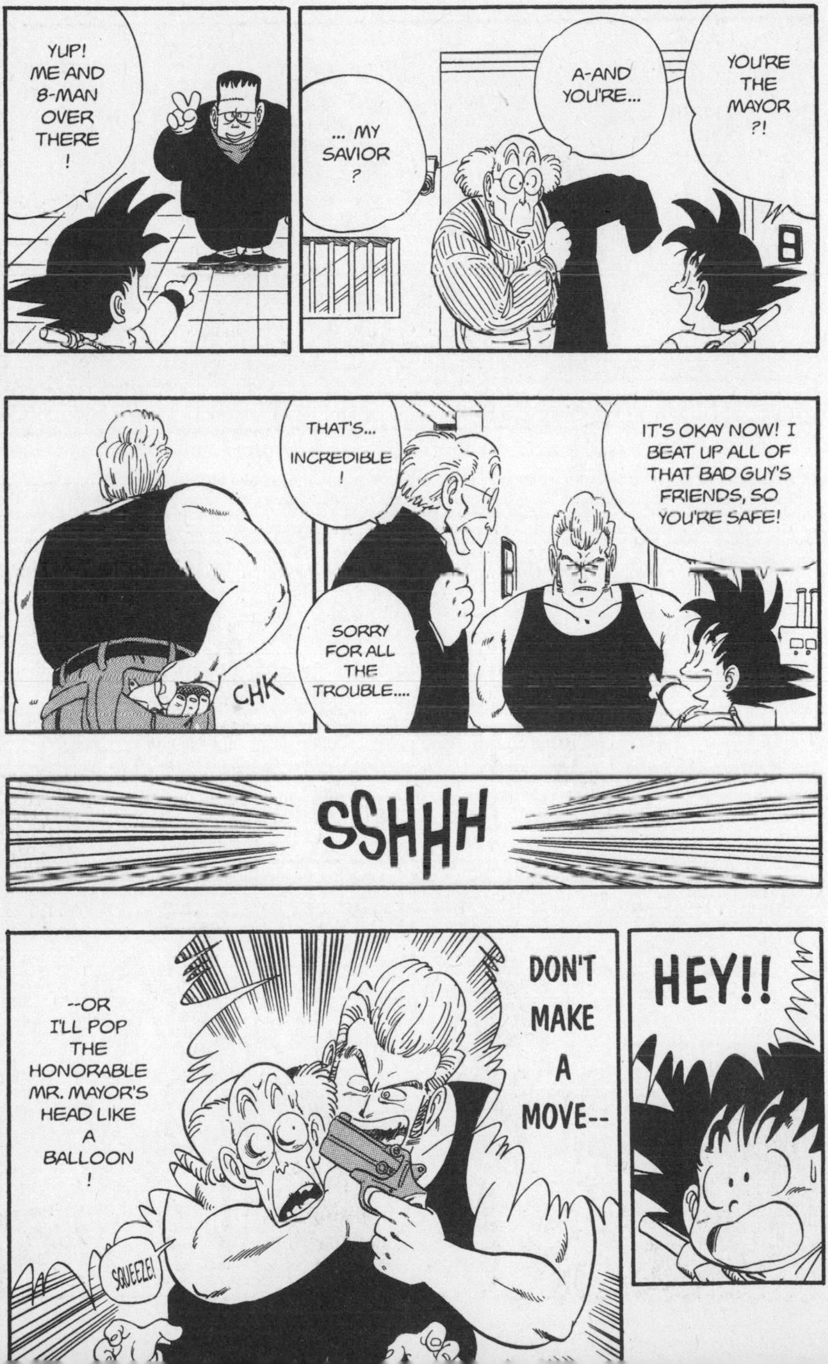
YOU'RE THE MAYOR ?!
A-AND YOU'RE...
... MY SAVIOR ?
YUP! ME AND 8-MAN OVER THERE !
IT'S OKAY NOW! I BEAT UP ALL OF THAT BAD GUY'S FRIENDS, SO YOU'RE SAFE!
THAT'S... INCREDIBLE !
SORRY FOR ALL THE TROUBLE....
CHK
SSHHH
HEY!!
DON'T MAKE A MOVE--
--OR I'LL POP THE HONORABLE MR. MAYOR'S HEAD LIKE A BALLOON !
SQUEEZE!

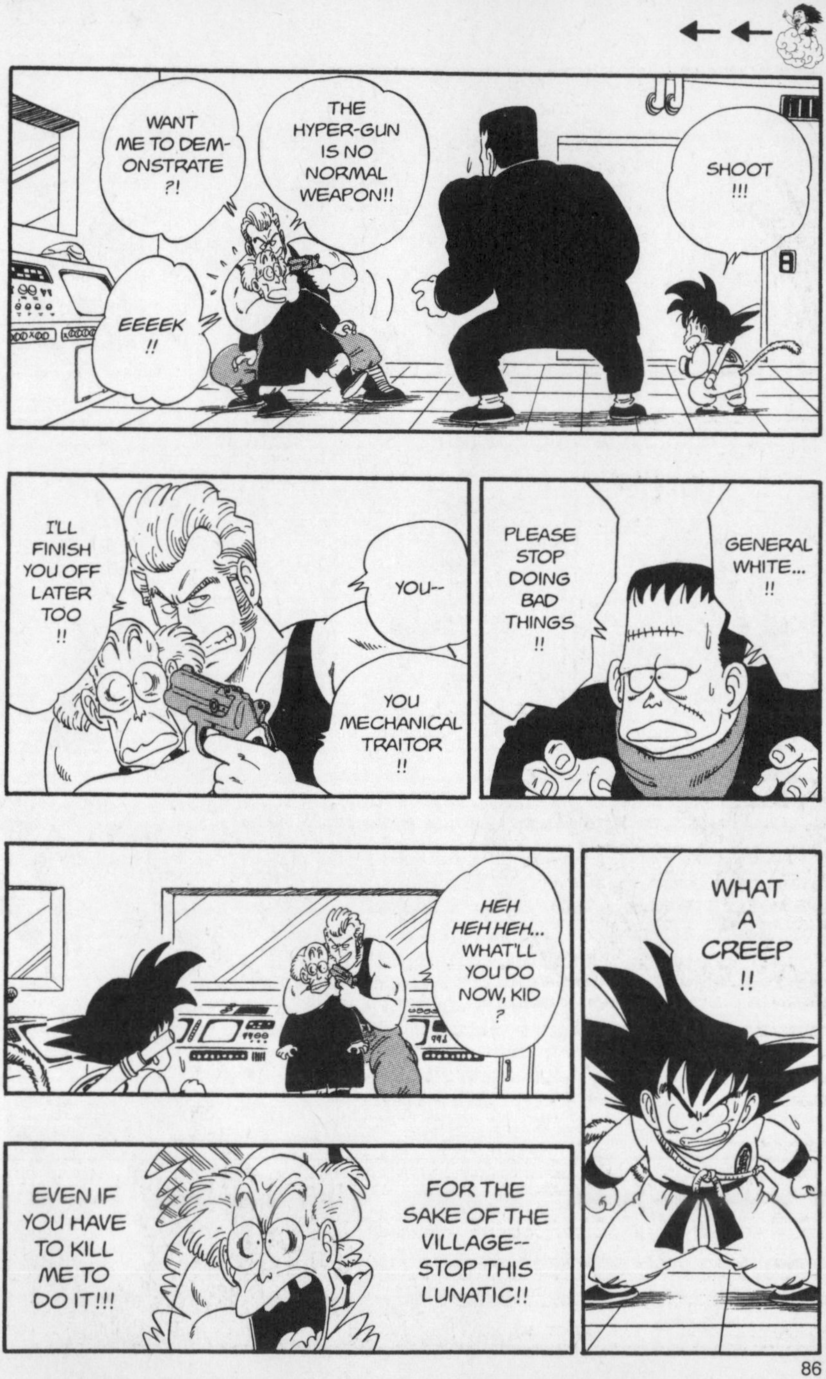
SHOOT !!!
THE HYPER-GUN IS NO NORMAL WEAPON!!
WANT ME TO DEMONSTRATE ?!
EEEEK !!
GENERAL WHITE... !!
PLEASE STOP DOING BAD THINGS !!
YOU--
YOU MECHANICAL TRAITOR !!
I'LL FINISH YOU OFF LATER TOO !!
WHAT A CREEP !!
HEH HEH HEH... WHAT'LL YOU DO NOW, KID ?
FOR THE SAKE OF THE VILLAGE-- STOP THIS LUNATIC!!
EVEN IF YOU HAVE TO KILL ME TO DO IT!!!

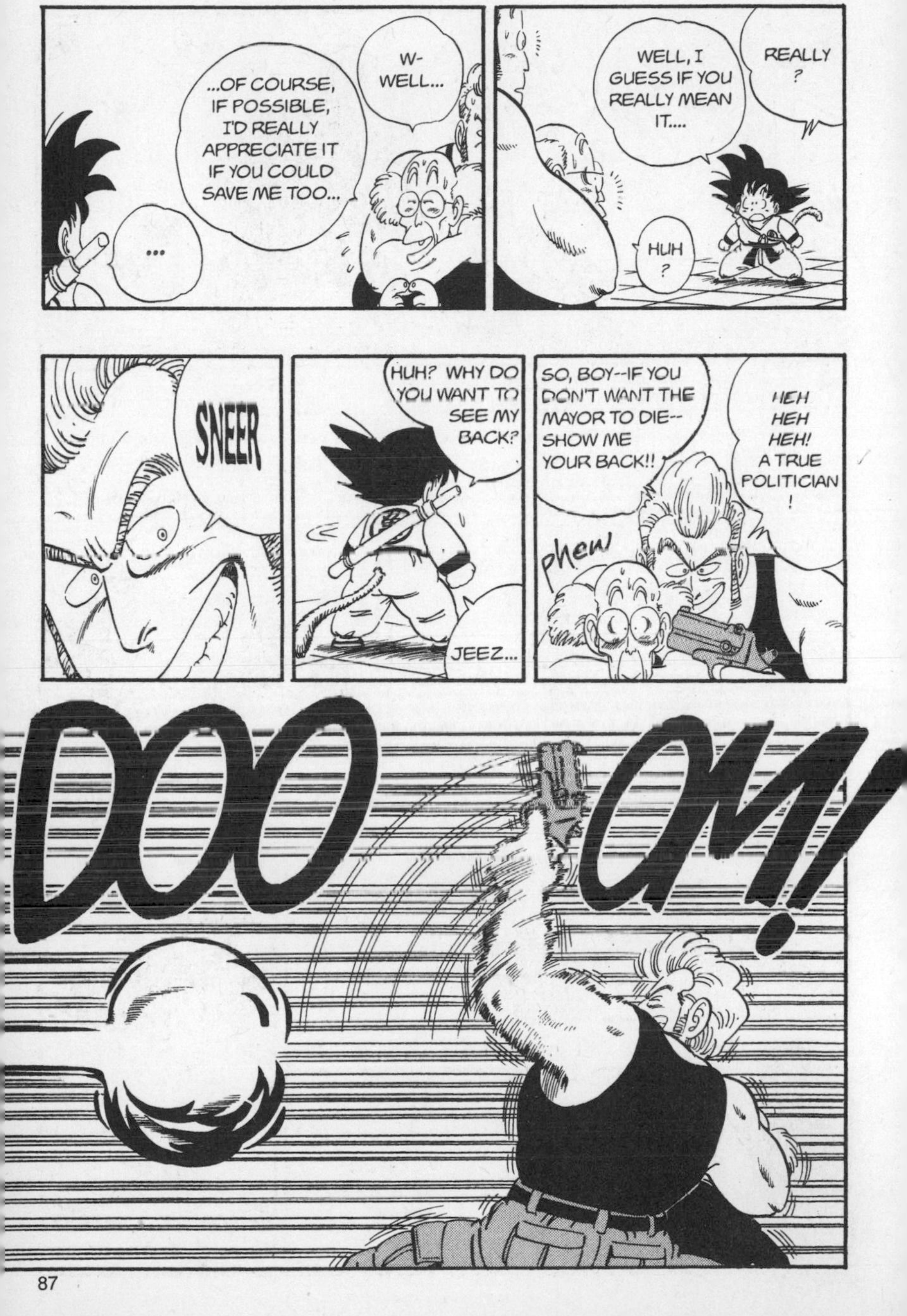
REALLY?
WELL, I GUESS IF YOU REALLY MEAN IT....
HUH?
W- WELL...
...OF COURSE, IF POSSIBLE, I'D REALLY APPRECIATE IT IF YOU COULD SAVE ME TOO...
...
HEH HEH HEH! A TRUE POLITICIAN!
SO, BOY--IF YOU DON'T WANT THE MAYOR TO DIE--SHOW ME YOUR BACK!!
phew
HUH? WHY DO YOU WANT TO SEE MY BACK?
JEEZ...
SNEER
DOO OM!!

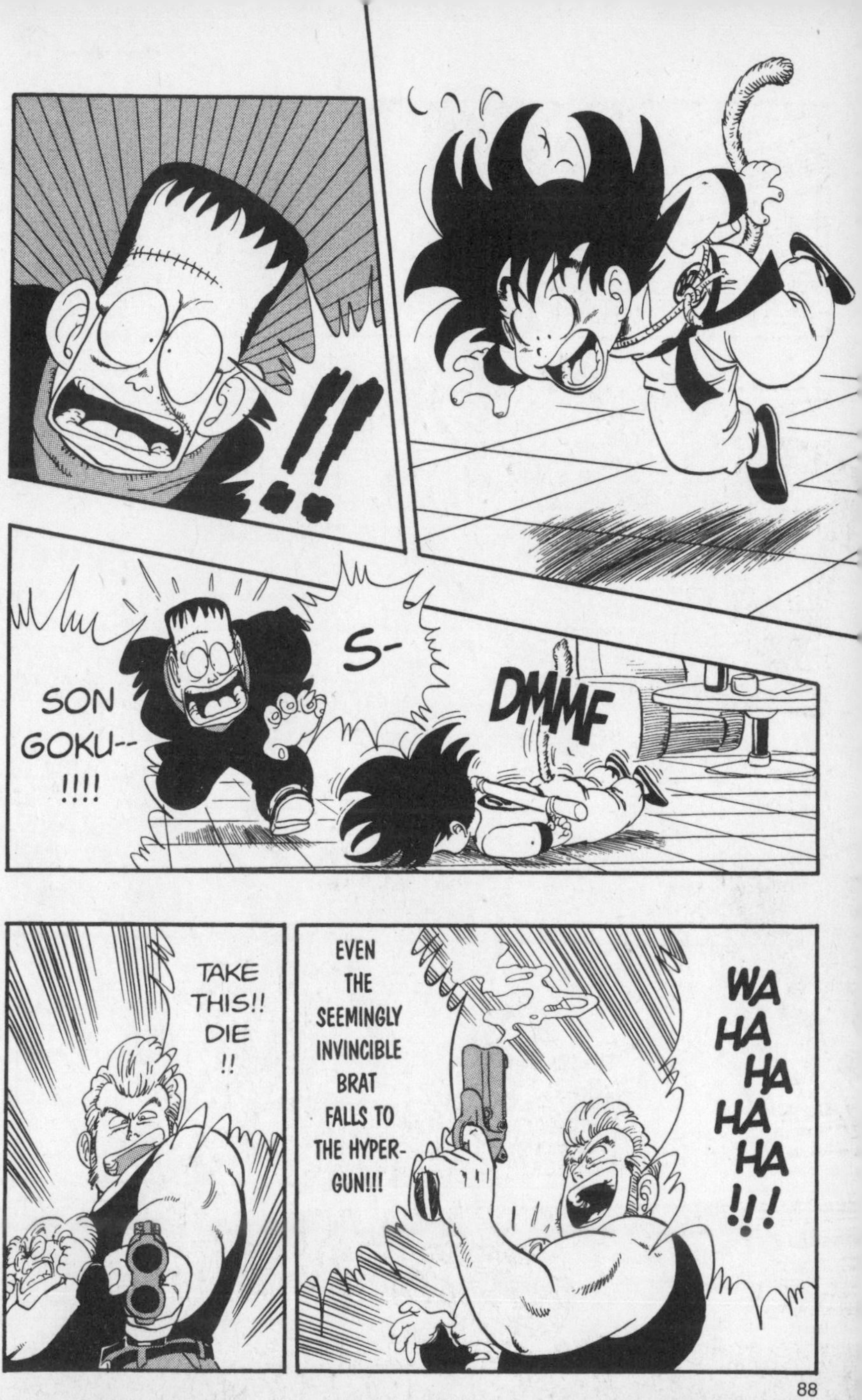
!!
DMMF
S-
SON GOKU--!!!!
WA HA HA HA HA!!!
EVEN THE SEEMINGLY INVINCIBLE BRAT FALLS TO THE HYPER-GUN!!!
TAKE THIS!! DIE!!

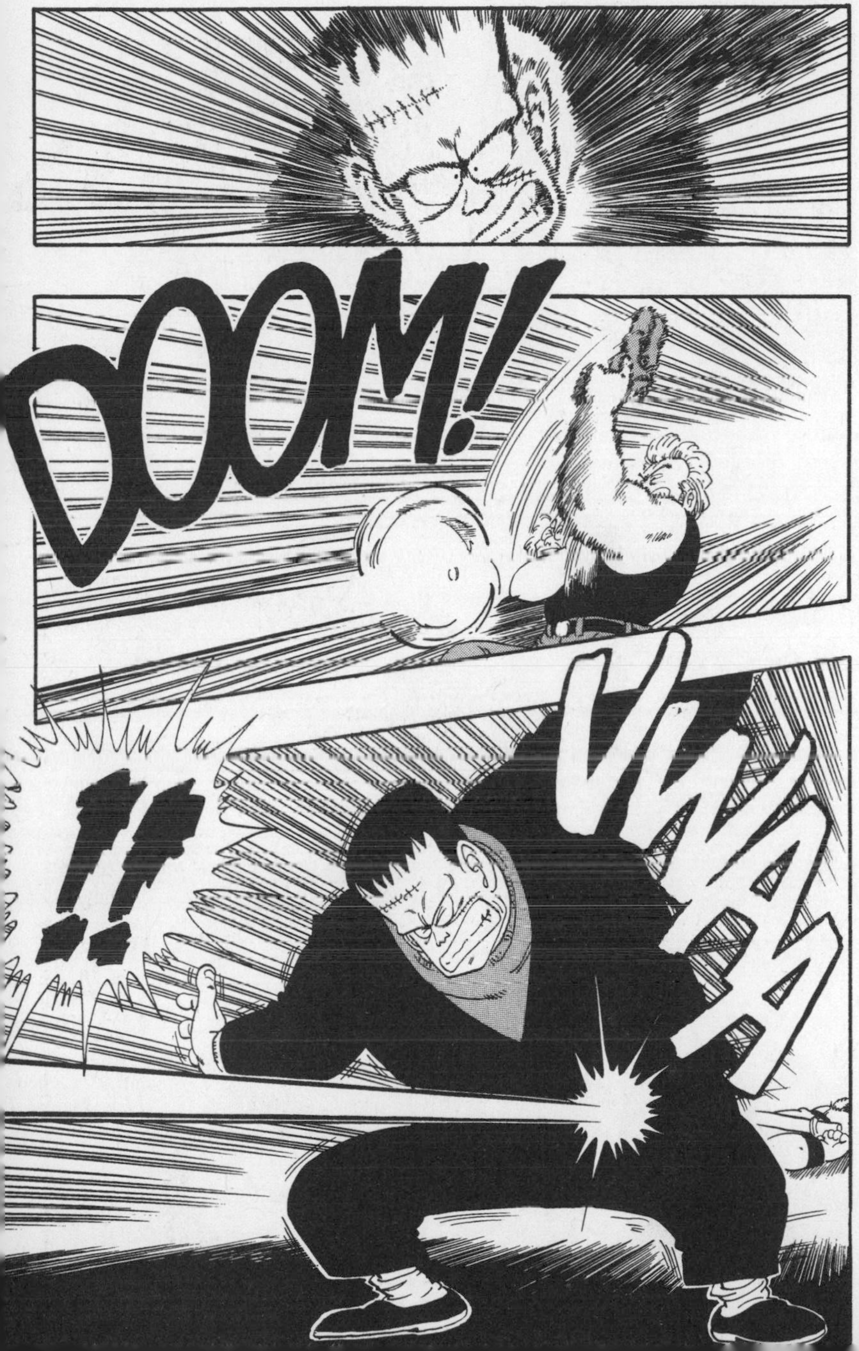
DOOM!
UWAA
!!

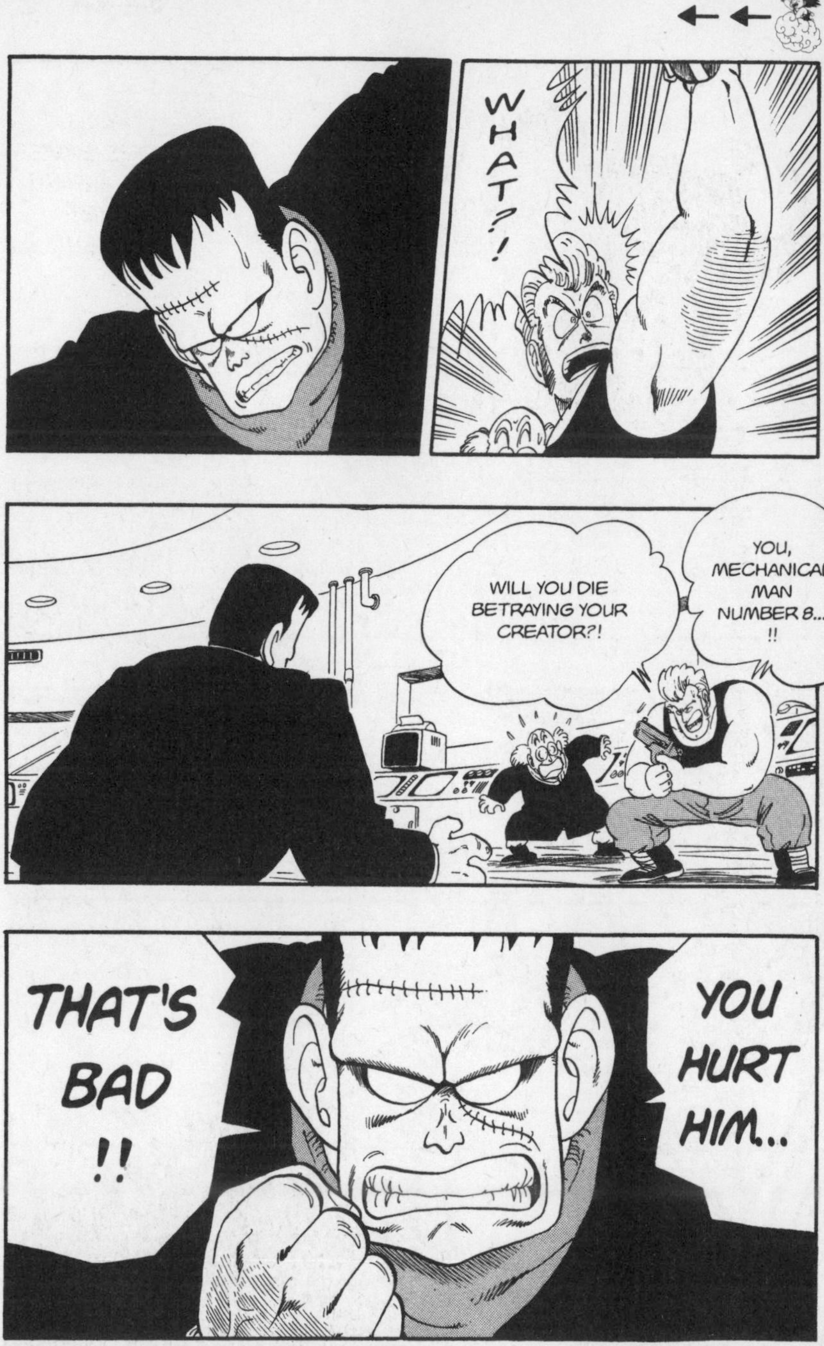
WHAT?!
YOU, MECHANICAL MAN NUMBER 8... !!
WILL YOU DIE BETRAYING YOUR CREATOR?!
YOU HURT HIM...
THAT'S BAD !!

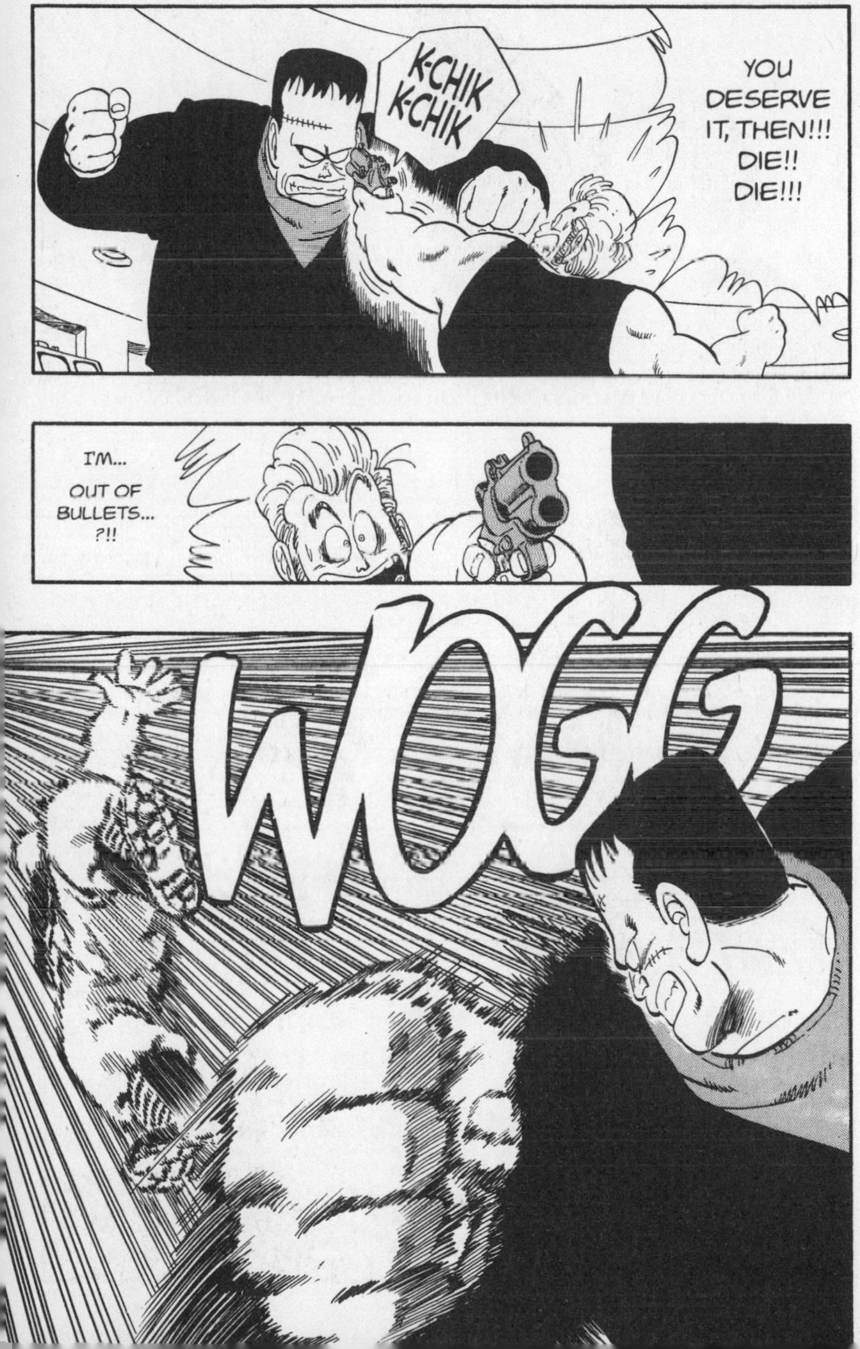
YOU DESERVE IT, THEN!!! DIE!! DIE!!!
K-CHIK K-CHIK
I'M...
OUT OF BULLETS... ?!!
WOGG

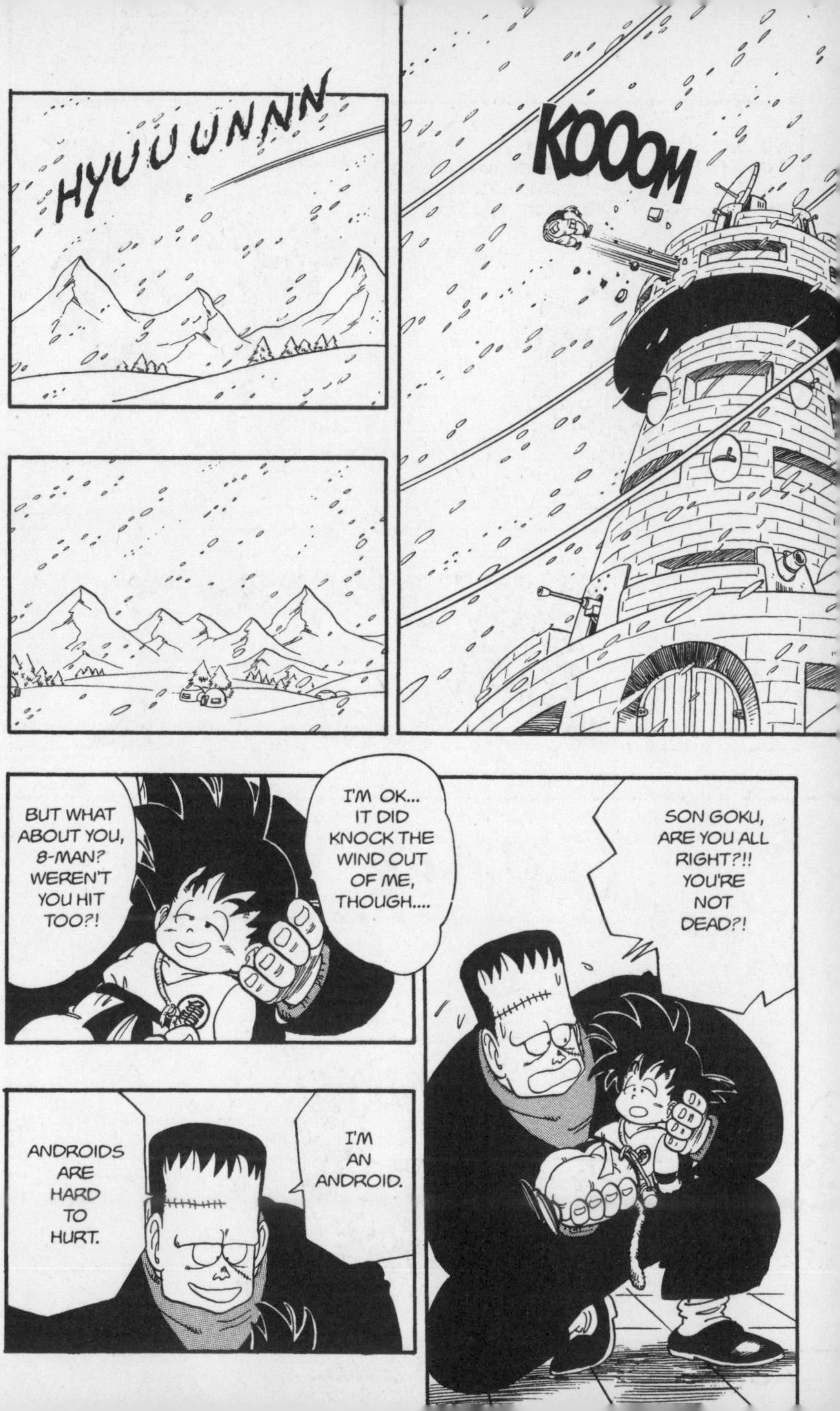
KOOOM
HYUUUNNN
SON GOKU, ARE YOU ALL RIGHT?!! YOU'RE NOT DEAD?!
I'M OK... IT DID KNOCK THE WIND OUT OF ME, THOUGH....
BUT WHAT ABOUT YOU, 8-MAN? WEREN'T YOU HIT TOO?!
I'M AN ANDROID.
ANDROIDS ARE HARD TO HURT.

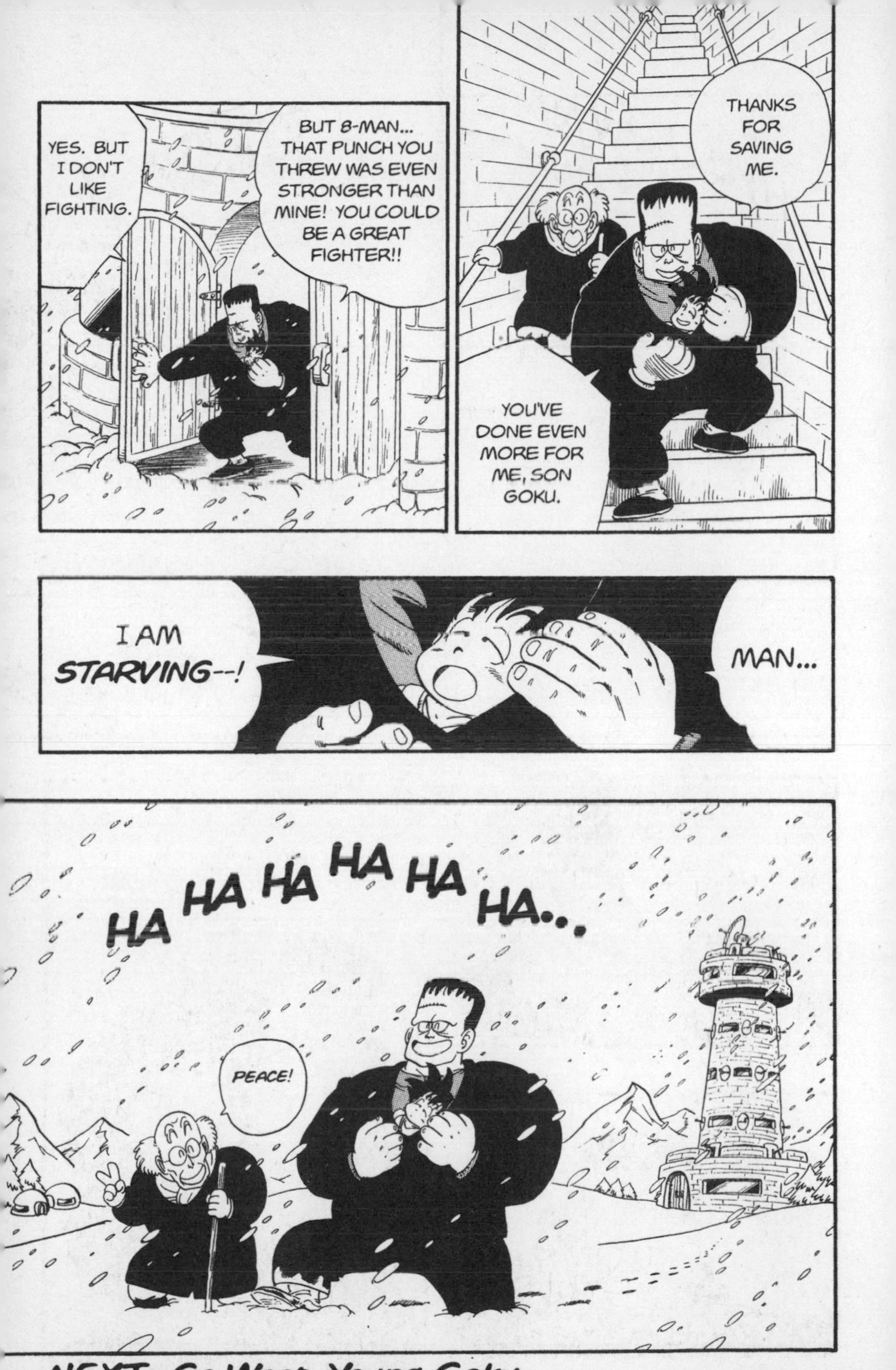
THANKS FOR SAVING ME.
YOU'VE DONE EVEN MORE FOR ME, SON GOKU.
BUT 8-MAN... THAT PUNCH YOU THREW WAS EVEN STRONGER THAN MINE! YOU COULD BE A GREAT FIGHTER!!
YES. BUT I DON'T LIKE FIGHTING.
MAN...
I AM STARVING--!
HA HA HA HA HA HA...
PEACE!

NEXT: Go West, Young Goku...

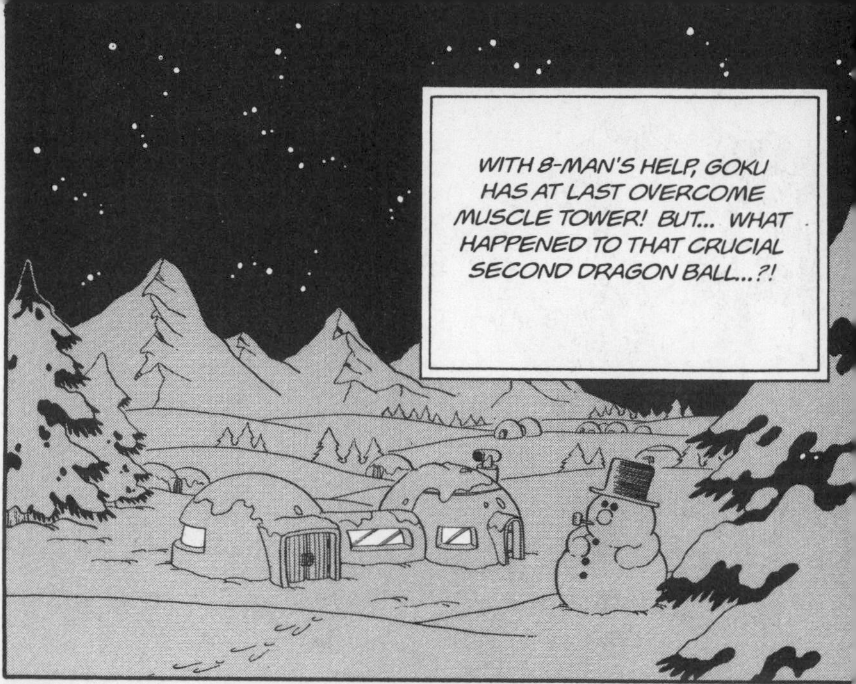
WITH 8-MAN'S HELP, GOKU HAS AT LAST OVERCOME MUSCLE TOWER! BUT... WHAT HAPPENED TO THAT CRUCIAL SECOND DRAGON BALL...?!

Tale 67 • Go West, Young Goku...

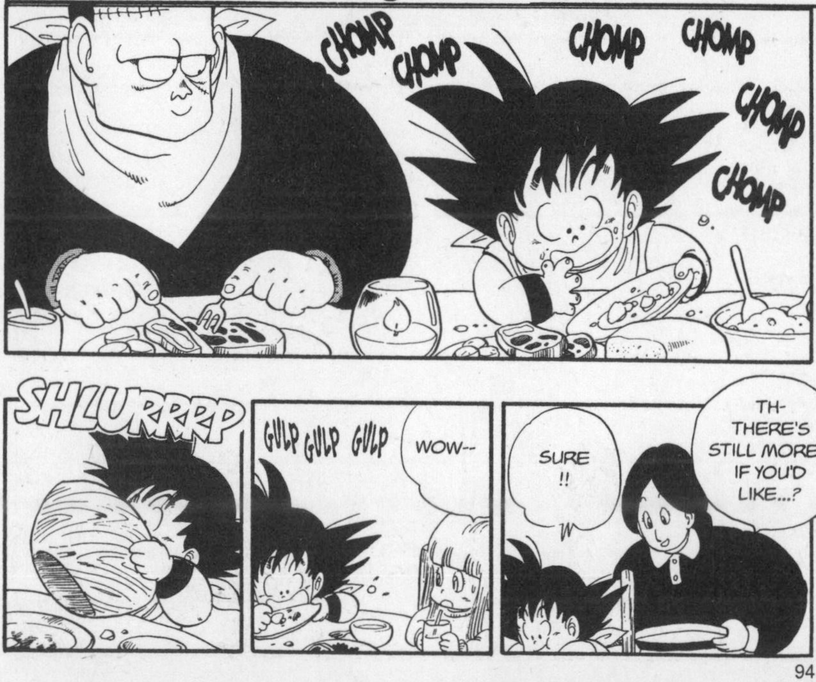
CHOMP
CHOMP
CHOMP
CHOMP
CHOMP
CHOMP
CHOMP
TH- THERE'S STILL MORE... IF YOU'D LIKE...?
SURE !!
WOW--
GULP GULP GULP
SHLURRRP

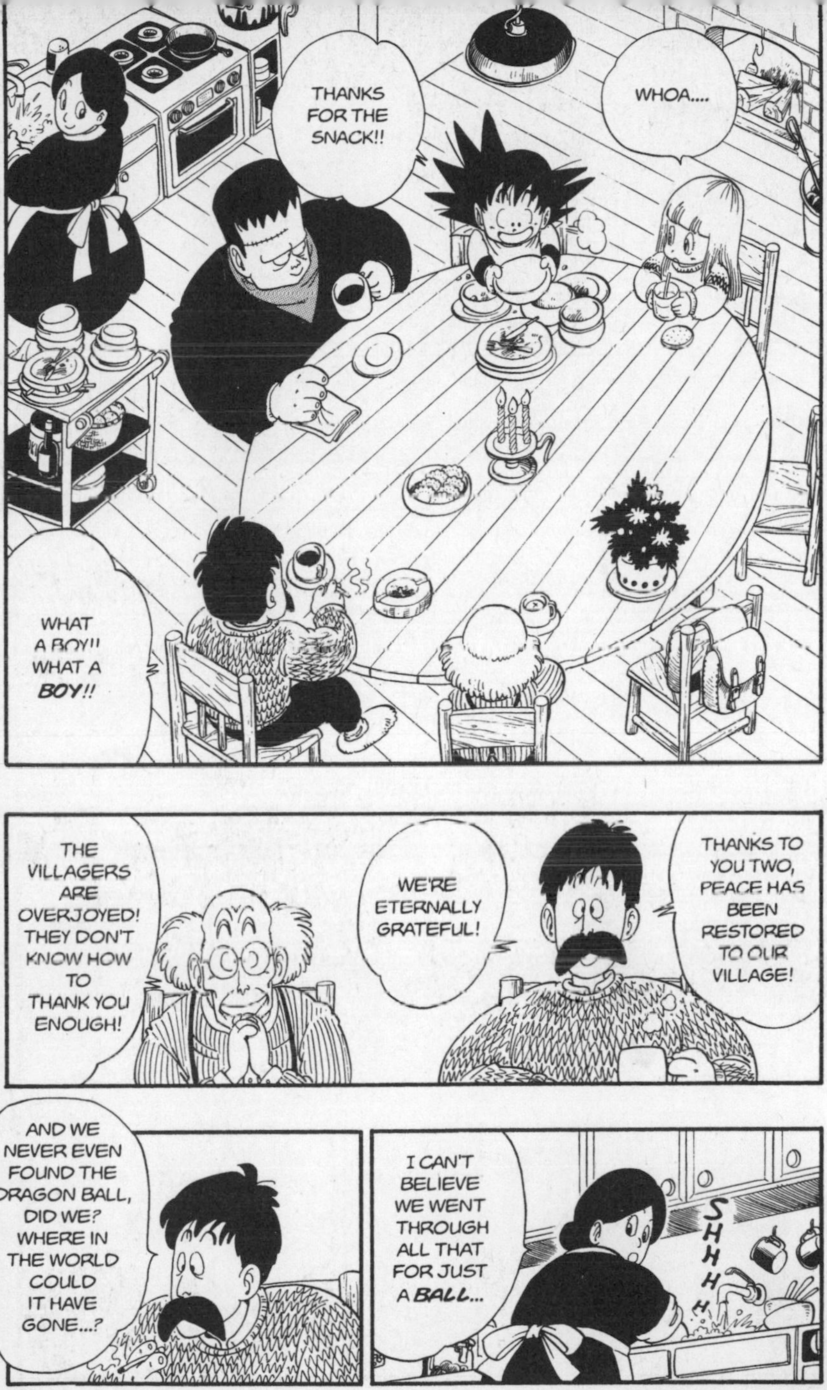
WHOA....
THANKS FOR THE SNACK!!
WHAT A BOY!! WHAT A BOY!!
THANKS TO YOU TWO, PEACE HAS BEEN RESTORED TO OUR VILLAGE!
WE'RE ETERNALLY GRATEFUL!
THE VILLAGERS ARE OVERJOYED! THEY DON'T KNOW HOW TO THANK YOU ENOUGH!
I CAN'T BELIEVE WE WENT THROUGH ALL THAT FOR JUST A BALL...
SHHHH
AND WE NEVER EVEN FOUND THE DRAGON BALL, DID WE? WHERE IN THE WORLD COULD IT HAVE GONE...?

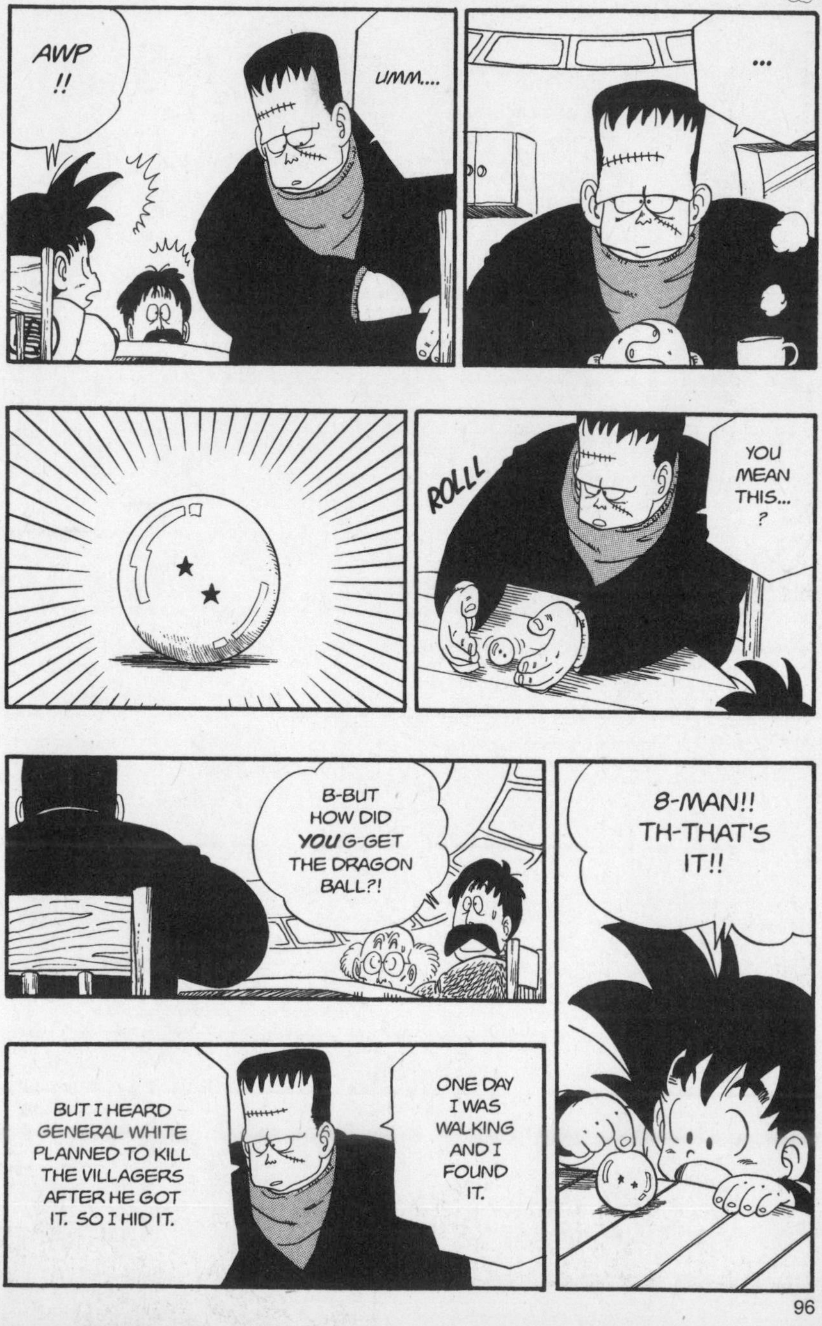
...
UMM....
AWP !!
YOU MEAN THIS... ?
ROLLL
8-MAN!! TH-THAT'S IT!!
B-BUT HOW DID YOU G-GET THE DRAGON BALL?!
ONE DAY I WAS WALKING AND I FOUND IT.
BUT I HEARD GENERAL WHITE PLANNED TO KILL THE VILLAGERS AFTER HE GOT IT. SO I HID IT.

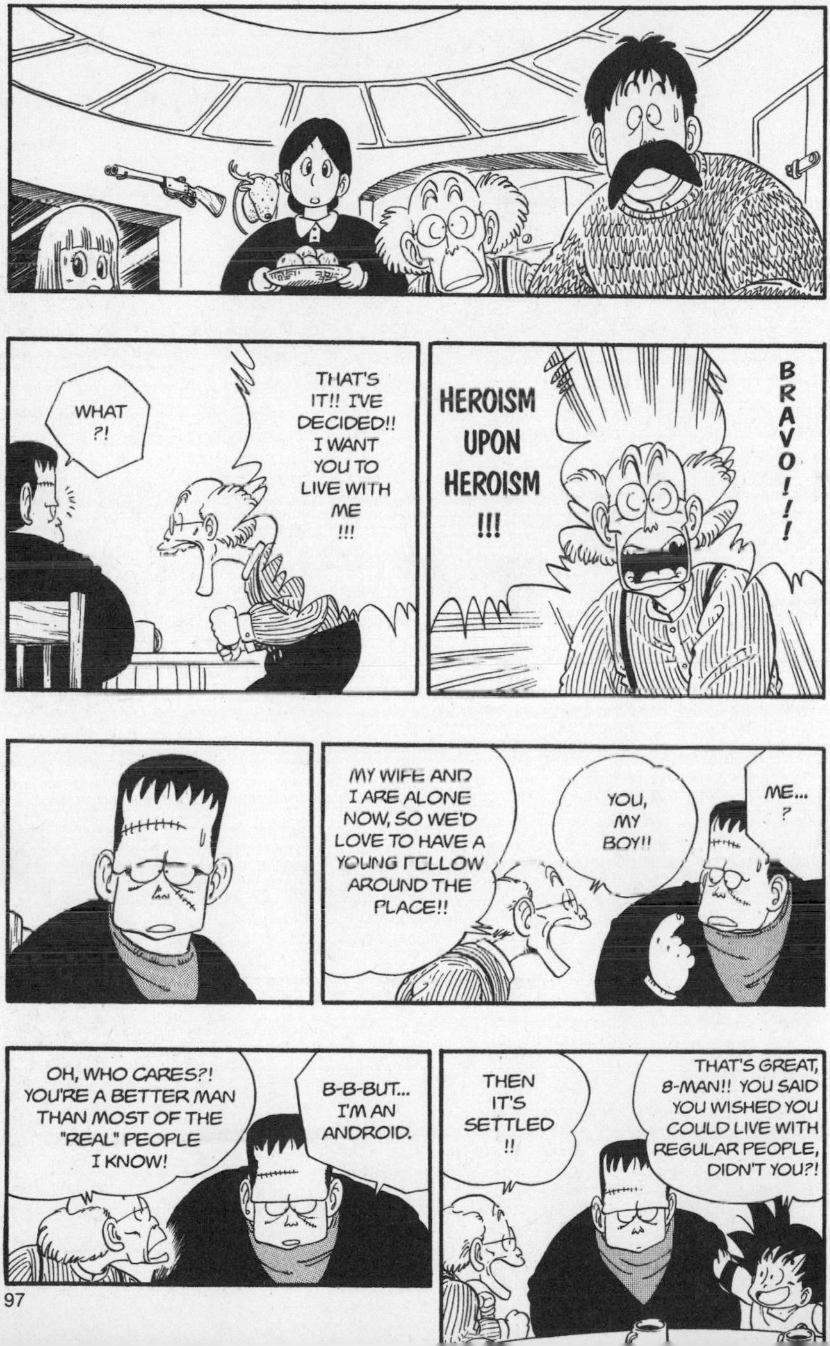
BRAVO!!!
HEROISM UPON HEROISM !!!
THAT'S IT!! I'VE DECIDED!! I WANT YOU TO LIVE WITH ME !!!
WHAT ?!
ME... ?
YOU, MY BOY!!
MY WIFE AND I ARE ALONE NOW, SO WE'D LOVE TO HAVE A YOUNG FELLOW AROUND THE PLACE!!
THAT'S GREAT, 8-MAN!! YOU SAID YOU WISHED YOU COULD LIVE WITH REGULAR PEOPLE, DIDN'T YOU?!
THEN IT'S SETTLED !!
B-B-BUT... I'M AN ANDROID.
OH, WHO CARES?! YOU'RE A BETTER MAN THAN MOST OF THE "REAL" PEOPLE I KNOW!

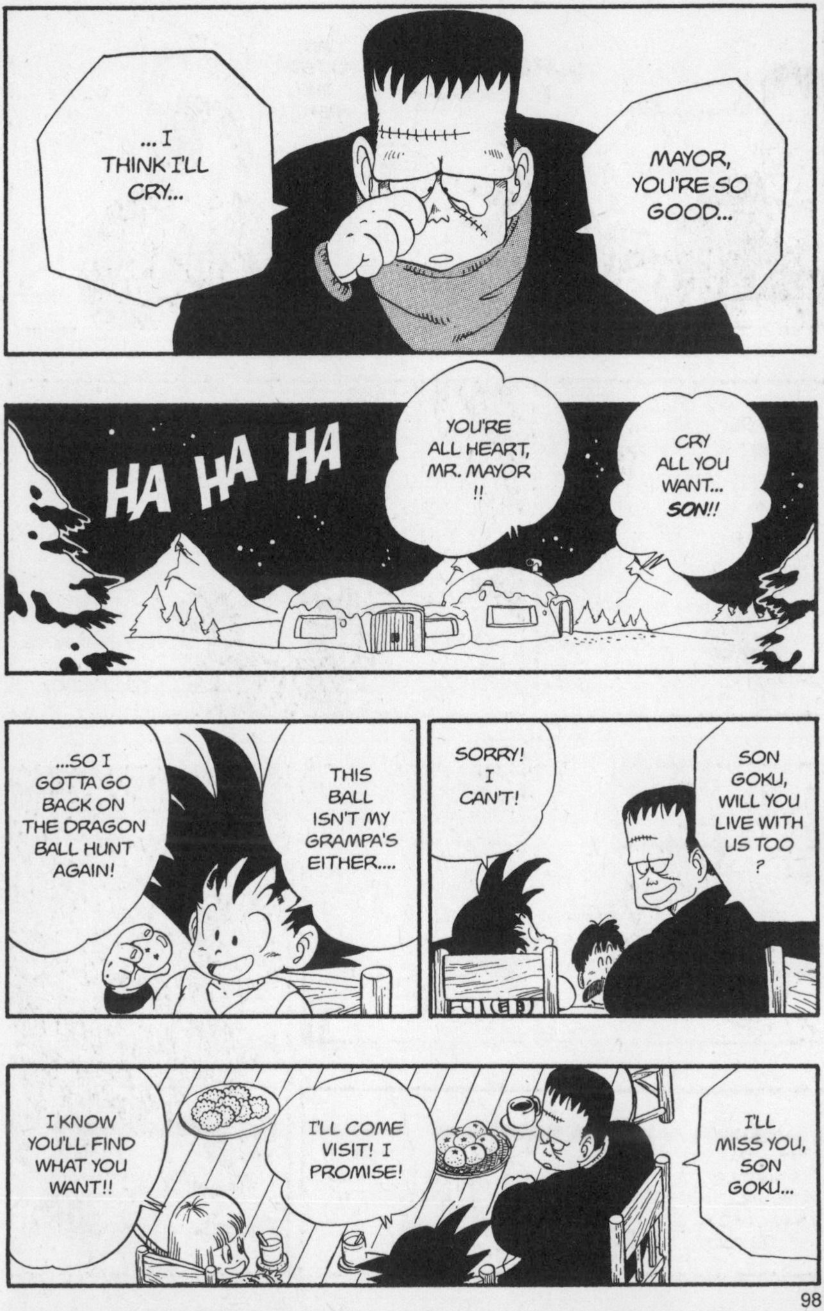
MAYOR, YOU'RE SO GOOD...
...I THINK I'LL CRY...
CRY ALL YOU WANT... *SON!!*
YOU'RE ALL HEART, MR. MAYOR !!
HA HA HA
SON GOKU, WILL YOU LIVE WITH US TOO ?
SORRY! I CAN'T!
THIS BALL ISN'T MY GRAMPA'S EITHER....
...SO I GOTTA GO BACK ON THE DRAGON BALL HUNT AGAIN!
I'LL MISS YOU, SON GOKU...
I'LL COME VISIT! I PROMISE!
I KNOW YOU'LL FIND WHAT YOU WANT!!

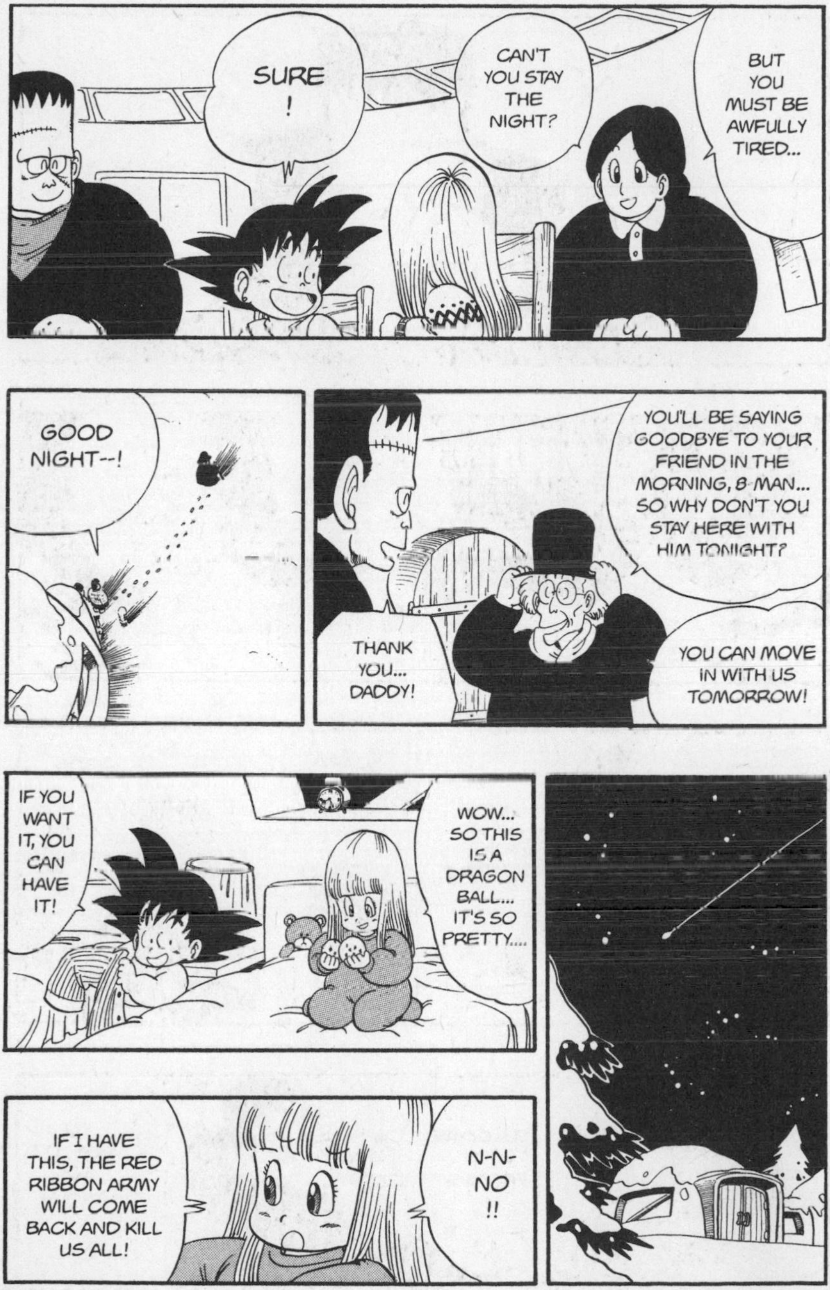
BUT YOU MUST BE AWFULLY TIRED...
CAN'T YOU STAY THE NIGHT?
SURE !
YOU'LL BE SAYING GOODBYE TO YOUR FRIEND IN THE MORNING, 8-MAN... SO WHY DON'T YOU STAY HERE WITH HIM TONIGHT?
YOU CAN MOVE IN WITH US TOMORROW!
THANK YOU... DADDY!
GOOD NIGHT--!
WOW... SO THIS IS A DRAGON BALL... IT'S SO PRETTY....
IF YOU WANT IT, YOU CAN HAVE IT!
N-N-NO !!
IF I HAVE THIS, THE RED RIBBON ARMY WILL COME BACK AND KILL US ALL!

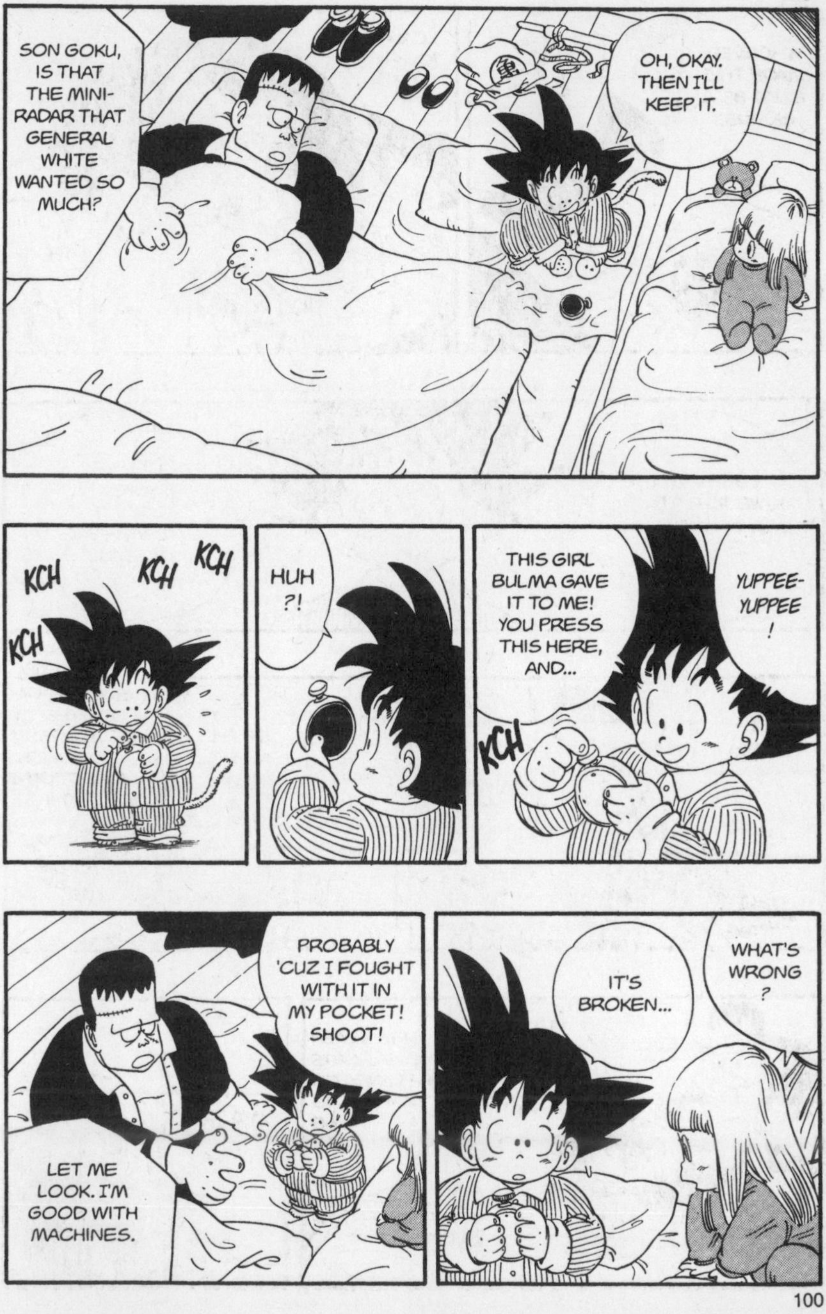
OH, OKAY. THEN I'LL KEEP IT.
SON GOKU, IS THAT THE MINI-RADAR THAT GENERAL WHITE WANTED SO MUCH?
YUPPEE-YUPPEE!
THIS GIRL BULMA GAVE IT TO ME! YOU PRESS THIS HERE, AND...
KCH
HUH ?!
KCH KCH KCH KCH
WHAT'S WRONG ?
IT'S BROKEN...
PROBABLY 'CUZ I FOUGHT WITH IT IN MY POCKET! SHOOT!
LET ME LOOK. I'M GOOD WITH MACHINES.

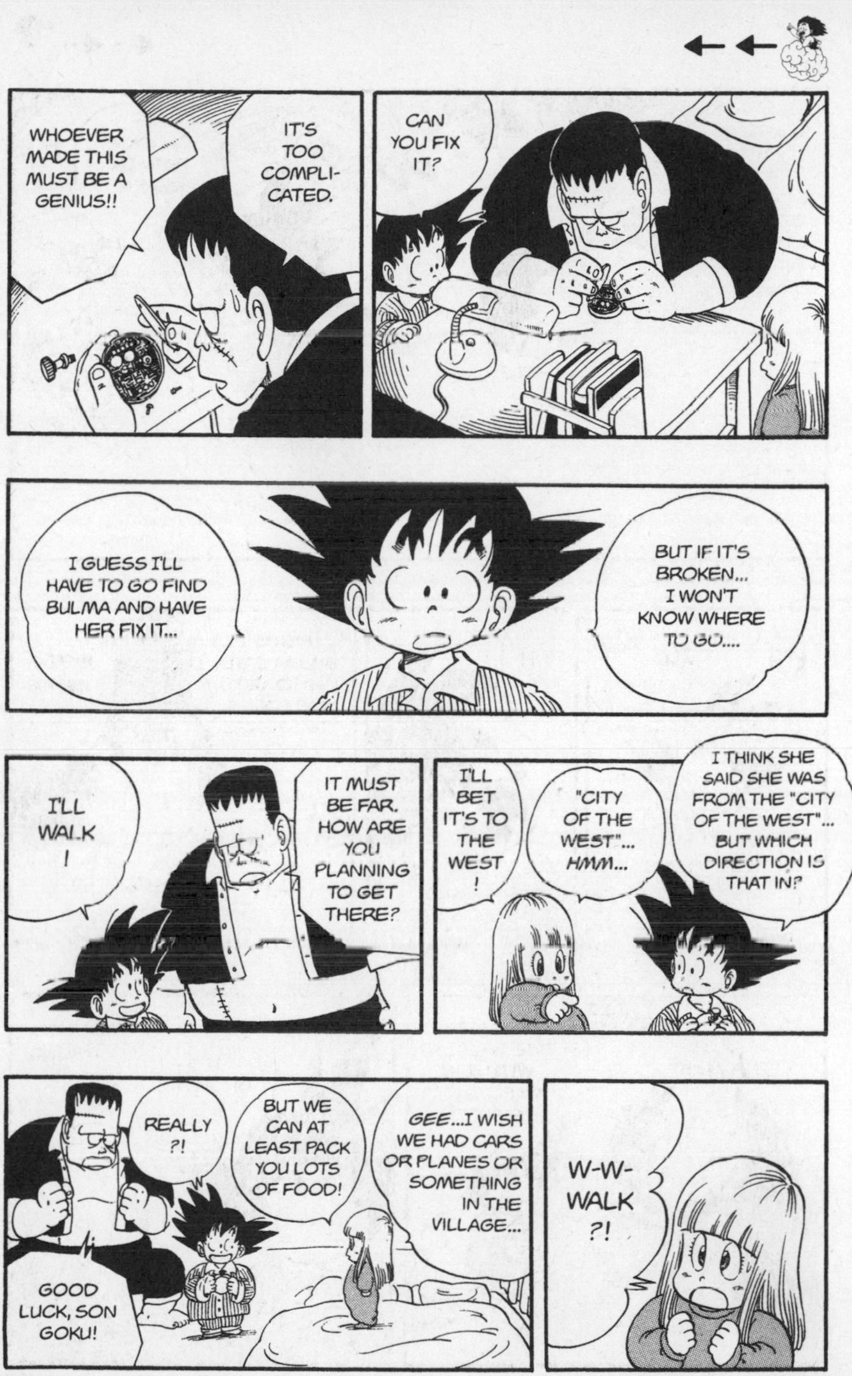
CAN YOU FIX IT?
IT'S TOO COMPLICATED.
WHOEVER MADE THIS MUST BE A GENIUS!!
BUT IF IT'S BROKEN... I WON'T KNOW WHERE TO GO....
I GUESS I'LL HAVE TO GO FIND BULMA AND HAVE HER FIX IT...
I THINK SHE SAID SHE WAS FROM THE "CITY OF THE WEST"... BUT WHICH DIRECTION IS THAT IN?
"CITY OF THE WEST"... *HMM...*
I'LL BET IT'S TO THE WEST!
IT MUST BE FAR. HOW ARE YOU PLANNING TO GET THERE?
I'LL WALK!
W-W-WALK?!
GEE...I WISH WE HAD CARS OR PLANES OR SOMETHING IN THE VILLAGE...
BUT WE CAN AT LEAST PACK YOU LOTS OF FOOD!
REALLY?!
GOOD LUCK, SON GOKU!

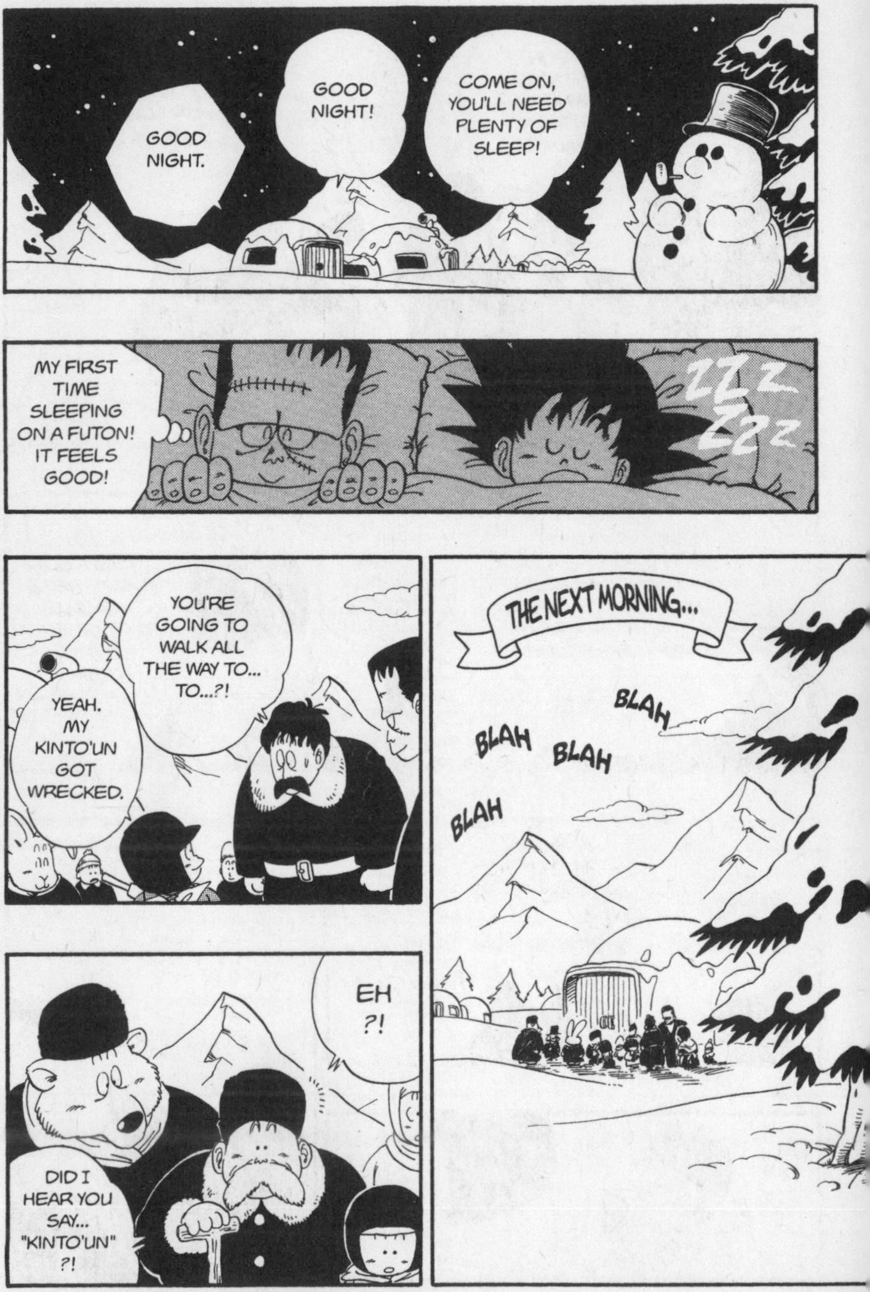
COME ON, YOU'LL NEED PLENTY OF SLEEP!
GOOD NIGHT!
GOOD NIGHT.
ZZZ ZZZ
MY FIRST TIME SLEEPING ON A FUTON! IT FEELS GOOD!
THE NEXT MORNING...
BLAH
BLAH
BLAH
BLAH
YOU'RE GOING TO WALK ALL THE WAY TO... TO...?!
YEAH. MY KINTO'UN GOT WRECKED.
EH ?!
DID I HEAR YOU SAY... "KINTO'UN" ?!

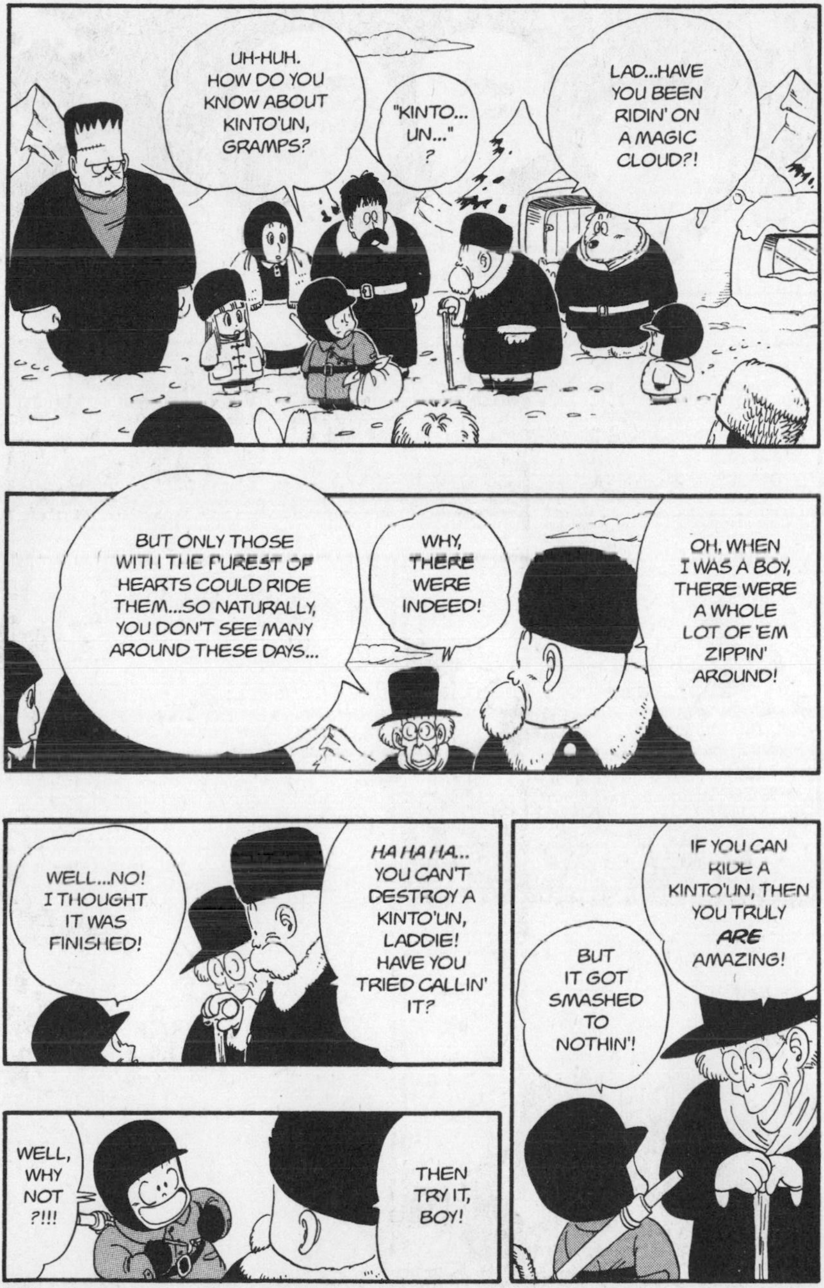
LAD...HAVE YOU BEEN RIDIN' ON A MAGIC CLOUD?!
"KINTO... UN..." ?
UH-HUH. HOW DO YOU KNOW ABOUT KINTO'UN, GRAMPS?
OH, WHEN I WAS A BOY, THERE WERE A WHOLE LOT OF 'EM ZIPPIN' AROUND!
WHY, THERE WERE INDEED!
BUT ONLY THOSE WITH THE PUREST OF HEARTS COULD RIDE THEM...SO NATURALLY, YOU DON'T SEE MANY AROUND THESE DAYS...
IF YOU CAN RIDE A KINTO'UN, THEN YOU TRULY *ARE* AMAZING!
BUT IT GOT SMASHED TO NOTHIN'!
HA HA HA... YOU CAN'T DESTROY A KINTO'UN, LADDIE! HAVE YOU TRIED CALLIN' IT?
WELL...NO! I THOUGHT IT WAS FINISHED!
THEN TRY IT, BOY!
WELL, WHY NOT ?!!!

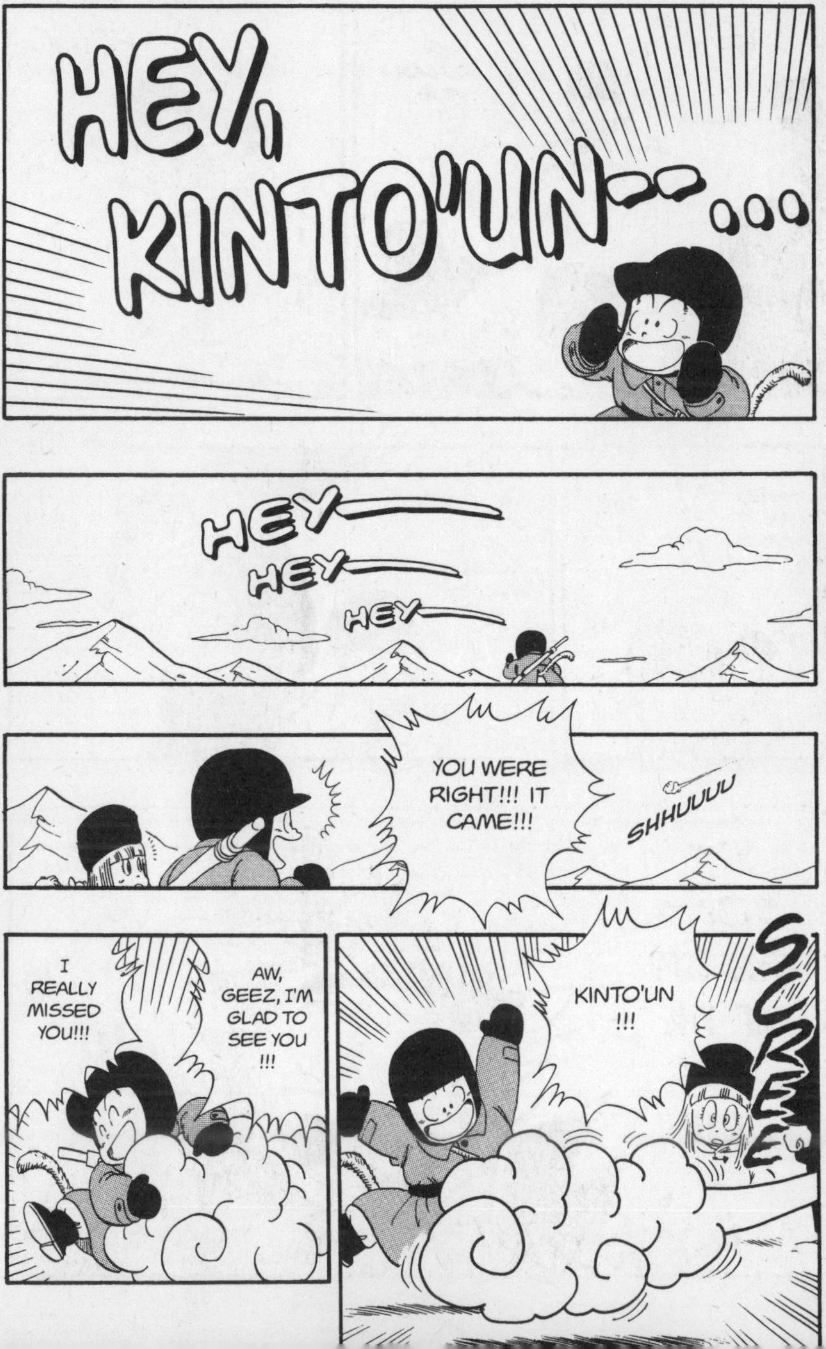
HEY, KINTO'UN--...
HEY— HEY— HEY—
SHHUUUU
YOU WERE RIGHT!!! IT CAME!!!
SCREE
KINTO'UN!!!
AW, GEEZ, I'M GLAD TO SEE YOU!!!
I REALLY MISSED YOU!!!

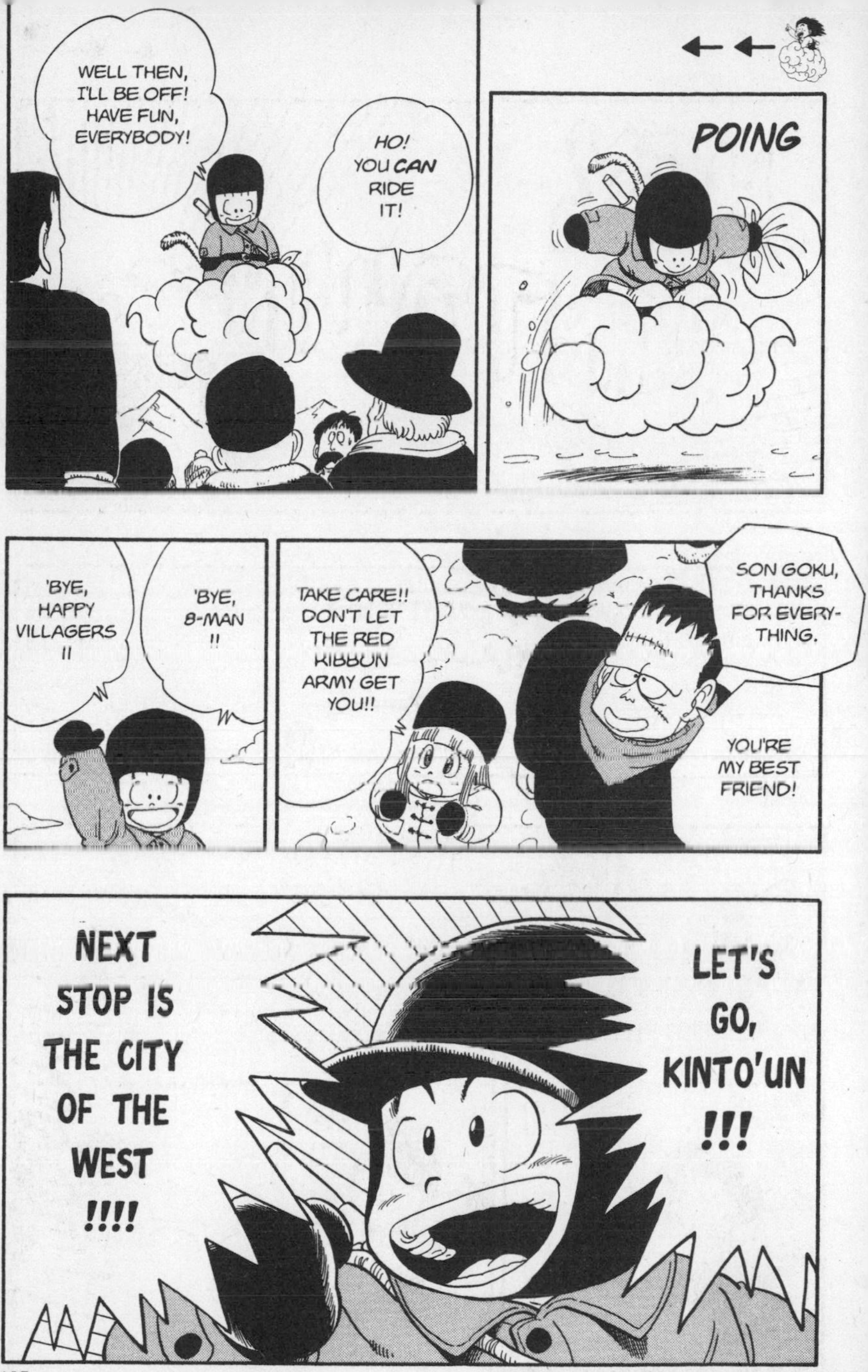
POING
HO! YOU CAN RIDE IT!
WELL THEN, I'LL BE OFF! HAVE FUN, EVERYBODY!
SON GOKU, THANKS FOR EVERY-THING.
YOU'RE MY BEST FRIEND!
TAKE CARE!! DON'T LET THE RED RIBBON ARMY GET YOU!!
'BYE, 8-MAN !!
'BYE, HAPPY VILLAGERS !!
LET'S GO, KINTO'UN !!!
NEXT STOP IS THE CITY OF THE WEST !!!!

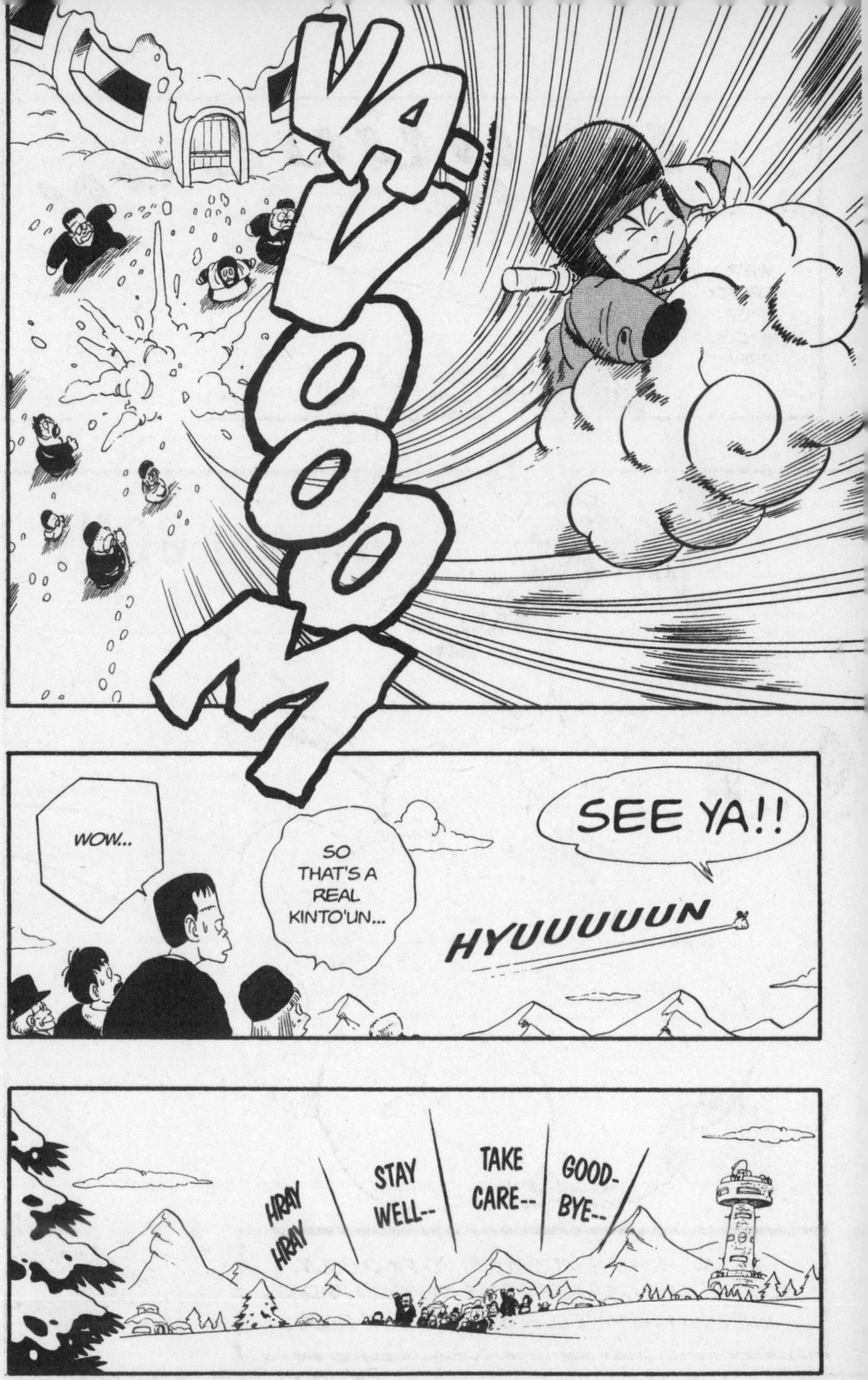
SEE YA!!
HYUUUUUN
SO THAT'S A REAL KINTO'UN...
WOW...
GOOD-BYE--
TAKE CARE--
STAY WELL--
HRAY HRAY

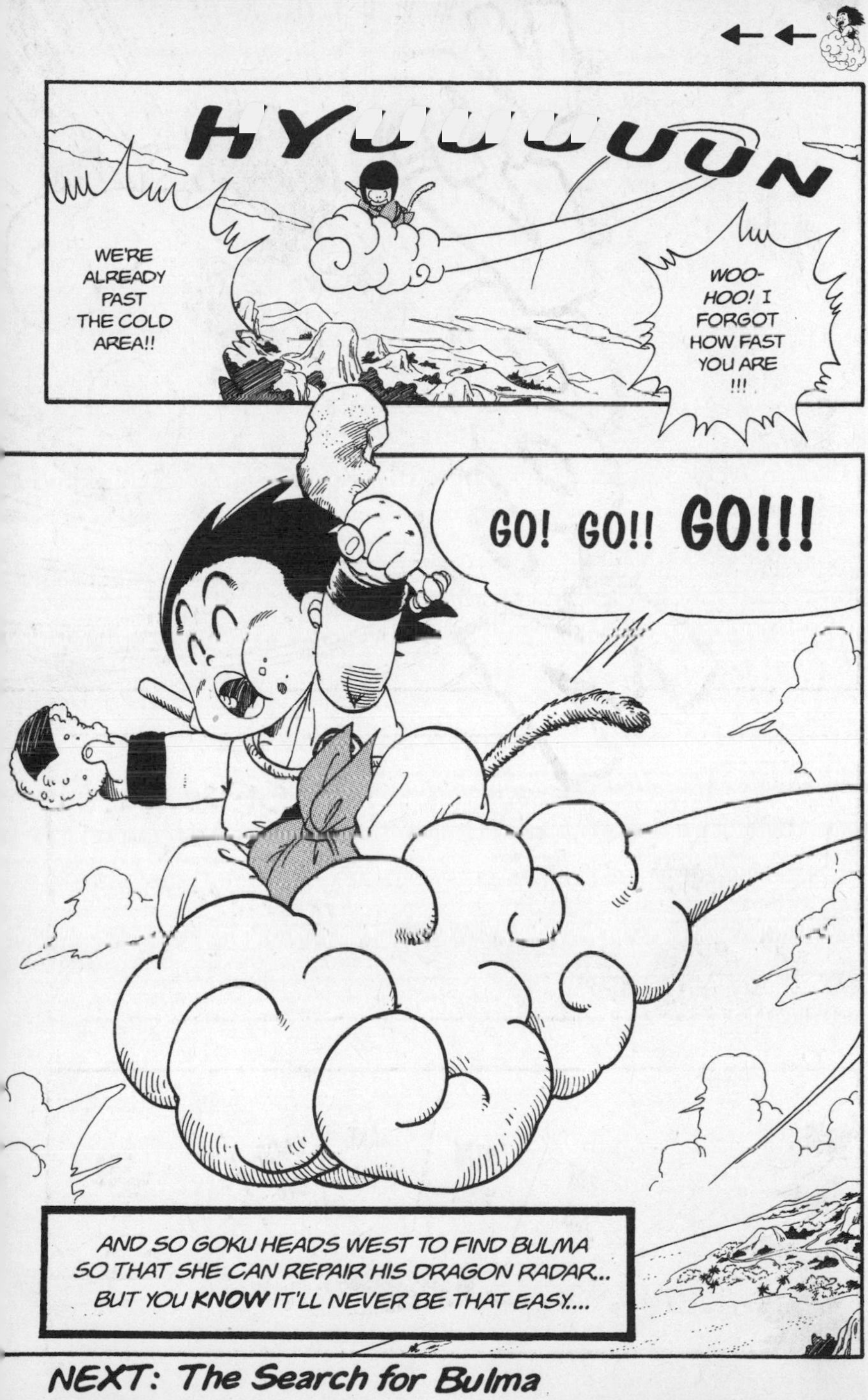
HYUUUUUUN
WOO-HOO! I FORGOT HOW FAST YOU ARE !!!
WE'RE ALREADY PAST THE COLD AREA!!
GO! GO!! GO!!!
AND SO GOKU HEADS WEST TO FIND BULMA SO THAT SHE CAN REPAIR HIS DRAGON RADAR... BUT YOU KNOW IT'LL NEVER BE THAT EASY....

NEXT: The Search for Bulma

Tale 68 • Monkey in the City

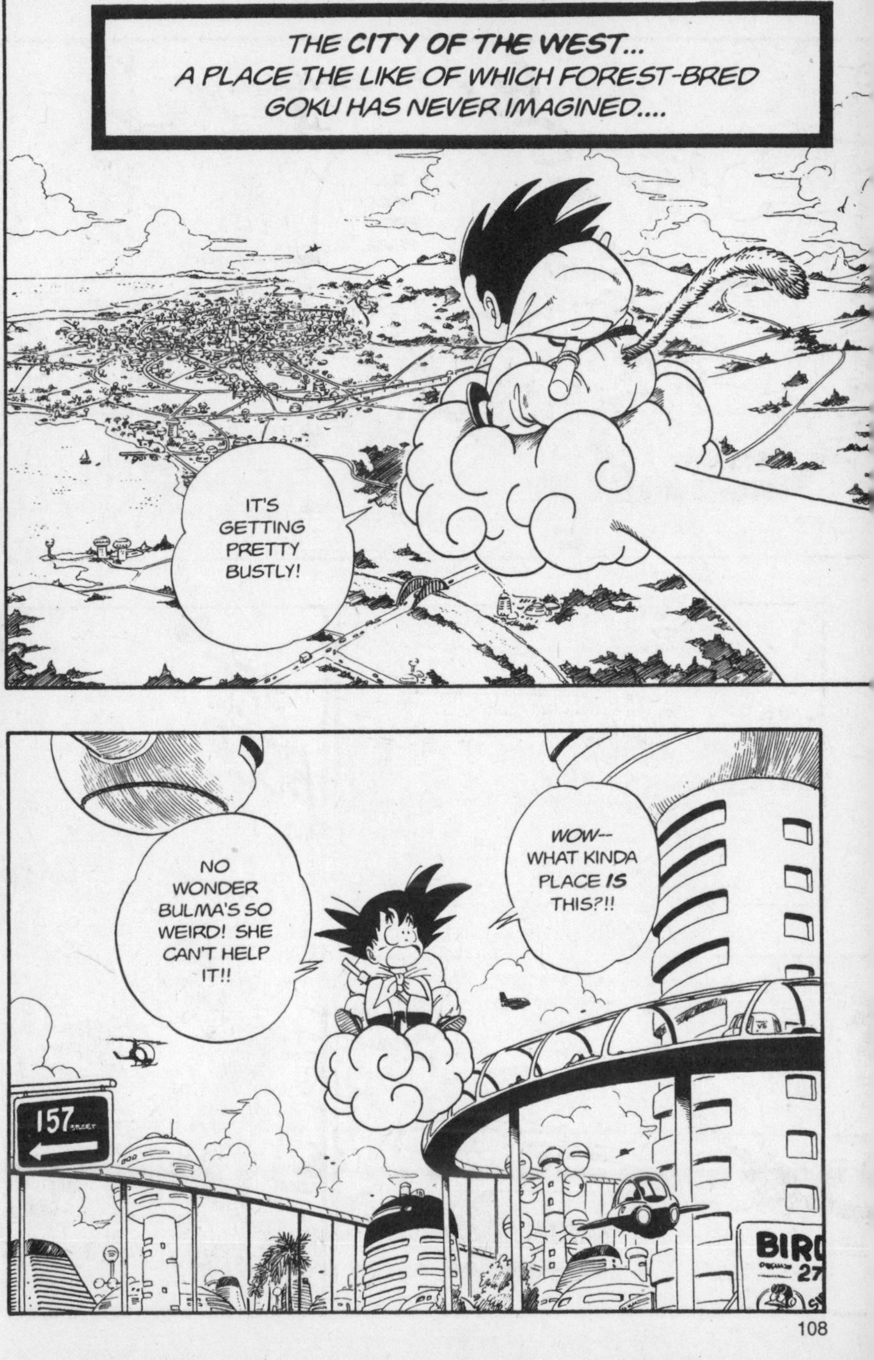
THE CITY OF THE WEST... A PLACE THE LIKE OF WHICH FOREST-BRED GOKU HAS NEVER IMAGINED....
IT'S GETTING PRETTY BUSTLY!
WOW-- WHAT KINDA PLACE *IS* THIS?!!
NO WONDER BULMA'S SO WEIRD! SHE CAN'T HELP IT!!
157

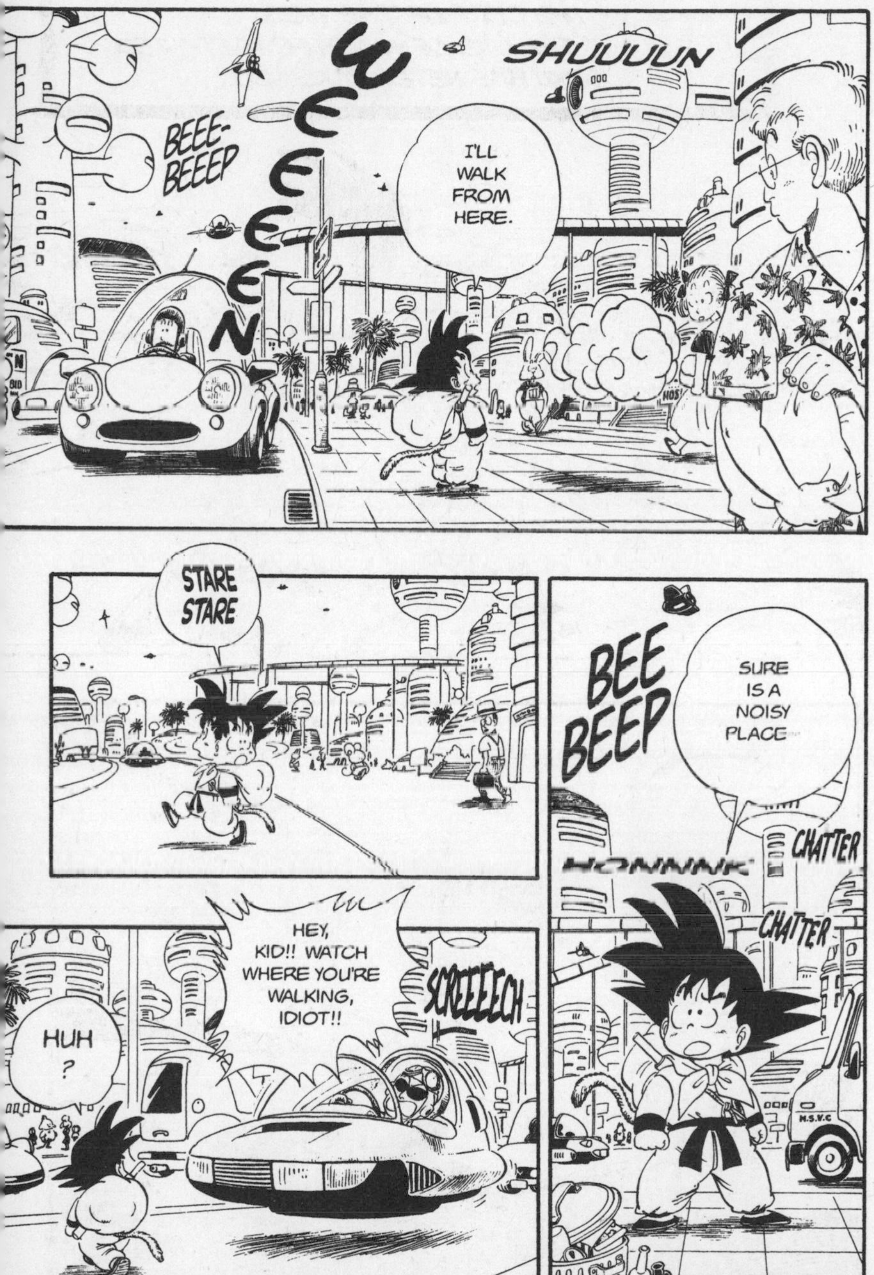
SHUUUUN
WEEEEEN
I'LL WALK FROM HERE.
BEEE-BEEEP
SURE IS A NOISY PLACE
BEE BEEP
CHATTER
CHATTER
STARE STARE
SCREEEECH
HEY, KID!! WATCH WHERE YOU'RE WALKING, IDIOT!!
HUH ?

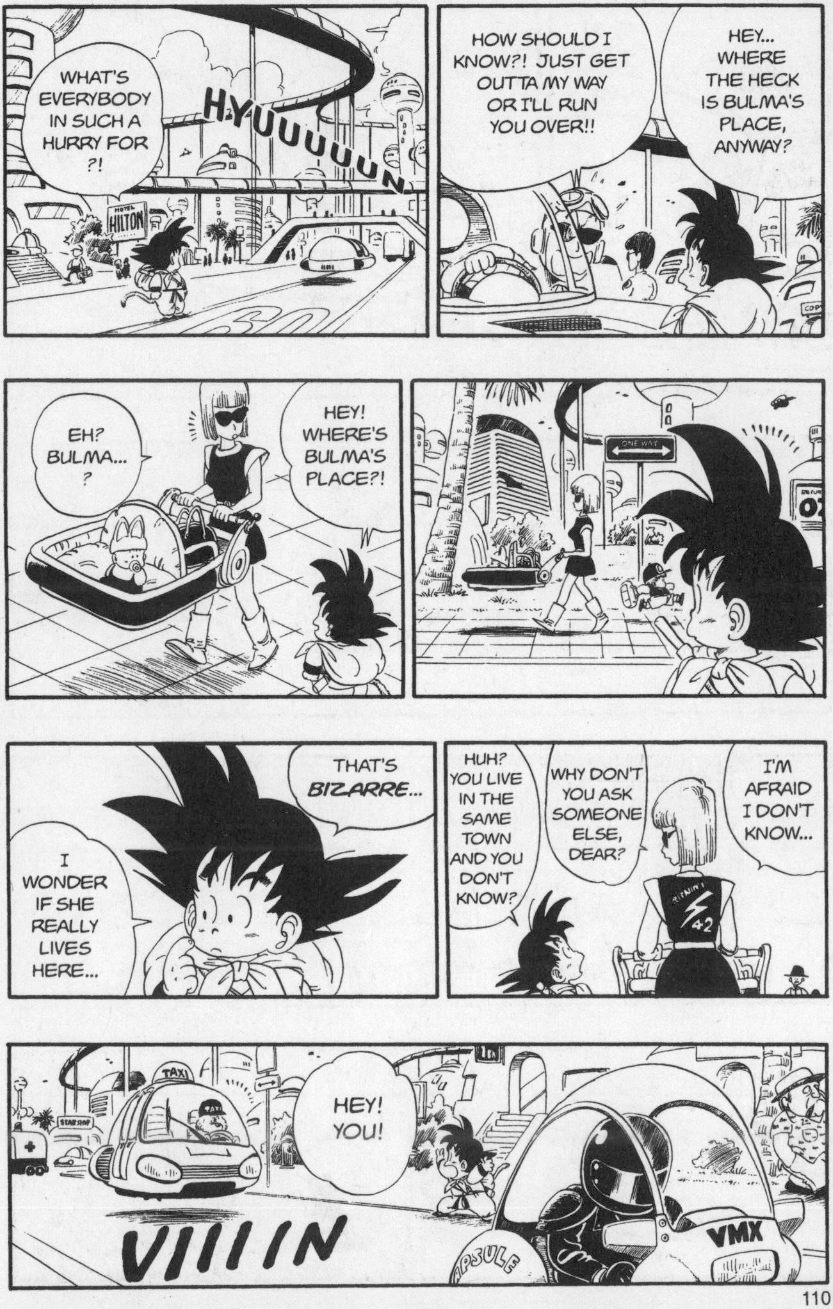
HEY... WHERE THE HECK IS BULMA'S PLACE, ANYWAY?
HOW SHOULD I KNOW?! JUST GET OUTTA MY WAY OR I'LL RUN YOU OVER!!
WHAT'S EVERYBODY IN SUCH A HURRY FOR ?!
HYUUUUUUN
HOTEL HILTON
ONE WAY
HEY! WHERE'S BULMA'S PLACE?!
EH? BULMA... ?
I'M AFRAID I DON'T KNOW...
WHY DON'T YOU ASK SOMEONE ELSE, DEAR?
HUH? YOU LIVE IN THE SAME TOWN AND YOU DON'T KNOW?
THAT'S *BIZARRE*...
I WONDER IF SHE REALLY LIVES HERE...
HEY! YOU!
TAXI
VIIIN
VMX

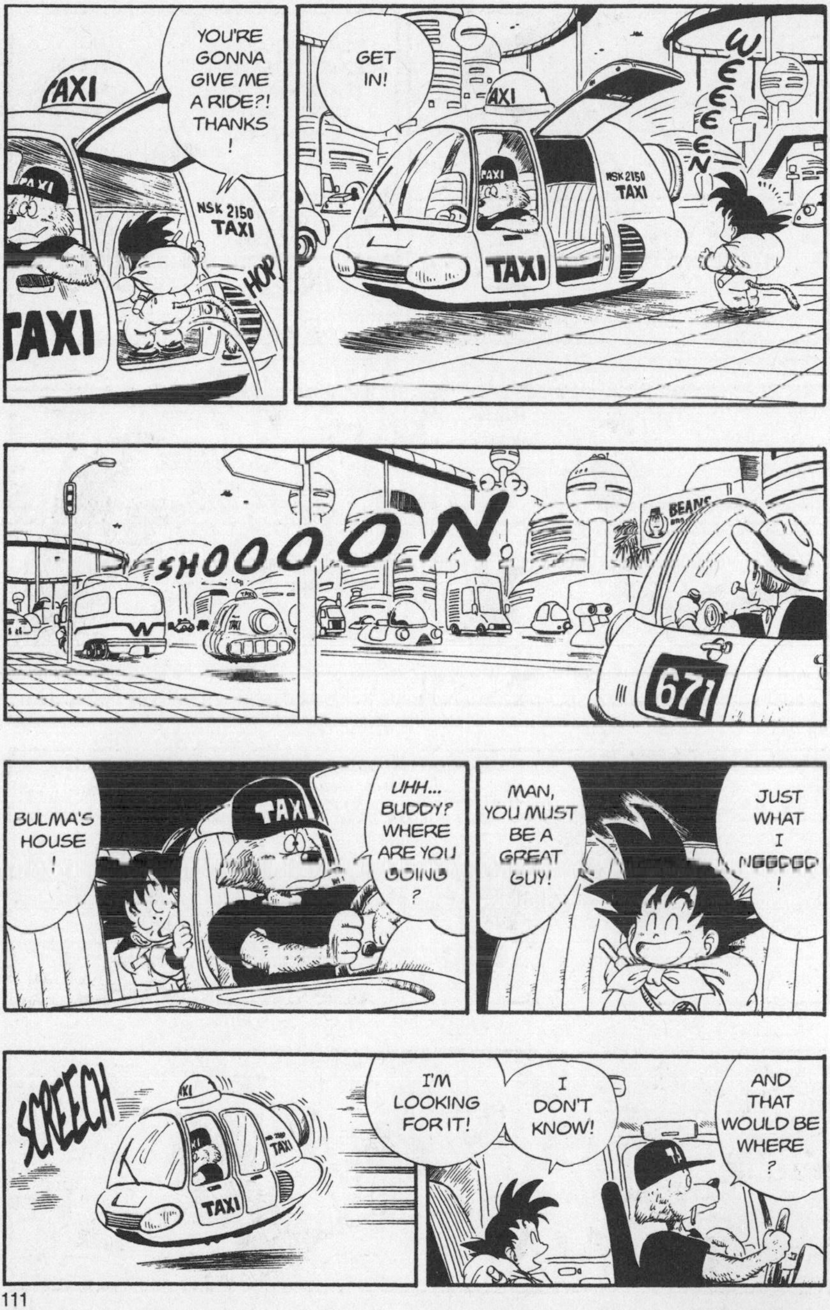
GET IN!
WEEEEEEN
TAXI
NSK 2150 TAXI
YOU'RE GONNA GIVE ME A RIDE?! THANKS!
HOP
NSK 2150 TAXI
SHOOOOON
BEANS
671
JUST WHAT I NEEEEED!
MAN, YOU MUST BE A GREAT GUY!
UHH... BUDDY? WHERE ARE YOU GOING?
BULMA'S HOUSE!
AND THAT WOULD BE WHERE?
I DON'T KNOW!
I'M LOOKING FOR IT!
SCREECH
TAXI

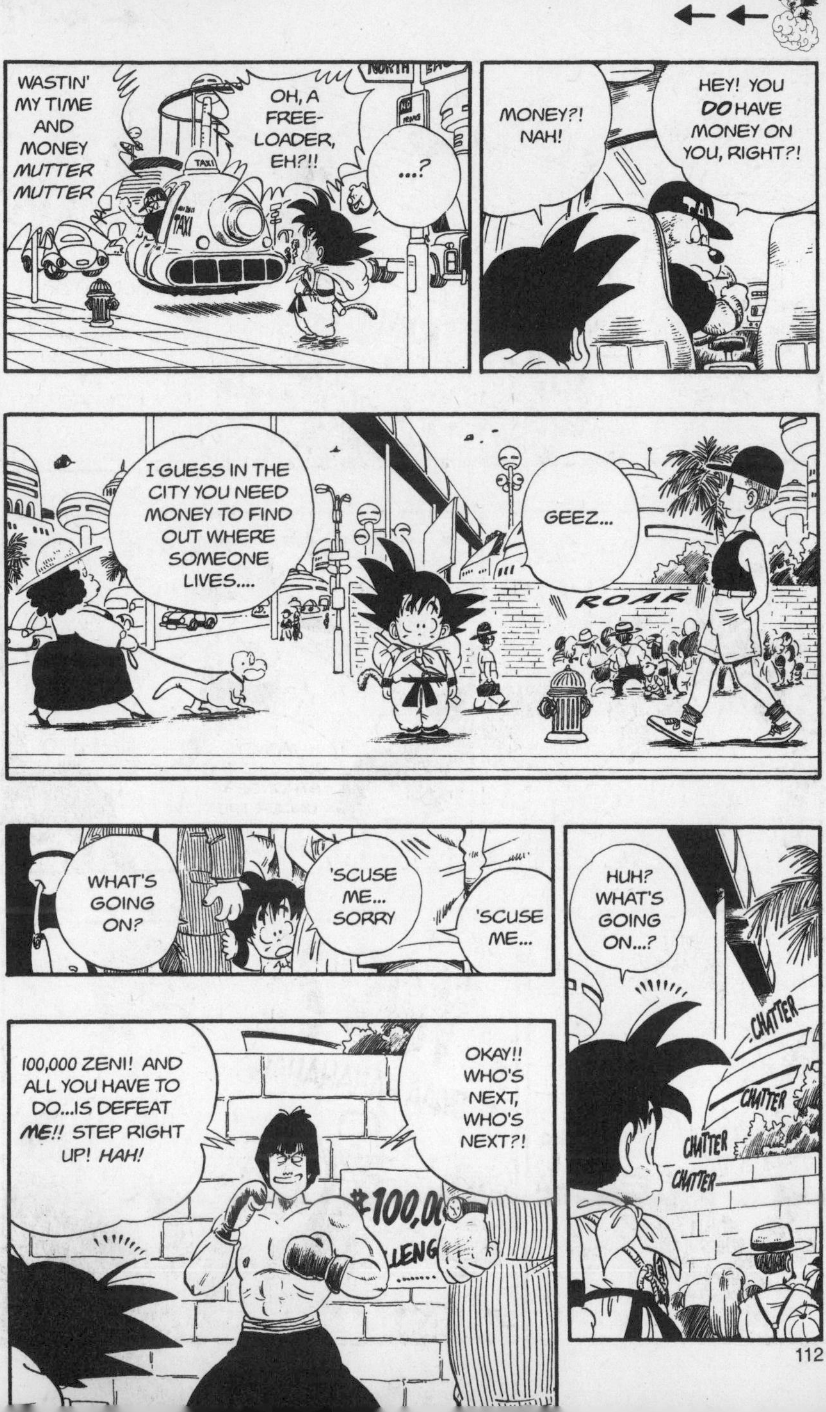
HEY! YOU DO HAVE MONEY ON YOU, RIGHT?!
MONEY?! NAH!
NORTH
...?
OH, A FREE-LOADER, EH?!!
WASTIN' MY TIME AND MONEY MUTTER MUTTER
TAXI
GEEZ...
I GUESS IN THE CITY YOU NEED MONEY TO FIND OUT WHERE SOMEONE LIVES....
ROAR
HUH? WHAT'S GOING ON...?
CHATTER
CHATTER
CHATTER
CHATTER
'SCUSE ME...
'SCUSE ME... SORRY
WHAT'S GOING ON?
OKAY!! WHO'S NEXT, WHO'S NEXT?!
100,000 ZENI! AND ALL YOU HAVE TO DO...IS DEFEAT ME!! STEP RIGHT UP! HAH!

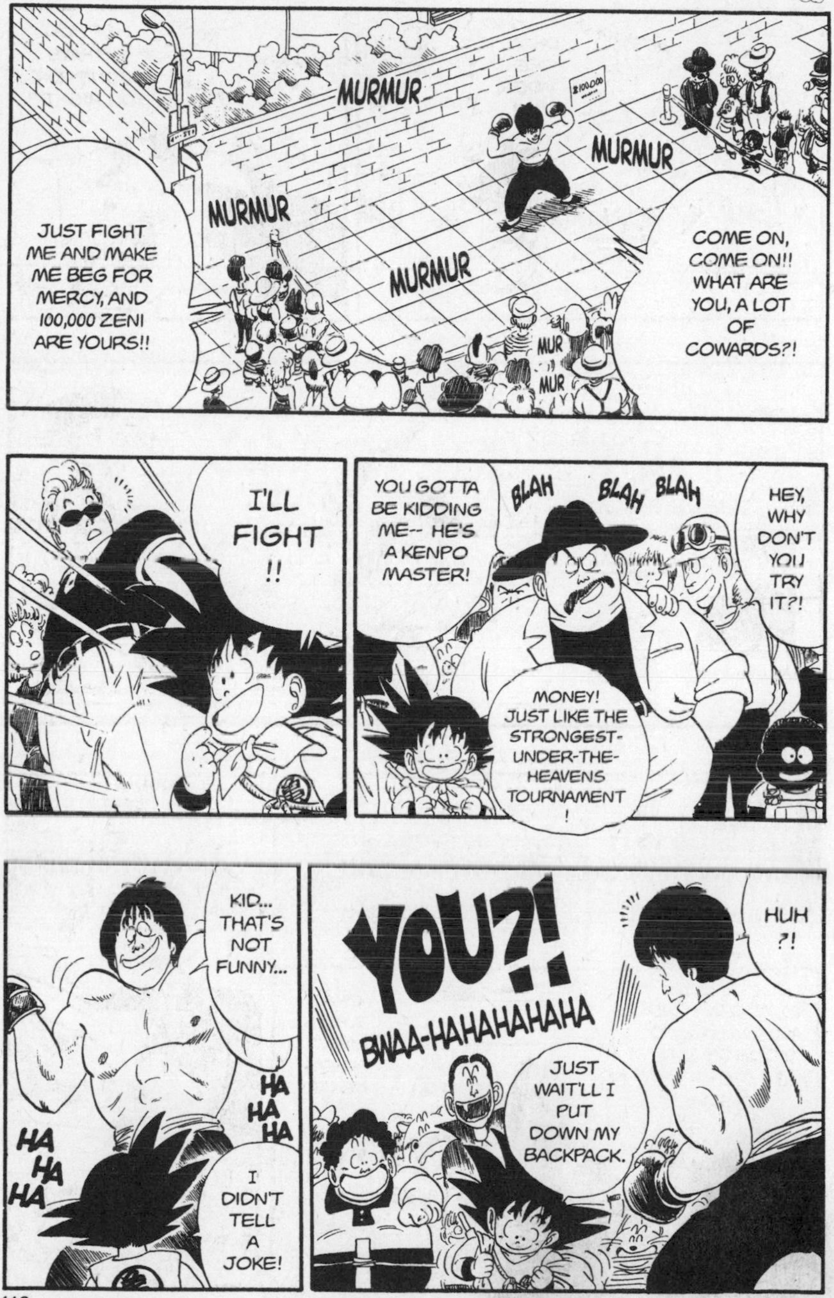
COME ON, COME ON!! WHAT ARE YOU, A LOT OF COWARDS?!
MURMUR
MURMUR
MURMUR
MURMUR
MUR MUR
JUST FIGHT ME AND MAKE ME BEG FOR MERCY, AND 100,000 ZENI ARE YOURS!!
HEY, WHY DON'T YOU TRY IT?!
BLAH BLAH BLAH
YOU GOTTA BE KIDDING ME-- HE'S A KENPO MASTER!
MONEY! JUST LIKE THE STRONGEST-UNDER-THE-HEAVENS TOURNAMENT!
I'LL FIGHT!!
HUH?!
YOU?!
BWAA-HAHAHAHAHA
JUST WAIT'LL I PUT DOWN MY BACKPACK.
KID... THAT'S NOT FUNNY...
HA HA HA
HA HA HA
I DIDN'T TELL A JOKE!

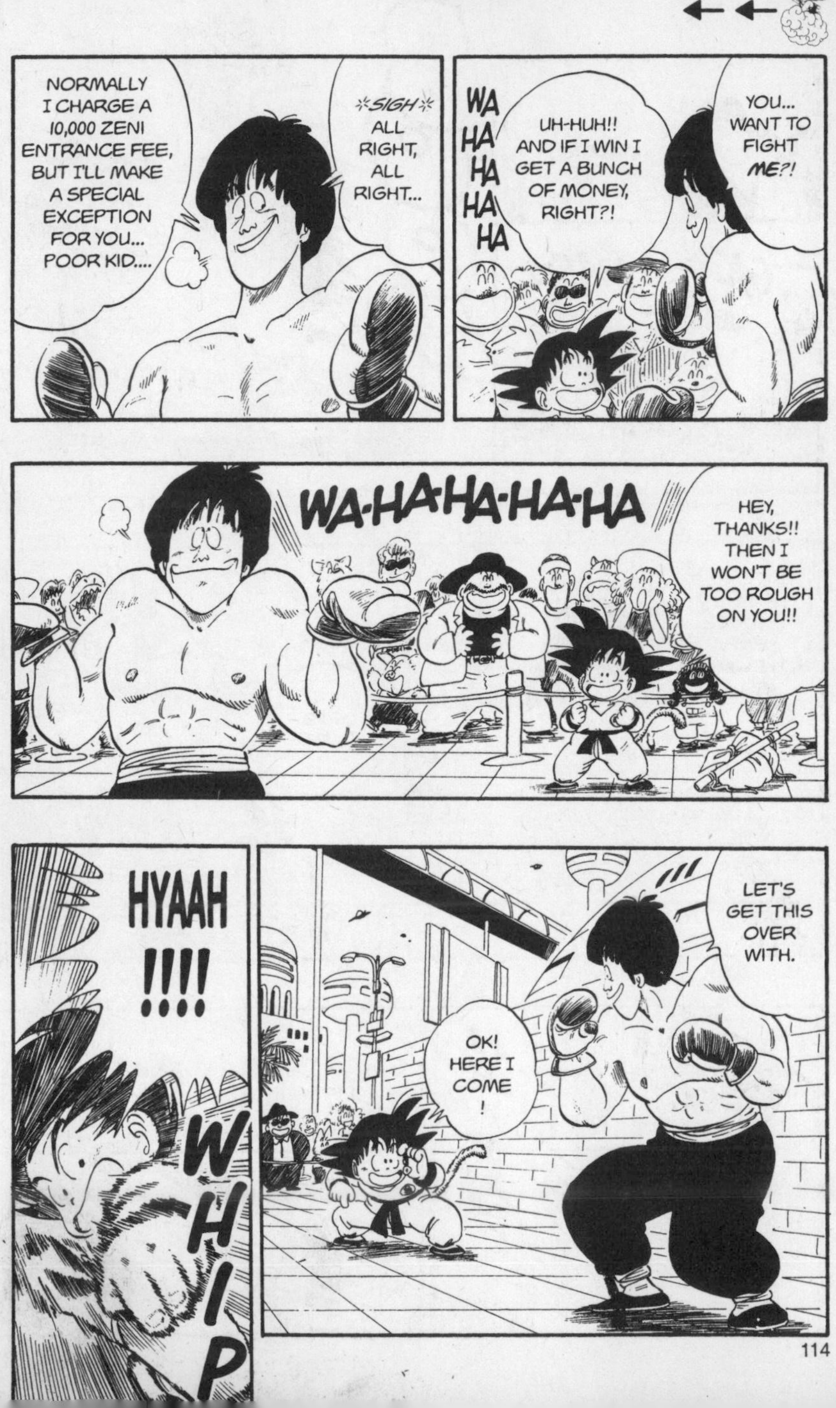
YOU... WANT TO FIGHT ME?!
UH-HUH!! AND IF I WIN I GET A BUNCH OF MONEY, RIGHT?!
WA HA HA HA HA
SIGH ALL RIGHT, ALL RIGHT...
NORMALLY I CHARGE A 10,000 ZENI ENTRANCE FEE, BUT I'LL MAKE A SPECIAL EXCEPTION FOR YOU... POOR KID....
HEY, THANKS!! THEN I WON'T BE TOO ROUGH ON YOU!!
WA-HA-HA-HA-HA
LET'S GET THIS OVER WITH.
OK! HERE I COME !
HYAAH !!!!
WHIP

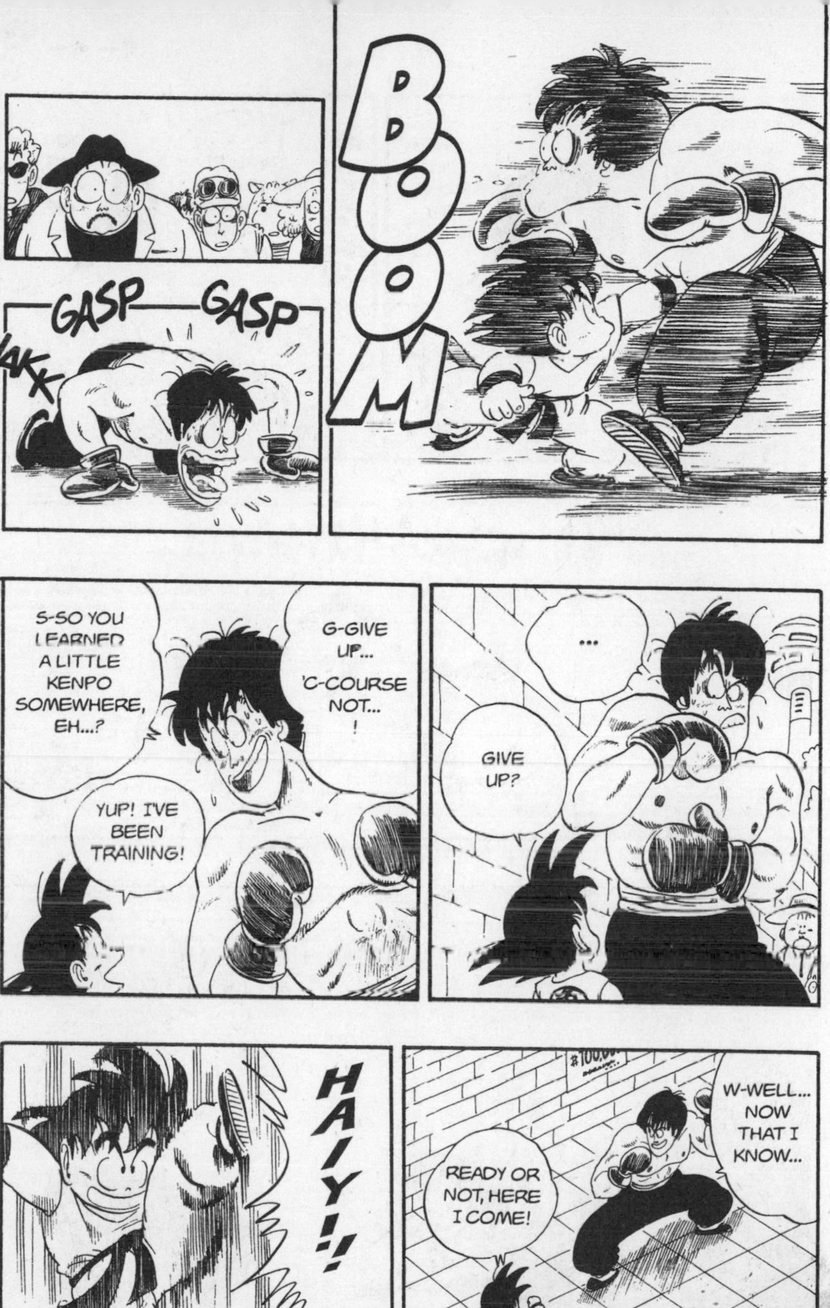
BOOM
GASP GASP
HAKK
...
GIVE UP?
G-GIVE UP... 'C-COURSE NOT... !
S-SO YOU LEARNED A LITTLE KENPO SOMEWHERE, EH...?
YUP! I'VE BEEN TRAINING!
W-WELL... NOW THAT I KNOW...
READY OR NOT, HERE I COME!
HAIYY!!!

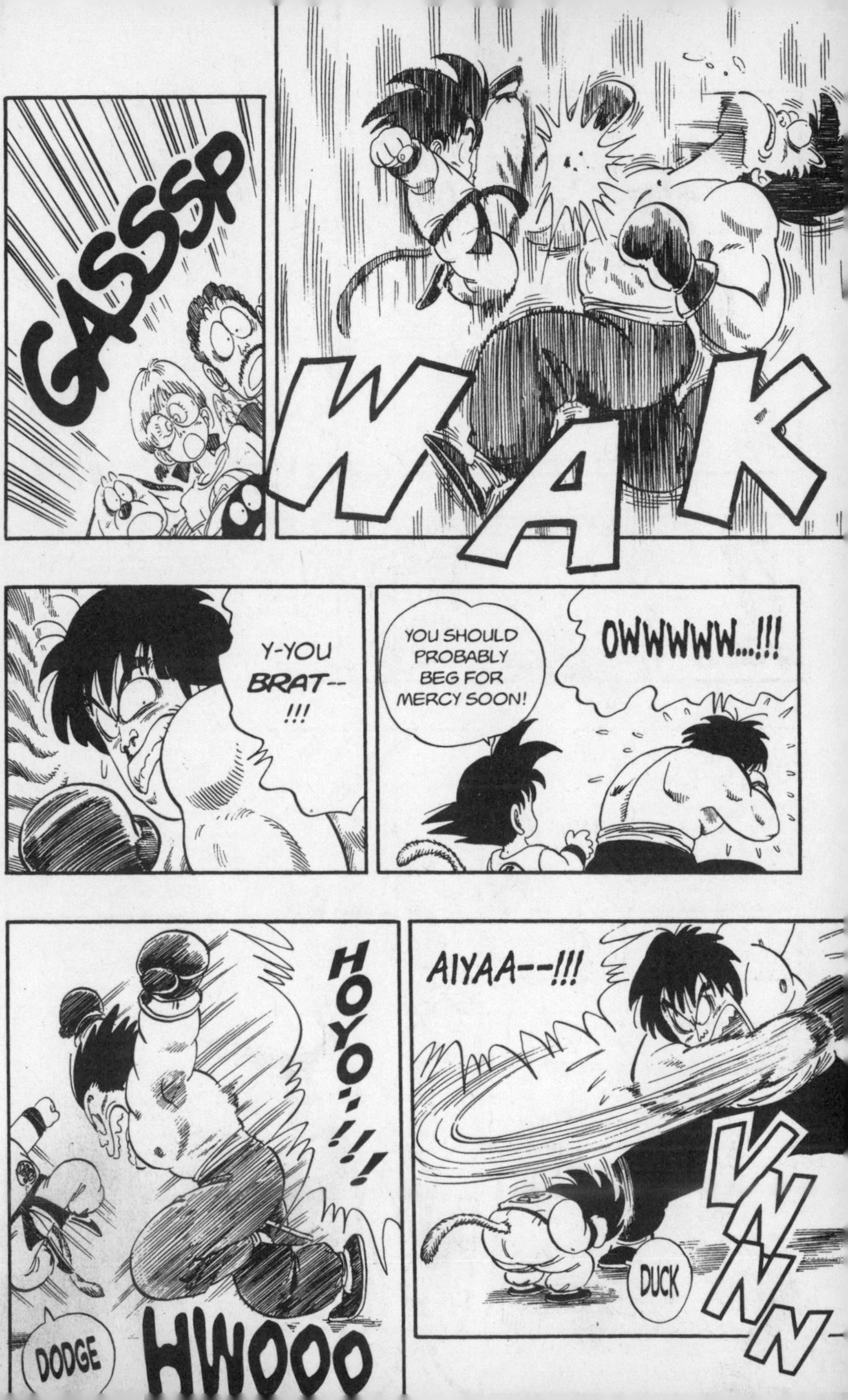
WAK
GASSSP
OWWWWW...!!!
YOU SHOULD PROBABLY BEG FOR MERCY SOON!
Y-YOU BRAT-- !!!
AIYAA--!!!
VNNNN-
DUCK
HOYO--!!!
HWOOO
DODGE

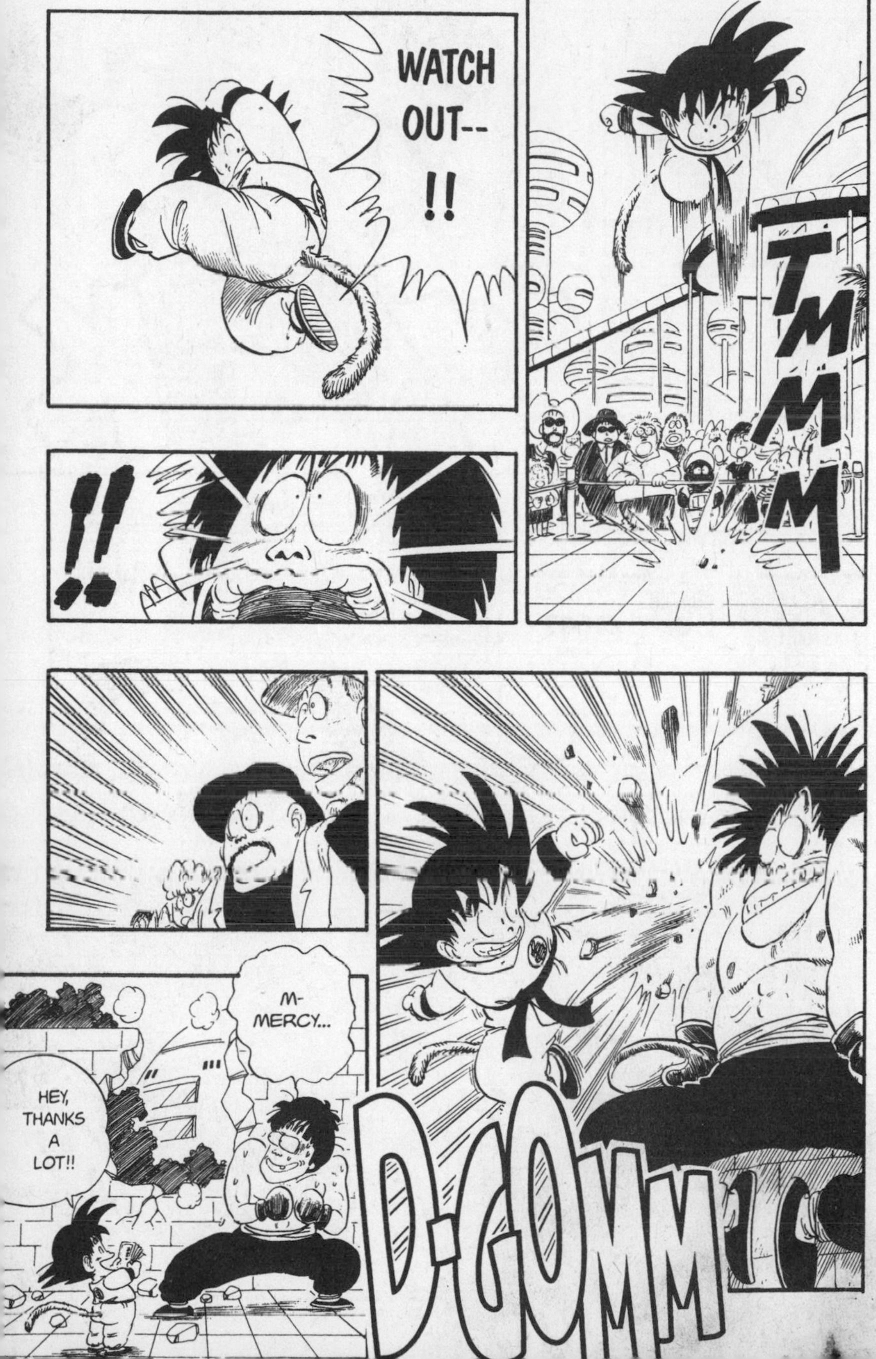
TMMM
WATCH OUT-- !!
!!
D-GOMM
M-MERCY...
HEY, THANKS A LOT!!

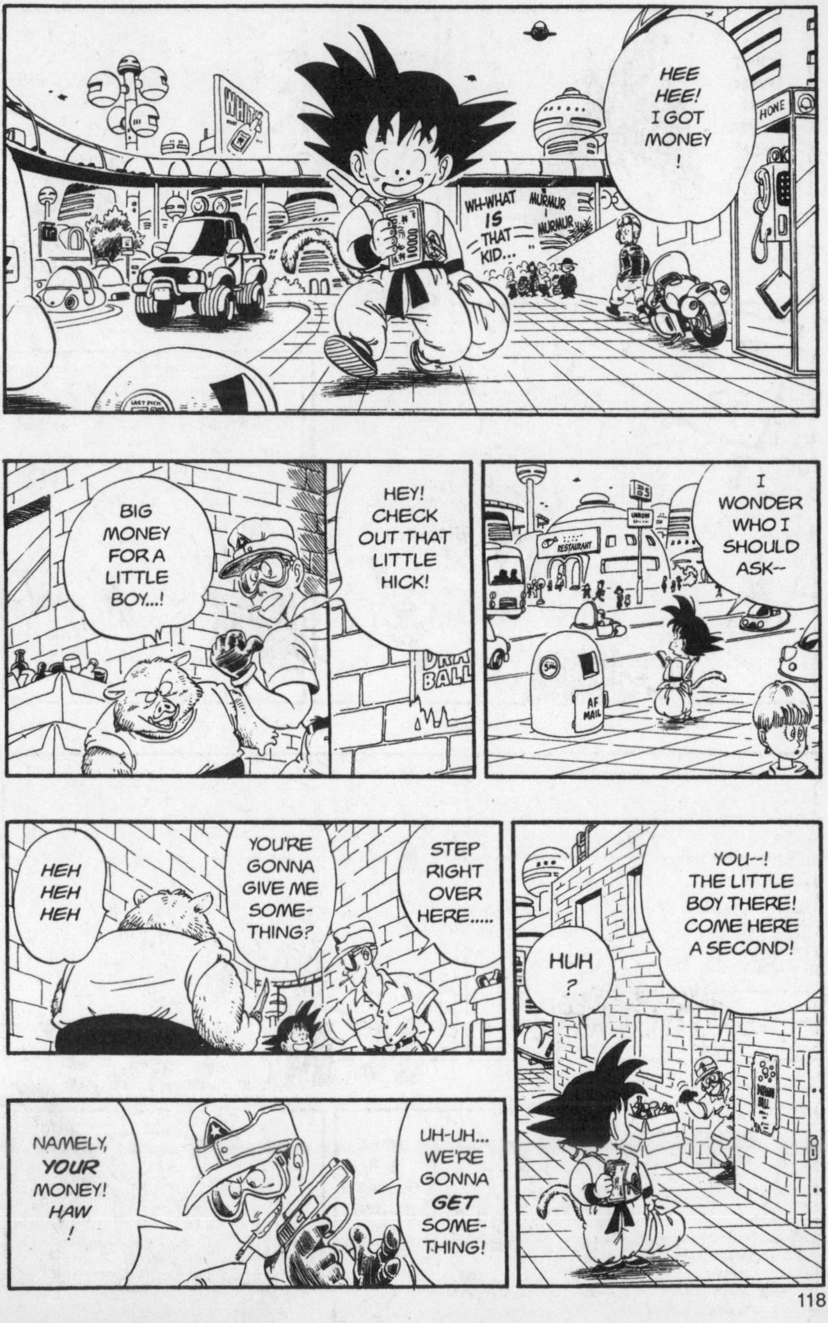
HEE HEE! I GOT MONEY!
WH-WHAT IS THAT KID...
MURMUR MURMUR
HONE
I WONDER WHO I SHOULD ASK--
RESTAURANT
AF MAIL
HEY! CHECK OUT THAT LITTLE HICK!
BIG MONEY FOR A LITTLE BOY...!
YOU--! THE LITTLE BOY THERE! COME HERE A SECOND!
HUH?
STEP RIGHT OVER HERE.....
YOU'RE GONNA GIVE ME SOME-THING?
HEH HEH HEH
UH-UH... WE'RE GONNA GET SOME-THING!
NAMELY, YOUR MONEY! HAW!

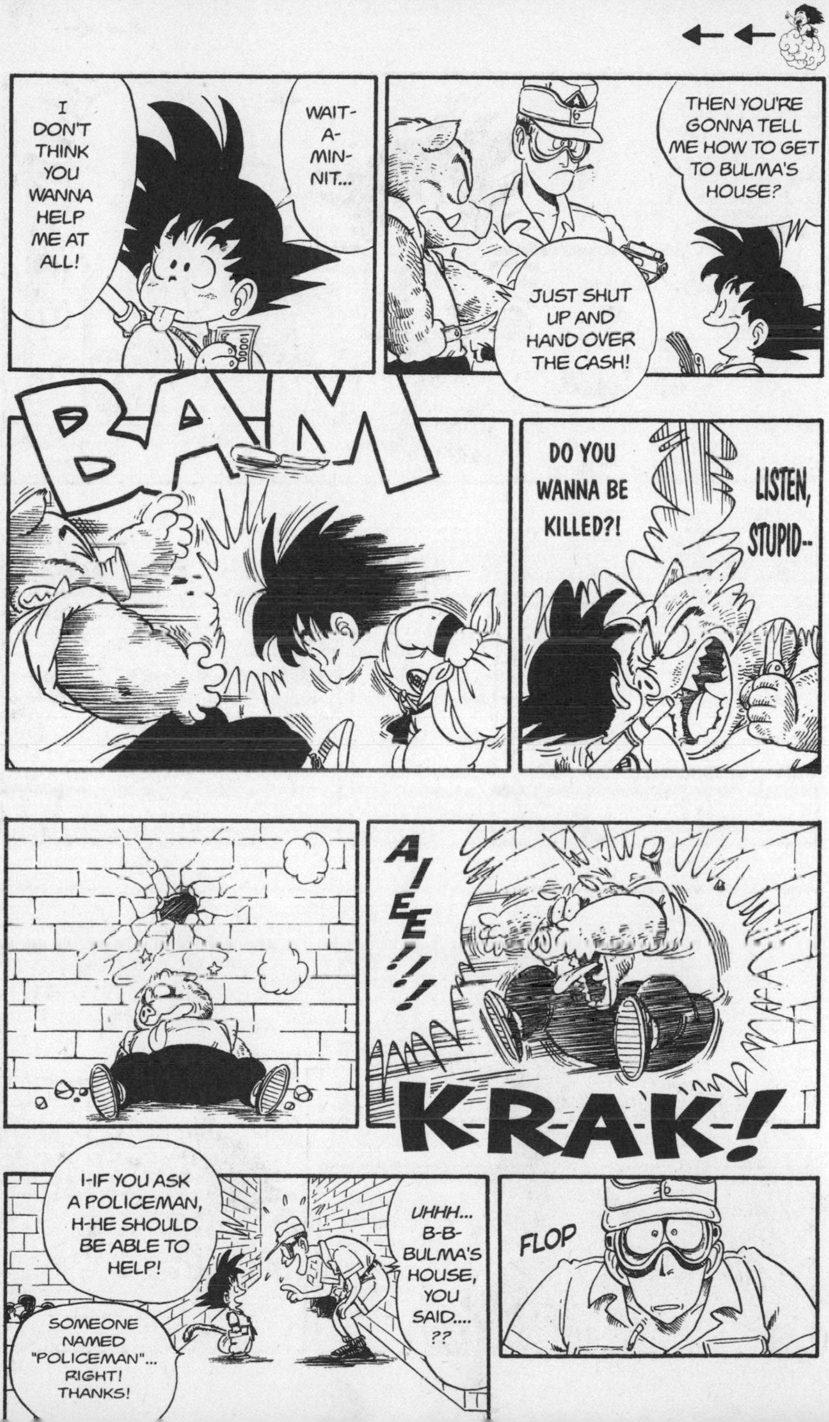
THEN YOU'RE GONNA TELL ME HOW TO GET TO BULMA'S HOUSE?
JUST SHUT UP AND HAND OVER THE CASH!
WAIT-A-MIN-NIT...
I DON'T THINK YOU WANNA HELP ME AT ALL!
LISTEN, STUPID--
DO YOU WANNA BE KILLED?!
BAM
AIEE!!!
KRAK!
FLOP
UHHH... B-B-BULMA'S HOUSE, YOU SAID....??
I-IF YOU ASK A POLICEMAN, H-HE SHOULD BE ABLE TO HELP!
SOMEONE NAMED "POLICEMAN"... RIGHT! THANKS!

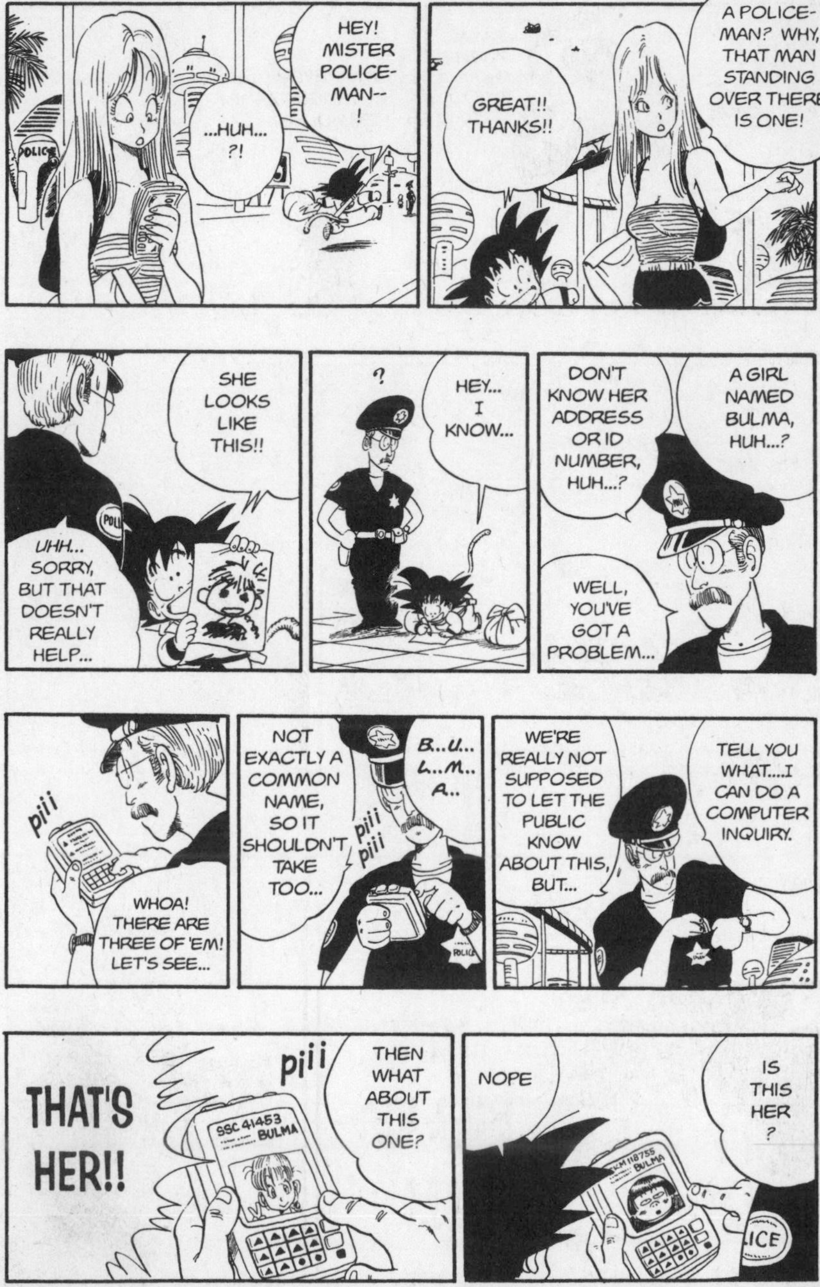
A POLICE-MAN? WHY, THAT MAN STANDING OVER THERE IS ONE!
GREAT!! THANKS!!
HEY! MISTER POLICE-MAN--!
...HUH...?!
POLICE
A GIRL NAMED BULMA, HUH...?
DON'T KNOW HER ADDRESS OR ID NUMBER, HUH...?
WELL, YOU'VE GOT A PROBLEM...
?
HEY... I KNOW...
SHE LOOKS LIKE THIS!!
UHH... SORRY, BUT THAT DOESN'T REALLY HELP...
TELL YOU WHAT....I CAN DO A COMPUTER INQUIRY.
WE'RE REALLY NOT SUPPOSED TO LET THE PUBLIC KNOW ABOUT THIS, BUT...
B..U... L..M... A..
NOT EXACTLY A COMMON NAME, SO IT SHOULDN'T TAKE TOO...
piii piii
POLICE
piii
WHOA! THERE ARE THREE OF 'EM! LET'S SEE...
IS THIS HER?
NOPE
KM 118755 BULMA
LICE
THEN WHAT ABOUT THIS ONE?
piii
SSC 41453 BULMA
THAT'S HER!!

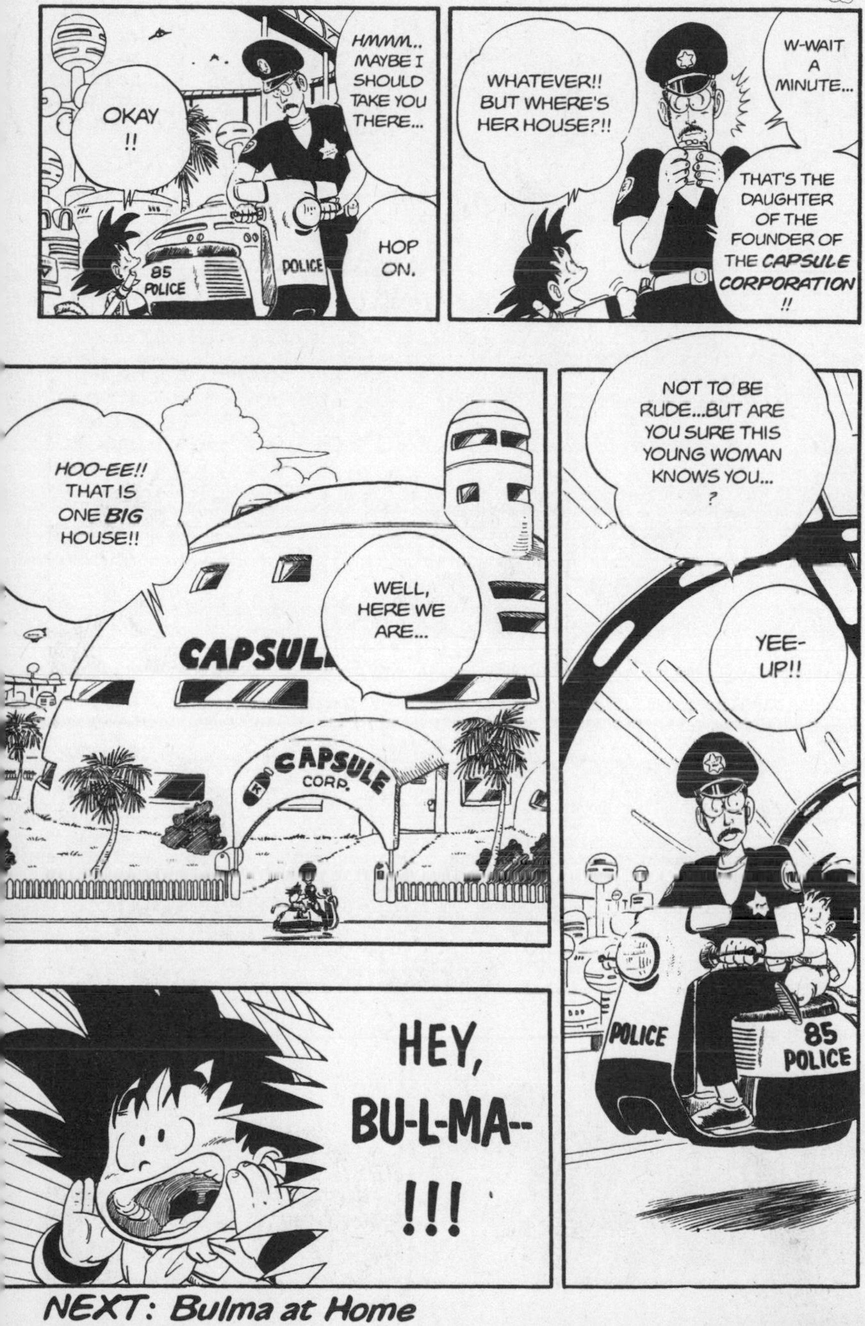
WHATEVER!! BUT WHERE'S HER HOUSE?!!
W-WAIT A MINUTE...
THAT'S THE DAUGHTER OF THE FOUNDER OF THE CAPSULE CORPORATION!!
HMMM.. MAYBE I SHOULD TAKE YOU THERE...
HOP ON.
OKAY!!
85 POLICE
POLICE
NOT TO BE RUDE...BUT ARE YOU SURE THIS YOUNG WOMAN KNOWS YOU...?
YEE-UP!!
POLICE
85 POLICE
WELL, HERE WE ARE...
HOO-EE!! THAT IS ONE BIG HOUSE!!
CAPSUL
CAPSULE CORP.
HEY, BU-L-MA--!!!

***NEXT*: Bulma at Home**

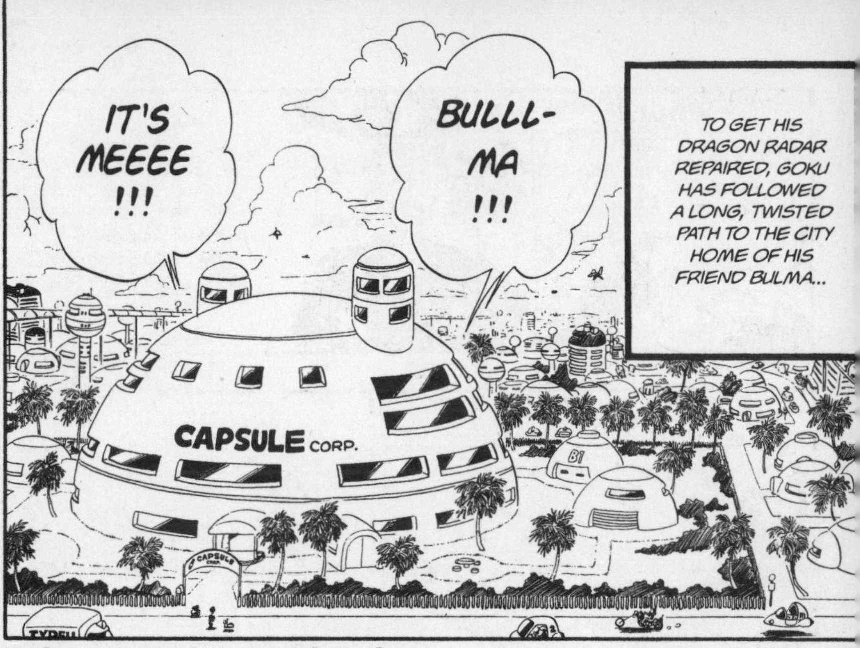
TO GET HIS DRAGON RADAR REPAIRED, GOKU HAS FOLLOWED A LONG, TWISTED PATH TO THE CITY HOME OF HIS FRIEND BULMA...
BULLL-MA !!!
IT'S MEEEE !!!
CAPSULE CORP.

Tale 69 • Bulma and Goku

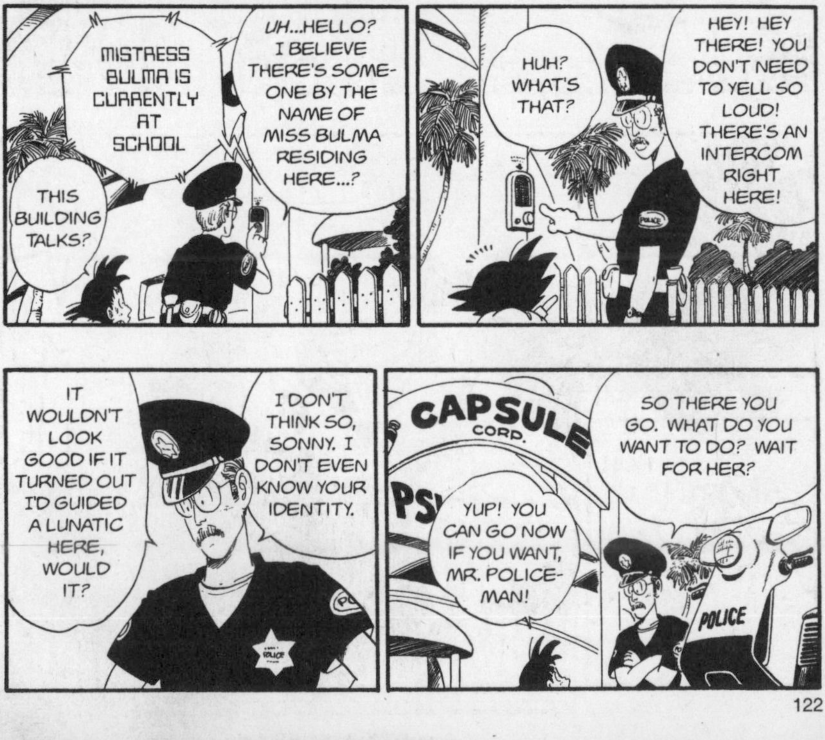
HEY! HEY THERE! YOU DON'T NEED TO YELL SO LOUD! THERE'S AN INTERCOM RIGHT HERE!
HUH? WHAT'S THAT?
UH...HELLO? I BELIEVE THERE'S SOME-ONE BY THE NAME OF MISS BULMA RESIDING HERE...?
MISTRESS BULMA IS CURRENTLY AT SCHOOL
THIS BUILDING TALKS?
SO THERE YOU GO. WHAT DO YOU WANT TO DO? WAIT FOR HER?
YUP! YOU CAN GO NOW IF YOU WANT, MR. POLICE-MAN!
CAPSULE CORP.
POLICE
I DON'T THINK SO, SONNY. I DON'T EVEN KNOW YOUR IDENTITY.
IT WOULDN'T LOOK GOOD IF IT TURNED OUT I'D GUIDED A LUNATIC HERE, WOULD IT?

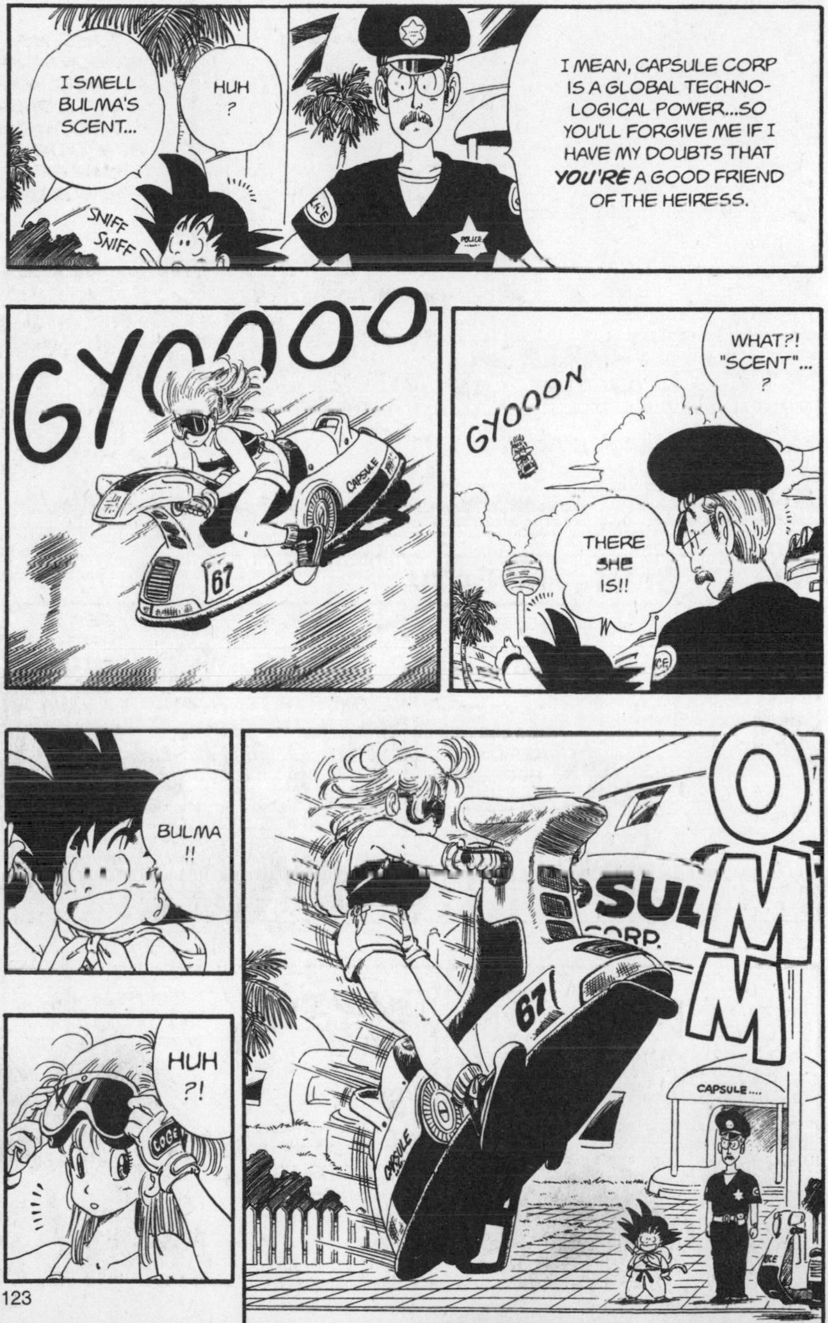
I MEAN, CAPSULE CORP IS A GLOBAL TECHNO-LOGICAL POWER...SO YOU'LL FORGIVE ME IF I HAVE MY DOUBTS THAT ***YOU'RE*** A GOOD FRIEND OF THE HEIRESS.
POLICE
HUH ?
I SMELL BULMA'S SCENT...
SNIFF SNIFF
WHAT?! "SCENT"... ?
GYOOON
THERE SHE IS!!
GYOOOO
CAPSULE
67
OMMM
CAPSULE....
67
CAPSULE
BULMA !!
HUH ?!

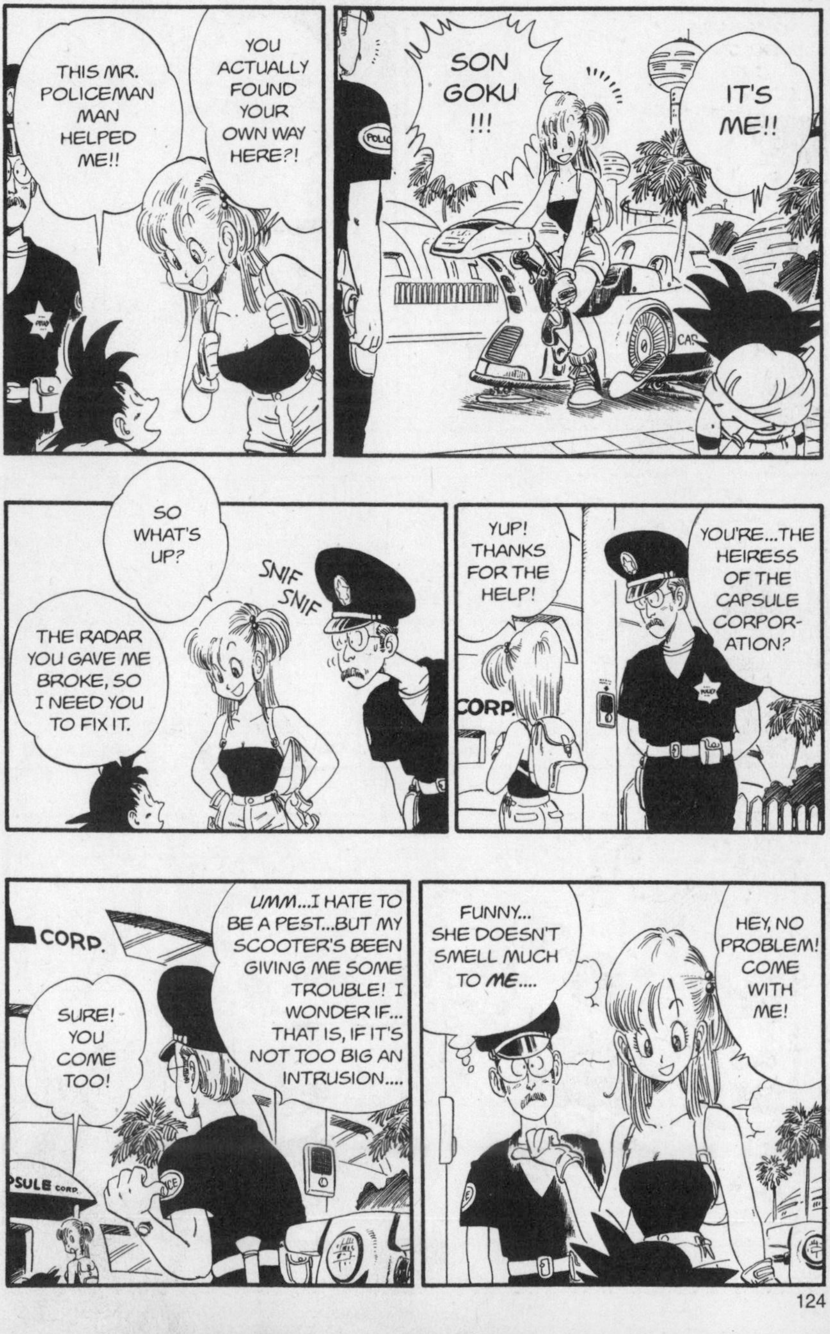
IT'S ME!!
SON GOKU !!!
YOU ACTUALLY FOUND YOUR OWN WAY HERE?!
THIS MR. POLICEMAN MAN HELPED ME!!
YOU'RE...THE HEIRESS OF THE CAPSULE CORPORATION?
YUP! THANKS FOR THE HELP!
CORP.
SO WHAT'S UP?
SNIF SNIF
THE RADAR YOU GAVE ME BROKE, SO I NEED YOU TO FIX IT.
HEY, NO PROBLEM! COME WITH ME!
FUNNY... SHE DOESN'T SMELL MUCH TO *ME*....
UMM...I HATE TO BE A PEST...BUT MY SCOOTER'S BEEN GIVING ME SOME TROUBLE! I WONDER IF... THAT IS, IF IT'S NOT TOO BIG AN INTRUSION....
CORP.
SURE! YOU COME TOO!

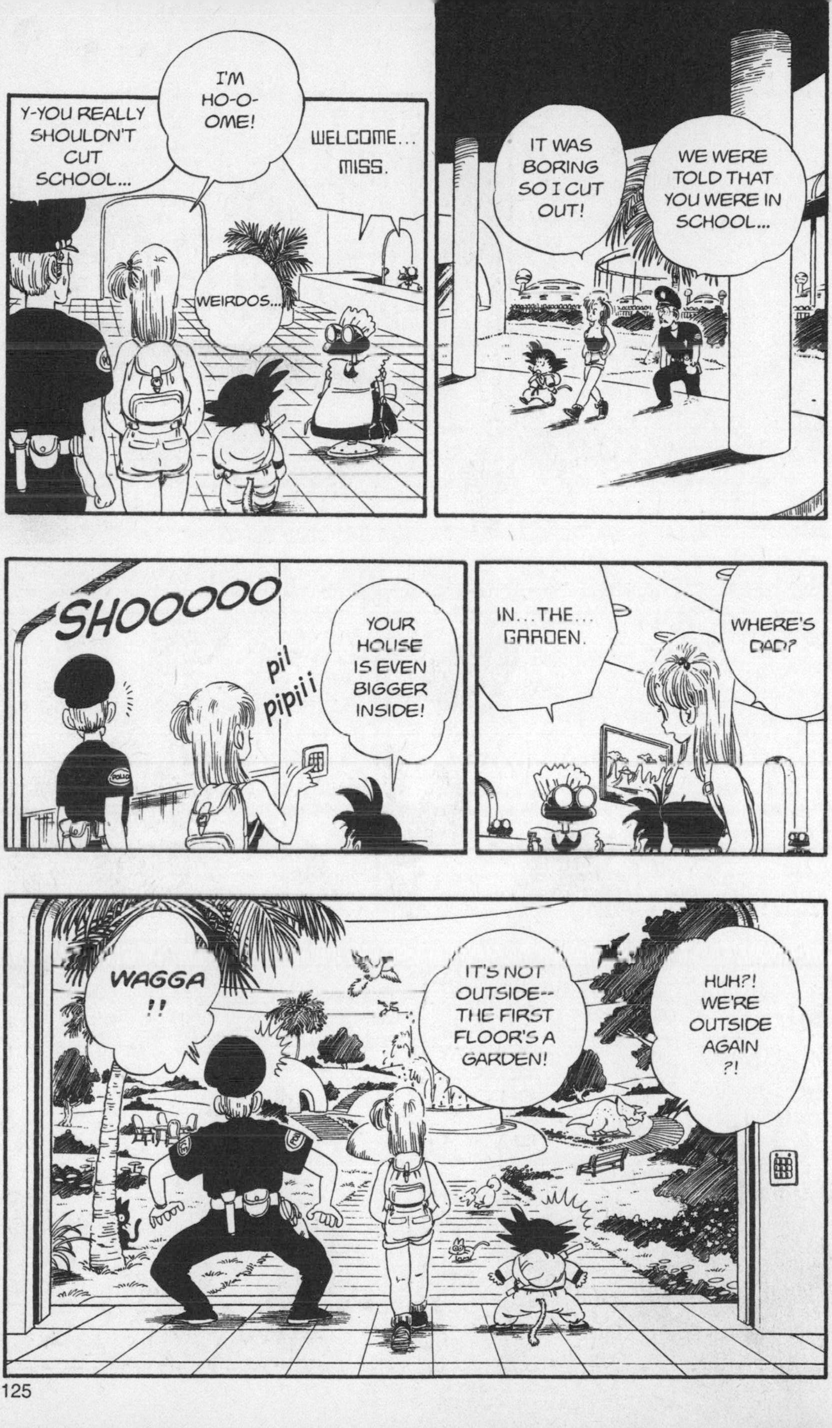
WE WERE TOLD THAT YOU WERE IN SCHOOL...
IT WAS BORING SO I CUT OUT!
WELCOME... MISS.
I'M HO-O-OME!
Y-YOU REALLY SHOULDN'T CUT SCHOOL...
WEIRDOS...
WHERE'S DAD?
IN... THE... GARDEN.
YOUR HOUSE IS EVEN BIGGER INSIDE!
pil pipiii
SHOOOOO
HUH?! WE'RE OUTSIDE AGAIN ?!
IT'S NOT OUTSIDE-- THE FIRST FLOOR'S A GARDEN!
WAGGA !!

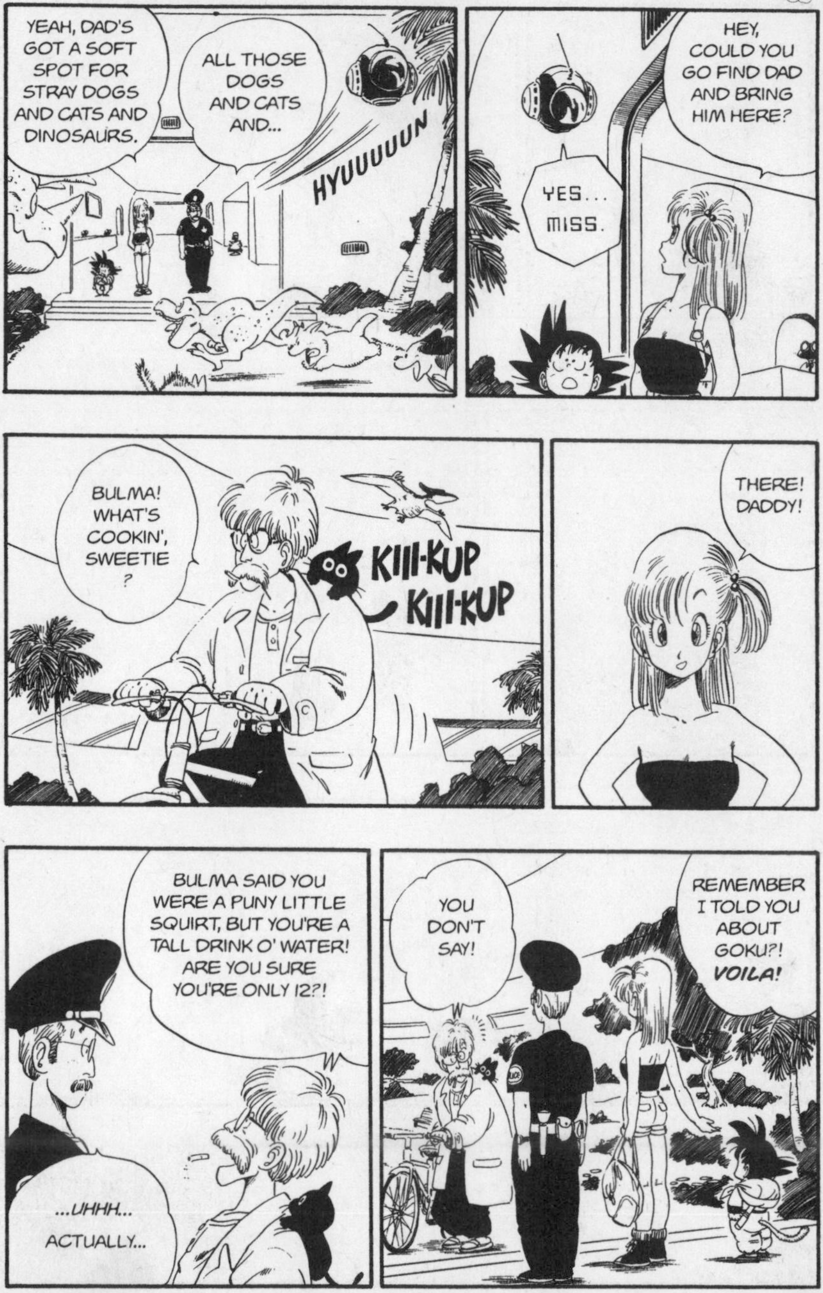
HEY, COULD YOU GO FIND DAD AND BRING HIM HERE?
YES... MISS.
ALL THOSE DOGS AND CATS AND...
YEAH, DAD'S GOT A SOFT SPOT FOR STRAY DOGS AND CATS AND DINOSAURS.
HYUUUUUN
THERE! DADDY!
BULMA! WHAT'S COOKIN', SWEETIE?
KIII-KUP
KIII-KUP
REMEMBER I TOLD YOU ABOUT GOKU?! *VOILA!*
YOU DON'T SAY!
BULMA SAID YOU WERE A PUNY LITTLE SQUIRT, BUT YOU'RE A TALL DRINK O' WATER! ARE YOU SURE YOU'RE ONLY 12?!
...UHHH... ACTUALLY...

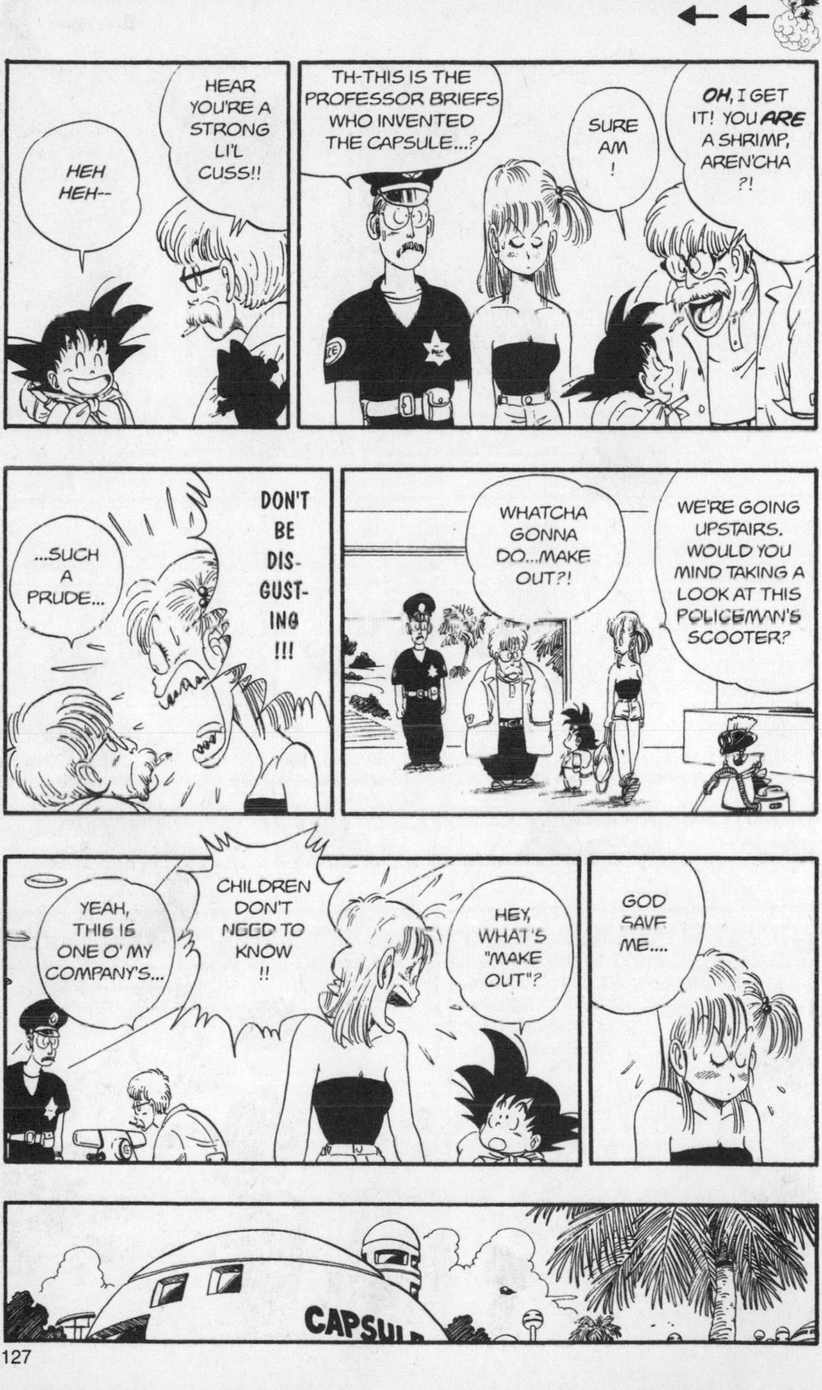
OH, I GET IT! YOU ARE A SHRIMP, AREN'CHA?!
SURE AM!
TH-THIS IS THE PROFESSOR BRIEFS WHO INVENTED THE CAPSULE...?
HEAR YOU'RE A STRONG LI'L CUSS!!
HEH HEH--
WE'RE GOING UPSTAIRS. WOULD YOU MIND TAKING A LOOK AT THIS POLICEMAN'S SCOOTER?
WHATCHA GONNA DO...MAKE OUT?!
DON'T BE DIS-GUST-ING!!!
...SUCH A PRUDE...
GOD SAVE ME....
HEY, WHAT'S "MAKE OUT"?
CHILDREN DON'T NEED TO KNOW!!
YEAH, THIS IS ONE O' MY COMPANY'S...
CAPSUL

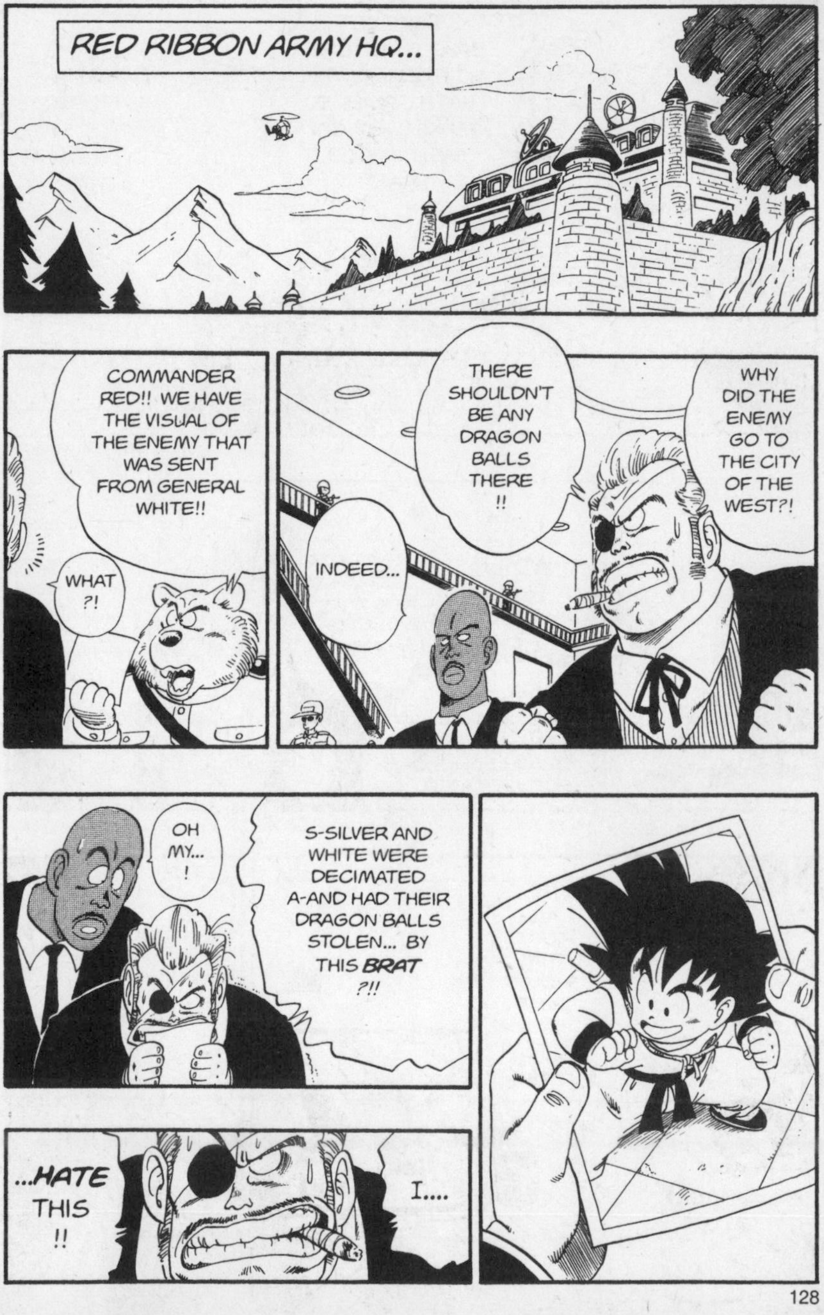
RED RIBBON ARMY HQ...
WHY DID THE ENEMY GO TO THE CITY OF THE WEST?!
THERE SHOULDN'T BE ANY DRAGON BALLS THERE!!
INDEED...
COMMANDER RED!! WE HAVE THE VISUAL OF THE ENEMY THAT WAS SENT FROM GENERAL WHITE!!
WHAT?!
S-SILVER AND WHITE WERE DECIMATED A-AND HAD THEIR DRAGON BALLS STOLEN... BY THIS *BRAT*?!!
OH MY...!
I....
...*HATE* THIS!!

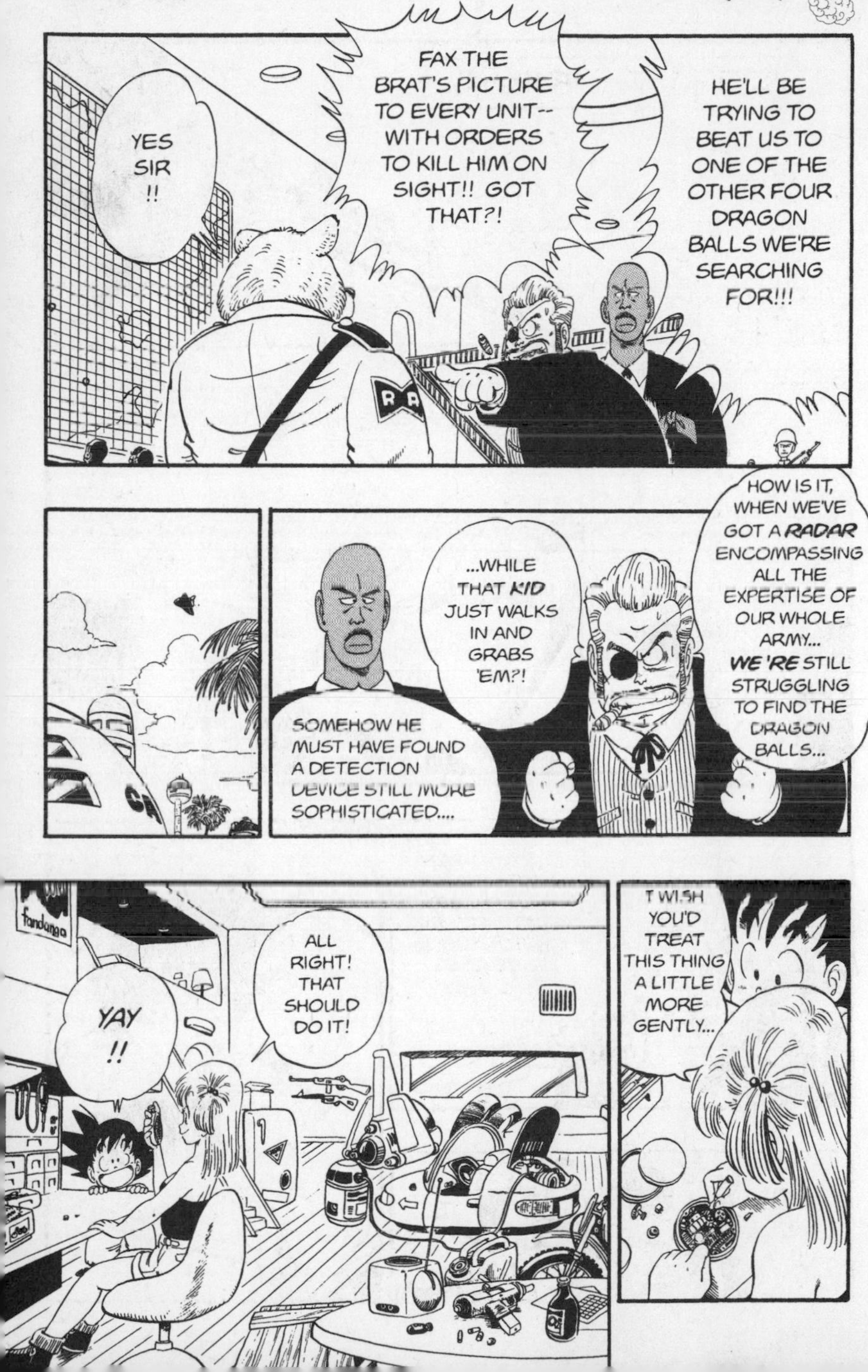
HE'LL BE TRYING TO BEAT US TO ONE OF THE OTHER FOUR DRAGON BALLS WE'RE SEARCHING FOR!!!
FAX THE BRAT'S PICTURE TO EVERY UNIT--WITH ORDERS TO KILL HIM ON SIGHT!! GOT THAT?!
YES SIR !!
HOW IS IT, WHEN WE'VE GOT A *RADAR* ENCOMPASSING ALL THE EXPERTISE OF OUR WHOLE ARMY... *WE'RE* STILL STRUGGLING TO FIND THE DRAGON BALLS...
...WHILE THAT *KID* JUST WALKS IN AND GRABS 'EM?!
SOMEHOW HE MUST HAVE FOUND A DETECTION DEVICE STILL MORE SOPHISTICATED....
I WISH YOU'D TREAT THIS THING A LITTLE MORE GENTLY...
fandango
ALL RIGHT! THAT SHOULD DO IT!
YAY !!

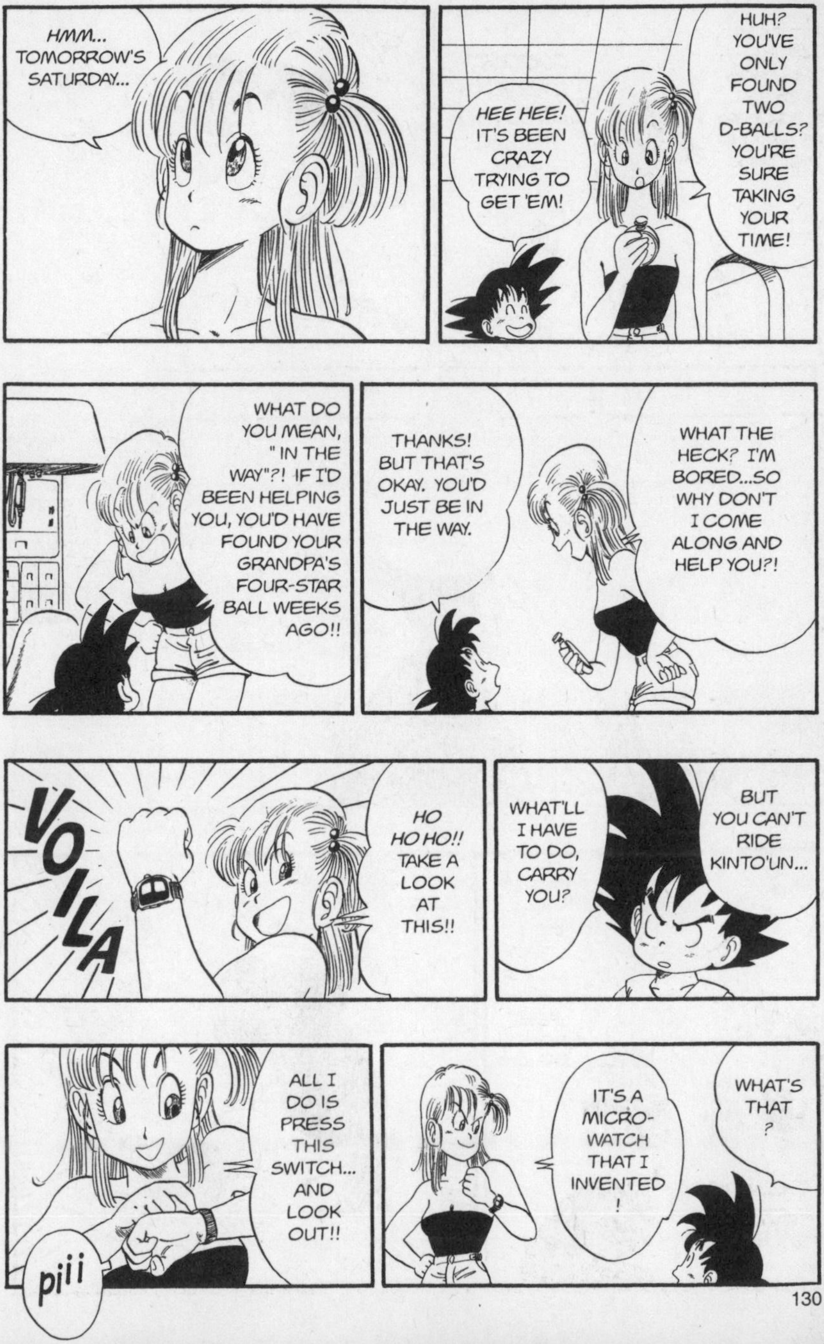
HUH? YOU'VE ONLY FOUND TWO D-BALLS? YOU'RE SURE TAKING YOUR TIME!
HEE HEE! IT'S BEEN CRAZY TRYING TO GET 'EM!
HMM... TOMORROW'S SATURDAY...
WHAT THE HECK? I'M BORED...SO WHY DON'T I COME ALONG AND HELP YOU?!
THANKS! BUT THAT'S OKAY. YOU'D JUST BE IN THE WAY.
WHAT DO YOU MEAN, "IN THE WAY"?! IF I'D BEEN HELPING YOU, YOU'D HAVE FOUND YOUR GRANDPA'S FOUR-STAR BALL WEEKS AGO!!
BUT YOU CAN'T RIDE KINTO'UN...
WHAT'LL I HAVE TO DO, CARRY YOU?
HO HO HO!! TAKE A LOOK AT THIS!!
VOILA
WHAT'S THAT ?
IT'S A MICRO-WATCH THAT I INVENTED !
ALL I DO IS PRESS THIS SWITCH... AND LOOK OUT!!
piii

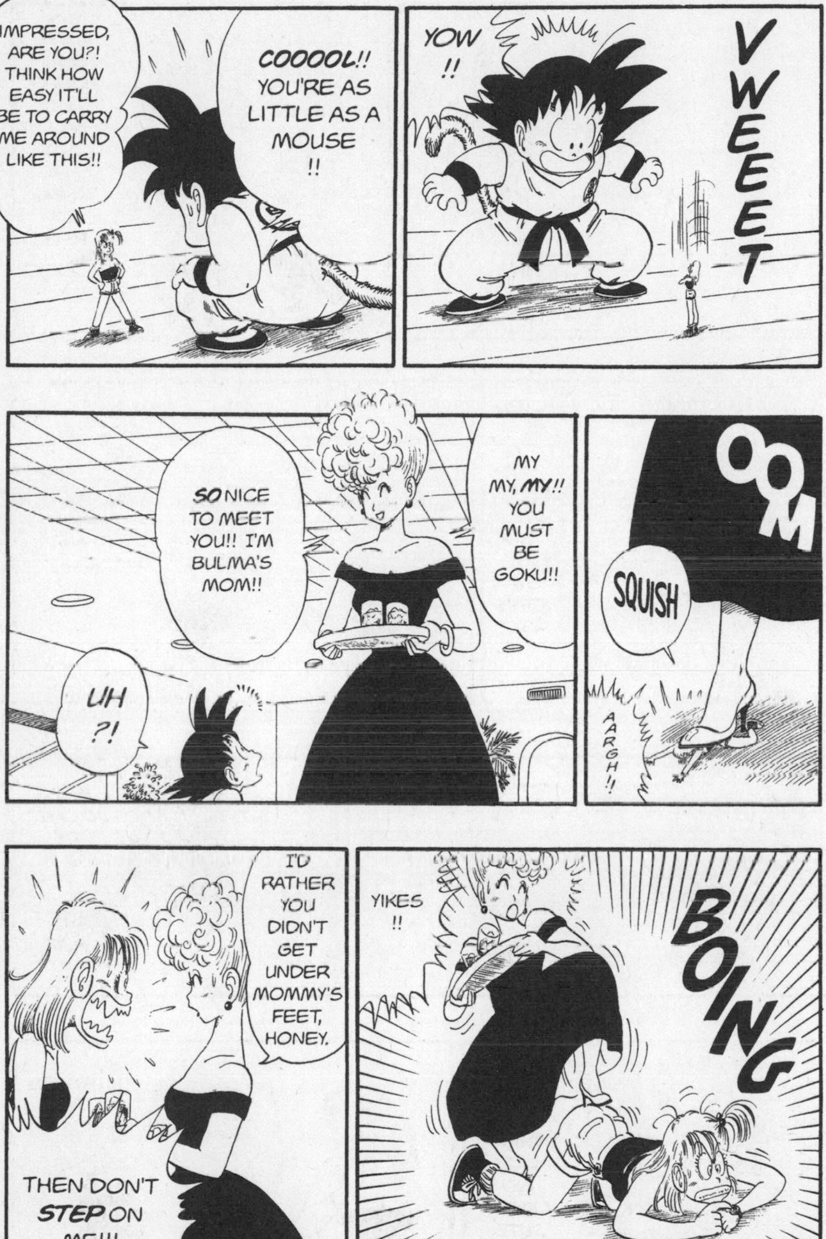
VWEEET
YOW !!
COOOOL!! YOU'RE AS LITTLE AS A MOUSE !!
IMPRESSED, ARE YOU?! THINK HOW EASY IT'LL BE TO CARRY ME AROUND LIKE THIS!!
OOM
SQUISH
AARGH!!
MY MY, MY!! YOU MUST BE GOKU!!
SO NICE TO MEET YOU!! I'M BULMA'S MOM!!
UH ?!
BOING
YIKES !!
I'D RATHER YOU DIDN'T GET UNDER MOMMY'S FEET, HONEY.
THEN DON'T STEP ON ME!!!

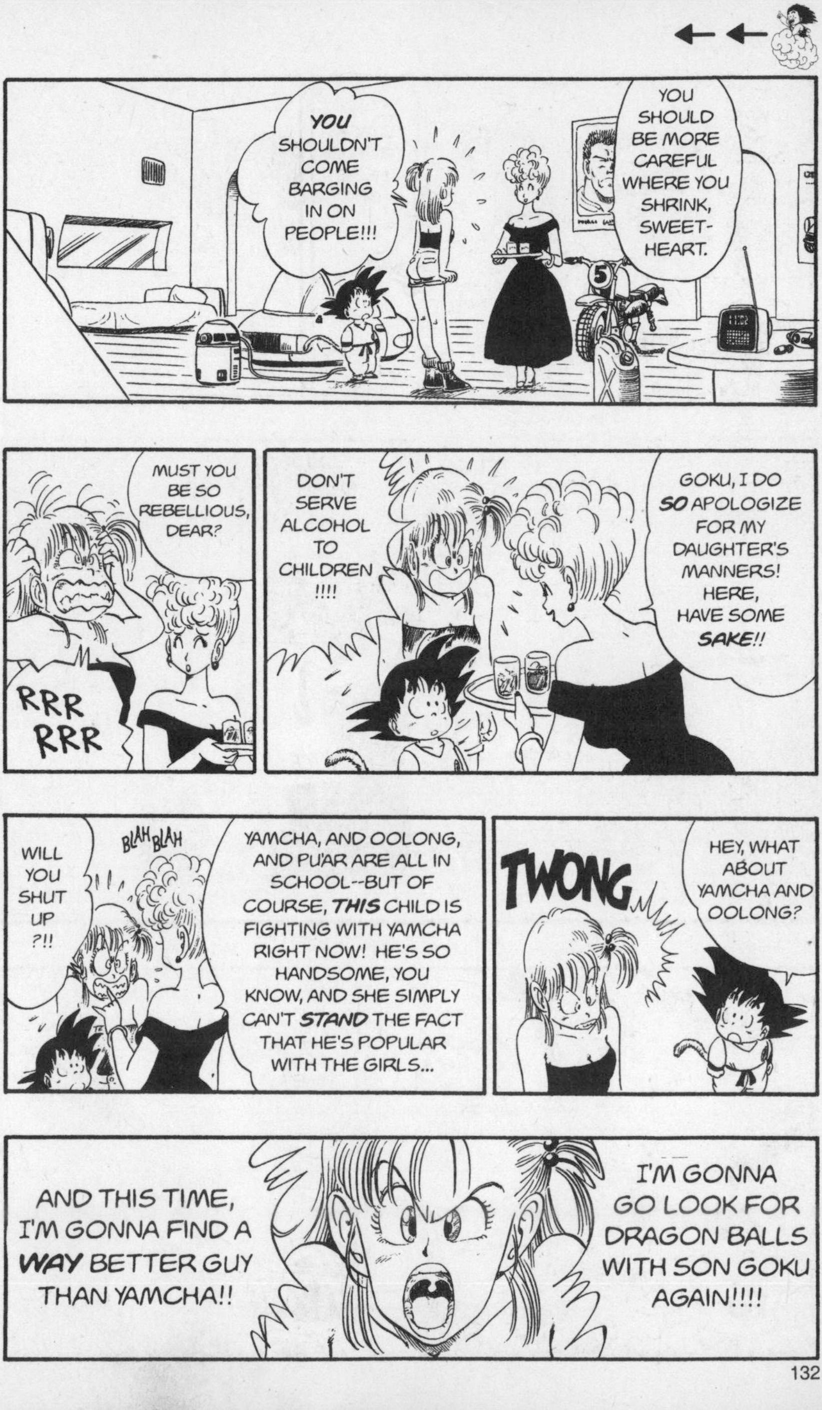
YOU SHOULD BE MORE CAREFUL WHERE YOU SHRINK, SWEET-HEART.
YOU SHOULDN'T COME BARGING IN ON PEOPLE!!!
GOKU, I DO SO APOLOGIZE FOR MY DAUGHTER'S MANNERS! HERE, HAVE SOME SAKE!!
DON'T SERVE ALCOHOL TO CHILDREN !!!!
MUST YOU BE SO REBELLIOUS, DEAR?
RRR RRR
HEY, WHAT ABOUT YAMCHA AND OOLONG?
TWONG
YAMCHA, AND OOLONG, AND PU'AR ARE ALL IN SCHOOL--BUT OF COURSE, THIS CHILD IS FIGHTING WITH YAMCHA RIGHT NOW! HE'S SO HANDSOME, YOU KNOW, AND SHE SIMPLY CAN'T STAND THE FACT THAT HE'S POPULAR WITH THE GIRLS...
BLAH BLAH
WILL YOU SHUT UP ?!!
I'M GONNA GO LOOK FOR DRAGON BALLS WITH SON GOKU AGAIN!!!!
AND THIS TIME, I'M GONNA FIND A WAY BETTER GUY THAN YAMCHA!!

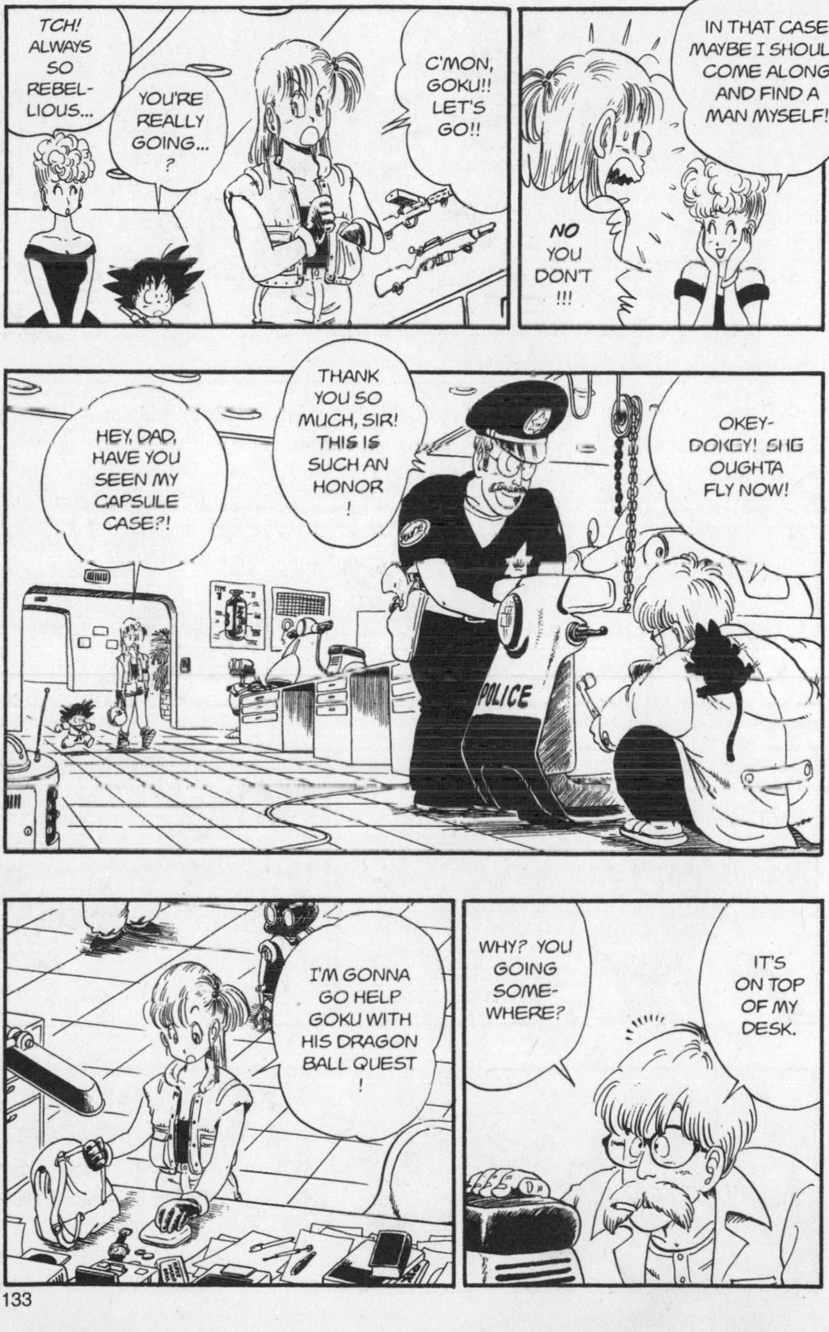
IN THAT CASE MAYBE I SHOULD COME ALONG AND FIND A MAN MYSELF!
NO YOU DON'T !!!
C'MON, GOKU!! LET'S GO!!
TCH! ALWAYS SO REBEL-LIOUS...
YOU'RE REALLY GOING... ?
OKEY-DOKEY! SHE OUGHTA FLY NOW!
THANK YOU SO MUCH, SIR! THIS IS SUCH AN HONOR !
HEY, DAD, HAVE YOU SEEN MY CAPSULE CASE?!
POLICE
IT'S ON TOP OF MY DESK.
WHY? YOU GOING SOME-WHERE?
I'M GONNA GO HELP GOKU WITH HIS DRAGON BALL QUEST !

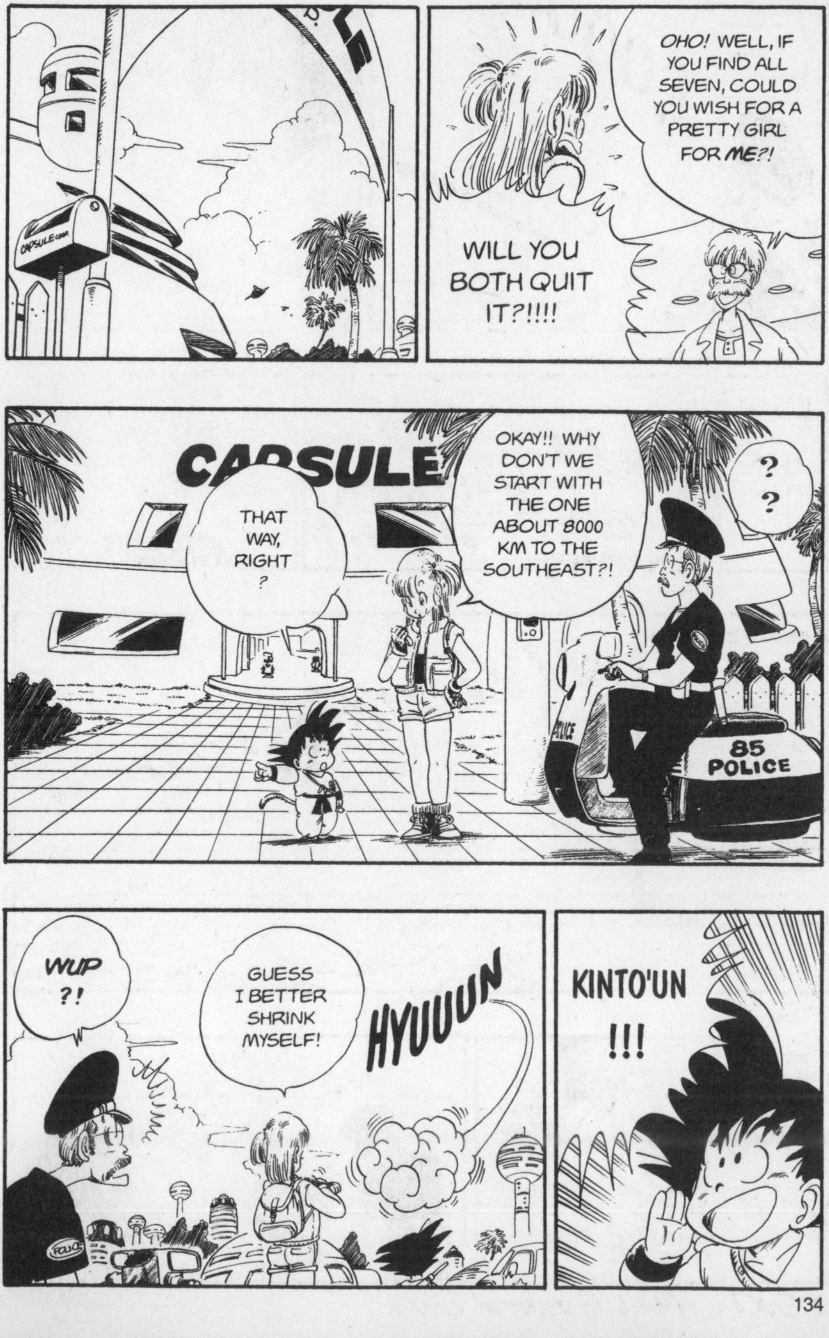
OHO! WELL, IF YOU FIND ALL SEVEN, COULD YOU WISH FOR A PRETTY GIRL FOR *ME*?!
WILL YOU BOTH QUIT IT?!!!!
CAPSULE CORP.
??
OKAY!! WHY DON'T WE START WITH THE ONE ABOUT 8000 KM TO THE SOUTHEAST?!
CAPSULE
THAT WAY, RIGHT?
85 POLICE
KINTO'UN !!!
HYUUUN
GUESS I BETTER SHRINK MYSELF!
WUP?!

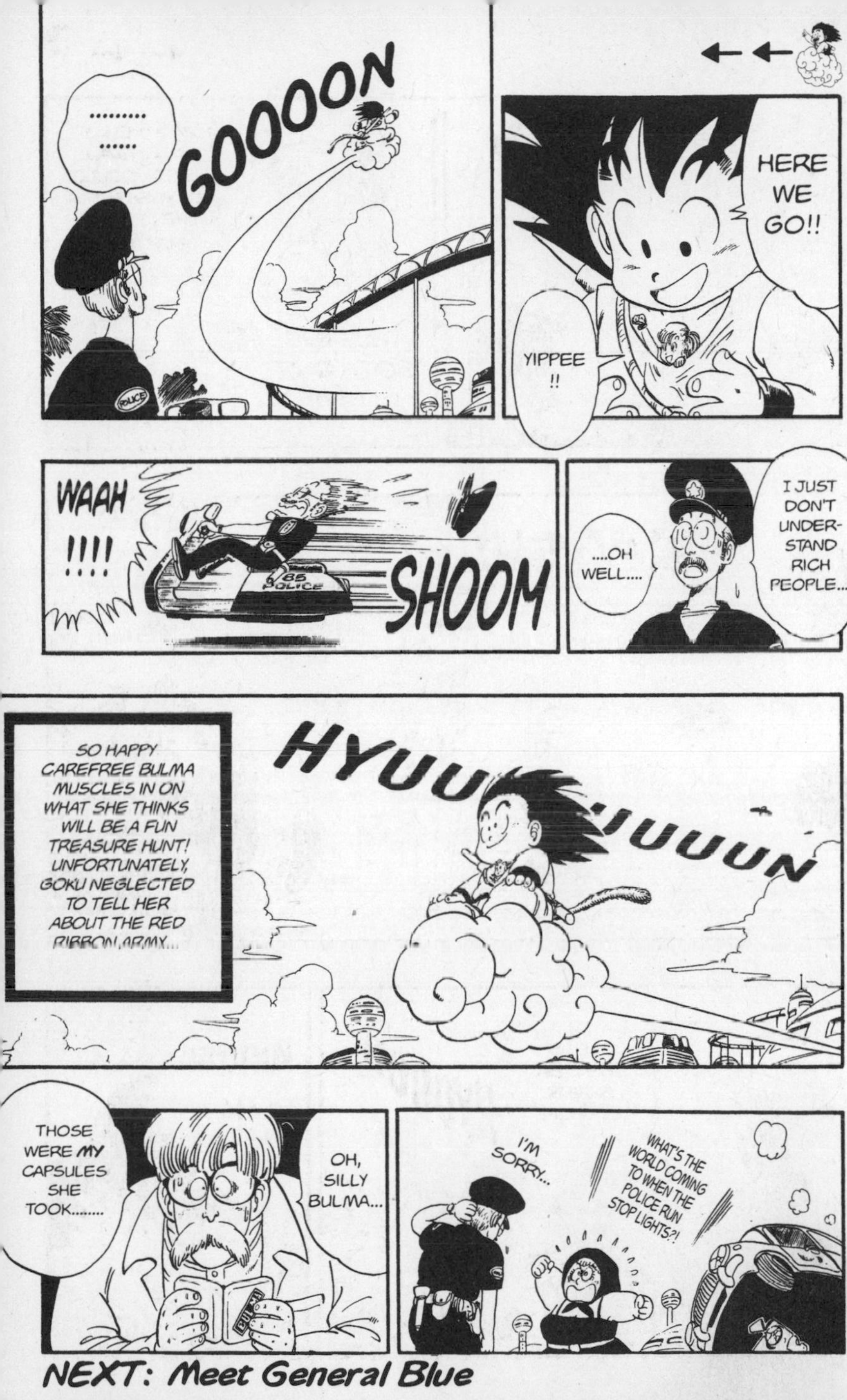
HERE WE GO!!
YIPPEE !!
....
....
GOOOON
I JUST DON'T UNDER-STAND RICH PEOPLE....
....OH WELL....
WAAH !!!!
SHOOM
HYUUUUUUUN
SO HAPPY CAREFREE BULMA MUSCLES IN ON WHAT SHE THINKS WILL BE A FUN TREASURE HUNT! UNFORTUNATELY, GOKU NEGLECTED TO TELL HER ABOUT THE RED RIBBON ARMY...
WHAT'S THE WORLD COMING TO WHEN THE POLICE RUN STOP LIGHTS?!
I'M SORRY...
THOSE WERE MY CAPSULES SHE TOOK........
OH, SILLY BULMA...

NEXT: Meet General Blue

Tale 70
Bulma's Big Mistake!!

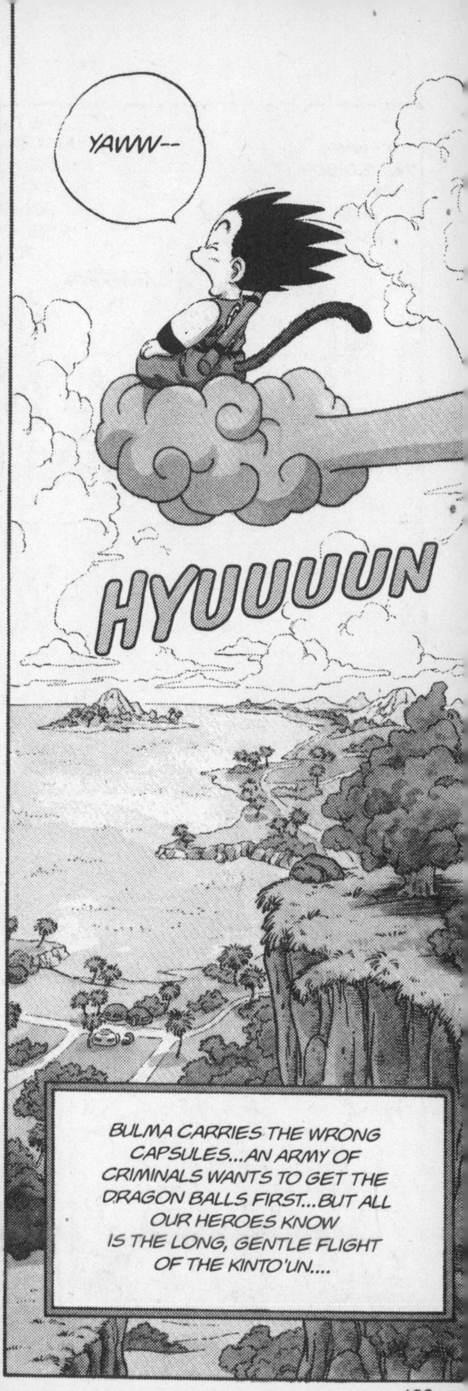
YAWW--
HYUUUUUN
BULMA CARRIES THE WRONG CAPSULES...AN ARMY OF CRIMINALS WANTS TO GET THE DRAGON BALLS FIRST...BUT ALL OUR HEROES KNOW IS THE LONG, GENTLE FLIGHT OF THE KINTO'UN....

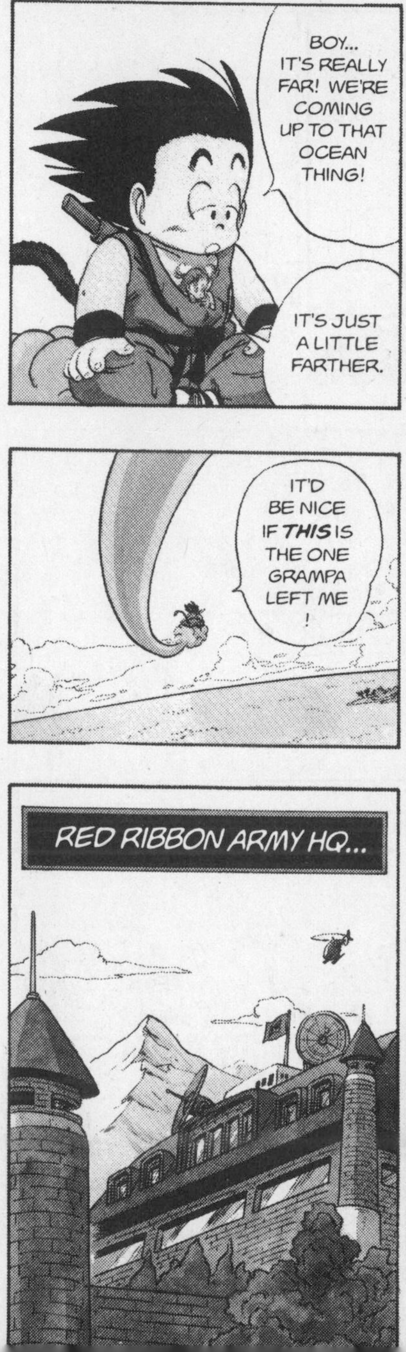
BOY... IT'S REALLY FAR! WE'RE COMING UP TO THAT OCEAN THING!
IT'S JUST A LITTLE FARTHER.
IT'D BE NICE IF **THIS** IS THE ONE GRAMPA LEFT ME!
RED RIBBON ARMY HQ...

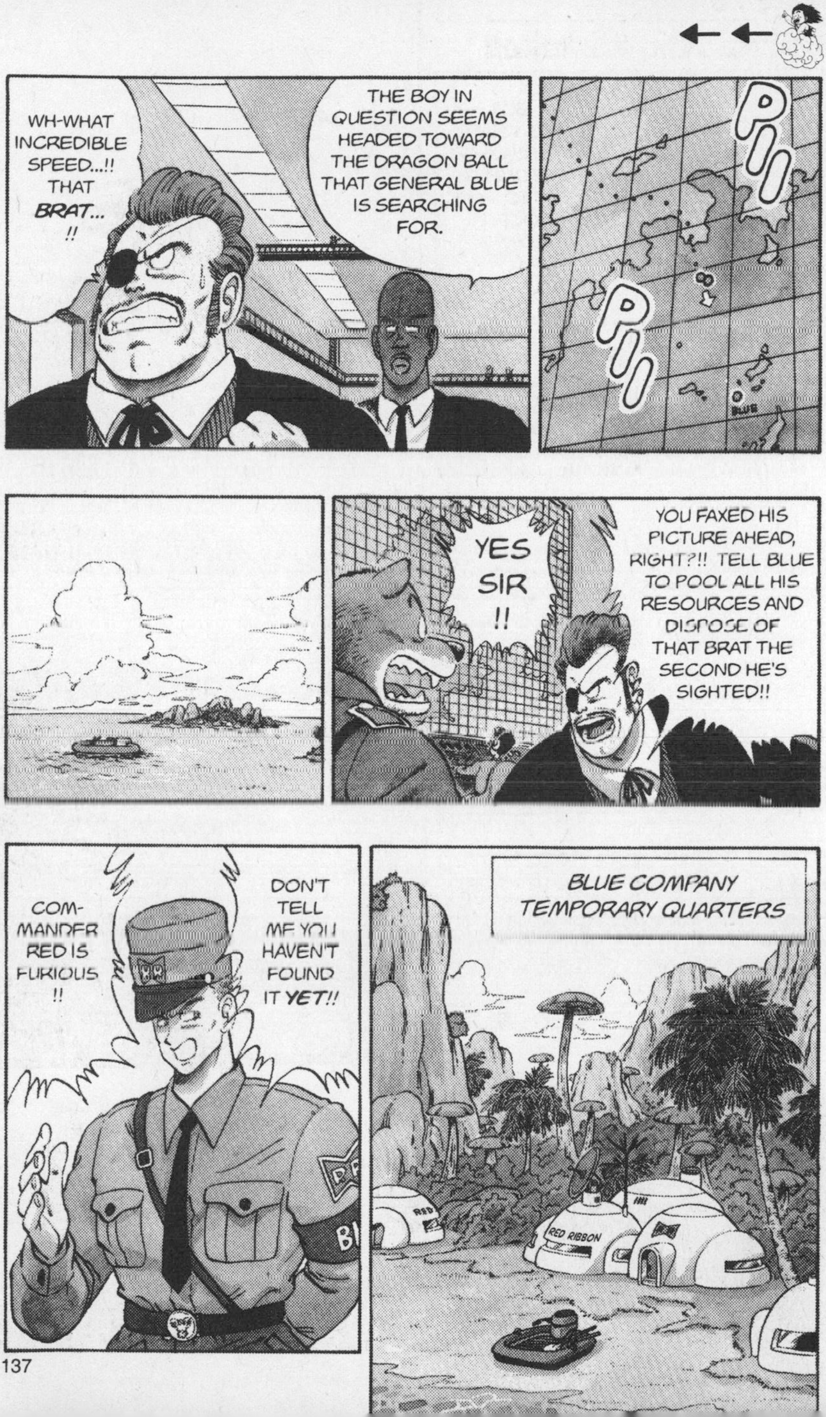
PI
PI
BLUE
THE BOY IN QUESTION SEEMS HEADED TOWARD THE DRAGON BALL THAT GENERAL BLUE IS SEARCHING FOR.
WH-WHAT INCREDIBLE SPEED...!! THAT *BRAT...* !!
YOU FAXED HIS PICTURE AHEAD, RIGHT?!! TELL BLUE TO POOL ALL HIS RESOURCES AND DISPOSE OF THAT BRAT THE SECOND HE'S SIGHTED!!
YES SIR !!
BLUE COMPANY TEMPORARY QUARTERS
RED RIBBON
DON'T TELL ME YOU HAVEN'T FOUND IT *YET*!!
COM-MANDER RED IS FURIOUS !!

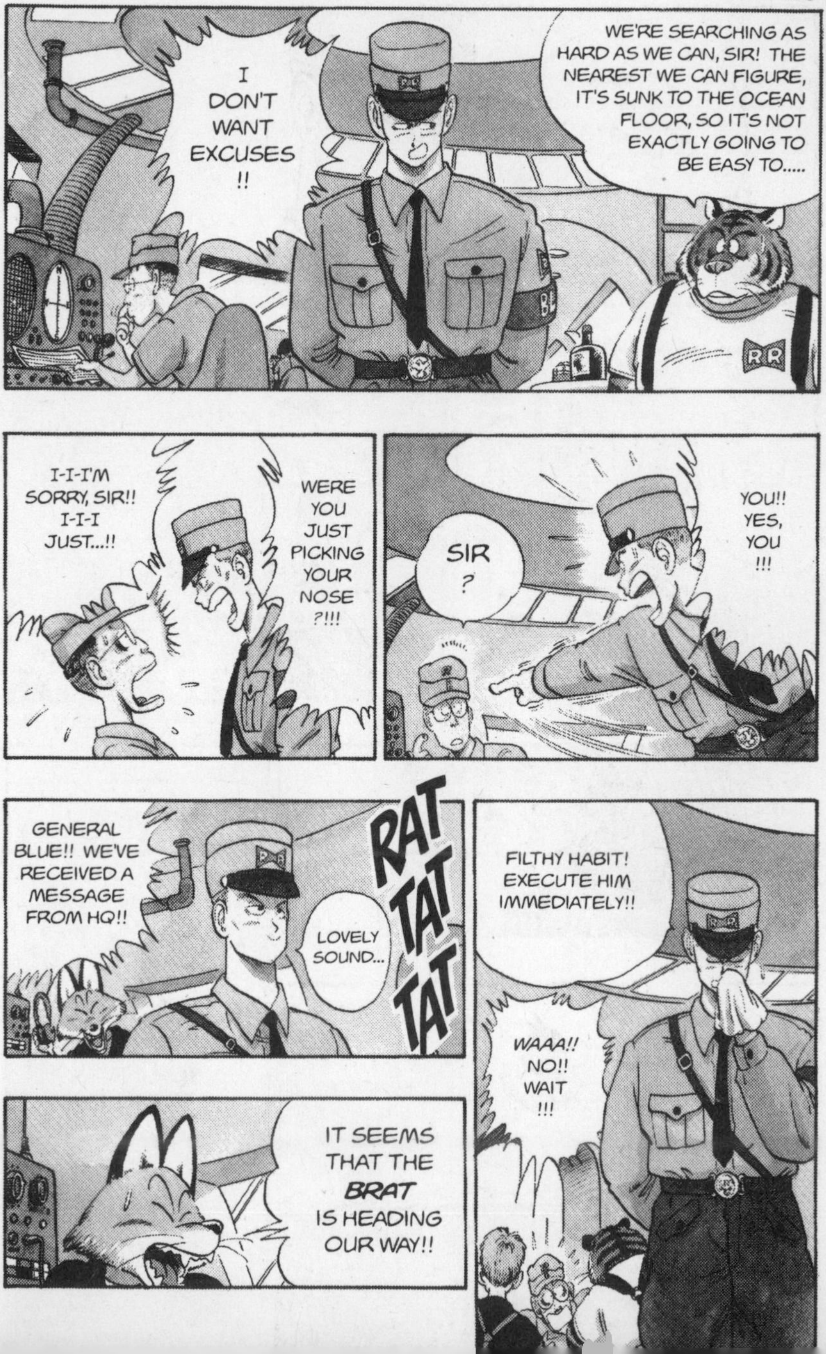
WE'RE SEARCHING AS HARD AS WE CAN, SIR! THE NEAREST WE CAN FIGURE, IT'S SUNK TO THE OCEAN FLOOR, SO IT'S NOT EXACTLY GOING TO BE EASY TO.....
I DON'T WANT EXCUSES!!
YOU!! YES, YOU!!!
SIR?
WERE YOU JUST PICKING YOUR NOSE?!!!
I-I-I'M SORRY, SIR!! I-I-I JUST...!!
FILTHY HABIT! EXECUTE HIM IMMEDIATELY!!
WAAA!! NO!! WAIT!!!
RAT TAT TAT
LOVELY SOUND...
GENERAL BLUE!! WE'VE RECEIVED A MESSAGE FROM HQ!!
IT SEEMS THAT THE *BRAT* IS HEADING OUR WAY!!

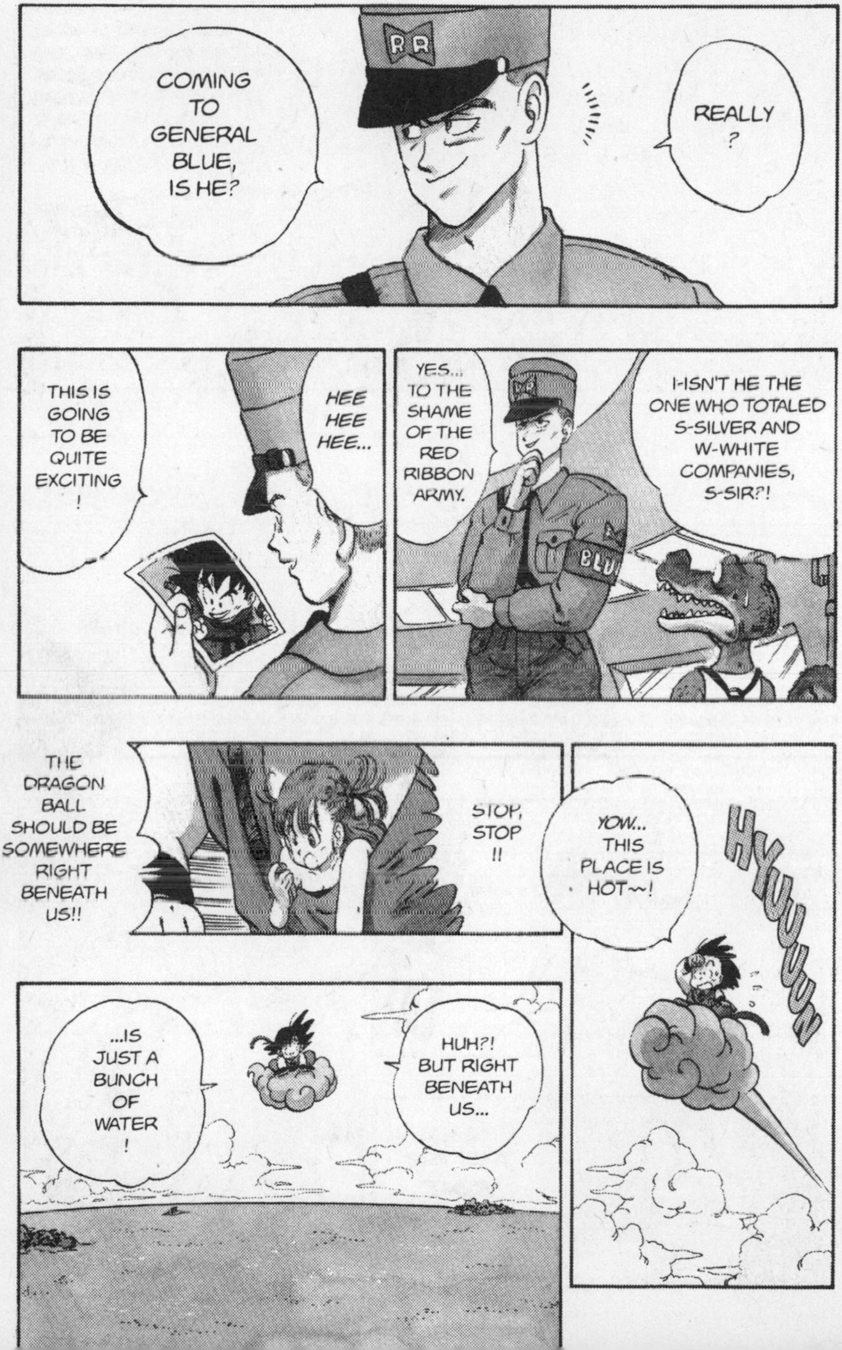
REALLY?
COMING TO GENERAL BLUE, IS HE?
I-ISN'T HE THE ONE WHO TOTALED S-SILVER AND W-WHITE COMPANIES, S-SIR?!
YES... TO THE SHAME OF THE RED RIBBON ARMY.
HEE HEE HEE...
THIS IS GOING TO BE QUITE EXCITING!
HYUUUUN
YOW... THIS PLACE IS HOT~!
STOP, STOP!!
THE DRAGON BALL SHOULD BE SOMEWHERE RIGHT BENEATH US!!
HUH?! BUT RIGHT BENEATH US...
...IS JUST A BUNCH OF WATER!

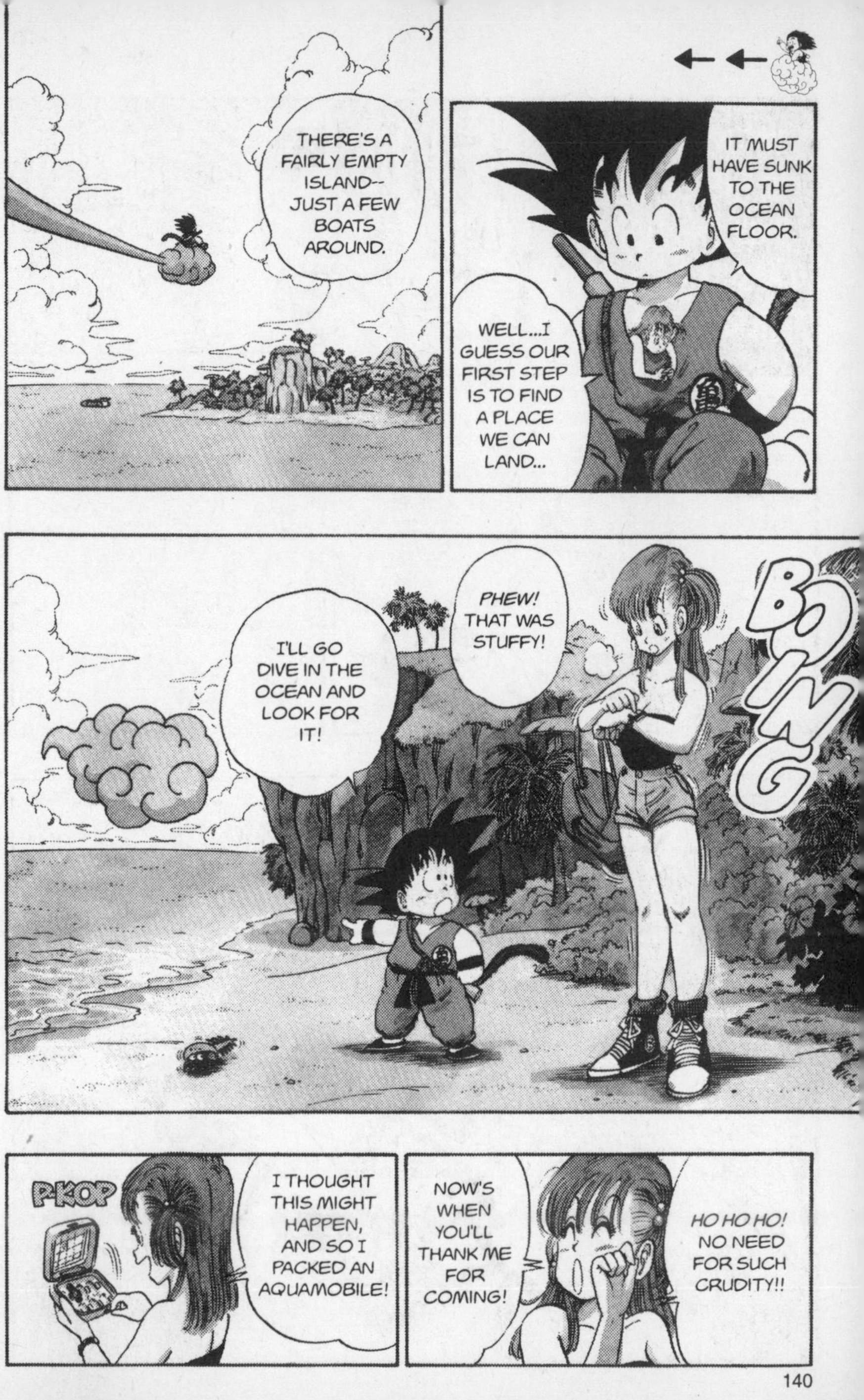
IT MUST HAVE SUNK TO THE OCEAN FLOOR.
WELL...I GUESS OUR FIRST STEP IS TO FIND A PLACE WE CAN LAND...
THERE'S A FAIRLY EMPTY ISLAND-- JUST A FEW BOATS AROUND.
BOING
PHEW! THAT WAS STUFFY!
I'LL GO DIVE IN THE OCEAN AND LOOK FOR IT!
HO HO HO! NO NEED FOR SUCH CRUDITY!!
NOW'S WHEN YOU'LL THANK ME FOR COMING!
P-KOP
I THOUGHT THIS MIGHT HAPPEN, AND SO I PACKED AN AQUAMOBILE!

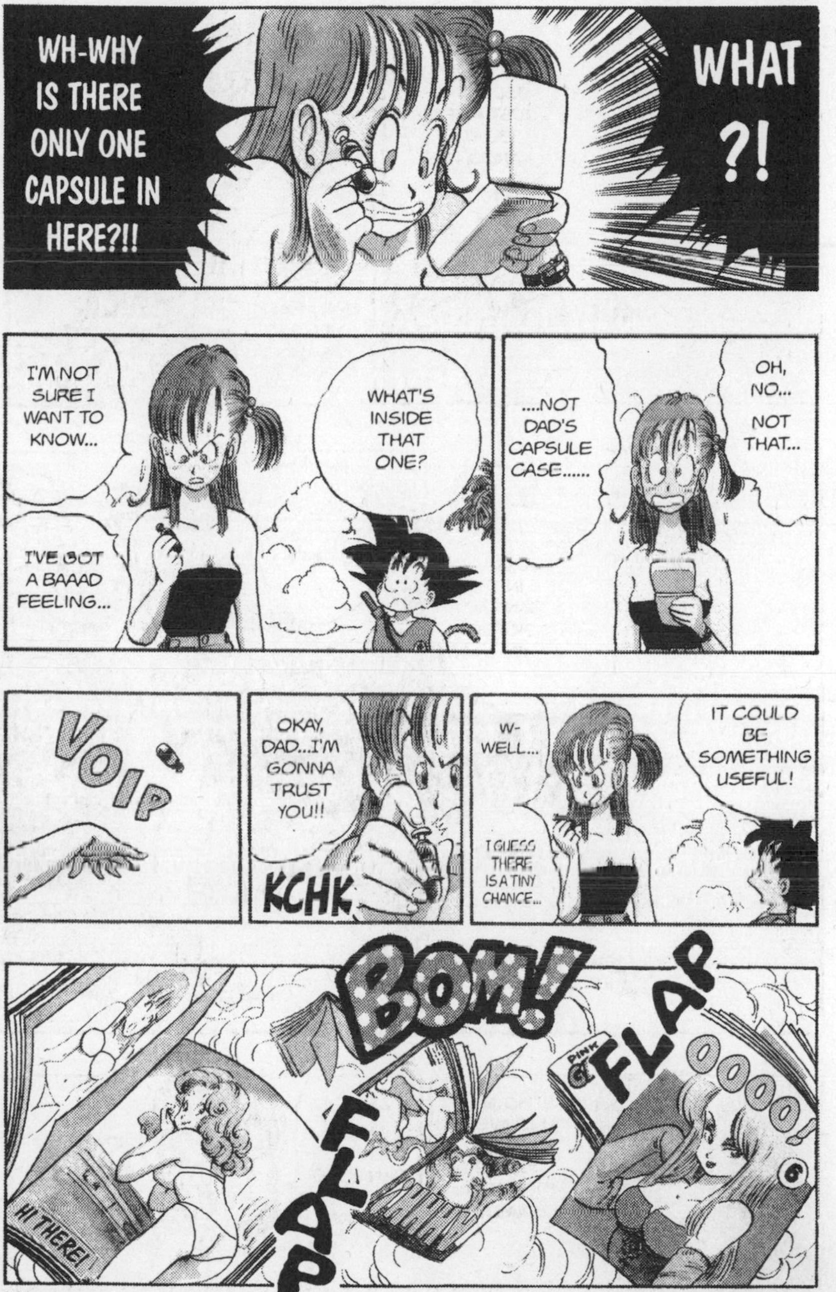
WHAT ?!
WH-WHY IS THERE ONLY ONE CAPSULE IN HERE?!!
OH, NO... NOT THAT...
....NOT DAD'S CAPSULE CASE......
WHAT'S INSIDE THAT ONE?
I'M NOT SURE I WANT TO KNOW...
I'VE GOT A BAAAD FEELING...
IT COULD BE SOMETHING USEFUL!
W-WELL...
I GUESS THERE IS A TINY CHANCE...
OKAY, DAD...I'M GONNA TRUST YOU!!
KCHK
VOIP
FLAP
BOM!
PINK
OOOOO!
FLAP FLAP
HI THERE!

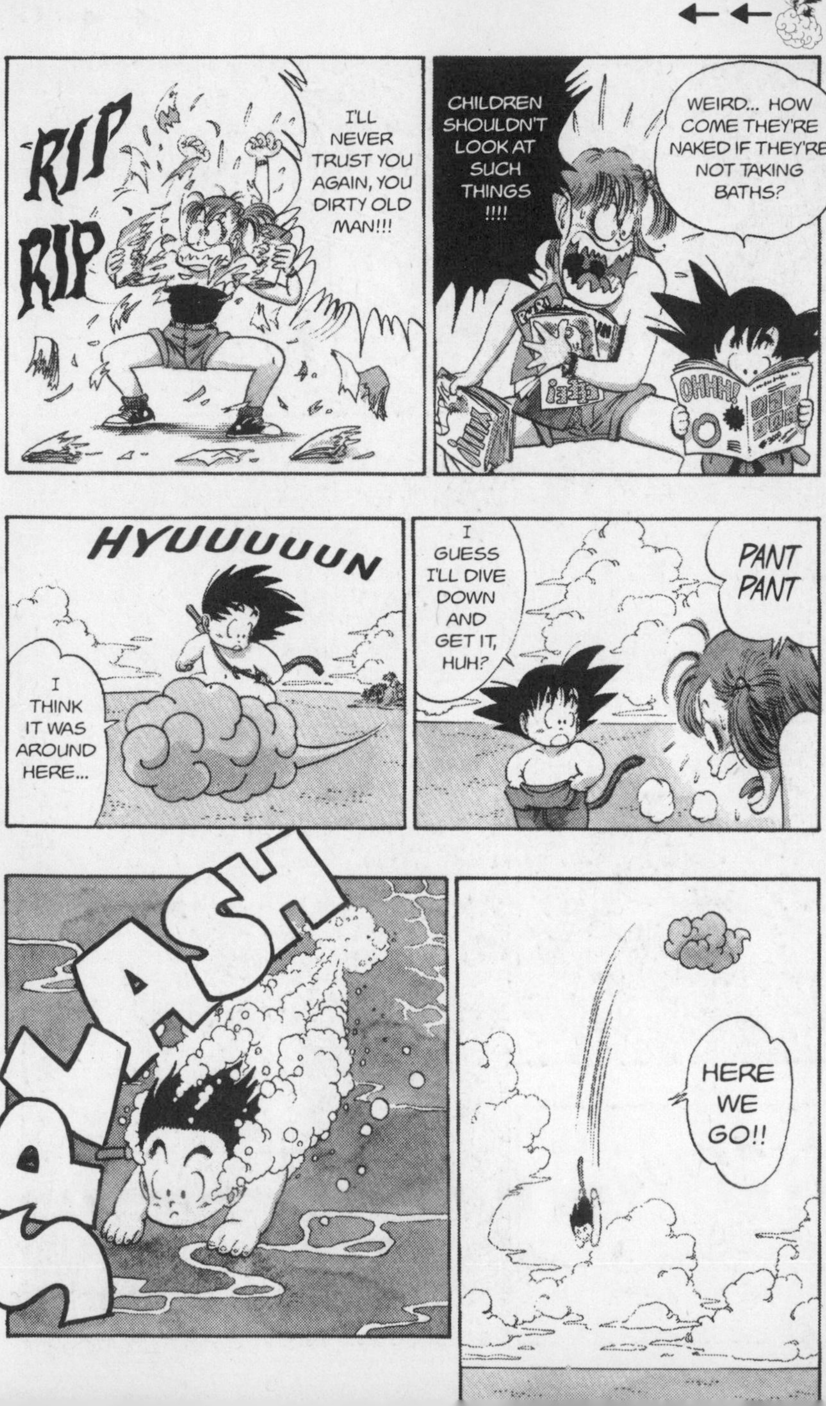
WEIRD... HOW COME THEY'RE NAKED IF THEY'RE NOT TAKING BATHS?
CHILDREN SHOULDN'T LOOK AT SUCH THINGS !!!!
OHHH!
I'LL NEVER TRUST YOU AGAIN, YOU DIRTY OLD MAN!!!
RIP RIP
PANT PANT
I GUESS I'LL DIVE DOWN AND GET IT, HUH?
HYUUUUUUN
I THINK IT WAS AROUND HERE...
HERE WE GO!!
SPLASH

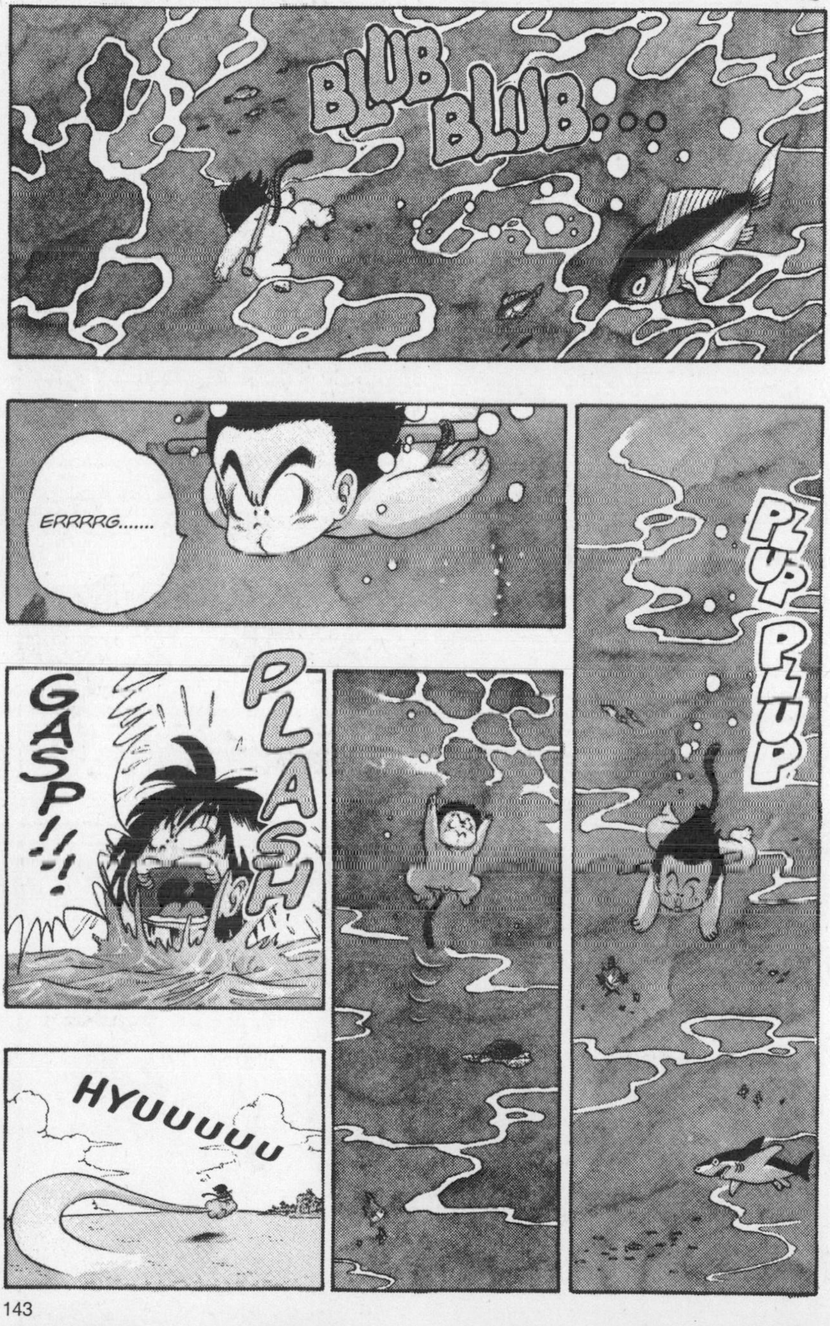
BLUB BLUB
PLUP PLUP PLUP
ERRRRG.......
PLASH
GASP!!!
HYUUUUUU

WE INTERRUPT THIS DULL STORY FOR A THRILLING ANNOUNCEMENT!

GENERAL BLUE IS APPROACHING!!

WHAT WILL HAPPEN?! READ THE NEXT DRAGON BALL!!

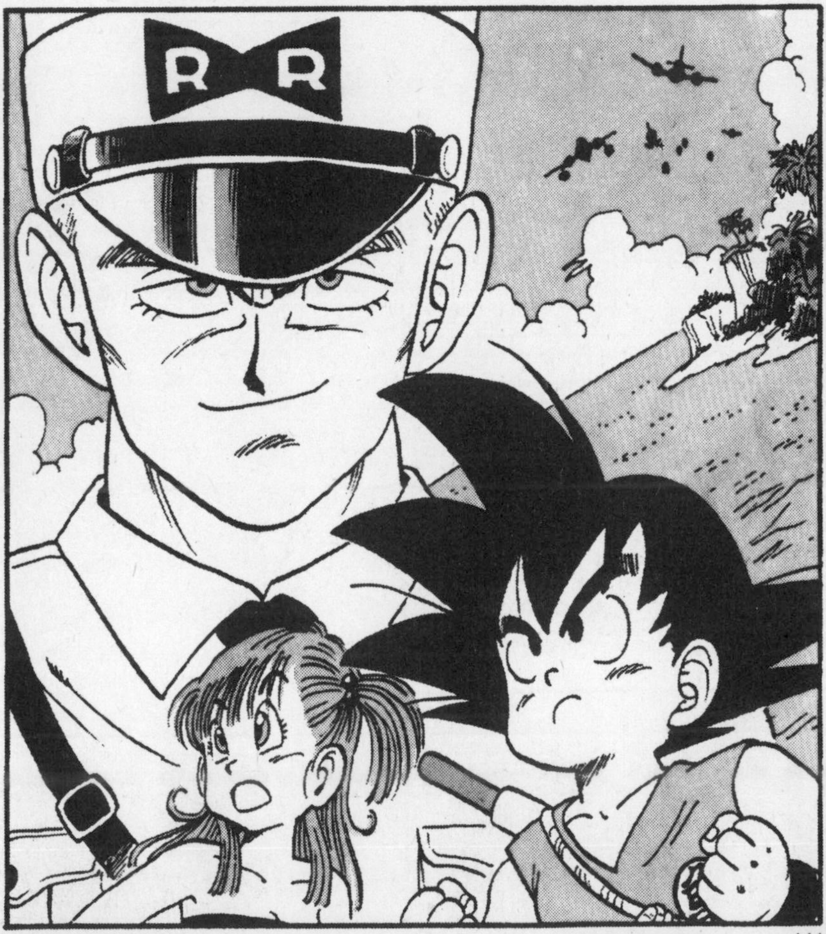

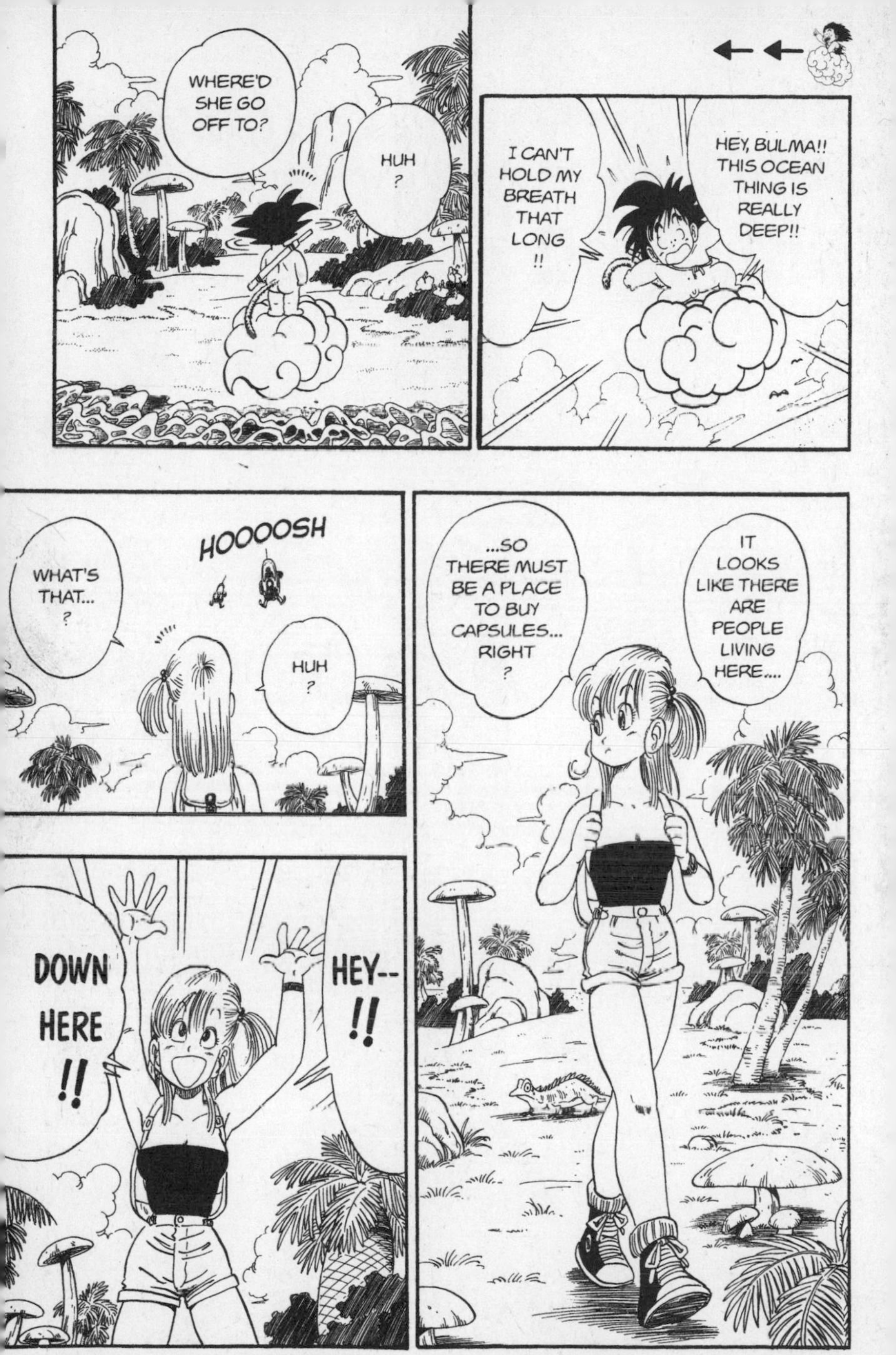
HEY, BULMA!! THIS OCEAN THING IS REALLY DEEP!!
I CAN'T HOLD MY BREATH THAT LONG !!
HUH ?
WHERE'D SHE GO OFF TO?
IT LOOKS LIKE THERE ARE PEOPLE LIVING HERE....
...SO THERE MUST BE A PLACE TO BUY CAPSULES... RIGHT ?
HOOOOSH
HUH ?
WHAT'S THAT... ?
HEY-- !!
DOWN HERE !!

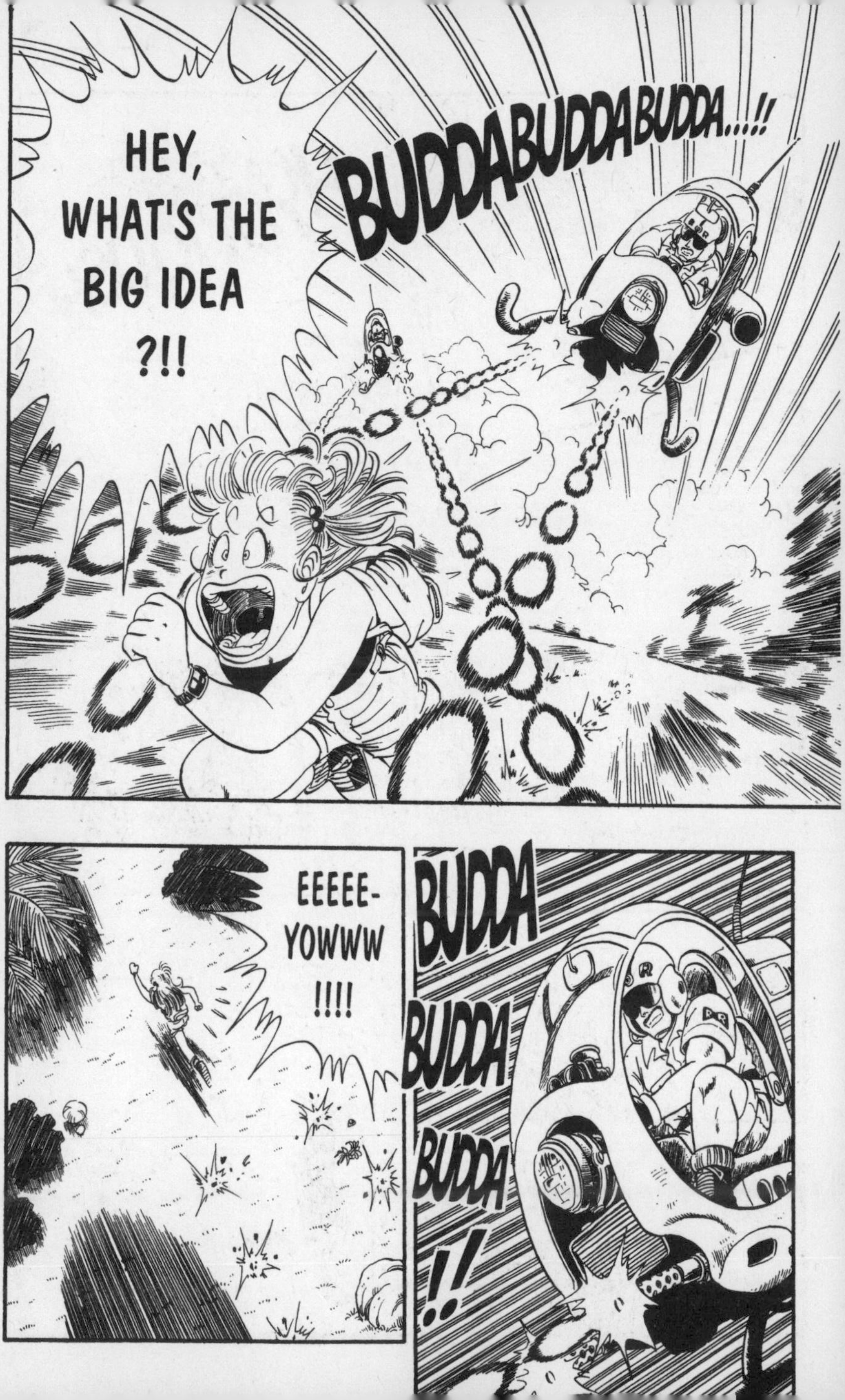
BUDDABUDDABUDDA...!!
HEY, WHAT'S THE BIG IDEA ?!!
BUDDA BUDDA BUDDA !!
EEEEE-YOWWW !!!!

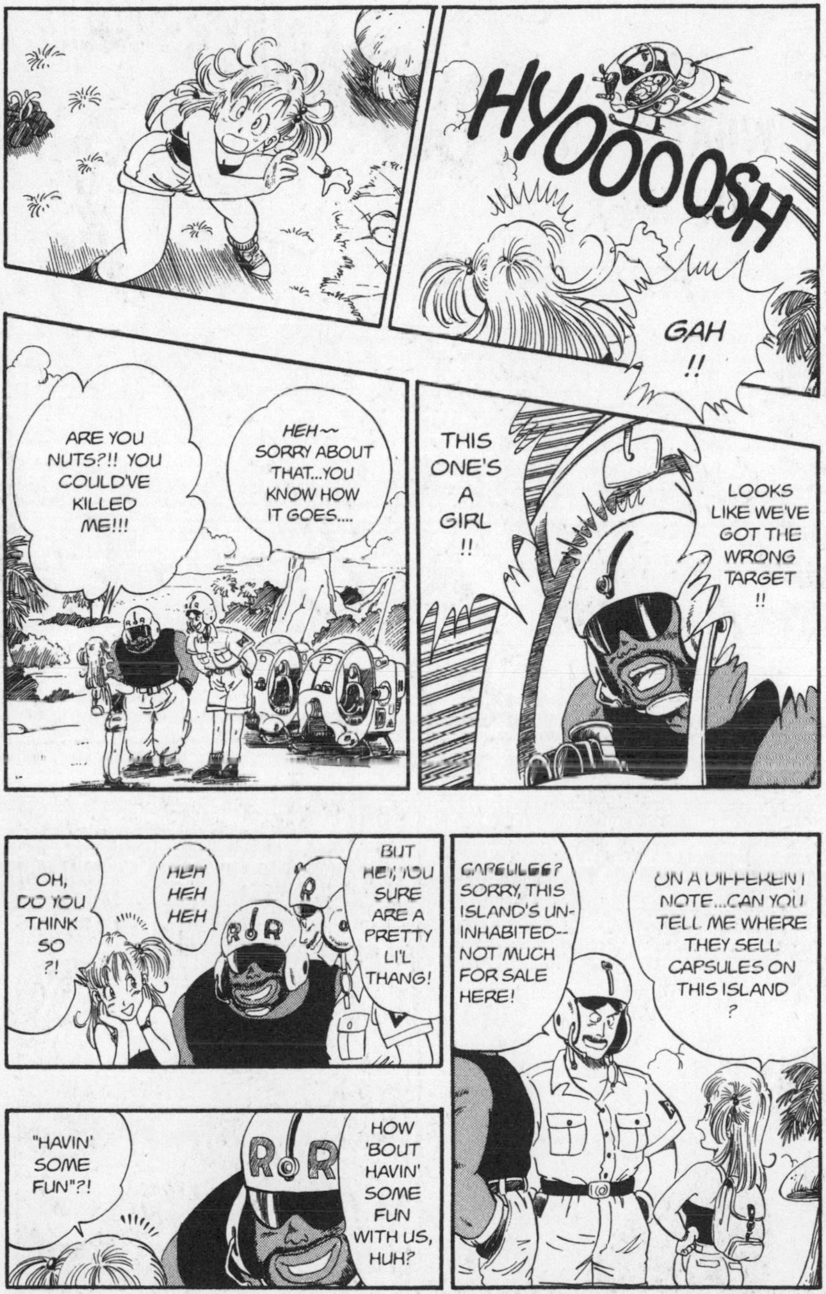
HYOOOOSH
GAH!!
LOOKS LIKE WE'VE GOT THE WRONG TARGET!!
THIS ONE'S A GIRL!!
HEH~ SORRY ABOUT THAT...YOU KNOW HOW IT GOES....
ARE YOU NUTS?!! YOU COULD'VE KILLED ME!!!
ON A DIFFERENT NOTE...CAN YOU TELL ME WHERE THEY SELL CAPSULES ON THIS ISLAND?
CAPSULES? SORRY, THIS ISLAND'S UN-INHABITED--NOT MUCH FOR SALE HERE!
BUT HEY, YOU SURE ARE A PRETTY LI'L THANG!
HEH HEH HEH
OH, DO YOU THINK SO?!
HOW 'BOUT HAVIN' SOME FUN WITH US, HUH?
"HAVIN' SOME FUN"?!

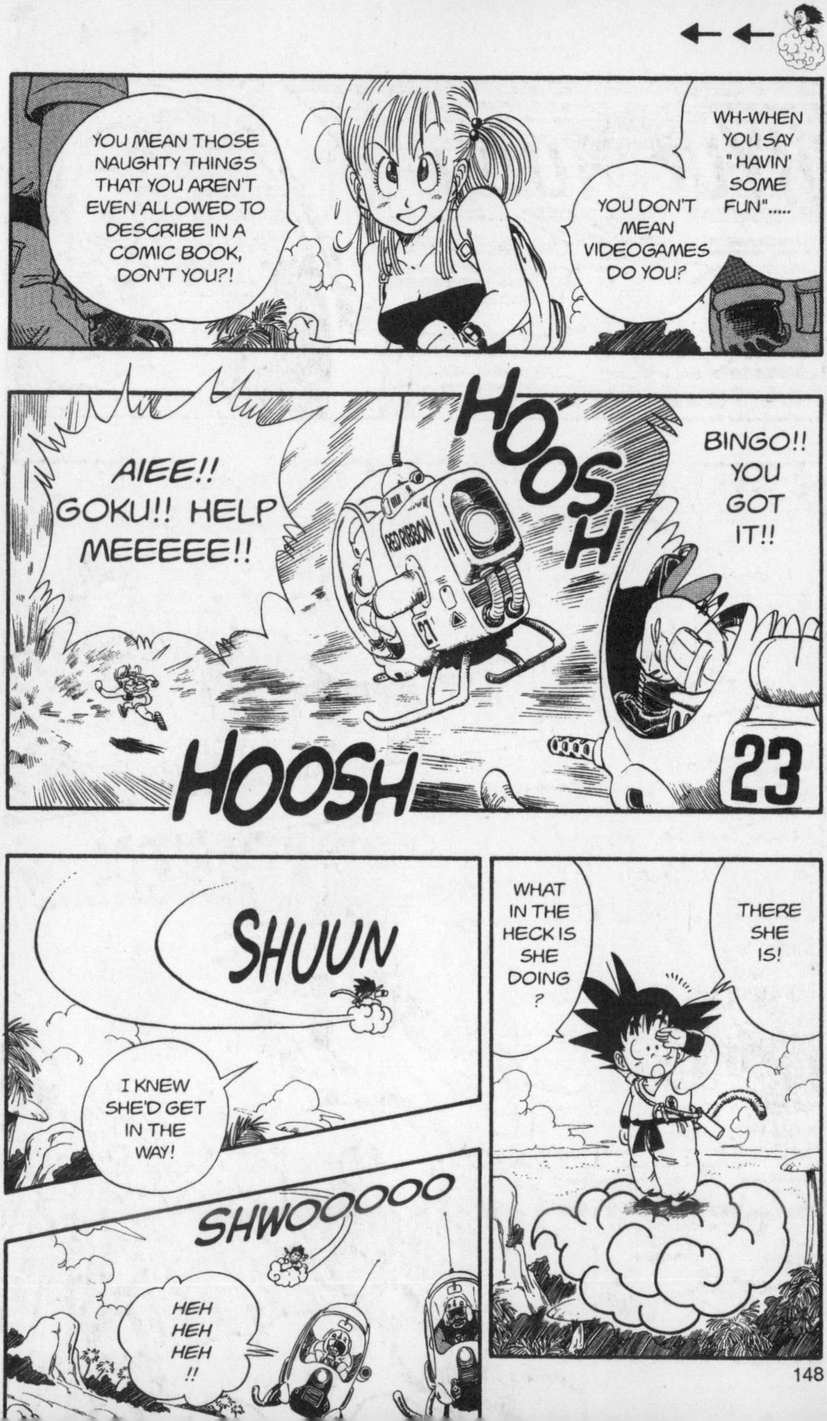
WH-WHEN YOU SAY "HAVIN' SOME FUN".....
YOU DON'T MEAN VIDEOGAMES DO YOU?
YOU MEAN THOSE NAUGHTY THINGS THAT YOU AREN'T EVEN ALLOWED TO DESCRIBE IN A COMIC BOOK, DON'T YOU?!
BINGO!! YOU GOT IT!!
HOOSH
RED RIBBON
27
AIEE!! GOKU!! HELP MEEEEE!!
HOOSH
23
THERE SHE IS!
WHAT IN THE HECK IS SHE DOING ?
SHUUN
I KNEW SHE'D GET IN THE WAY!
SHWOOOOO
HEH HEH HEH !!

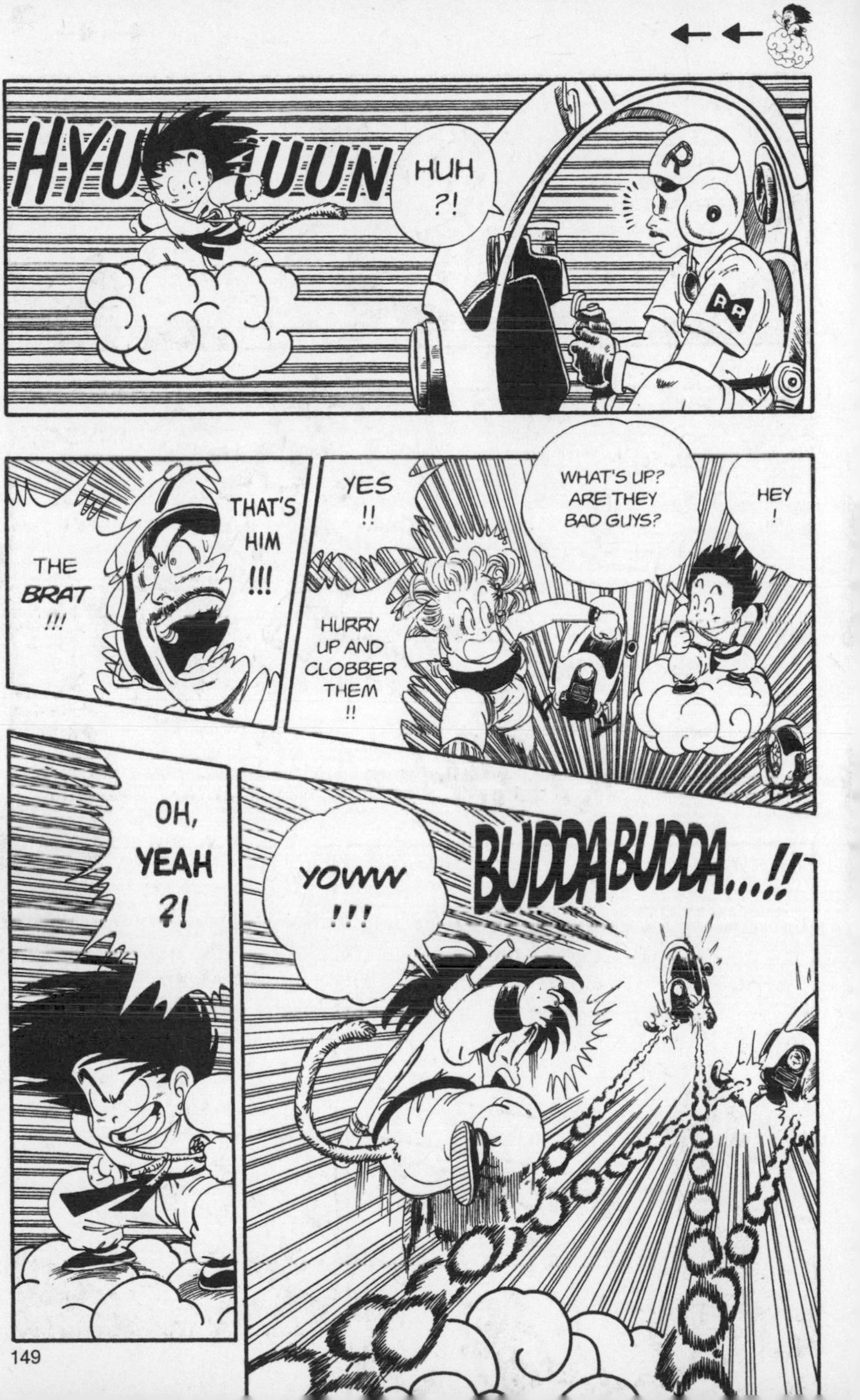
HUH ?!
HYU UUN
HEY !
WHAT'S UP? ARE THEY BAD GUYS?
YES !!
HURRY UP AND CLOBBER THEM !!
THAT'S HIM !!!
THE *BRAT* !!!
BUDDABUDDA...!!
YOWW !!!
OH, YEAH ?!

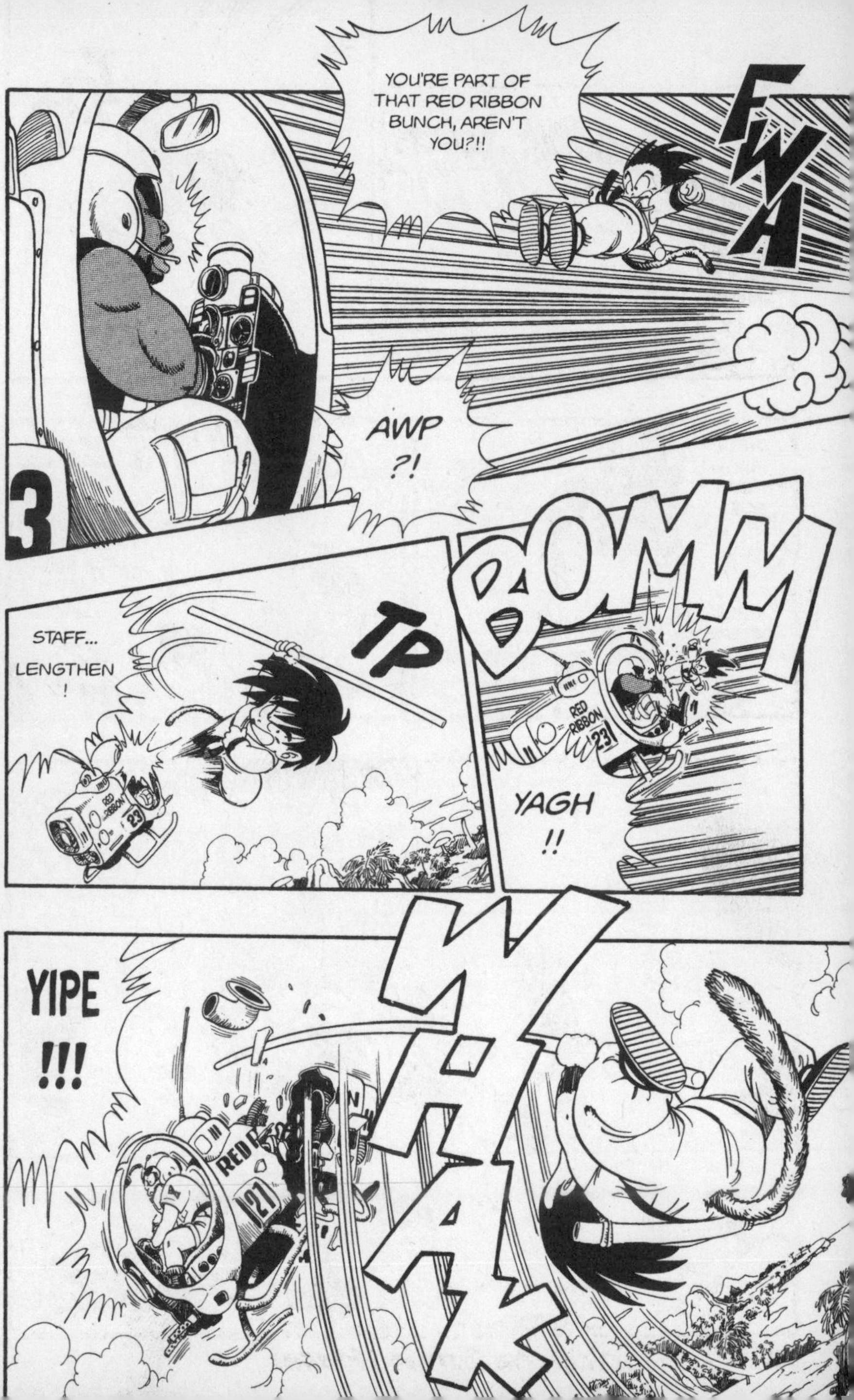
YOU'RE PART OF THAT RED RIBBON BUNCH, AREN'T YOU?!!
FWA
AWP ?!
BOMM
YAGH !!
TP
STAFF... LENGTHEN !
WHAK
YIPE !!!

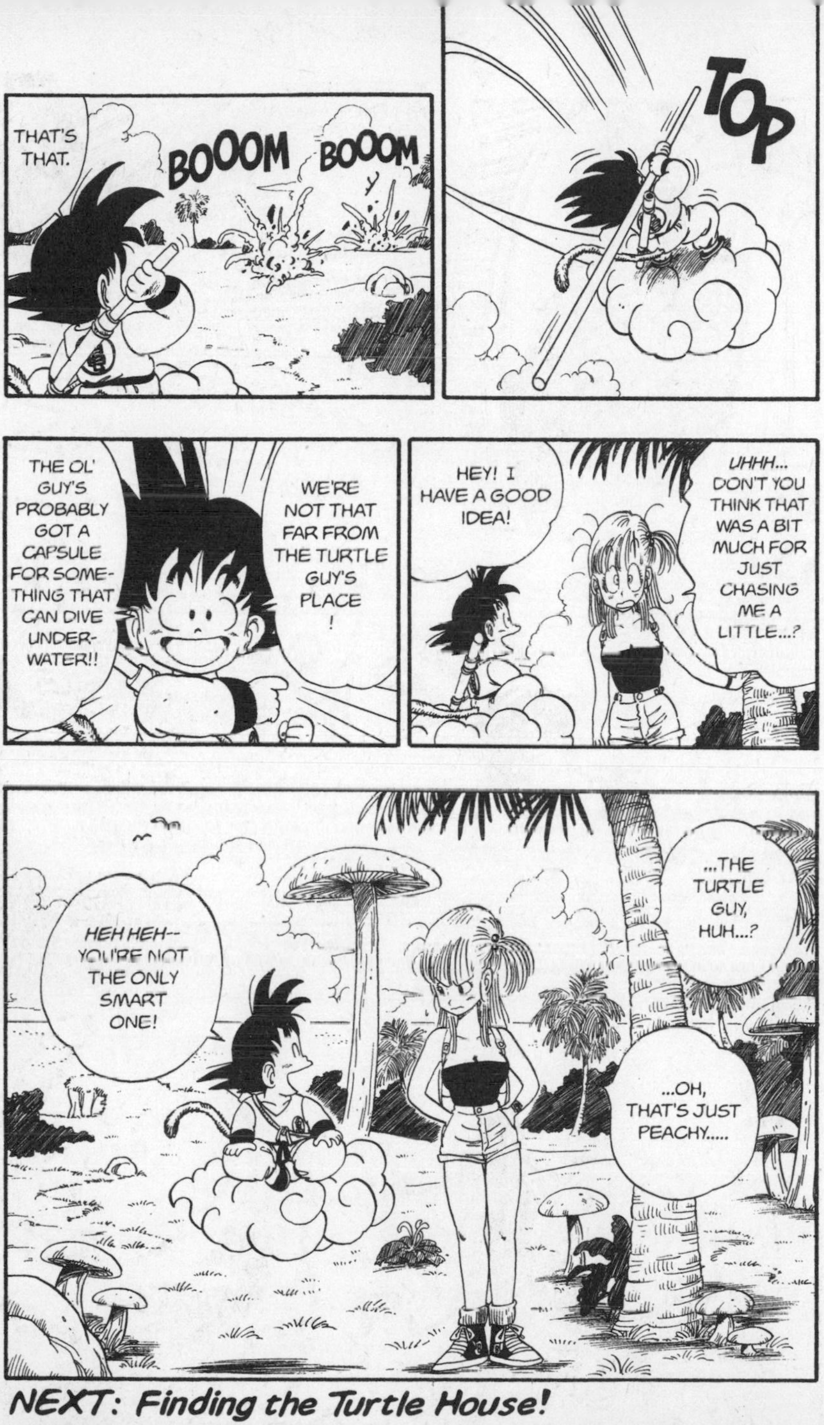
TOP
THAT'S THAT.
BOOOM
BOOOM
UHHH... DON'T YOU THINK THAT WAS A BIT MUCH FOR JUST CHASING ME A LITTLE...?
HEY! I HAVE A GOOD IDEA!
WE'RE NOT THAT FAR FROM THE TURTLE GUY'S PLACE!
THE OL' GUY'S PROBABLY GOT A CAPSULE FOR SOMETHING THAT CAN DIVE UNDERWATER!!
...THE TURTLE GUY, HUH...?
HEH HEH-- YOU'RE NOT THE ONLY SMART ONE!
...OH, THAT'S JUST PEACHY.....

NEXT: Finding the Turtle House!

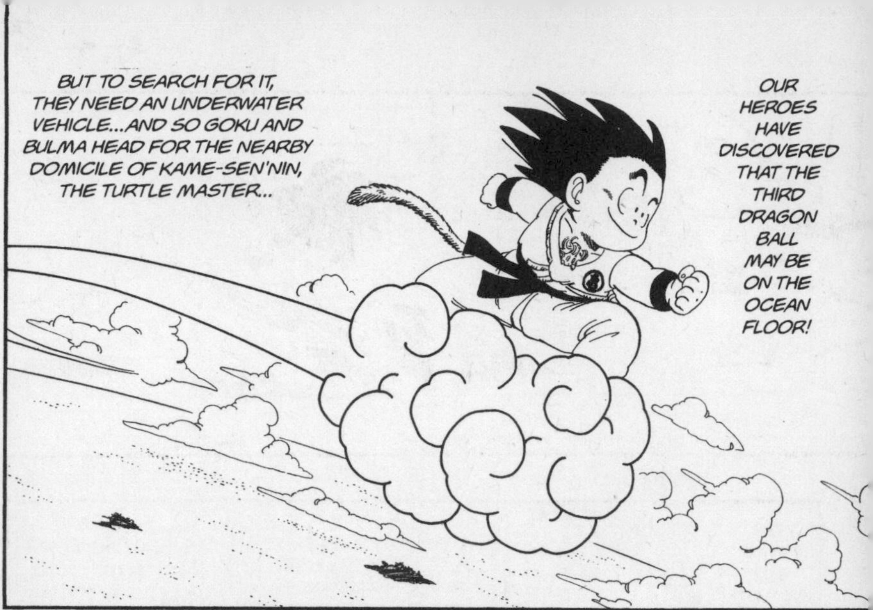
OUR HEROES HAVE DISCOVERED THAT THE THIRD DRAGON BALL MAY BE ON THE OCEAN FLOOR!
BUT TO SEARCH FOR IT, THEY NEED AN UNDERWATER VEHICLE...AND SO GOKU AND BULMA HEAD FOR THE NEARBY DOMICILE OF KAME-SEN'NIN, THE TURTLE MASTER...

Tale 71 • The Turtle is Spotted!

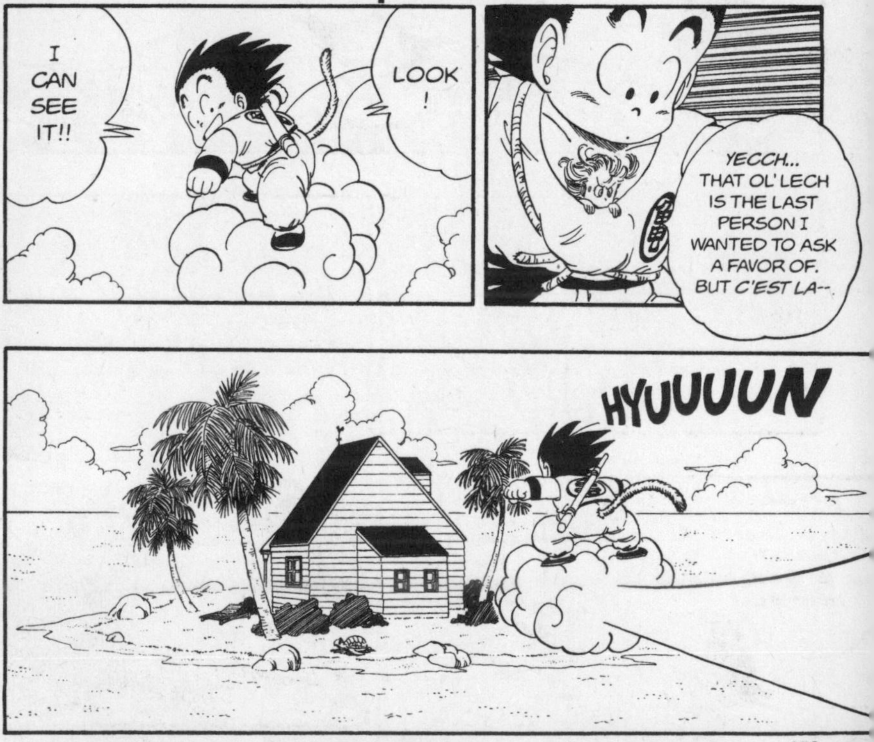
YECCH... THAT OL' LECH IS THE LAST PERSON I WANTED TO ASK A FAVOR OF. BUT C'EST LA--
LOOK!
I CAN SEE IT!!
HYUUUUN

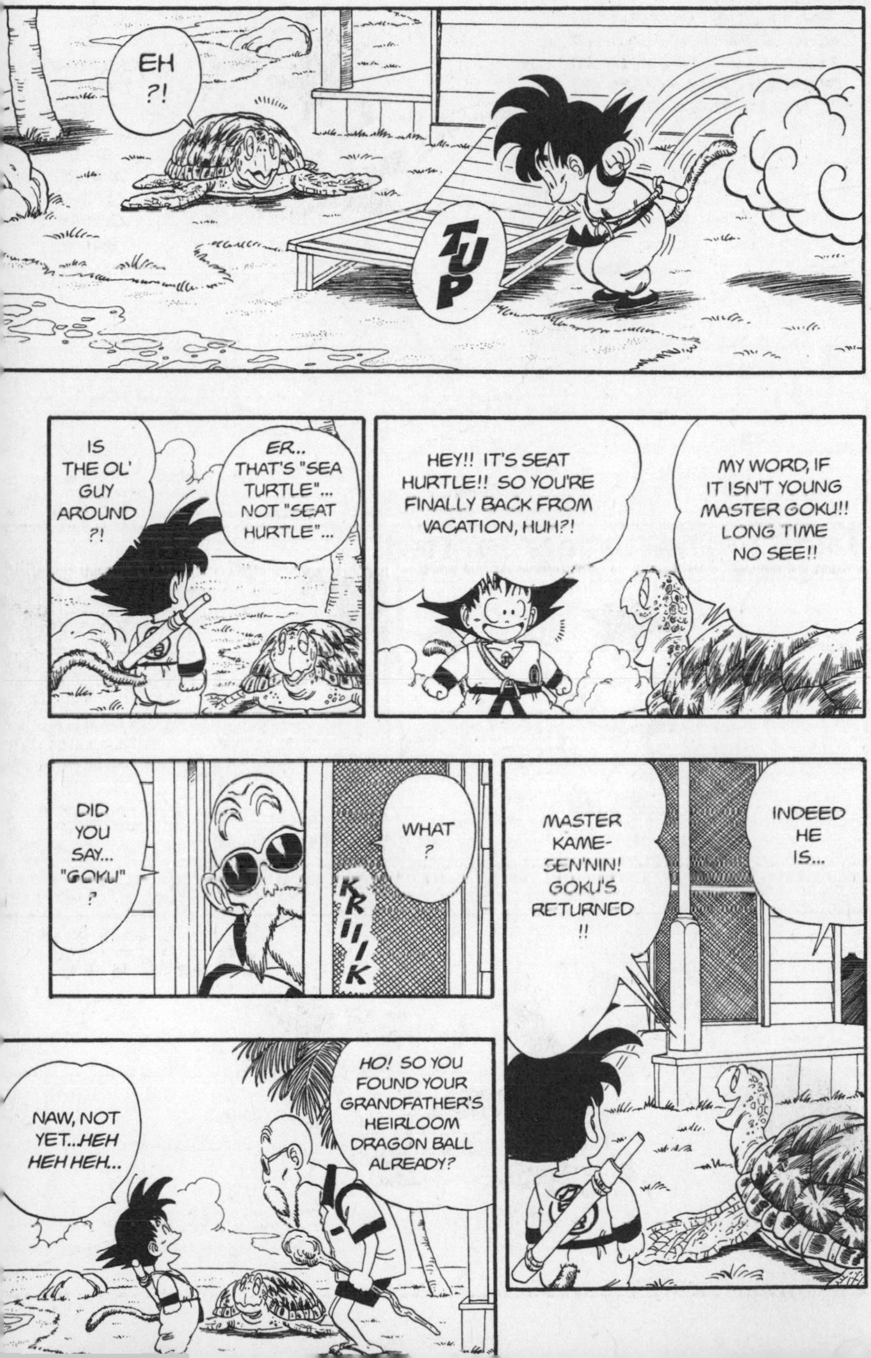
EH ?!
TUP
MY WORD, IF IT ISN'T YOUNG MASTER GOKU!! LONG TIME NO SEE!!
HEY!! IT'S SEAT HURTLE!! SO YOU'RE FINALLY BACK FROM VACATION, HUH?!
ER.. THAT'S "SEA TURTLE"... NOT "SEAT HURTLE"...
IS THE OL' GUY AROUND ?!
INDEED HE IS...
MASTER KAME-SEN'NIN! GOKU'S RETURNED !!
WHAT ?
KRIIIK
DID YOU SAY... "GOKU" ?
HO! SO YOU FOUND YOUR GRANDFATHER'S HEIRLOOM DRAGON BALL ALREADY?
NAW, NOT YET...HEH HEH HEH...

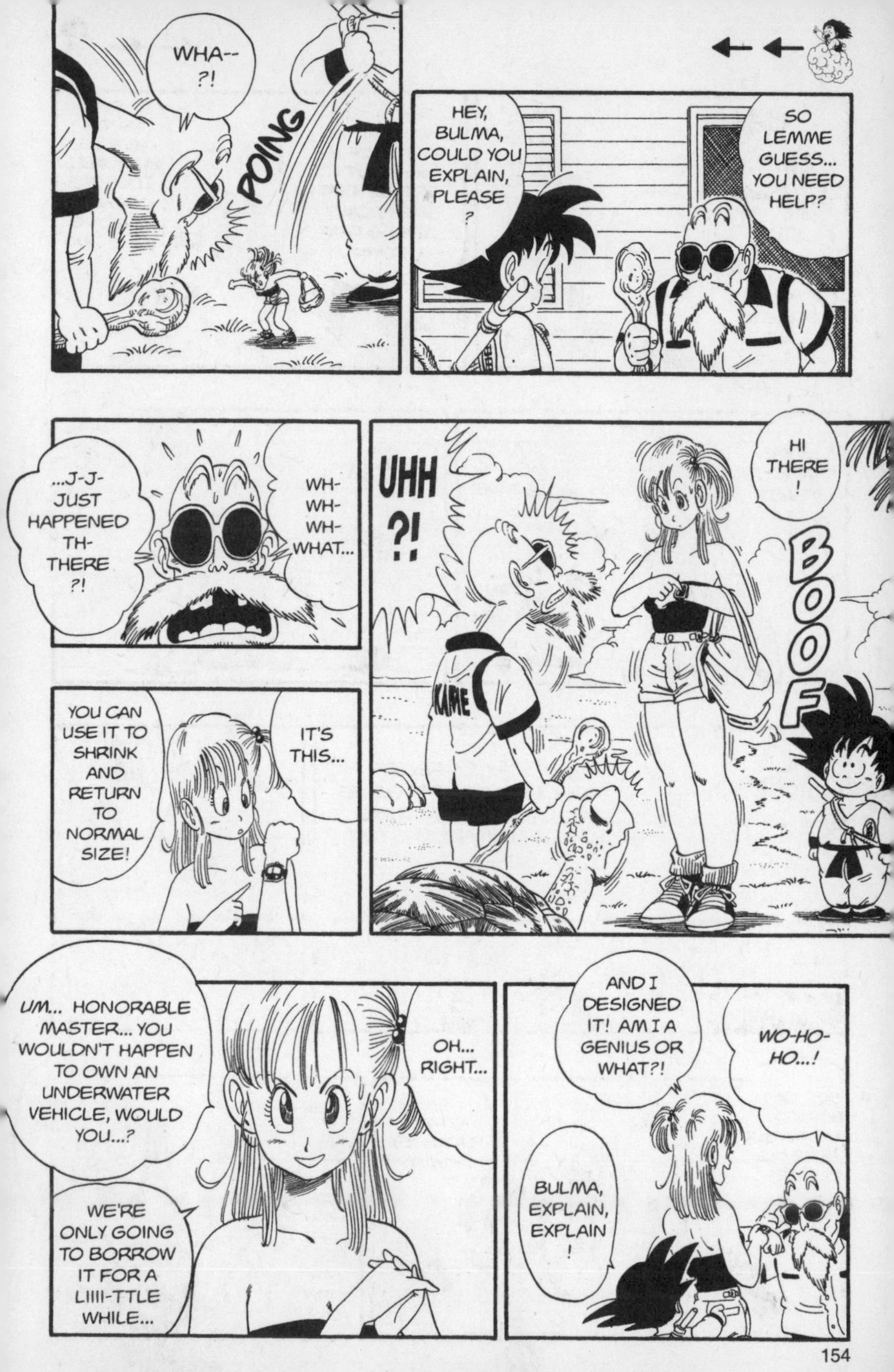
SO LEMME GUESS... YOU NEED HELP?
HEY, BULMA, COULD YOU EXPLAIN, PLEASE ?
POING
WHA-- ?!
HI THERE !
BOOF
UHH ?!
WH- WH- WH- WHAT...
...J-J- JUST HAPPENED TH- THERE ?!
IT'S THIS...
YOU CAN USE IT TO SHRINK AND RETURN TO NORMAL SIZE!
WO-HO-HO...!
AND I DESIGNED IT! AM I A GENIUS OR WHAT?!
BULMA, EXPLAIN, EXPLAIN !
OH... RIGHT...
UM... HONORABLE MASTER... YOU WOULDN'T HAPPEN TO OWN AN UNDERWATER VEHICLE, WOULD YOU...?
WE'RE ONLY GOING TO BORROW IT FOR A LIIII-TTLE WHILE...

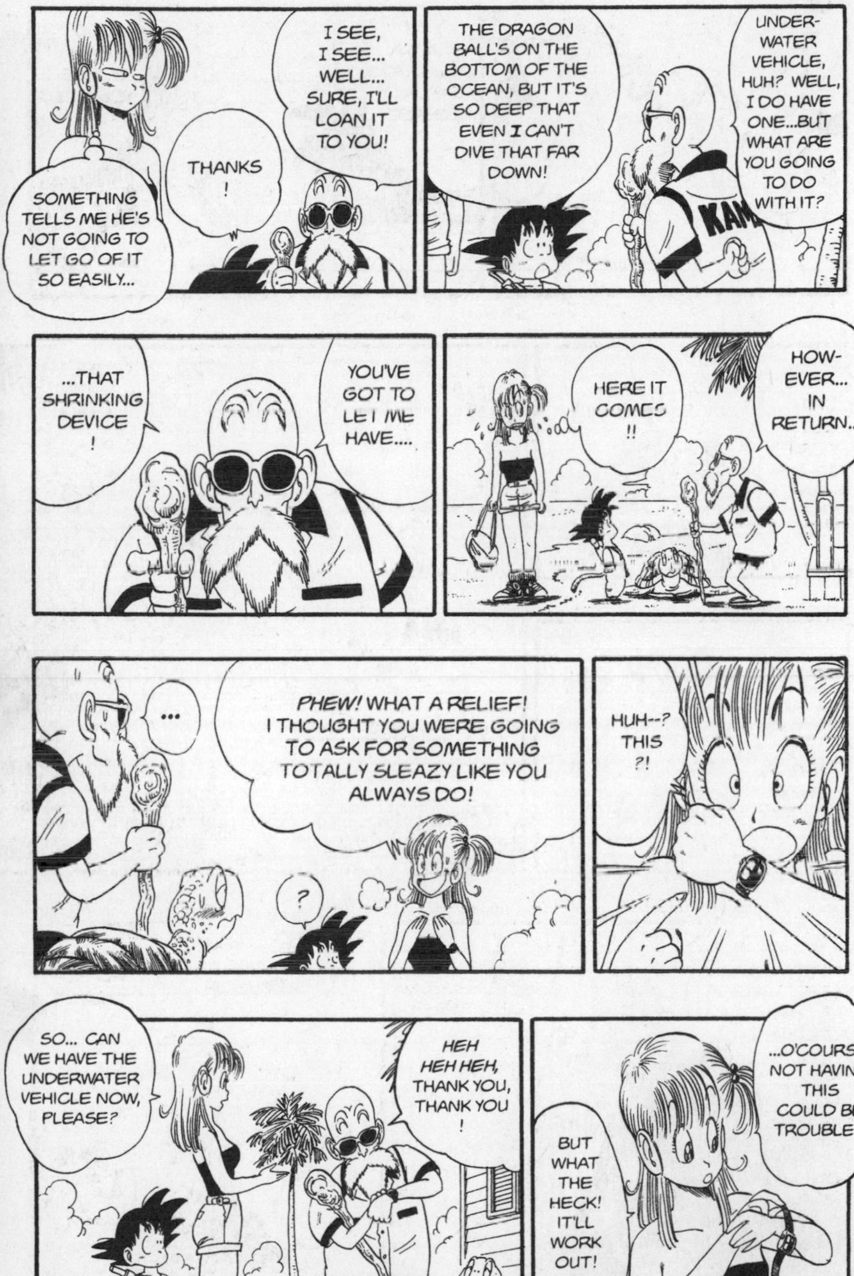
UNDER-WATER VEHICLE, HUH? WELL, I DO HAVE ONE...BUT WHAT ARE YOU GOING TO DO WITH IT?
THE DRAGON BALL'S ON THE BOTTOM OF THE OCEAN, BUT IT'S SO DEEP THAT EVEN I CAN'T DIVE THAT FAR DOWN!
I SEE, I SEE... WELL... SURE, I'LL LOAN IT TO YOU!
THANKS!
SOMETHING TELLS ME HE'S NOT GOING TO LET GO OF IT SO EASILY...
HOW-EVER... IN RETURN...
HERE IT COMES!!
YOU'VE GOT TO LET ME HAVE....
...THAT SHRINKING DEVICE!
HUH--? THIS?!
PHEW! WHAT A RELIEF! I THOUGHT YOU WERE GOING TO ASK FOR SOMETHING TOTALLY SLEAZY LIKE YOU ALWAYS DO!
...
?
...O'COURSE, NOT HAVING THIS COULD BE TROUBLE...
BUT WHAT THE HECK! IT'LL WORK OUT!
HEH HEH HEH, THANK YOU, THANK YOU!
SO... CAN WE HAVE THE UNDERWATER VEHICLE NOW, PLEASE?

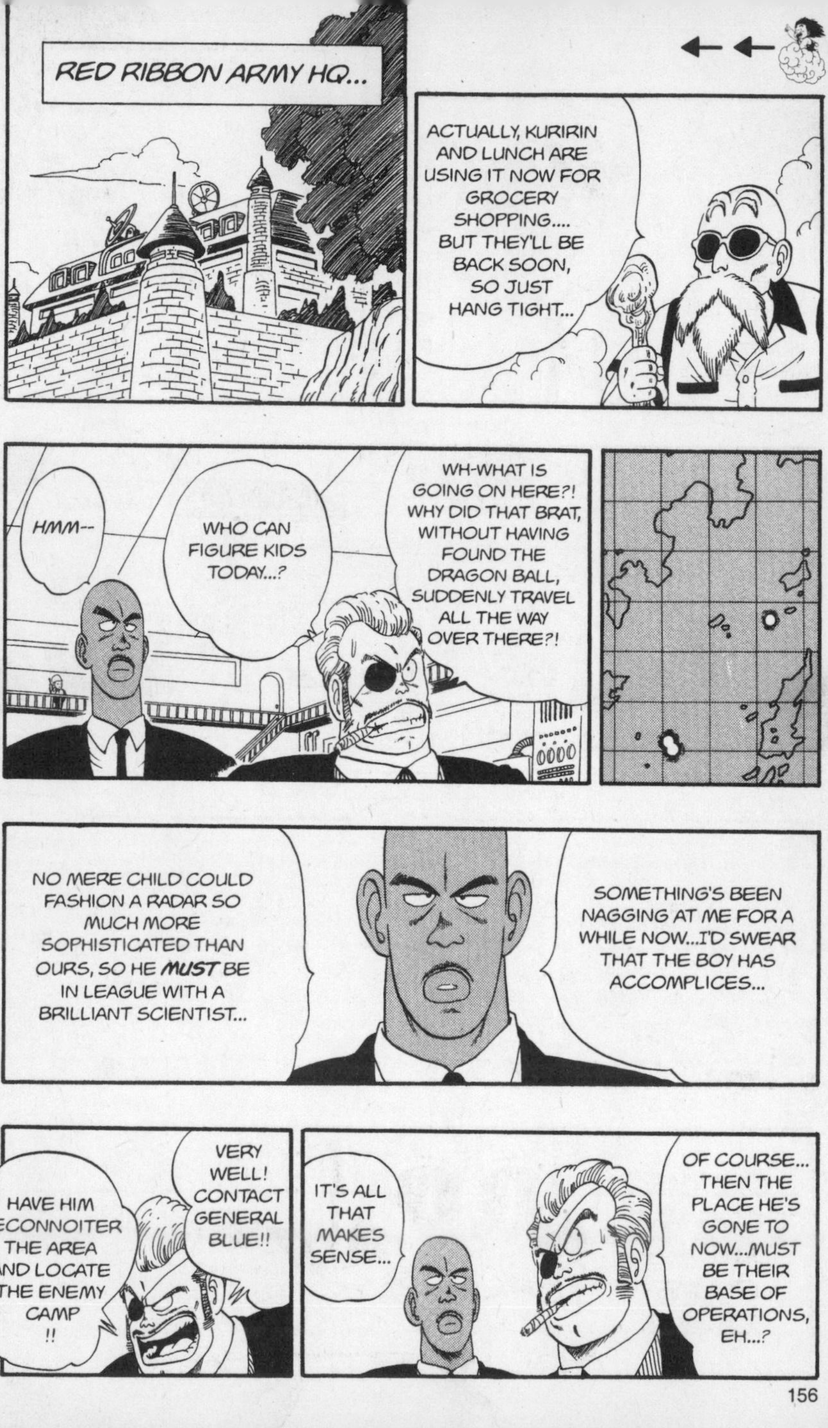

ACTUALLY, KURIRIN AND LUNCH ARE USING IT NOW FOR GROCERY SHOPPING.... BUT THEY'LL BE BACK SOON, SO JUST HANG TIGHT...
RED RIBBON ARMY HQ...
WH-WHAT IS GOING ON HERE?! WHY DID THAT BRAT, WITHOUT HAVING FOUND THE DRAGON BALL, SUDDENLY TRAVEL ALL THE WAY OVER THERE?!
WHO CAN FIGURE KIDS TODAY...?
HMM--
SOMETHING'S BEEN NAGGING AT ME FOR A WHILE NOW...I'D SWEAR THAT THE BOY HAS ACCOMPLICES...
NO MERE CHILD COULD FASHION A RADAR SO MUCH MORE SOPHISTICATED THAN OURS, SO HE *MUST* BE IN LEAGUE WITH A BRILLIANT SCIENTIST...
OF COURSE... THEN THE PLACE HE'S GONE TO NOW...MUST BE THEIR BASE OF OPERATIONS, EH...?
IT'S ALL THAT MAKES SENSE...
VERY WELL! CONTACT GENERAL BLUE!!
HAVE HIM RECONNOITER THE AREA AND LOCATE THE ENEMY CAMP !!

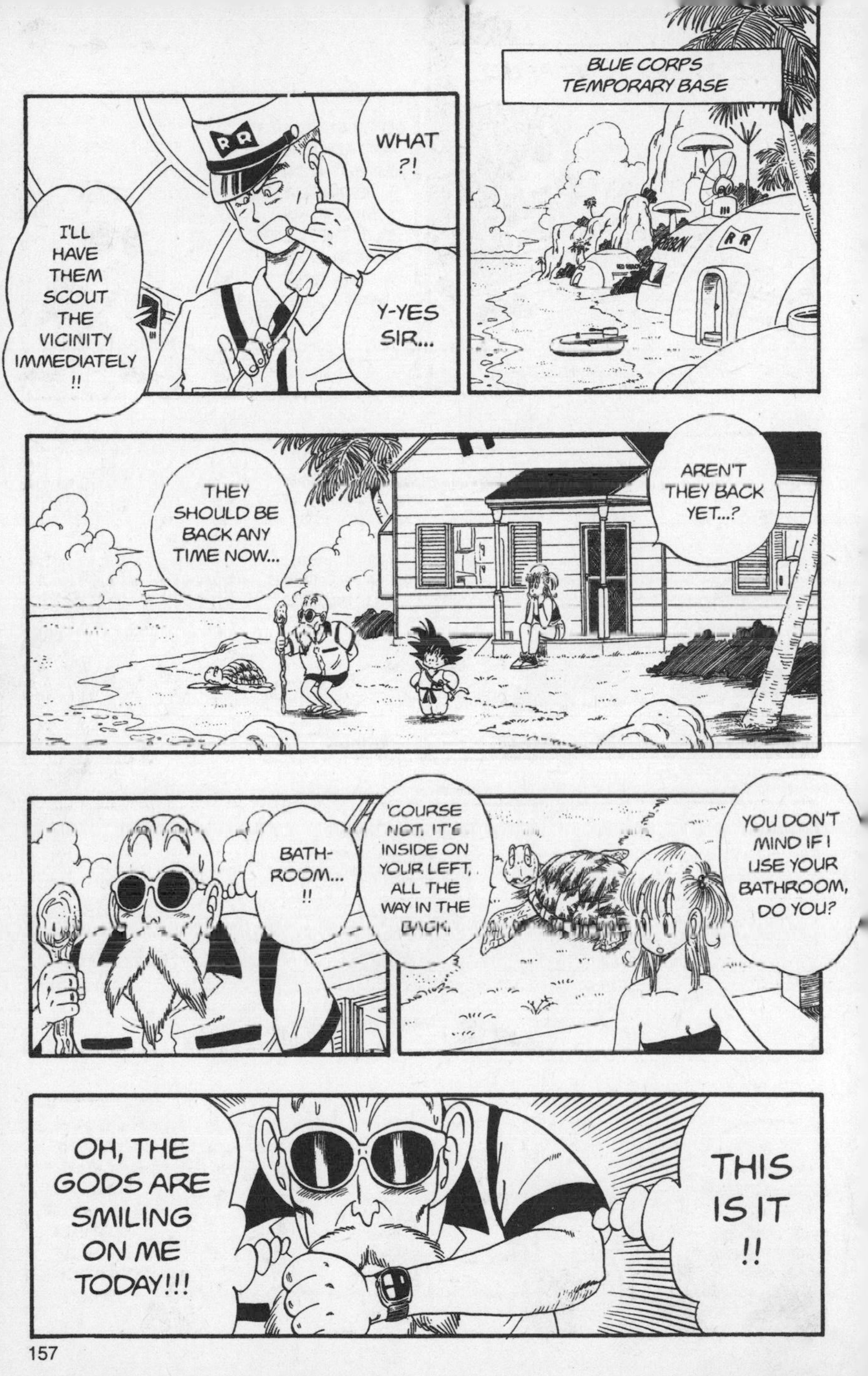
BLUE CORPS TEMPORARY BASE
WHAT ?!
Y-YES SIR...
I'LL HAVE THEM SCOUT THE VICINITY IMMEDIATELY !!
AREN'T THEY BACK YET...?
THEY SHOULD BE BACK ANY TIME NOW...
YOU DON'T MIND IF I USE YOUR BATHROOM, DO YOU?
'COURSE NOT. IT'S INSIDE ON YOUR LEFT, ALL THE WAY IN THE BACK.
BATH-ROOM... !!
THIS IS IT !!
OH, THE GODS ARE SMILING ON ME TODAY!!!

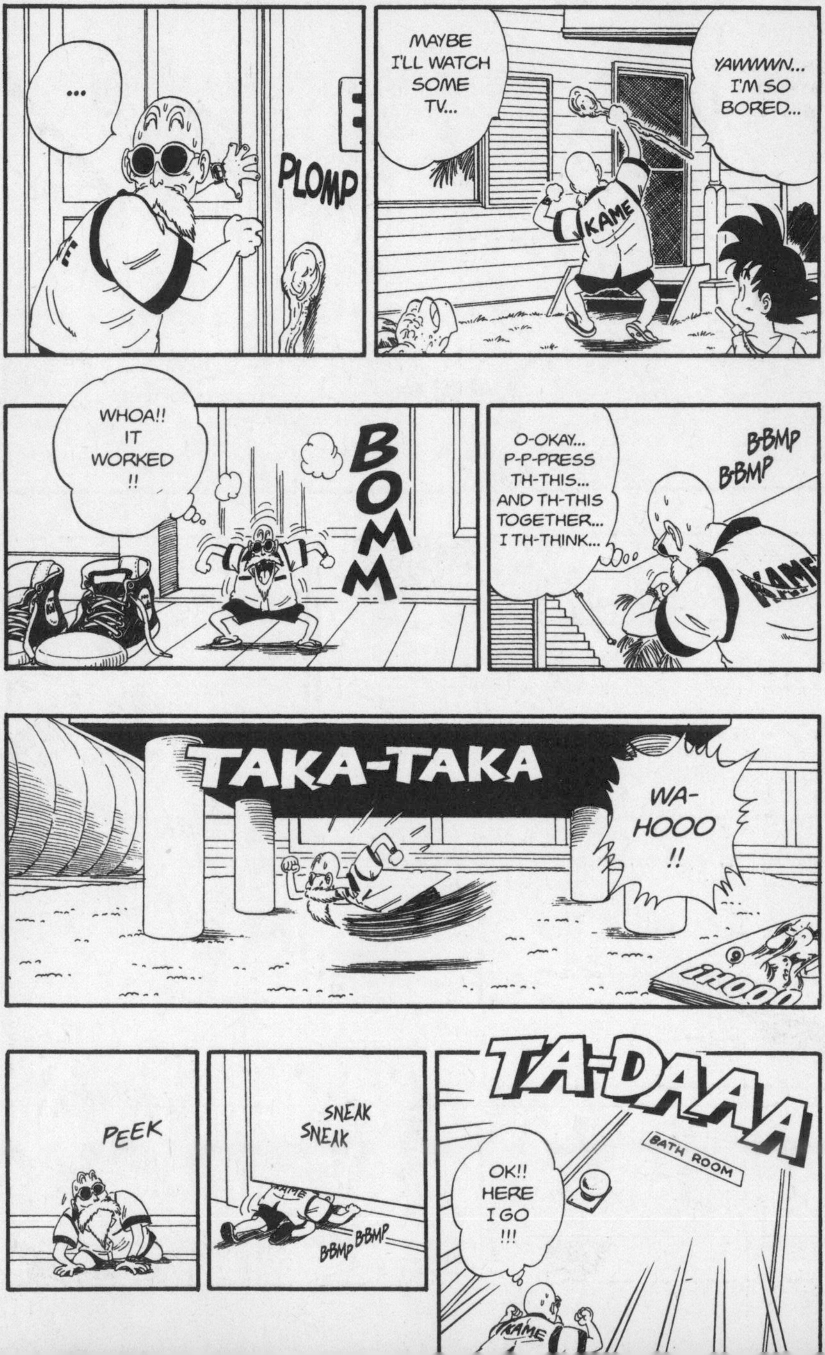
YAWWWN... I'M SO BORED...
MAYBE I'LL WATCH SOME TV...
...
PLOMP
B-BMP B-BMP
O-OKAY... P-P-PRESS TH-THIS... AND TH-THIS TOGETHER... I TH-THINK...
BOMM
WHOA!! IT WORKED !!
TAKA-TAKA
WA-HOOO !!
TA-DAAA
BATH ROOM
OK!! HERE I GO !!!
SNEAK SNEAK
B-BMP B-BMP
PEEK

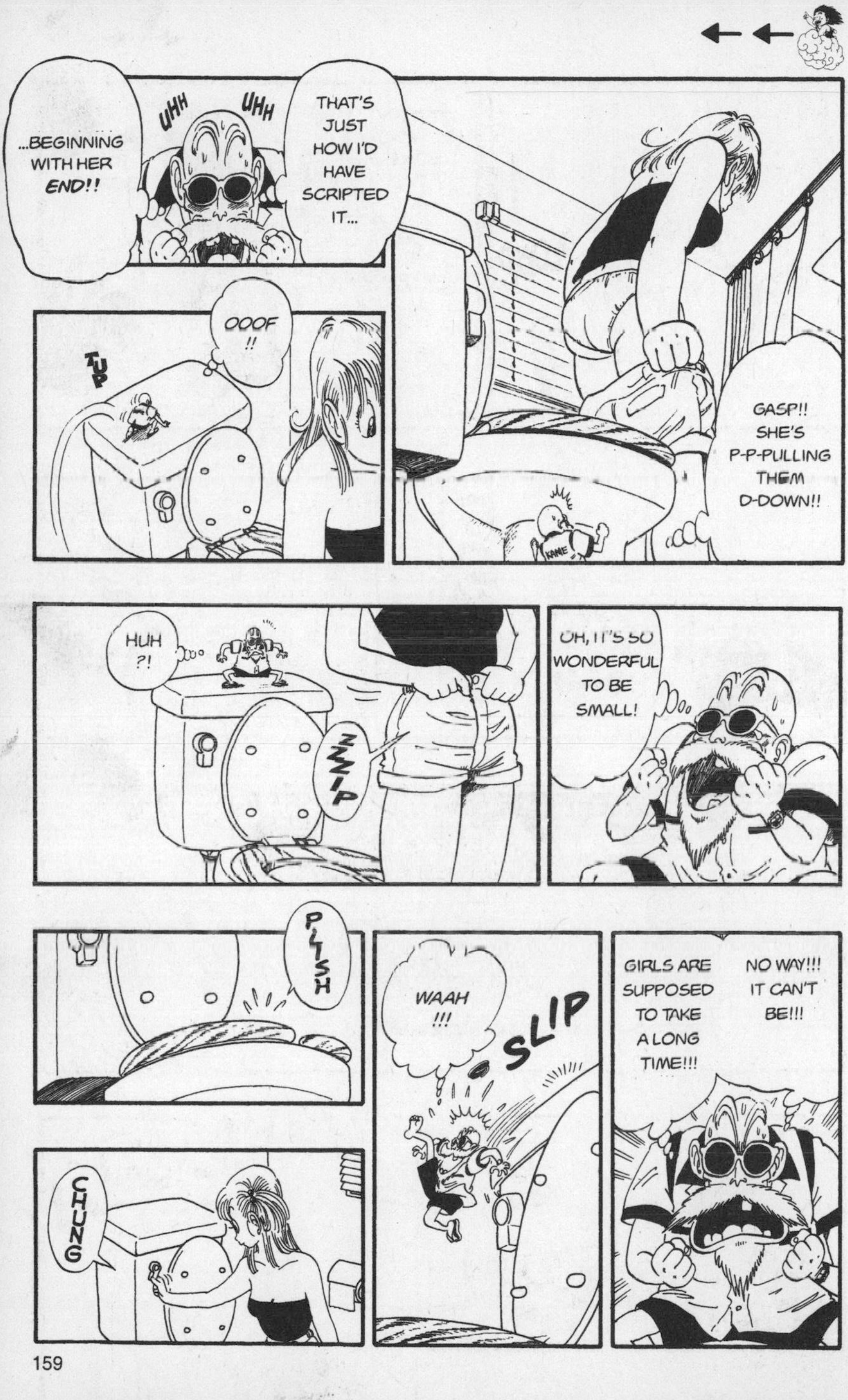
GASP!! SHE'S P-P-PULLING THEM D-DOWN!!
UHH UHH
THAT'S JUST HOW I'D HAVE SCRIPTED IT...
...BEGINNING WITH HER END!!
TUP
OOOF!!
OH, IT'S SO WONDERFUL TO BE SMALL!
HUH?!
ZZZIP
NO WAY!!! IT CAN'T BE!!!
GIRLS ARE SUPPOSED TO TAKE A LONG TIME!!!
SLIP
WAAH!!!
PLISH
CHUNG

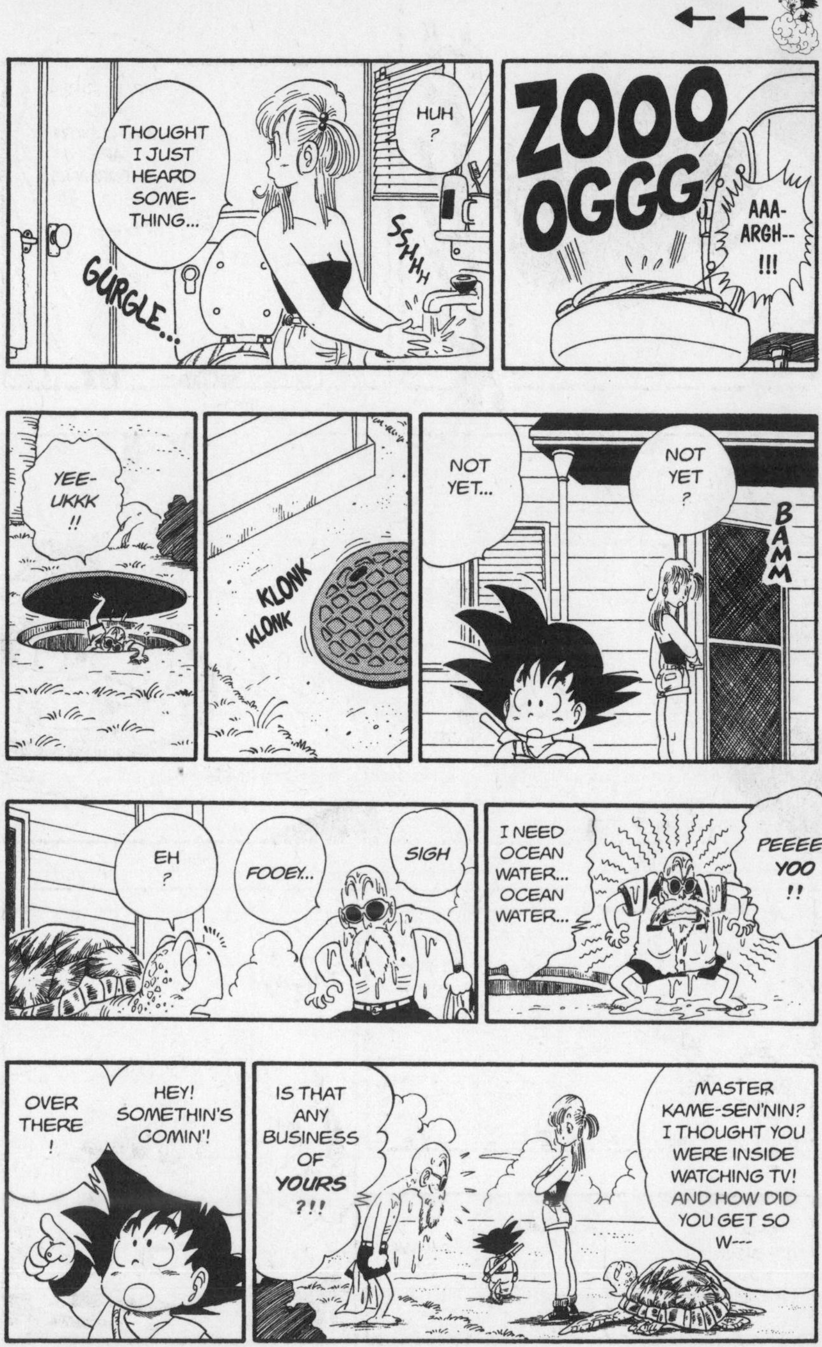
ZOOO OGGG
AAA-ARGH--!!!
HUH ?
THOUGHT I JUST HEARD SOME-THING...
SSHHH
GURGLE...
NOT YET ?
BAMM
NOT YET...
KLONK
KLONK
YEE-UKKK !!
PEEEE-YOO !!
I NEED OCEAN WATER... OCEAN WATER...
SIGH
FOOEY...
EH ?
MASTER KAME-SEN'NIN? I THOUGHT YOU WERE INSIDE WATCHING TV! AND HOW DID YOU GET SO W---
IS THAT ANY BUSINESS OF *YOURS* ?!!
HEY! SOMETHIN'S COMIN'!
OVER THERE !

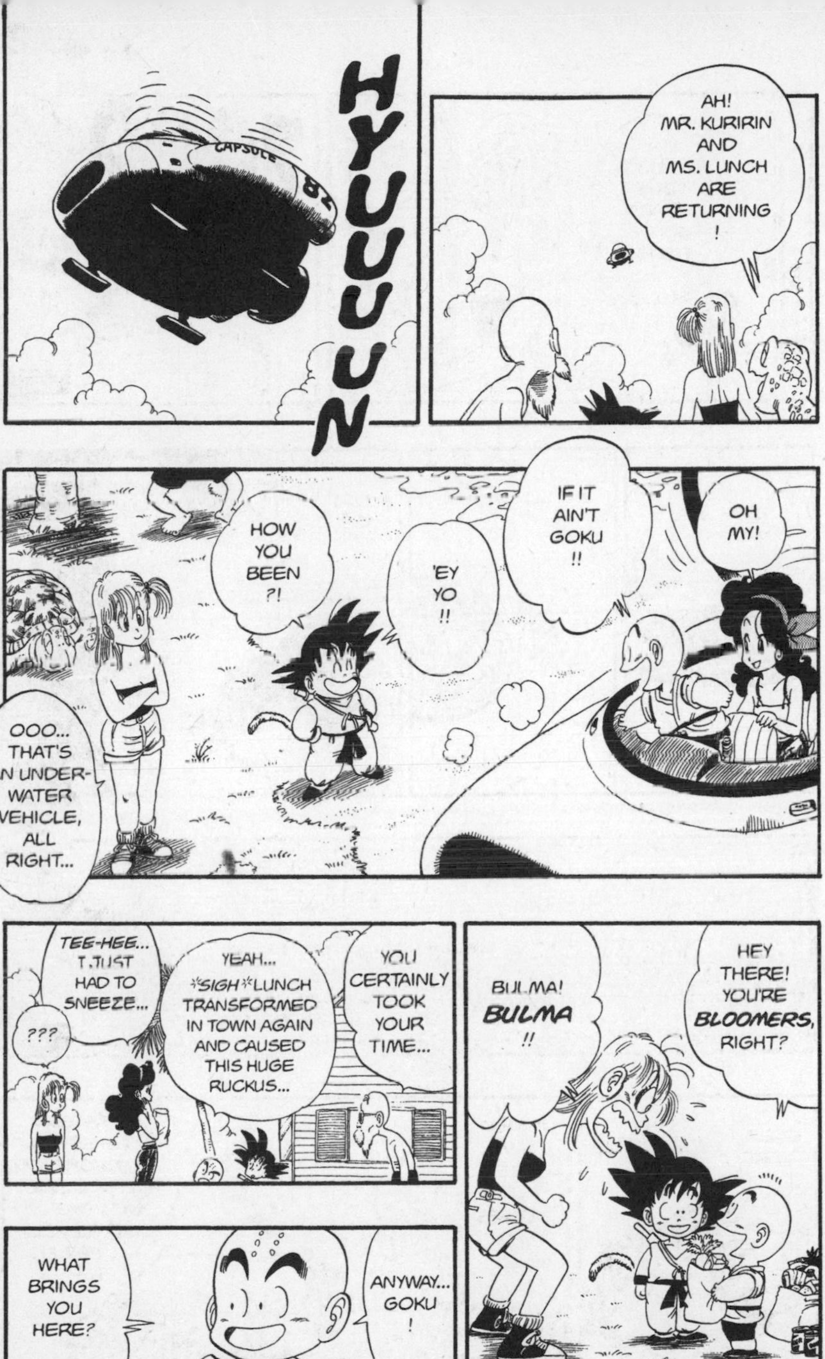
AH! MR. KURIRIN AND MS. LUNCH ARE RETURNING !
HYUUUN
OH MY!
IF IT AIN'T GOKU !!
'EY YO !!
HOW YOU BEEN ?!
OOO... THAT'S AN UNDER-WATER VEHICLE, ALL RIGHT...
HEY THERE! YOU'RE *BLOOMERS*, RIGHT?
BULMA! *BULMA* !!
YOU CERTAINLY TOOK YOUR TIME...
YEAH... *SIGH* LUNCH TRANSFORMED IN TOWN AGAIN AND CAUSED THIS HUGE RUCKUS...
TEE-HEE... I JUST HAD TO SNEEZE...
???
ANYWAY... GOKU !
WHAT BRINGS YOU HERE?

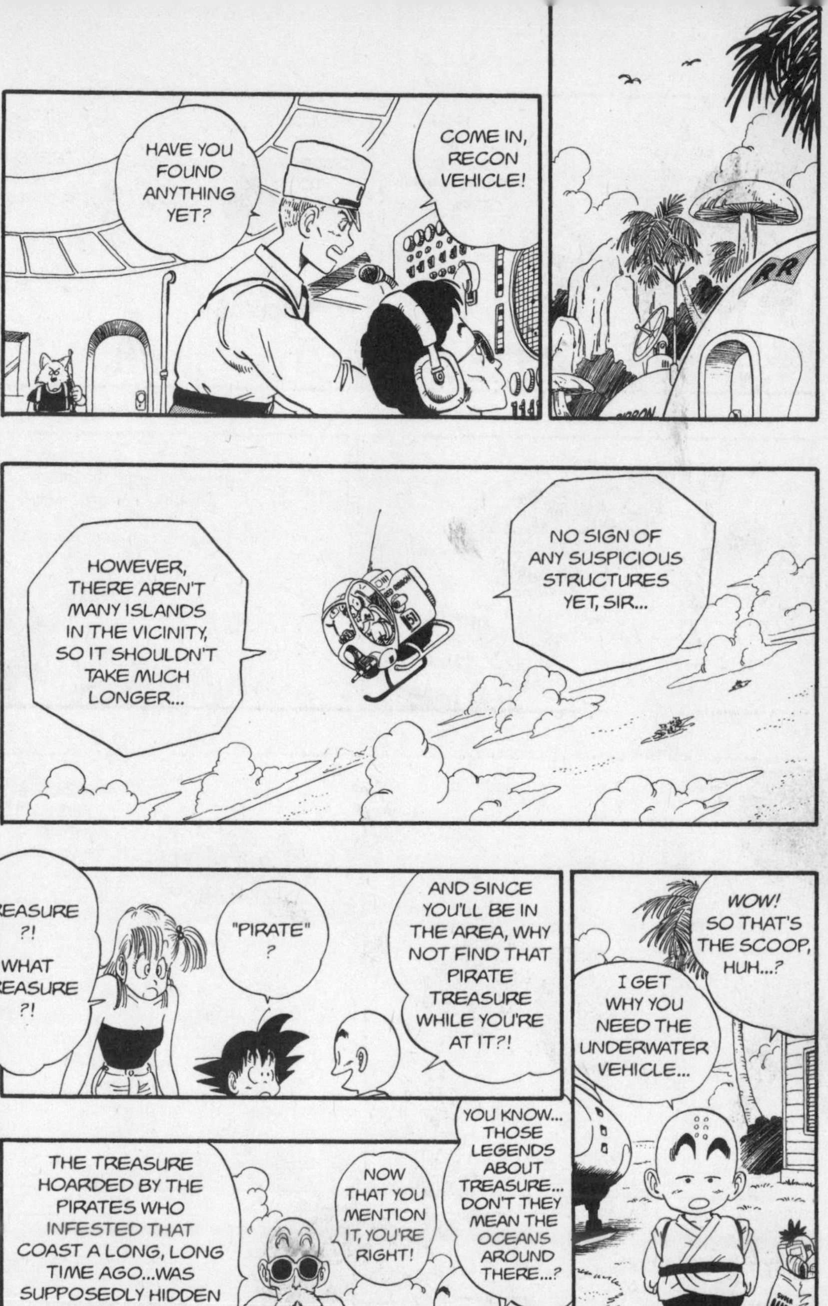
COME IN, RECON VEHICLE!
HAVE YOU FOUND ANYTHING YET?
NO SIGN OF ANY SUSPICIOUS STRUCTURES YET, SIR...
HOWEVER, THERE AREN'T MANY ISLANDS IN THE VICINITY, SO IT SHOULDN'T TAKE MUCH LONGER...
WOW! SO THAT'S THE SCOOP, HUH...?
I GET WHY YOU NEED THE UNDERWATER VEHICLE...
AND SINCE YOU'LL BE IN THE AREA, WHY NOT FIND THAT PIRATE TREASURE WHILE YOU'RE AT IT?!
"PIRATE" ?
TREASURE ?! WHAT TREASURE ?!
YOU KNOW... THOSE LEGENDS ABOUT TREASURE... DON'T THEY MEAN THE OCEANS AROUND THERE...?
NOW THAT YOU MENTION IT, YOU'RE RIGHT!
THE TREASURE HOARDED BY THE PIRATES WHO INFESTED THAT COAST A LONG, LONG TIME AGO...WAS SUPPOSEDLY HIDDEN SOMEWHERE IN THE OCEAN!

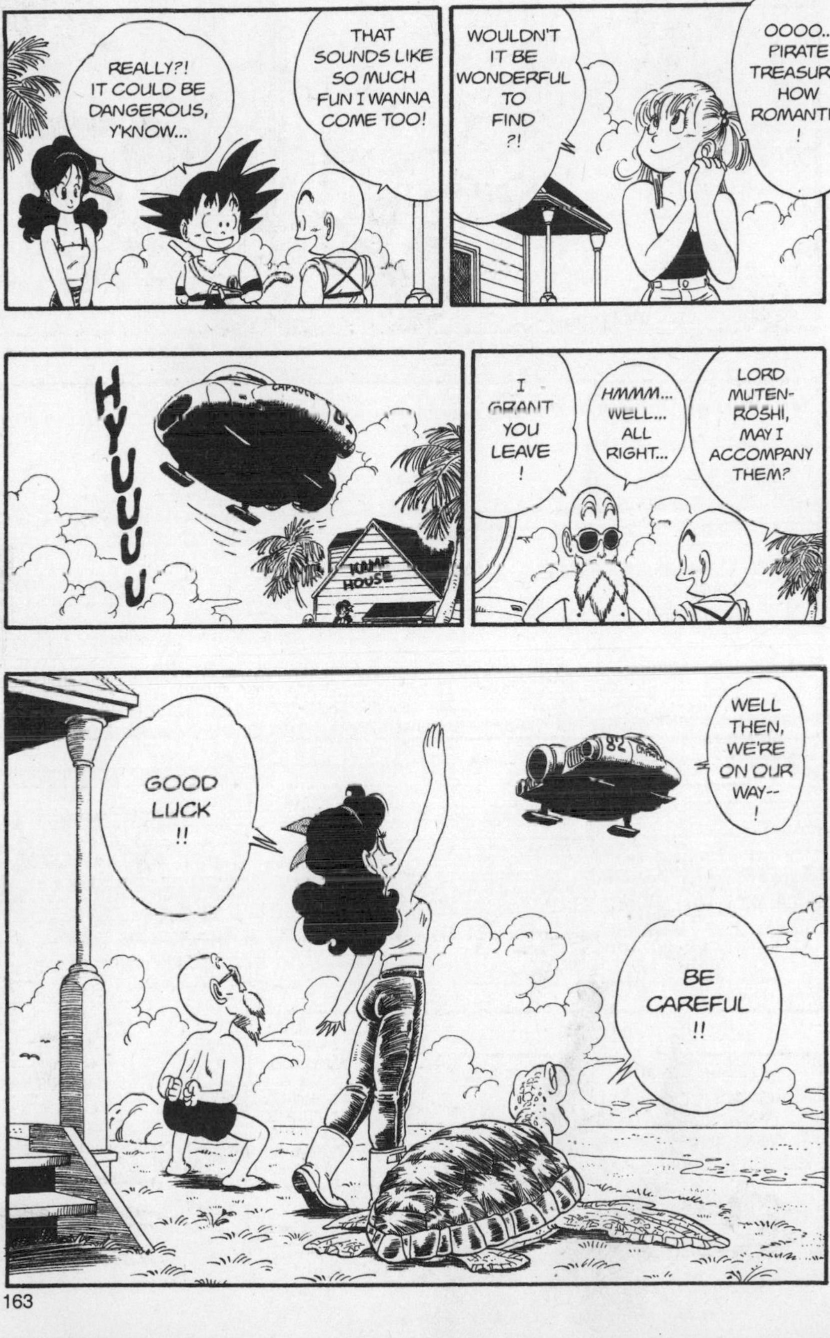
OOOO... PIRATE TREASURE! HOW ROMANTIC!
WOULDN'T IT BE WONDERFUL TO FIND?!
THAT SOUNDS LIKE SO MUCH FUN I WANNA COME TOO!
REALLY?! IT COULD BE DANGEROUS, Y'KNOW...
LORD MUTEN-ROSHI, MAY I ACCOMPANY THEM?
HMMM... WELL... ALL RIGHT...
I GRANT YOU LEAVE!
CAPSULE
KAME HOUSE
HYUUUU
WELL THEN, WE'RE ON OUR WAY--!
GOOD LUCK!!
BE CAREFUL!!

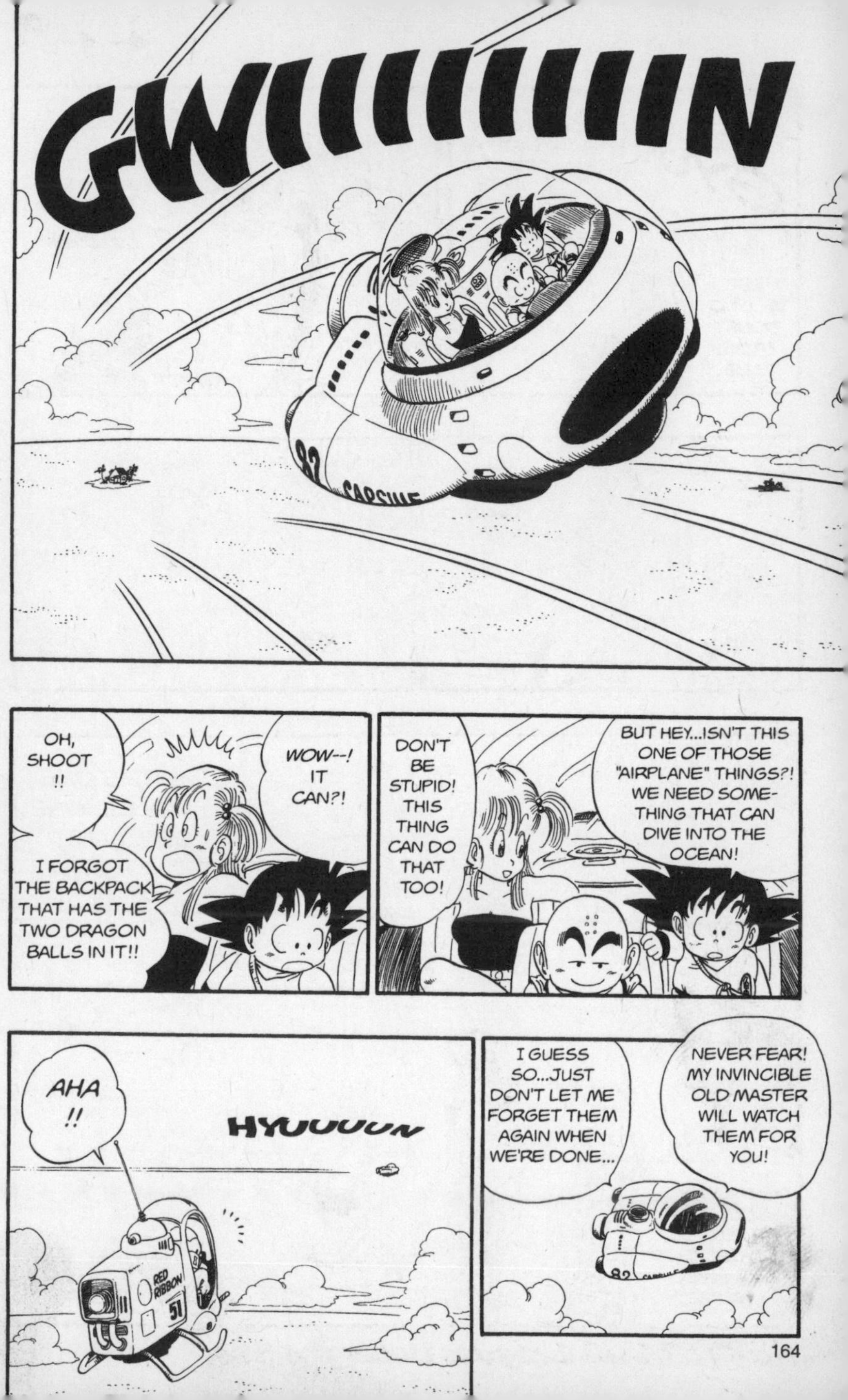
GWIIIIIIIN
82
BUT HEY...ISN'T THIS ONE OF THOSE "AIRPLANE" THINGS?! WE NEED SOME-THING THAT CAN DIVE INTO THE OCEAN!
DON'T BE STUPID! THIS THING CAN DO THAT TOO!
WOW--! IT CAN?!
OH, SHOOT !!
I FORGOT THE BACKPACK THAT HAS THE TWO DRAGON BALLS IN IT!!
NEVER FEAR! MY INVINCIBLE OLD MASTER WILL WATCH THEM FOR YOU!
I GUESS SO...JUST DON'T LET ME FORGET THEM AGAIN WHEN WE'RE DONE...
HYUUUUN
AHA !!
RED RIBBON
51

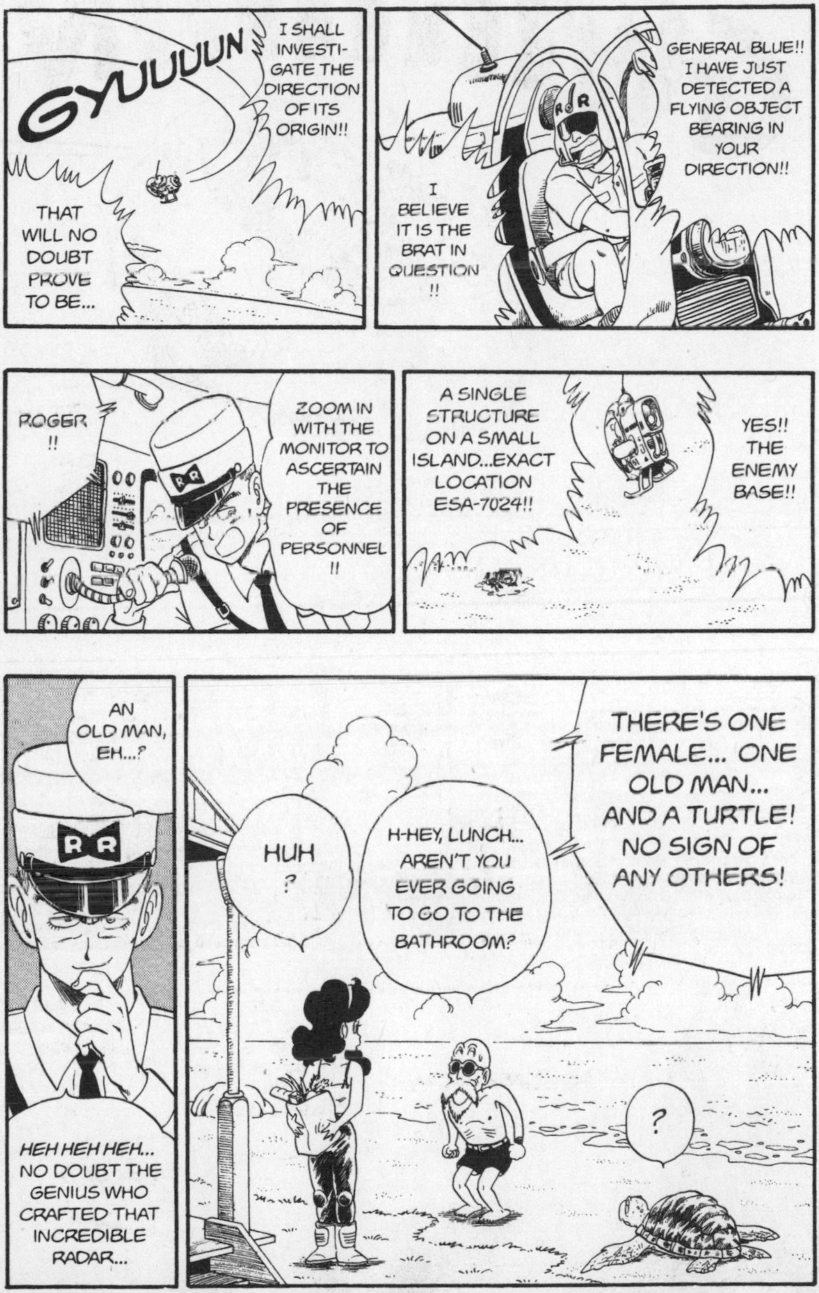
GENERAL BLUE!! I HAVE JUST DETECTED A FLYING OBJECT BEARING IN YOUR DIRECTION!!
I BELIEVE IT IS THE BRAT IN QUESTION!!
I SHALL INVESTI-GATE THE DIRECTION OF ITS ORIGIN!!
GYUUUUN
THAT WILL NO DOUBT PROVE TO BE...
YES!! THE ENEMY BASE!!
A SINGLE STRUCTURE ON A SMALL ISLAND...EXACT LOCATION ESA-7024!!
ZOOM IN WITH THE MONITOR TO ASCERTAIN THE PRESENCE OF PERSONNEL!!
ROGER!!
THERE'S ONE FEMALE... ONE OLD MAN... AND A TURTLE! NO SIGN OF ANY OTHERS!
H-HEY, LUNCH... AREN'T YOU EVER GOING TO GO TO THE BATHROOM?
HUH?
?
AN OLD MAN, EH...?
HEH HEH HEH... NO DOUBT THE GENIUS WHO CRAFTED THAT INCREDIBLE RADAR...

NEXT: 7,000 Leagues Under the Sea!

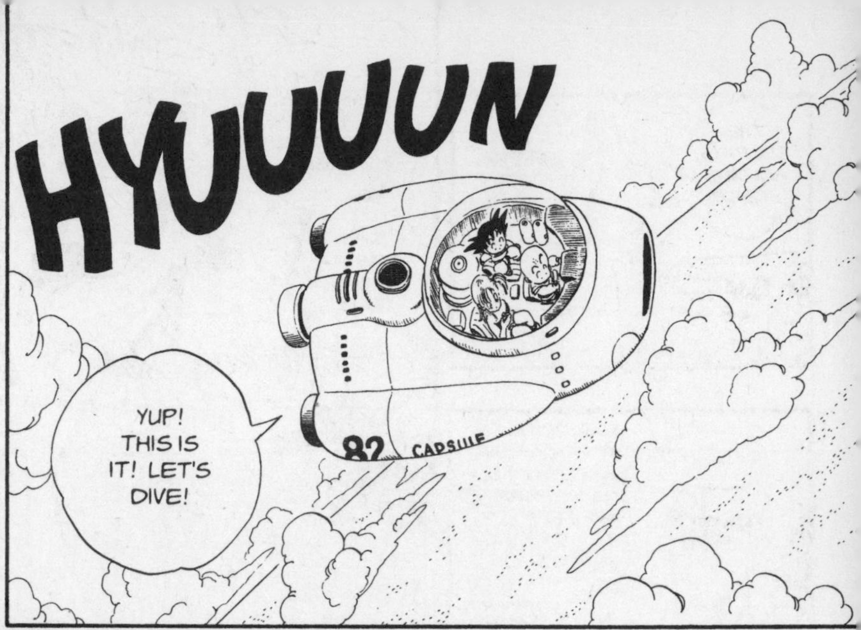
HYUUUUN
82 CAPSULE
YUP! THIS IS IT! LET'S DIVE!

Tale 72 • The Blue Meanies

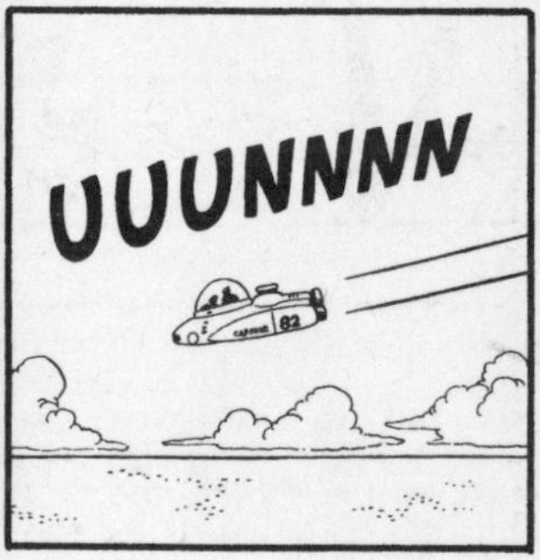
UUUNNNN

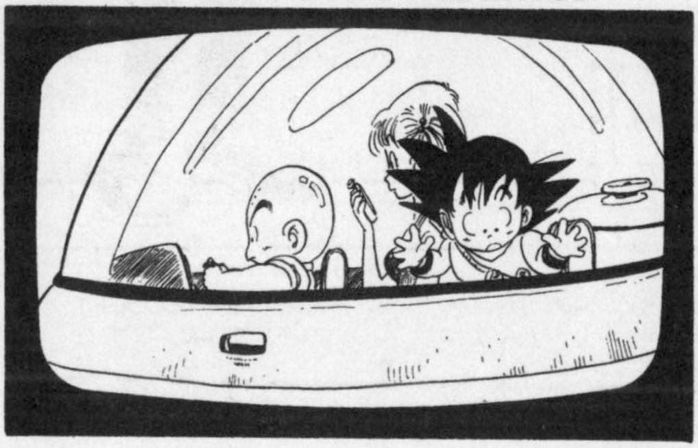

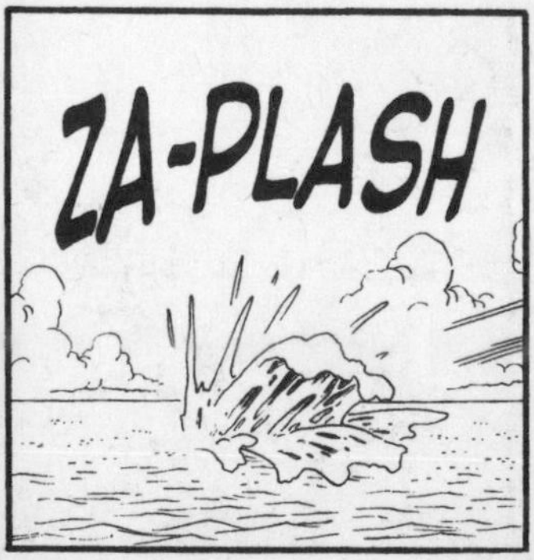
ZA-PLASH

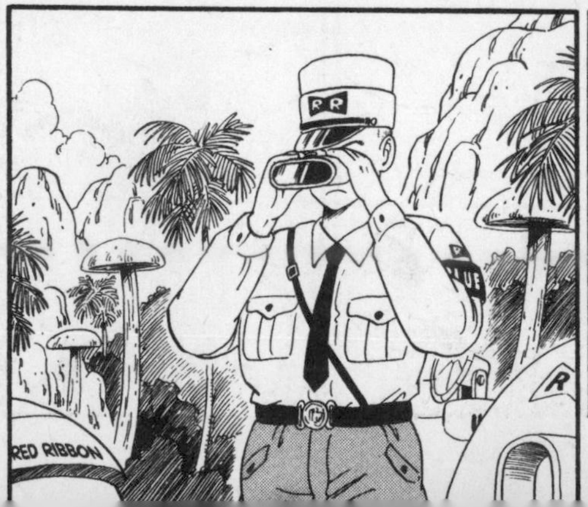
RED RIBBON

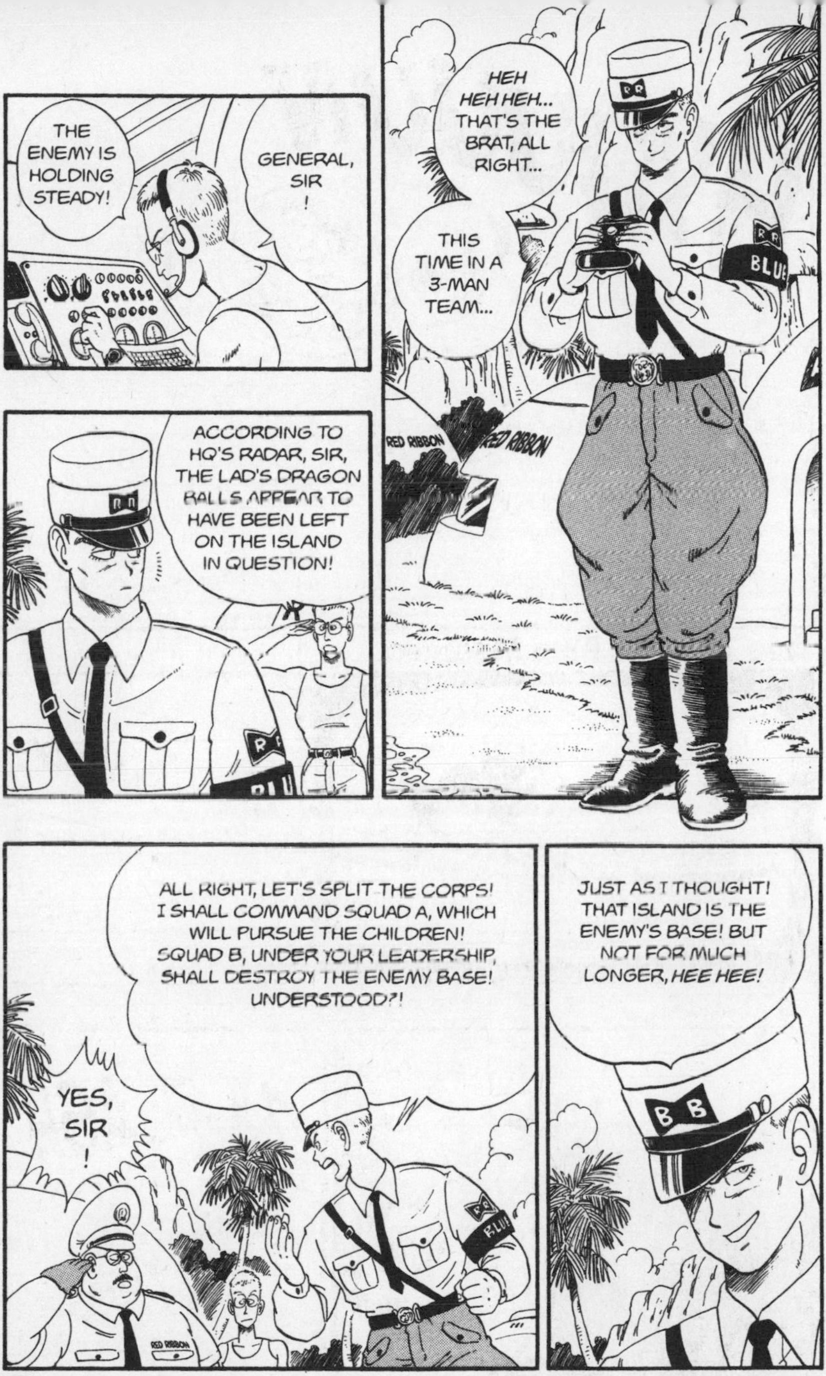
HEH HEH HEH... THAT'S THE BRAT, ALL RIGHT...
THIS TIME IN A 3-MAN TEAM...
GENERAL, SIR!
THE ENEMY IS HOLDING STEADY!
ACCORDING TO HQ'S RADAR, SIR, THE LAD'S DRAGON BALLS APPEAR TO HAVE BEEN LEFT ON THE ISLAND IN QUESTION!
JUST AS I THOUGHT! THAT ISLAND IS THE ENEMY'S BASE! BUT NOT FOR MUCH LONGER, HEE HEE!
ALL RIGHT, LET'S SPLIT THE CORPS! I SHALL COMMAND SQUAD A, WHICH WILL PURSUE THE CHILDREN! SQUAD B, UNDER YOUR LEADERSHIP, SHALL DESTROY THE ENEMY BASE! UNDERSTOOD?!
YES, SIR!

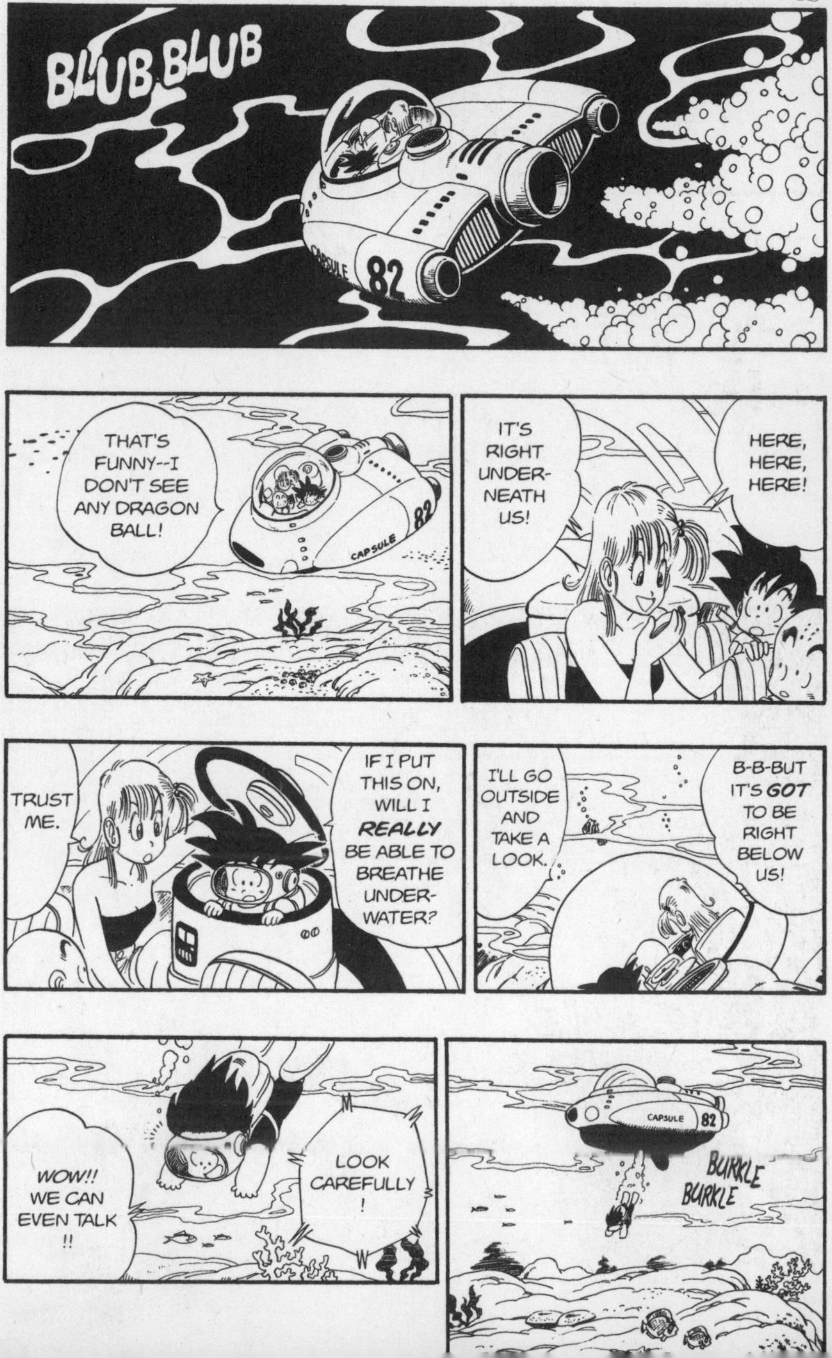
BLUB BLUB
CAPSULE 82
HERE, HERE, HERE!
IT'S RIGHT UNDERNEATH US!
THAT'S FUNNY--I DON'T SEE ANY DRAGON BALL!
CAPSULE 82
B-B-BUT IT'S GOT TO BE RIGHT BELOW US!
I'LL GO OUTSIDE AND TAKE A LOOK.
IF I PUT THIS ON, WILL I REALLY BE ABLE TO BREATHE UNDERWATER?
TRUST ME.
CAPSULE 82
BURKLE BURKLE
LOOK CAREFULLY!
WOW!! WE CAN EVEN TALK!!

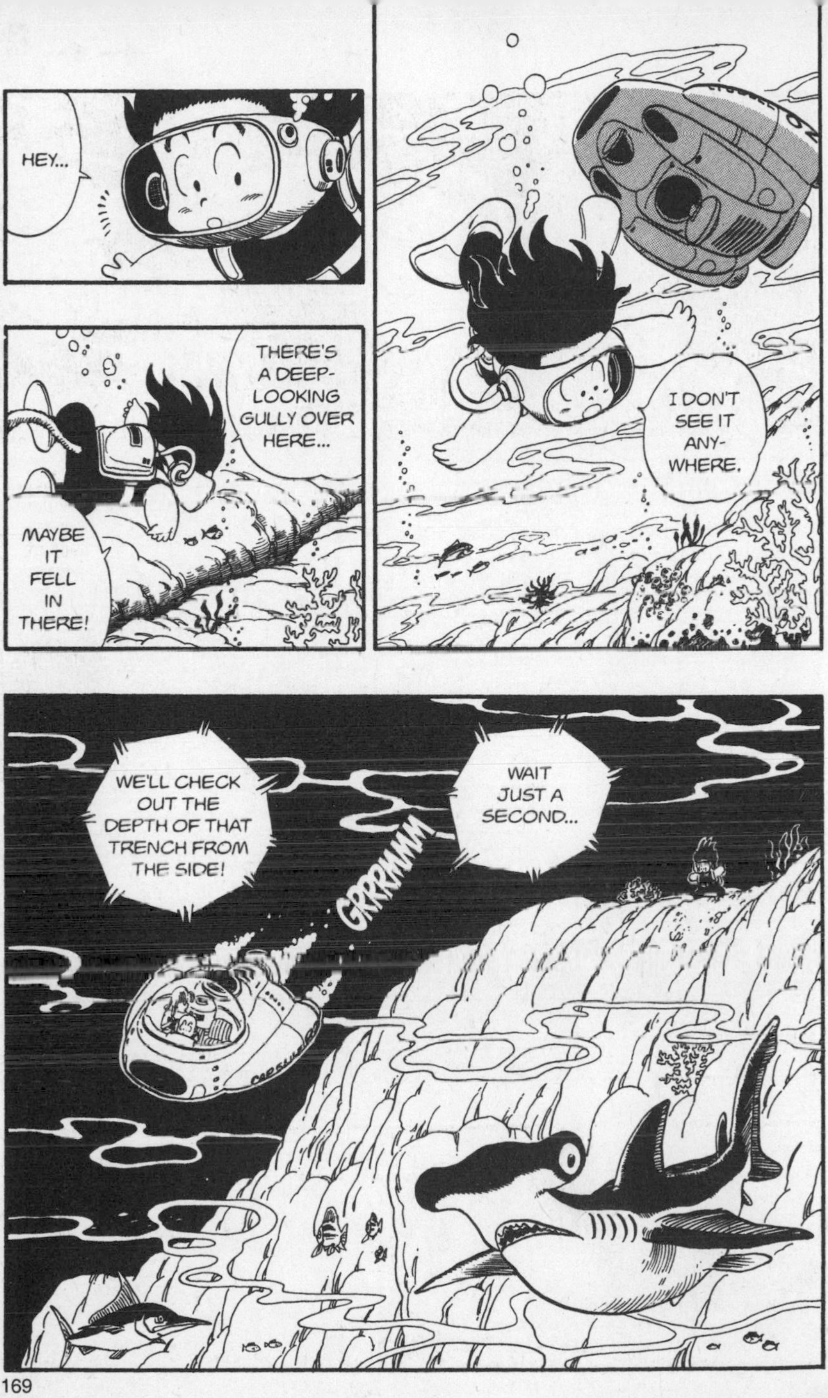
I DON'T SEE IT ANY-WHERE.
HEY...
THERE'S A DEEP-LOOKING GULLY OVER HERE...
MAYBE IT FELL IN THERE!
WAIT JUST A SECOND...
WE'LL CHECK OUT THE DEPTH OF THAT TRENCH FROM THE SIDE!
GRRRMMM

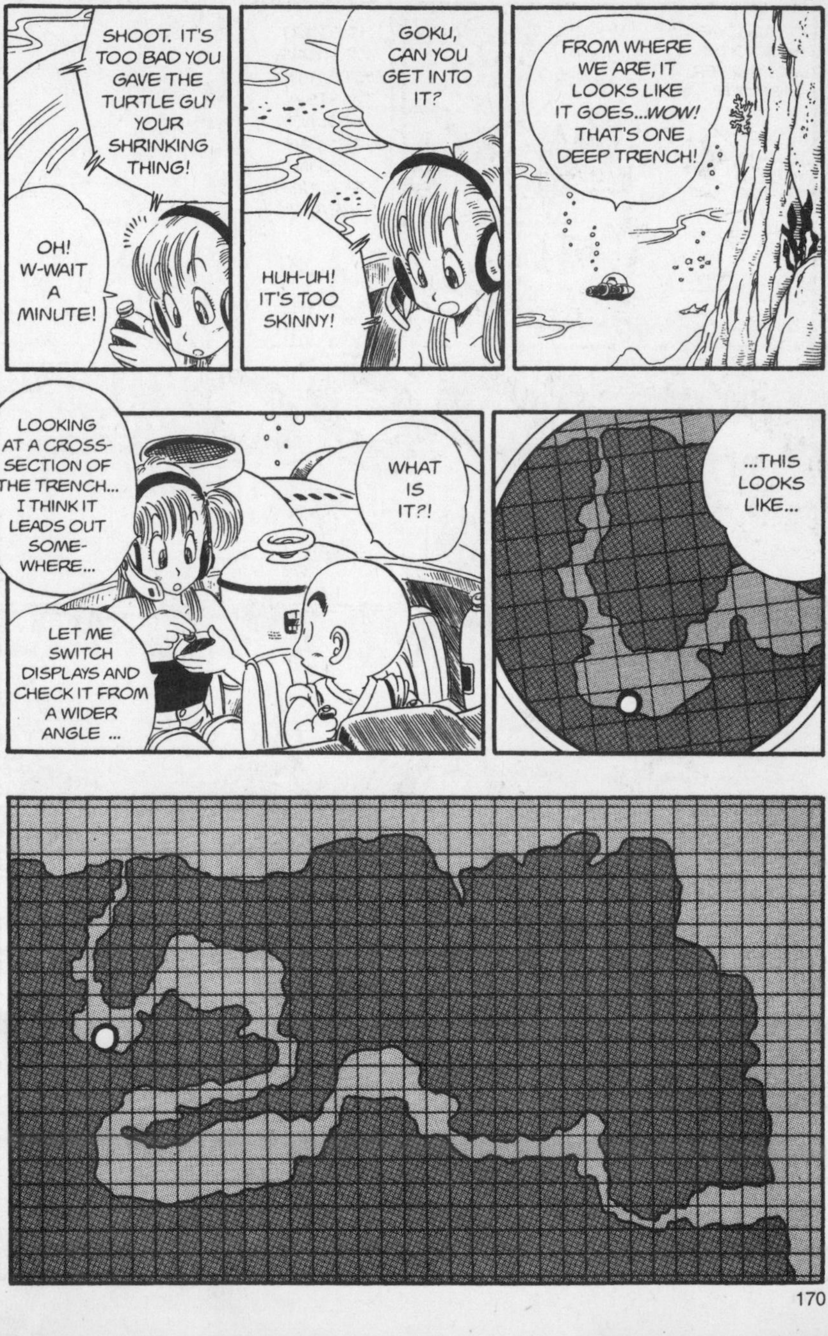
FROM WHERE WE ARE, IT LOOKS LIKE IT GOES...WOW! THAT'S ONE DEEP TRENCH!
GOKU, CAN YOU GET INTO IT?
HUH-UH! IT'S TOO SKINNY!
SHOOT. IT'S TOO BAD YOU GAVE THE TURTLE GUY YOUR SHRINKING THING!
OH! W-WAIT A MINUTE!
...THIS LOOKS LIKE...
LOOKING AT A CROSS-SECTION OF THE TRENCH... I THINK IT LEADS OUT SOMEWHERE...
WHAT IS IT?!
LET ME SWITCH DISPLAYS AND CHECK IT FROM A WIDER ANGLE ...

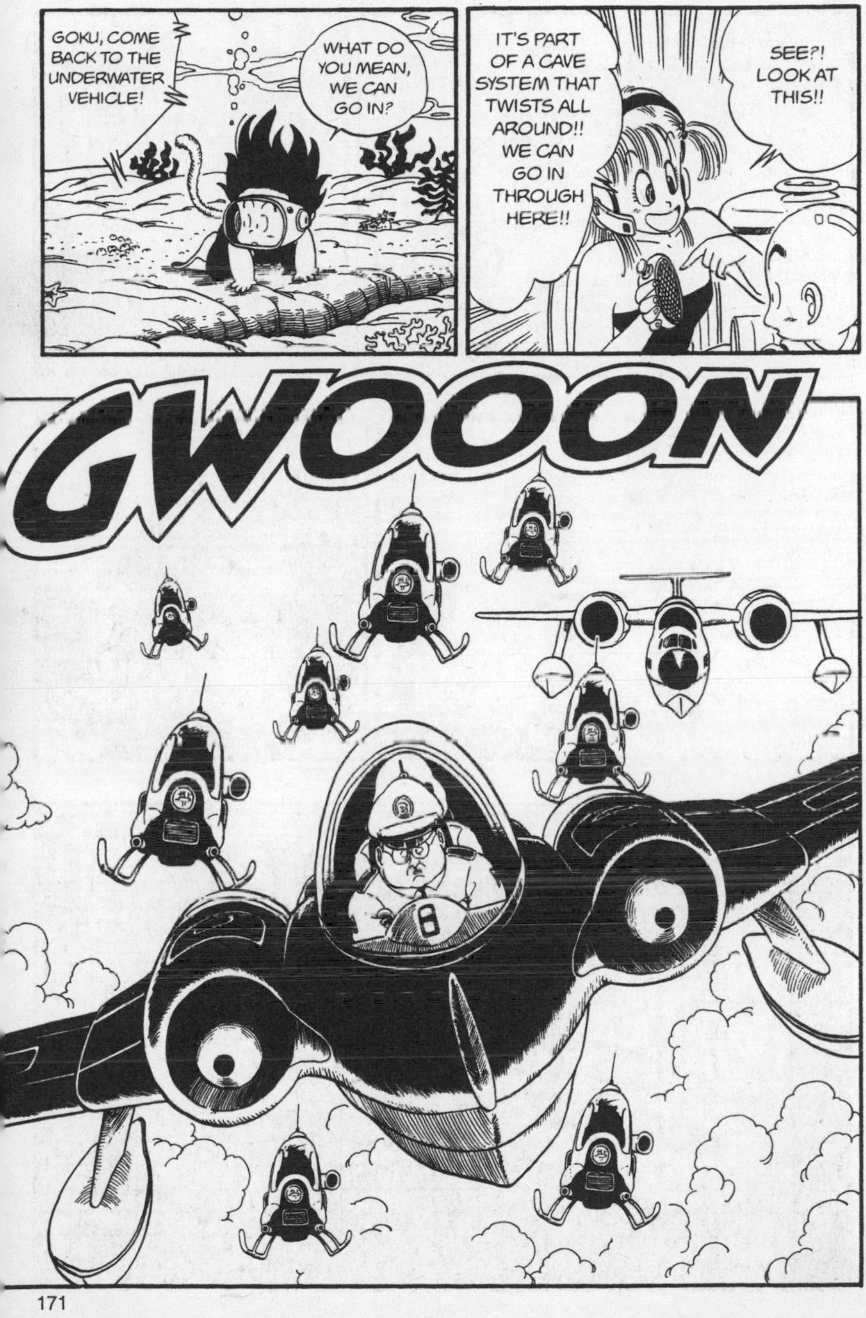
SEE?! LOOK AT THIS!!
IT'S PART OF A CAVE SYSTEM THAT TWISTS ALL AROUND!! WE CAN GO IN THROUGH HERE!!
GOKU, COME BACK TO THE UNDERWATER VEHICLE!
WHAT DO YOU MEAN, WE CAN GO IN?
GWOOON

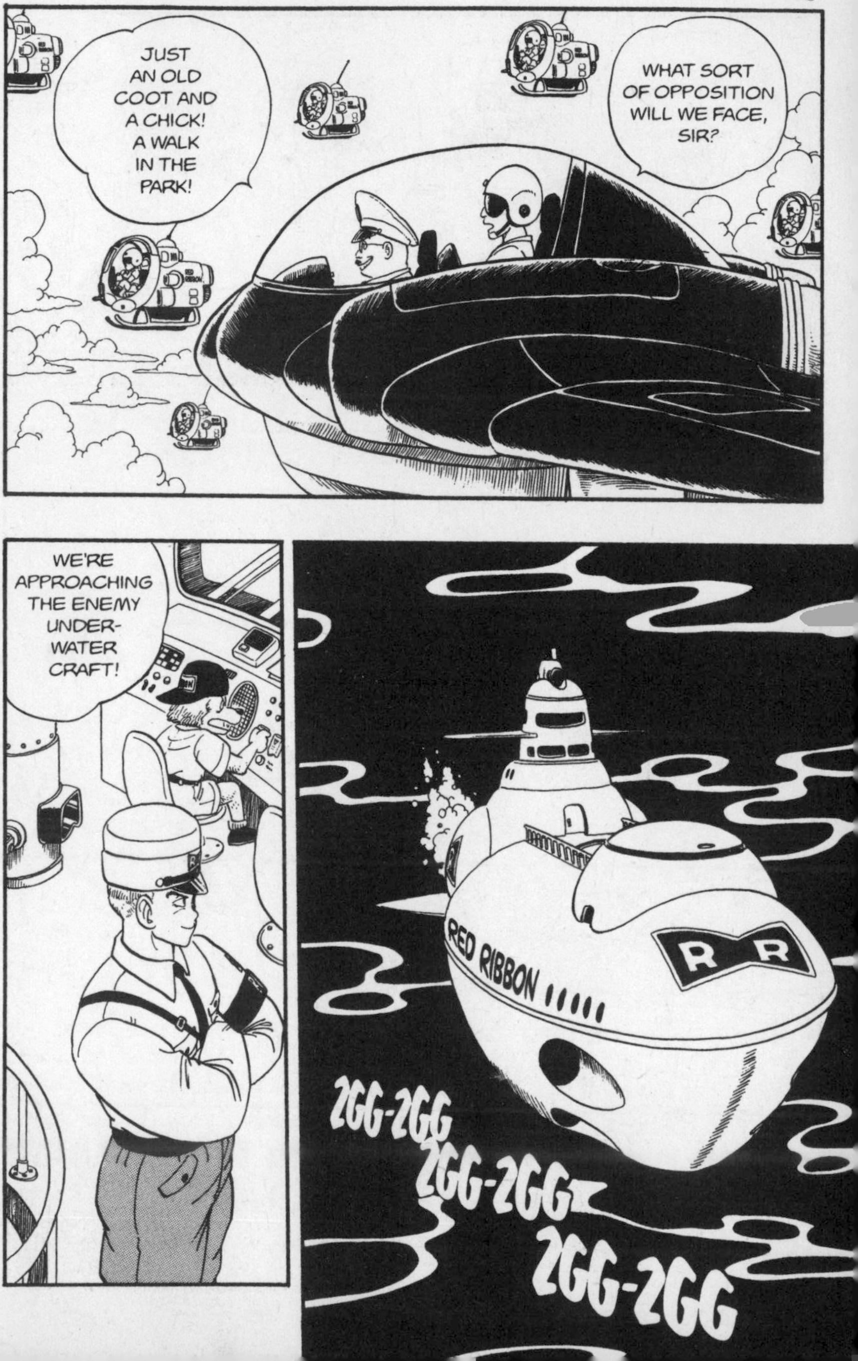
WHAT SORT OF OPPOSITION WILL WE FACE, SIR?
JUST AN OLD COOT AND A CHICK! A WALK IN THE PARK!
RED RIBBON
ZGG-ZGG
ZGG-ZGG
ZGG-ZGG
WE'RE APPROACHING THE ENEMY UNDER-WATER CRAFT!

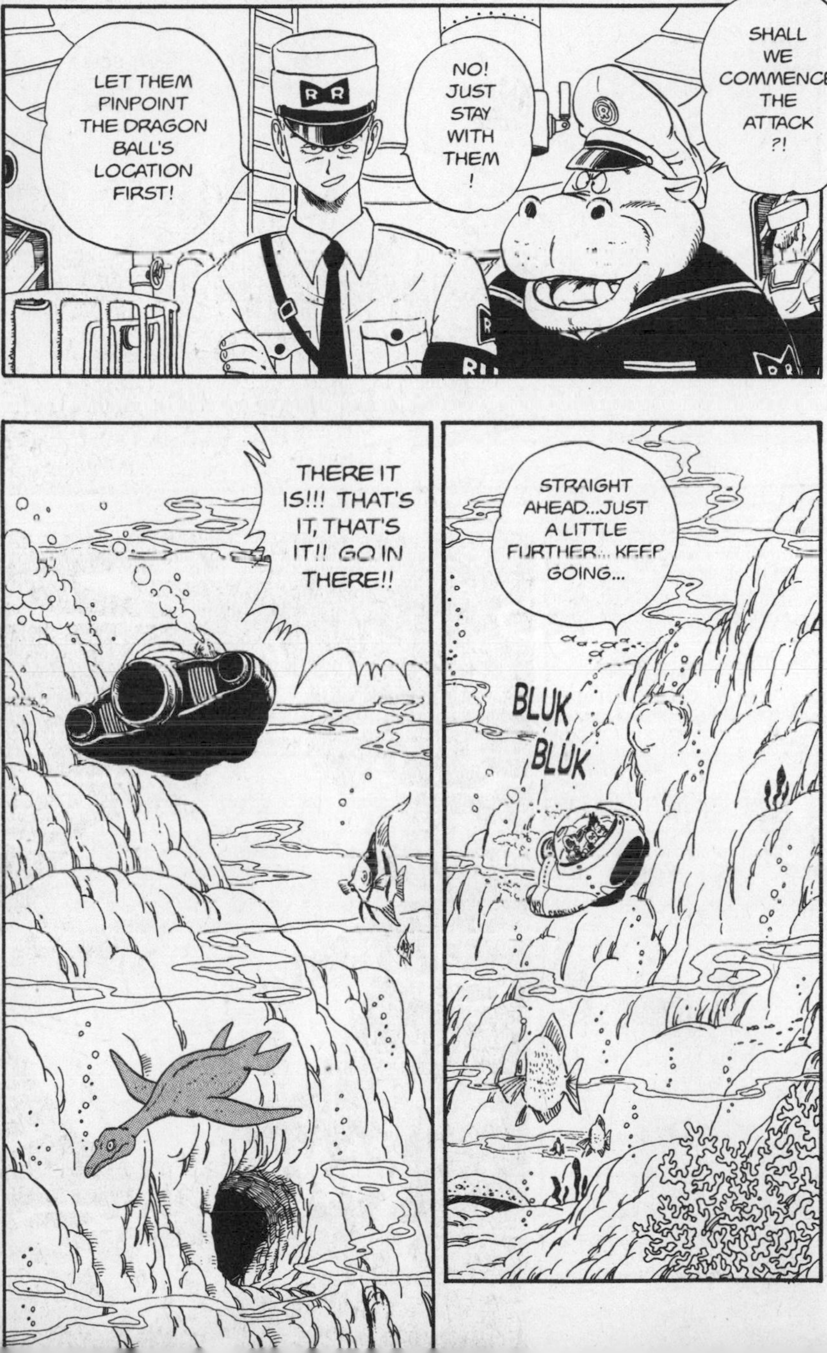
SHALL WE COMMENCE THE ATTACK?!
NO! JUST STAY WITH THEM!
LET THEM PINPOINT THE DRAGON BALL'S LOCATION FIRST!
STRAIGHT AHEAD...JUST A LITTLE FURTHER... KEEP GOING...
BLUK BLUK
THERE IT IS!!! THAT'S IT, THAT'S IT!! GO IN THERE!!

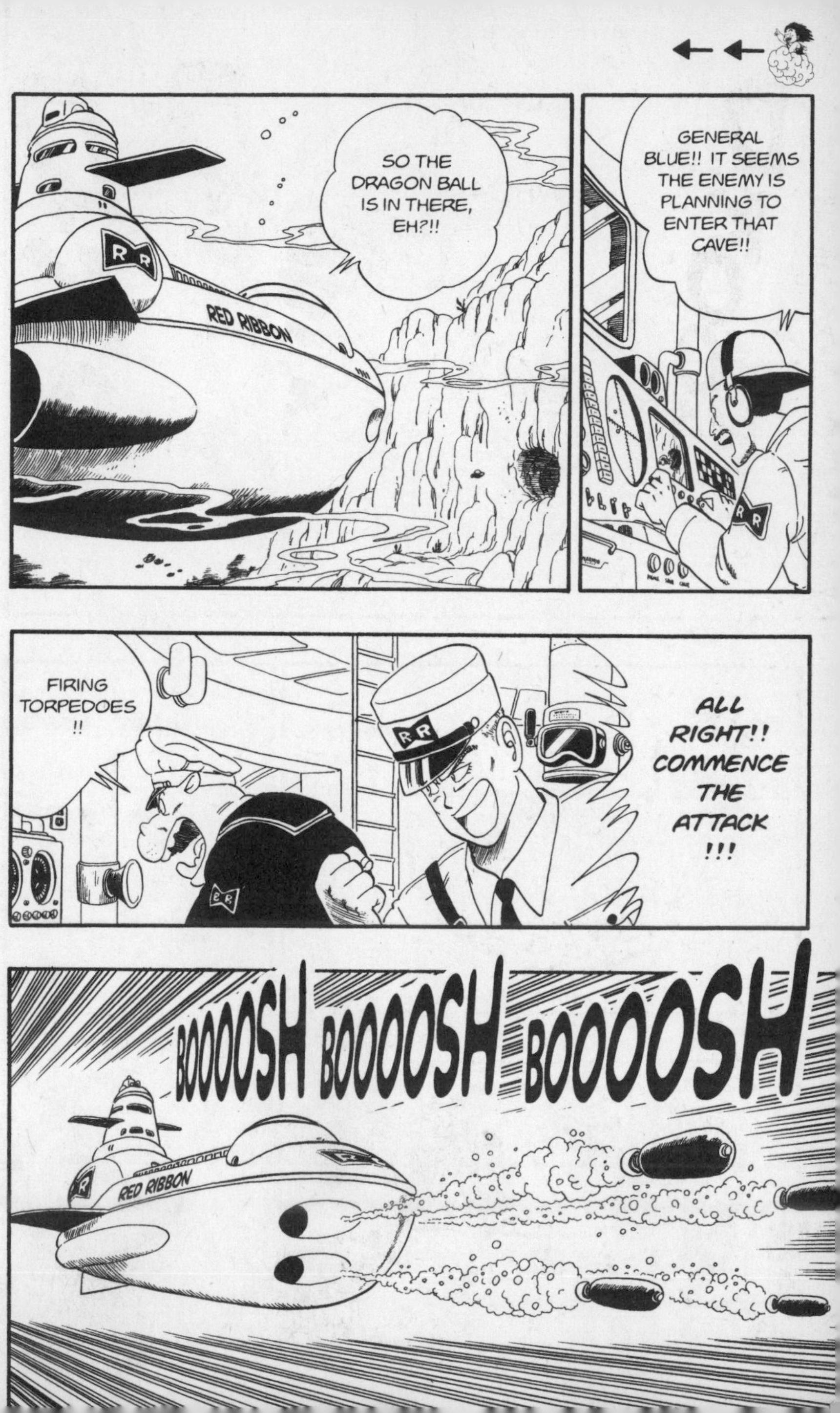
GENERAL BLUE!! IT SEEMS THE ENEMY IS PLANNING TO ENTER THAT CAVE!!
SO THE DRAGON BALL IS IN THERE, EH?!!
RED RIBBON
ALL RIGHT!! COMMENCE THE ATTACK!!!
FIRING TORPEDOES!!
BOOOOSH BOOOOSH BOOOOSH
RED RIBBON

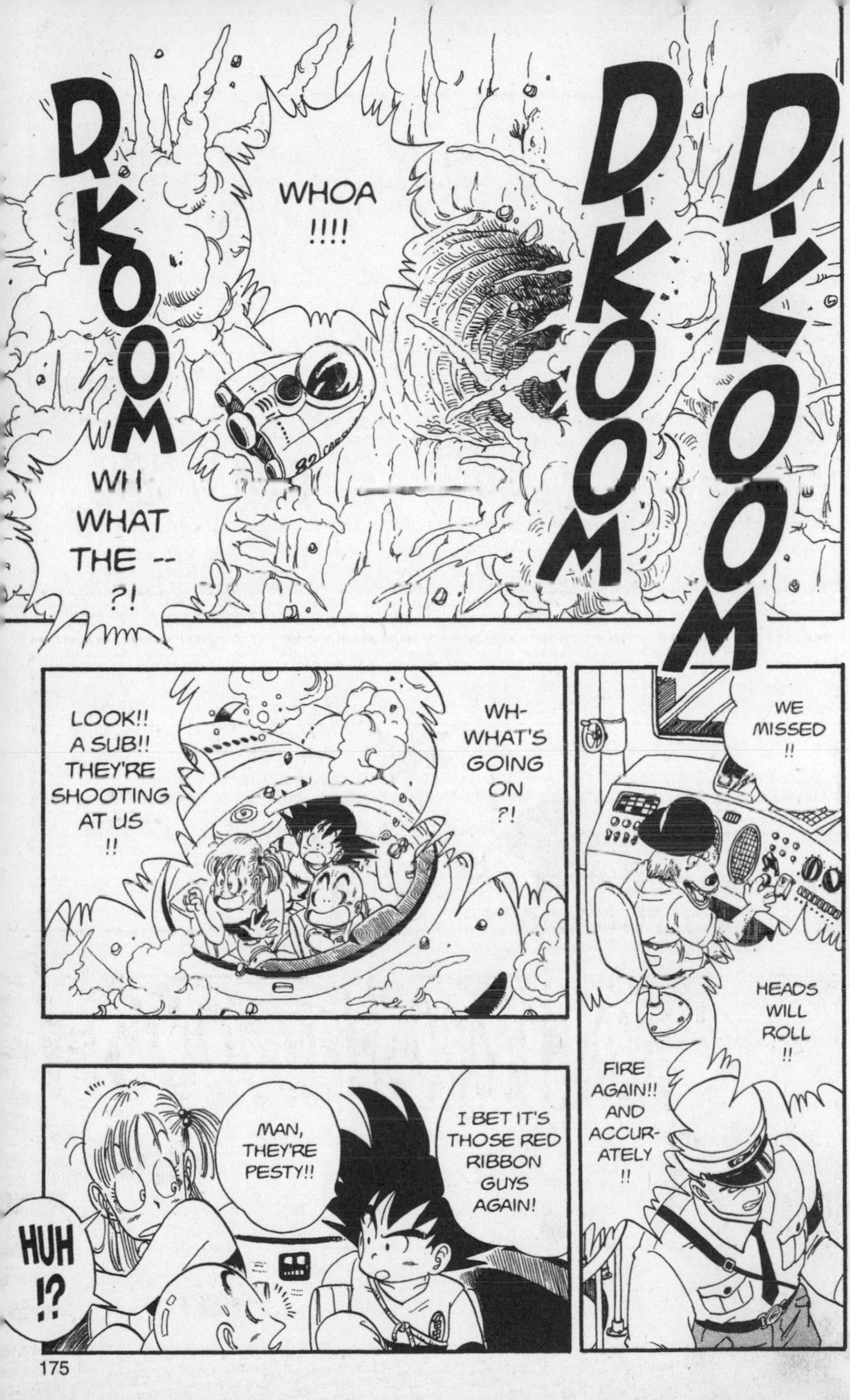

DKOOM
DKOOM
WHOA!!!!
DKOOM
WH WHAT THE --?!
WE MISSED!!
HEADS WILL ROLL!!
FIRE AGAIN!! AND ACCUR-ATELY!!
WH-WHAT'S GOING ON?!
LOOK!! A SUB!! THEY'RE SHOOTING AT US!!
I BET IT'S THOSE RED RIBBON GUYS AGAIN!
MAN, THEY'RE PESTY!!
HUH!?

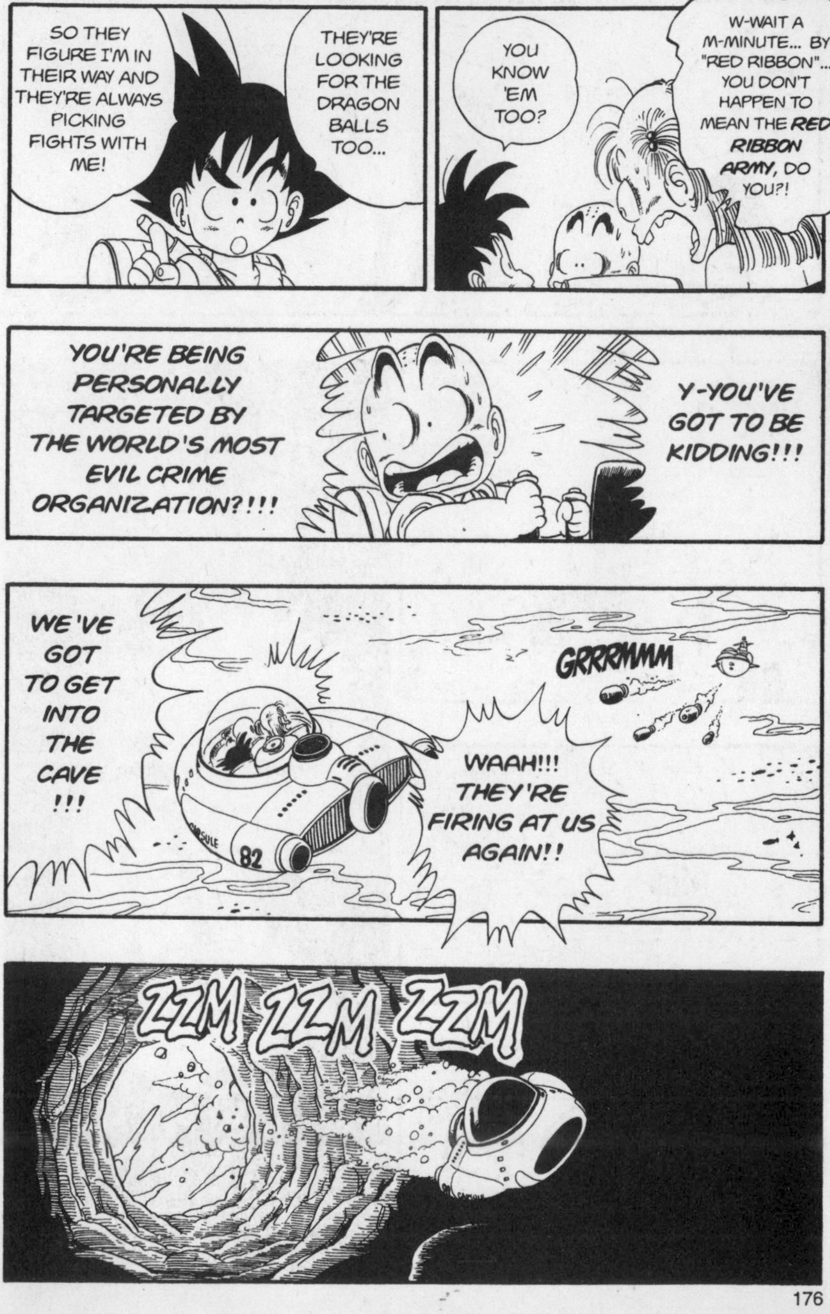

W-WAIT A M-MINUTE... BY "RED RIBBON"... YOU DON'T HAPPEN TO MEAN THE **RED RIBBON ARMY**, DO YOU?!
YOU KNOW 'EM TOO?
THEY'RE LOOKING FOR THE DRAGON BALLS TOO...
SO THEY FIGURE I'M IN THEIR WAY AND THEY'RE ALWAYS PICKING FIGHTS WITH ME!
Y-YOU'VE GOT TO BE KIDDING!!!
YOU'RE BEING PERSONALLY TARGETED BY THE WORLD'S MOST EVIL CRIME ORGANIZATION?!!!
GRRRMMM
WAAH!!! THEY'RE FIRING AT US AGAIN!!
WE'VE GOT TO GET INTO THE CAVE!!!
CAPSULE 82
ZZM ZZM ZZM

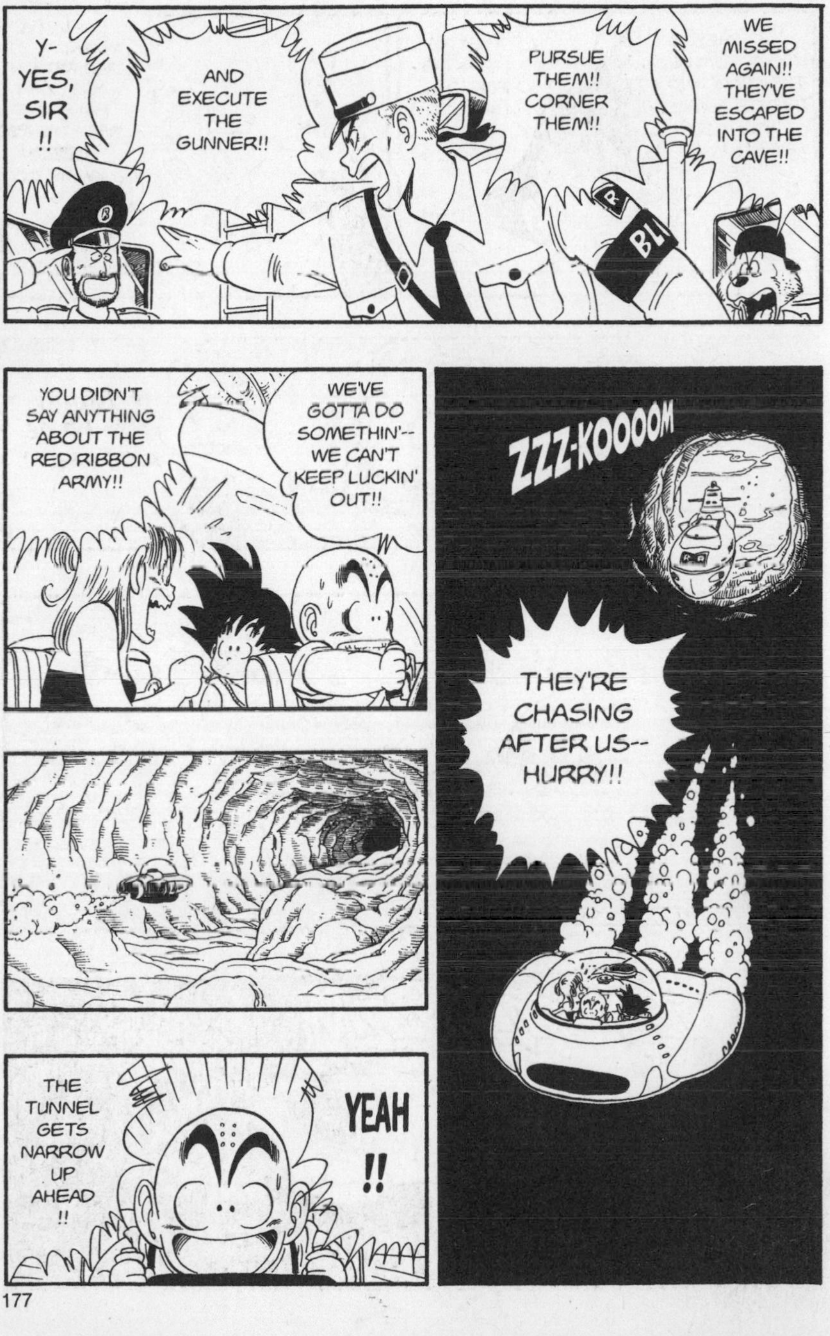
WE MISSED AGAIN!! THEY'VE ESCAPED INTO THE CAVE!!
PURSUE THEM!! CORNER THEM!!
AND EXECUTE THE GUNNER!!
Y- YES, SIR!!
ZZZ-KOOOM
THEY'RE CHASING AFTER US-- HURRY!!
WE'VE GOTTA DO SOMETHIN'-- WE CAN'T KEEP LUCKIN' OUT!!
YOU DIDN'T SAY ANYTHING ABOUT THE RED RIBBON ARMY!!
YEAH!!
THE TUNNEL GETS NARROW UP AHEAD!!

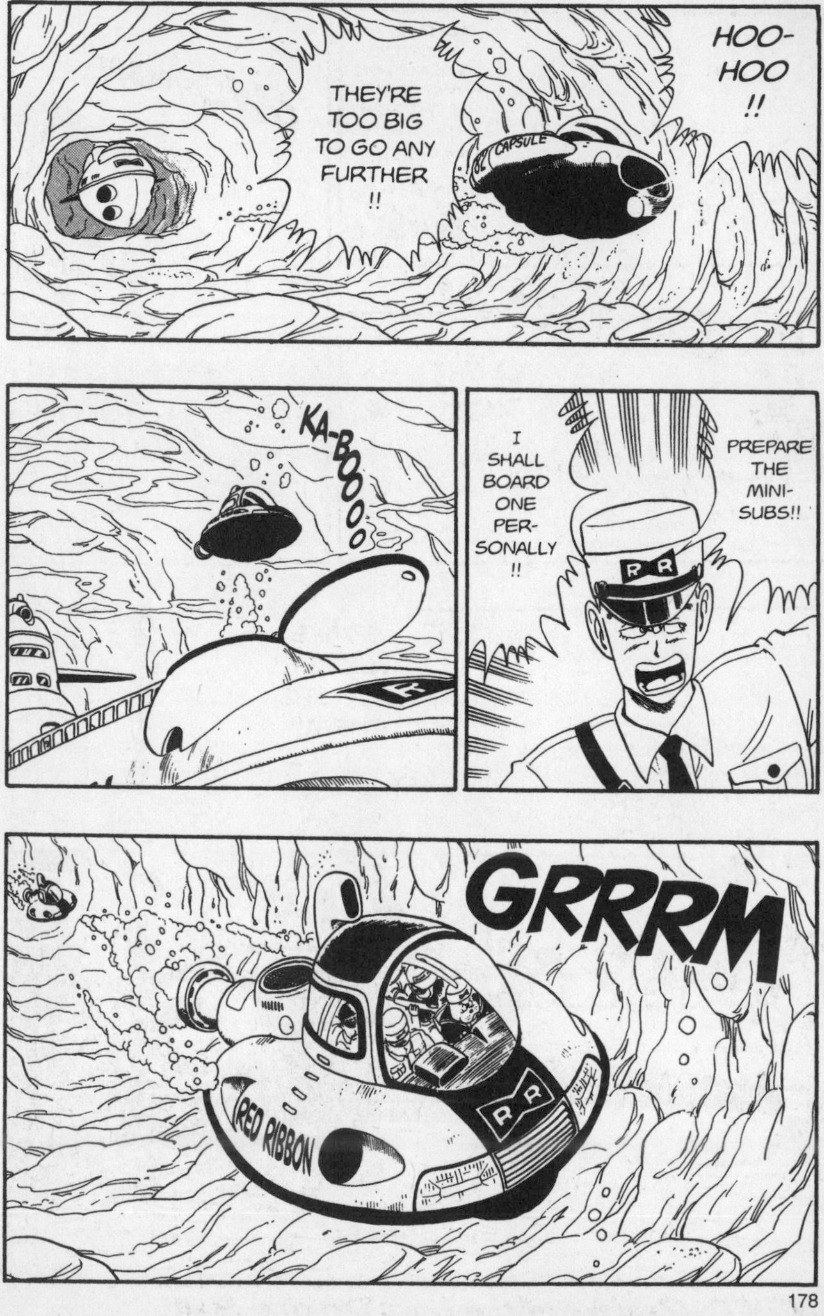
HOO-HOO!!
CAPSULE
THEY'RE TOO BIG TO GO ANY FURTHER!!
PREPARE THE MINI-SUBS!!
I SHALL BOARD ONE PER-SONALLY!!
KA-BOOOOO
GRRRM
RED RIBBON

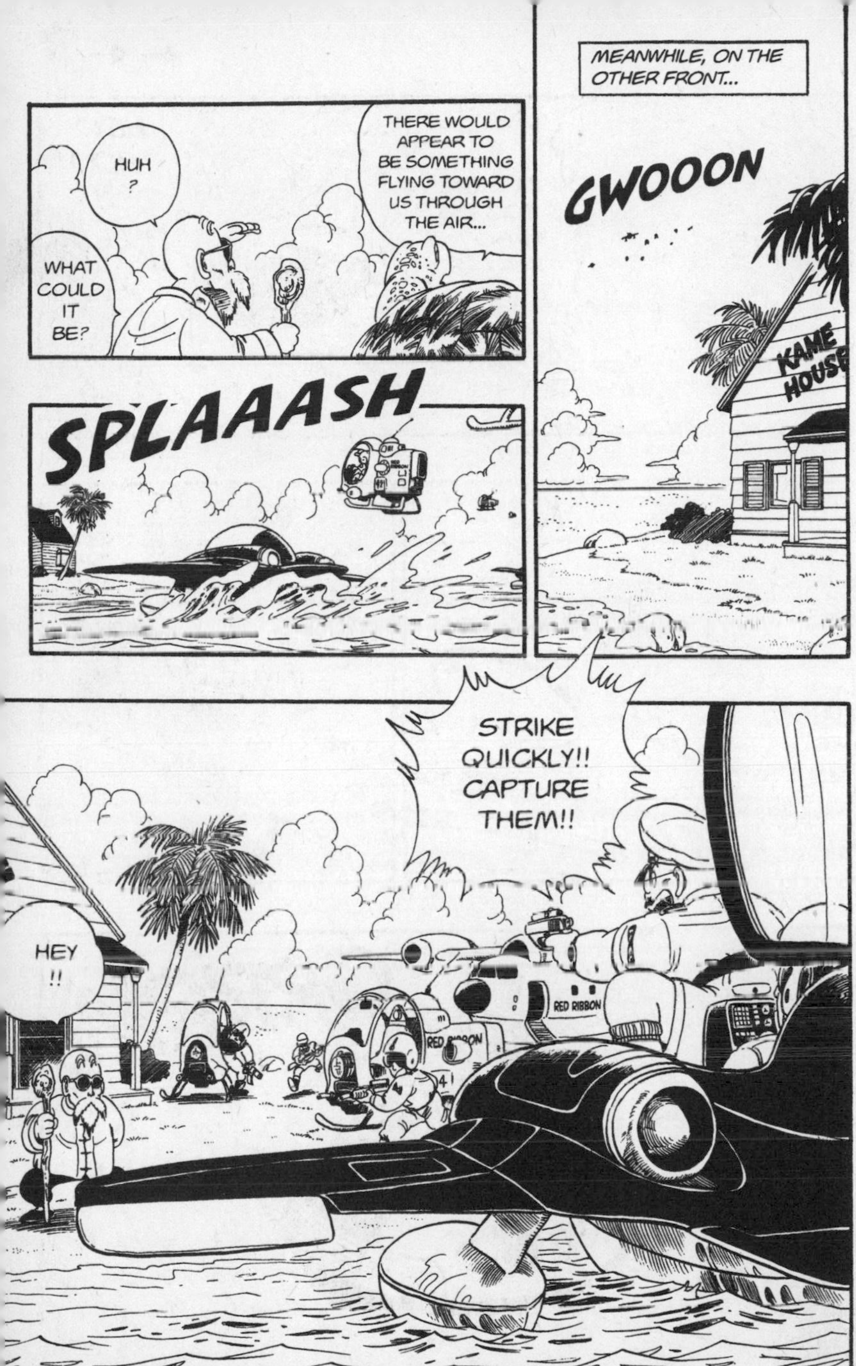

MEANWHILE, ON THE OTHER FRONT...
GWOOON
KAME HOUSE
THERE WOULD APPEAR TO BE SOMETHING FLYING TOWARD US THROUGH THE AIR...
HUH ?
WHAT COULD IT BE?
SPLAAASH
STRIKE QUICKLY!! CAPTURE THEM!!
RED RIBBON
HEY !!

NEXT: Raiders of the Lost Dragon Ball!

Title Page Gallery

Here are some of the chapter title pages which were used when these chapters of **Dragon Ball** were originally published in Japan in 1986 in **Weekly Shonen Jump** magazine.

IT'S ALIVE!!!

THE SHOCKING MECHANICAL MAN!!!

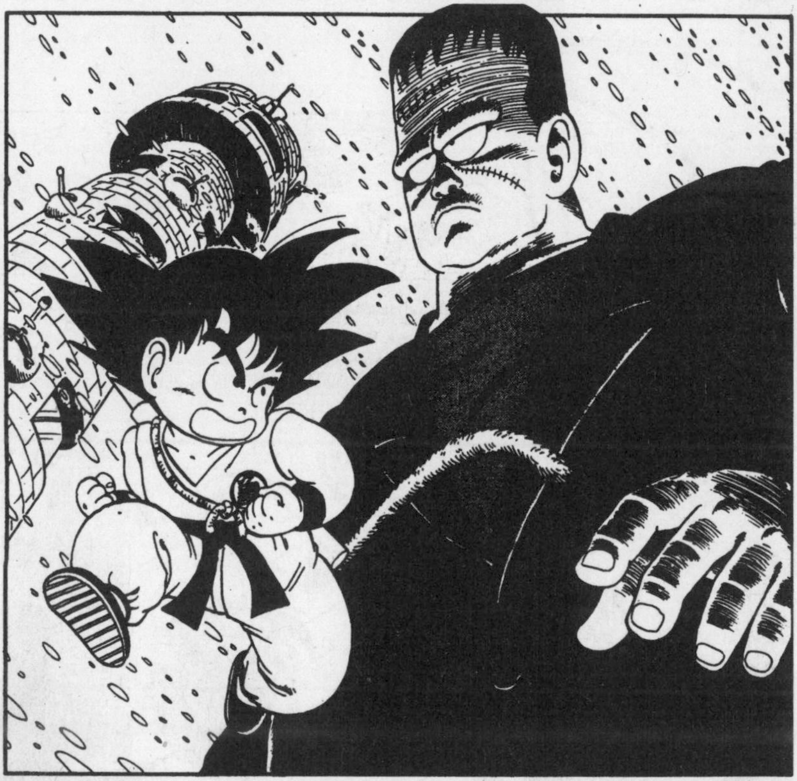

Tale 63 • Mechanical Man No.8

Akira Toriyama
鳥山明

ドラゴンボール

DRAGON BALL

HEY! WHAT AM I DOING IN THAT BOX?

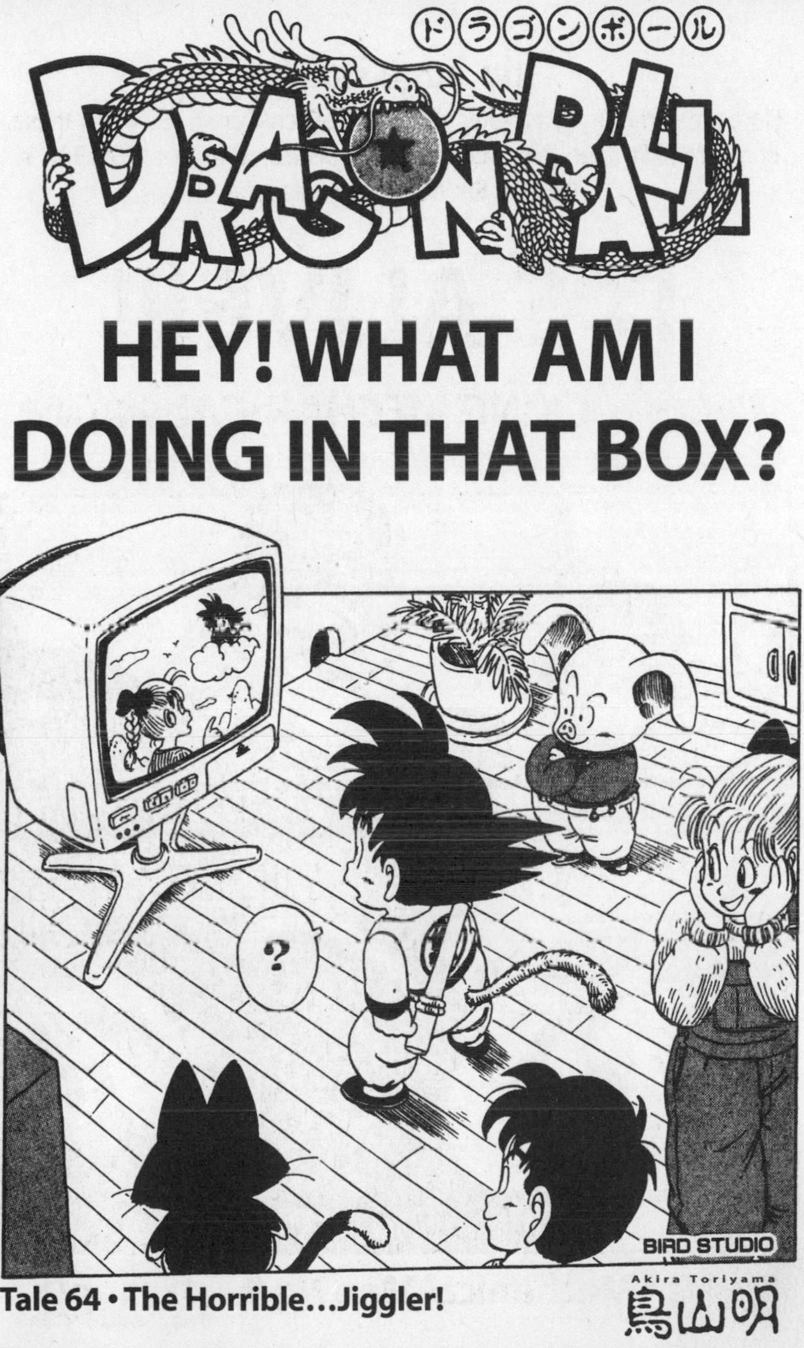
?
BIRD STUDIO

WATCH GOKU ON TV ON WEDNESDAYS!*

Tale 64 • The Horrible…Jiggler!

Akira Toriyama
鳥山明

* In Japan, the Dragon Ball TV series originally played every Wednesday at 7 PM.

CAN NO MOVE DEFEAT...THE JIGGLER?!?

Tale 65 • How to Unjiggle a Jiggler

Akira Toriyama
鳥山明 BIRD STUDIO

OOPS! I MADE A MISTAKE!

In two earlier issues, I accidentally referred to General White as "General Silver!" I didn't notice it until a lot of people wrote in about it (including my editor)...luckily it was fixed for the American version! But still...I'M SORRY!

IF I HAVE TO LOSE, AT LEAST GET MY NAME RIGHT!

ドラゴンボール

DRAGON BALL

YOU'LL HAVE MANY MORE ADVENTURES!

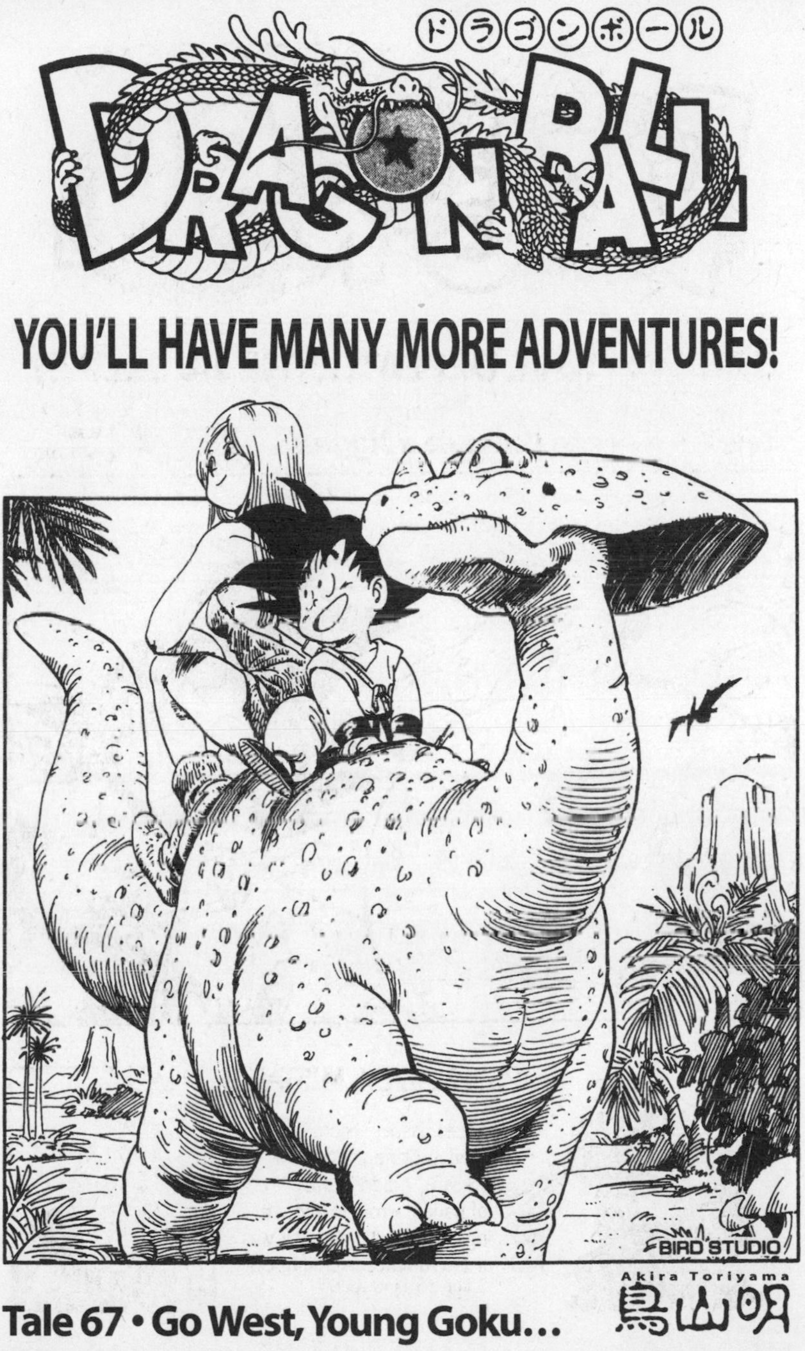
BIRD STUDIO

Akira Toriyama
鳥山明

Tale 67 • Go West, Young Goku…

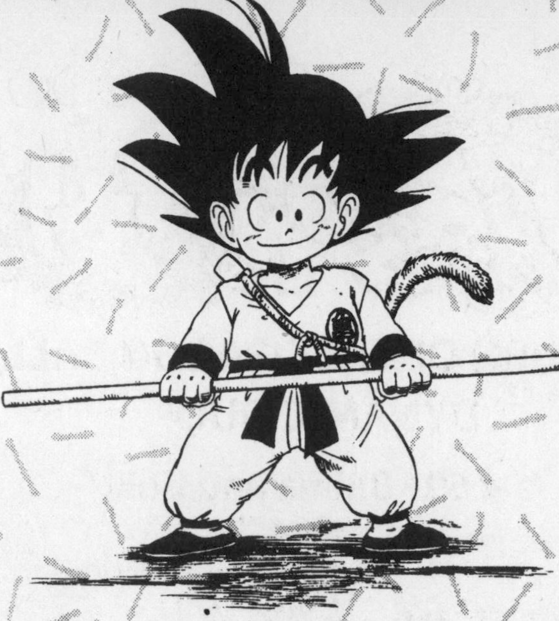

I'M SON GOKU, WITH MY NYOIBÔ AND KINTO'UN

DRAGON BALL

Tale 68 • Monkey in the City

Akira Toriyama

鳥山明

BIRD STUDIO

ドラゴンボール

DRAGON BALL

RETURN OF THE DRAGON BALL DYNAMIC DUO!

Tale 69 • Bulma and Goku

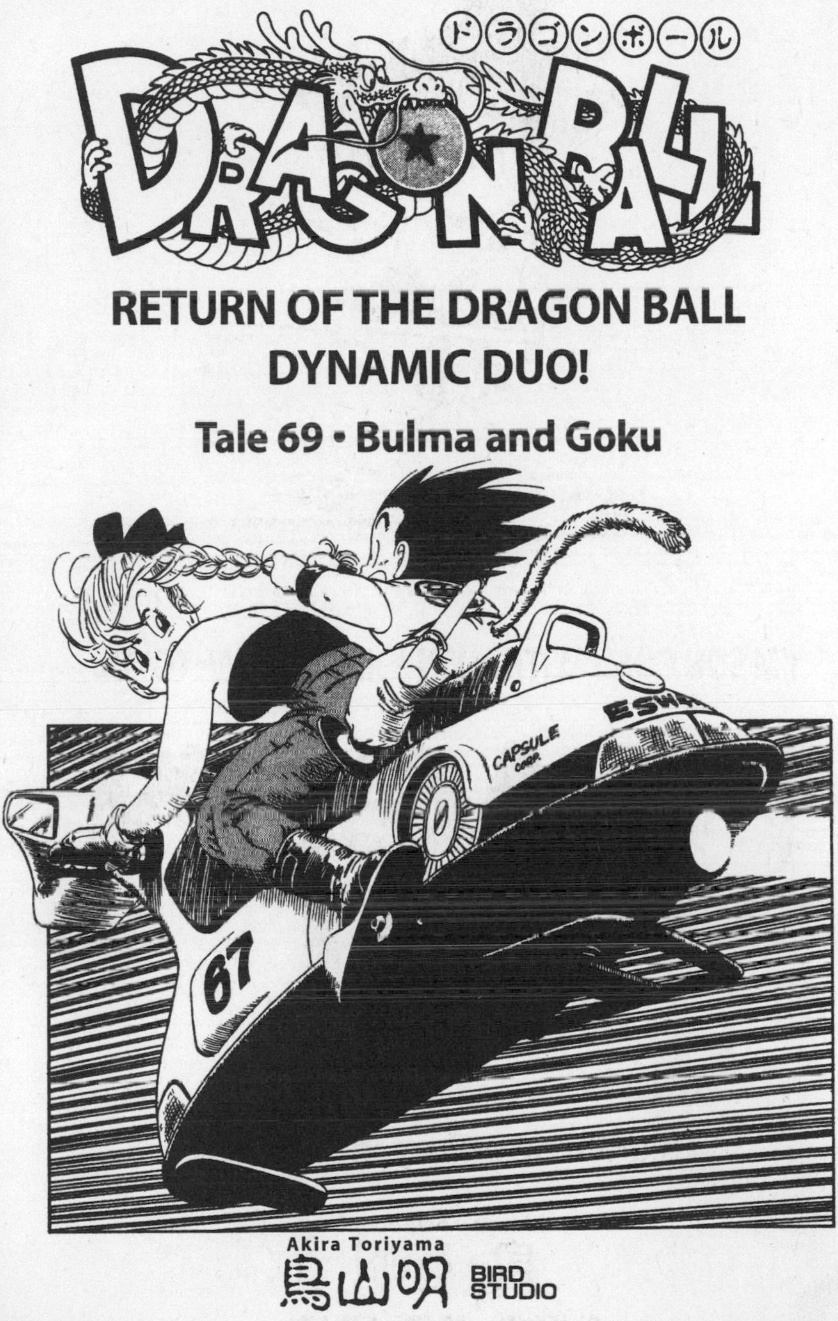
CAPSULE
CORP.
67

Akira Toriyama
鳥山明 BIRD STUDIO

DRAGON BALL

ALL RIGHT! LET'S GET THAT THIRD DRAGON BALL!

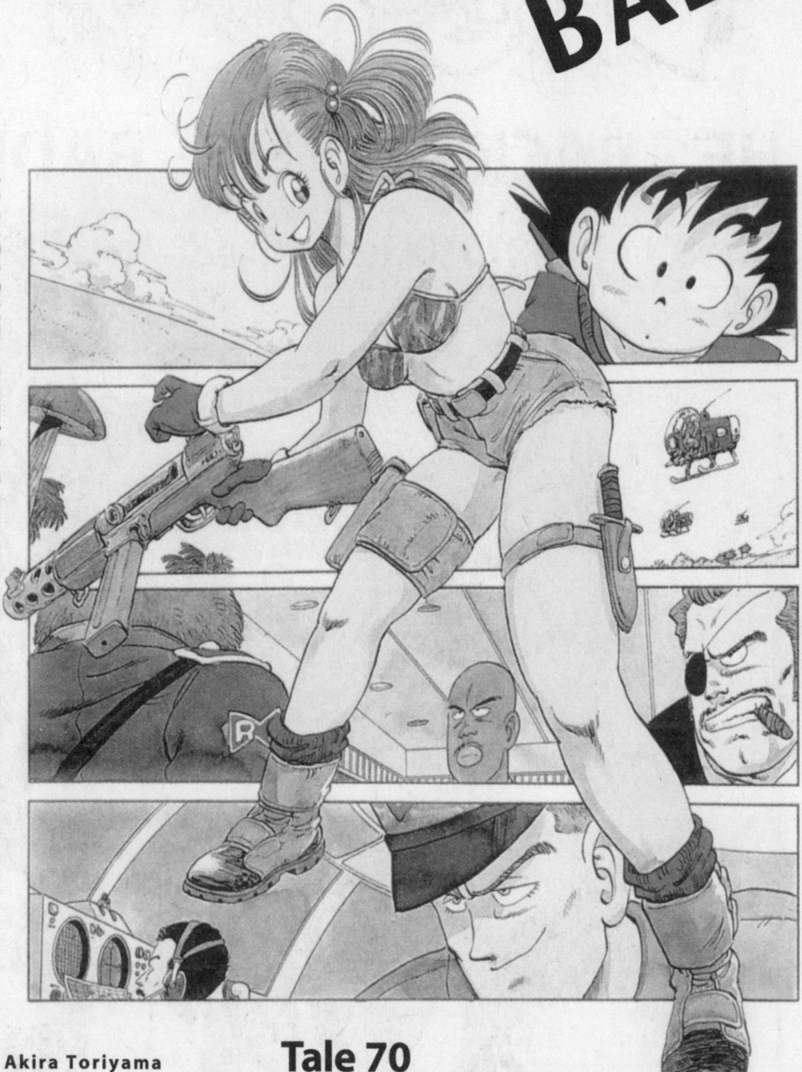

Akira Toriyama
鳥山明
BIRD STUDIO

Tale 70
Bulma's Big Mistake!

ドラゴンボール

DRAGON BALL

HE'S BACK AND HE'S BAD!

Akira Toriyama

Tale 71 • The Turtle is Spotted!

鳥山明
BIRD STUDIO

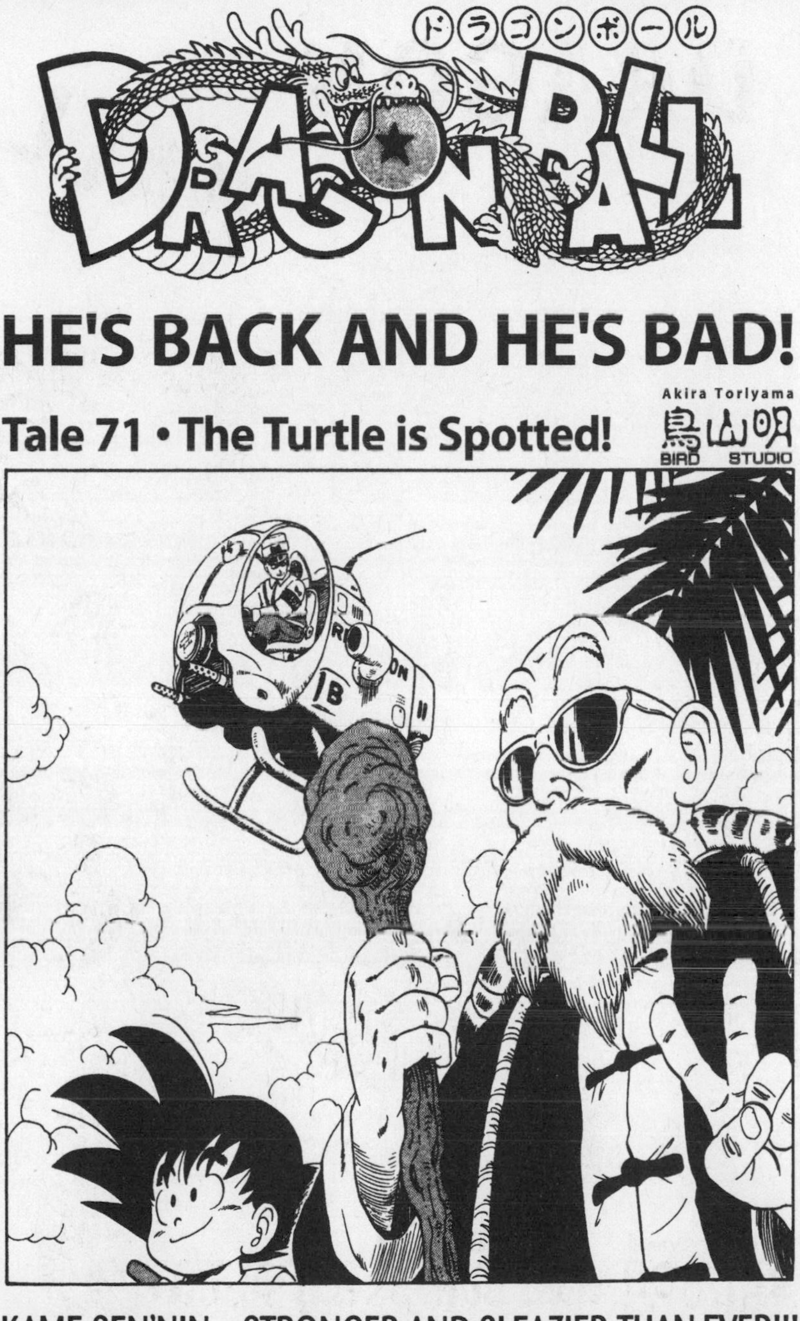

KAME-SEN'NIN...STRONGER AND SLEAZIER THAN EVER!!!

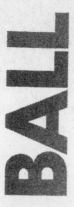

DRAGON BALL

Tale 72

The Blue Meanies

JUST 'CUZ YOU'RE LITTLE DOESN'T MEAN YOU'RE WEAK!

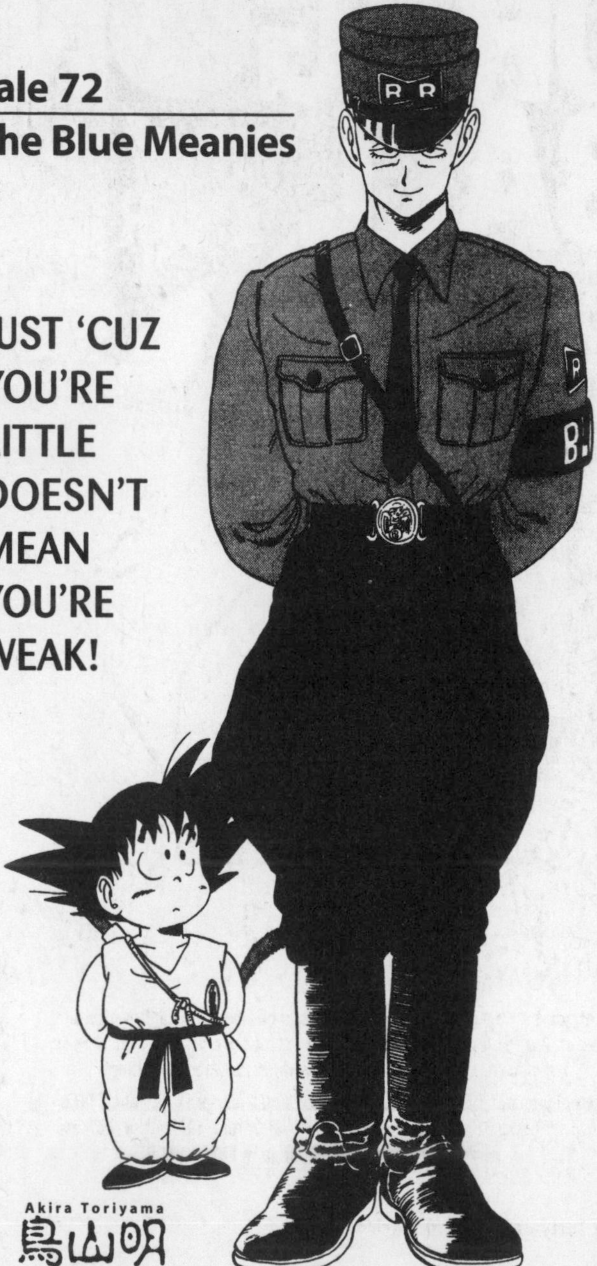

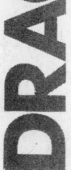

Akira Toriyama
鳥山明
BIRD STUDIO

DRAGON BALL
FULL COLOR
SAIYAN ARC
ARRH

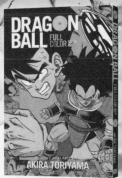

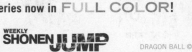

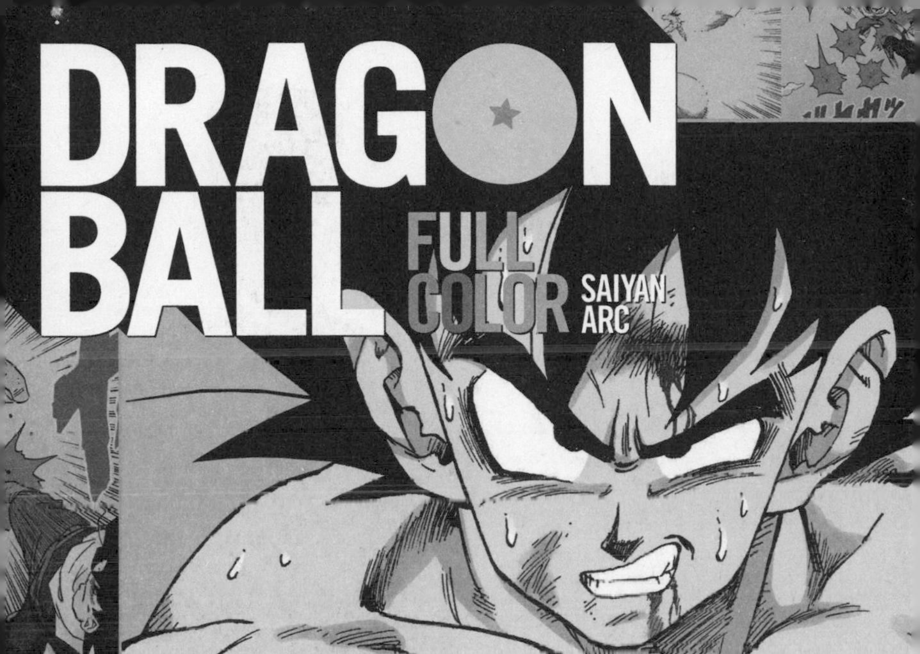

You're Reading in the Wrong Direction!!

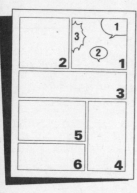

Whoops! Guess what? You're starting at the wrong end of the comic!

...It's true! In keeping with the original Japanese format, Akira Toriyama's world-famous **Dragon Ball** series is meant to be read from right to left, starting in the upper-right corner.

Unlike English, which is read from left to right, Japanese is read from right to left, meaning that action, sound effects, and word-balloon order are completely reversed...something which can make readers unfamiliar with Japanese feel pretty backwards themselves. For this reason, manga or Japanese comics published in the U.S. in English have traditionally been published "flopped"—that is, printed in exact reverse order, as though seen from the other side of a mirror.

By flopping pages, U.S. publishers can avoid confusing readers, but the compromise is not without its downside. For one thing, a character in a flopped manga series who once wore in the original Japanese version a T-shirt emblazoned with "M A Y" (as in "the merry month of") now wears one which reads "Y A M"! Additionally, many manga creators in Japan are themselves unhappy with the process, as some feel the mirror-imaging of their art alters their original intentions.

In recognition of the importance and popularity of **Dragon Ball**, we are proud to bring it to you in the original unflopped format.

For now, though, turn to the other side of the book and let the adventure begin...!

—Editor